The Richmond Stage, 1784-1812

The BURNING of the THEATRE in RICHMOND, VIRGINIA, on the Night of the 26th December 1811, *By which awful Calamity upwards of* SEVENTY FIVE *of its most valuable Citizens suddenly lost their lives, and many others were much injured.*

The Richmond Stage

1784–1812

Martin Staples Shockley

University Press of Virginia

Charlottesville

THE UNIVERSITY PRESS OF VIRGINIA
Copyright ©1977 by the Rector and Visitors
of the University of Virginia

First published 1977

Frontispiece: The Burning of the Richmond Theatre,
1811. (Courtesy Virginia State Library.)

Library of Congress Cataloging in Publication Data

Shockley, Martin.
The Richmond Stage, 1784-1812.

Includes indexes.
1. Theater—Virginia—Richmond—History. 2. Richmond—History. I. Title.
PN2277.R54S5   792'.09755'451   76-16866   ISBN 0-8139-0686-5

Printed in the United States of America

Preface

My interest in the Richmond theatre began when I was a student at the University of Richmond, 1924-28. My dissertation at the University of North Carolina (1938) was a history of the Richmond theatre, 1819-38. Between 1938 and 1976 I have researched the period before 1819 and completed this history covering the years 1784-1812, from the arrival of the first professional acting company to the famous fire of 1811.

Clarence Brigham's bibliography of early American newspapers has been indispensable. Following his listings, I have searched extant copies of Richmond newspapers for theatre advertisements and related news. I have been assisted by Mr. Brigham in person at the American Antiquarian Society and by many curators of newspaper files. Musicologists whom I consulted advised that in view of frequent precopyright borrowing, stealing, and unacknowledged collaboration, ascriptions of musical comedies of this period to individual composers are often inaccurate and generally suspect. I gratefully acknowledge valuable and courteous assistance from the Virginia State Library, the Virginia Historical Society, the Valentine Museum, the College of William and Mary, Harvard University, the New York Public Library, the Library of Congress, and many others.

Striving for accuracy and completeness, I acknowledge the inevitability of error, and trust my colleagues to supply omissions and correct mistakes.

Contents

Illustrations

The Richmond Stage, 1784–1812

1784–1789

FIRST SEASON

Dennis Ryan Company

June–December 1784

Interest in the theatre in Williamsburg, site of America's first theatre, has been great; and much has been written about the theatre in the capital of colonial Virginia. Less research has been devoted to the early theatre in Richmond, partly because Richmond, being inland, developed later than the coastal cities of New York, Philadelphia, and Charleston, all of which had well-established theatres before the first company of actors came to Richmond.

Richmond's importance as a cultural center may be dated from 1779, when Richmond superseded Williamsburg as the state capital. Burned by Benedict Arnold in 1781, Richmond was rebuilt after the war, and at the time of the earliest recorded theatrical activity it was a flourishing little city of about two thousand, the capital, and, despite the claims of such competitors as Alexandria and Petersburg, the cultural center of Virginia.

The date and circumstances of the beginning of the theatre in Richmond are unknown. We may conjecture that colonial acting companies, which usually traveled by water, came up the river from Williamsburg to play in the little village at the falls of the James. If they did, they left no record, which certainly does not prove that they did not. It may be equally reasonable to assume that the first company of actors came after the war to play in the new capital city some time in the early 1780s. Where they acted and what sort of building they performed in are also unknown. Samuel Mordecai says, "The very first dramatic performance in Richmond was as I have heard, in a wooden house, large in that day, which stood in the rear of the old jail (Rose's Brig), and which, if I mistake not, was demolished only a few years ago."[1] What other early, lost performances there may have been remain in the realm of hearsay and conjecture.

Who the first company of actors was can be established, I believe, beyond reasonable doubt, although the earliest reliable evidence, the records of the Richmond Common Hall, or City

Council, is vague. Under the date of June 3, 1784, appears the following entry:

Application having been made to the Hall by Mr. Dennis Ryan, Manager of a Company of Comedians for permission to perform public exhibitions on the Stage, theatrical and amusing, within this City, under such restraint as the Common Hall shall deem expedient, and it being the sense of the Hall that such permission be extended to them and that a Committee to confer with Mr. Ryan may best adopt and devise the necessary restraints.

Resolved that Mr. Recorder, Mr. Foushee, Mr. Buchanan, Mr. Mitchell, and Mr. Adams, or any three of them be appointed a Committee to prepare and devise necessary restraints or regulations and report the same to the Mayor, who is thereupon authorized to License such exhibitions in conformity thereto.[2]

There is no record of whatever "restraints or regulations" may have been devised. That Ryan may have intended to mollify or persuade the Hall is indicated by the following entry for Saturday, July 10, 1784:

Mr. Ryan having applied for permission to present a piece for the benefit of the City.

Ordered that it be signified to Mr. Ryan upon his particular desire that he hath permission of the Hall to present any theatrical piece or pieces for the benefit of the City, And that Mr. Boyd be appointed to receive the amount of such benefits and make report thereof to the next Hall.[3]

If such were his intention, his Saturday success was turned into Monday failure, as indicated by the following entry on the next page, dated July 12:

Resolved that Mr. Ryan be informed, that the Hall are convinced, from his offer of a benefit, for the use of the City, of his polite attention to it; but that they do not conceive themselves at liberty to apply any part of the produce thereof to the emolument of the Corporation.

Resolved that the Order of Saturday last upon which the foregoing Resolution is founded, be Rescinded.

Thomas Clark Pollock tells us that Dennis Ryan had had similar difficulties in Philadelphia: "In November, 1783, Dennis Ryan— who had succeeded to the management of the Baltimore theatre after Lindsay and Wall's regime, that is, early in 1783—attempted to open the Theatre in Southwark. His petition to the Assembly for a repeal of the prohibitory law was opposed by a 'Memorial and Remonstrance from the people called Quakers.' The Assembly tabled Ryan's petition, so chloroforming it."[4]

George O. Seilhamer says that Mr. and Mrs. Dennis Ryan came from Ireland. He records the Ryan Company in Baltimore between November 15, 1782, and April 15, 1783; in Annapolis from April 19 to 26, 1783; in Baltimore from May 13 to June 9, 1783; in New York from June 19 to October 25, 1783; in Baltimore from December 2, 1783 to February 14, 1784. Of what happened after February, 1784, he says: "It is probable the company was either disbanded or went in search of new pastures. Indeed, it is not unlikely that Ryan carried his forces as far away as Canada, for in the autumn of 1784 the American papers announced a regular company of players as giving performances in Quebec. As no files of the Quebec papers seem to have been preserved, it is impossible to identify the company, but the probabilities favor this supposition."[5]

I do not think that Dennis Ryan went from Baltimore to Quebec in February 1784. There is evidence that some time early in 1784 (probably in March) Ryan wrote to Governor Benjamin Harrison requesting permission to bring his company to Virginia. Ryan's letter has apparently not survived, but Governor Harrison's, dated March 13, 1784, has:

> The permission you request of introducing into this State your company of Comedians is most readily granted so far as it rests with me. I am sensible that these kind of entertainments are objected to by some very good men as tending to corrupt the morals of the people. These arguments however lose their weight with me being fixed in an opinion that a well chosen & well acted play is amongst the first of moral Lessons and tend greatly to inculcate & fix on the mind the most virtuous principles.
>
> I am &c
> B. H.[6]

I doubt that Ryan, an experienced actor-manager, would have come to Richmond before he wrote the governor requesting permission to come. Considering that prejudice against the theatre was common and that players were frequently in difficulties with the authorities, to have done so would have been an indiscretion that

Ryan would have known not to commit. On receiving the governor's favorable reply, Ryan probably proceeded by ship with his company to Richmond, and some time before June 3 petitioned the Common Hall for permission to perform plays. The Common Hall's instructing its Committee "to confer with Mr. Ryan" is evidence that he was in Richmond in June. It seems reasonable to assume that his "company of Comedians" was with him, ready to perform as soon as the Committee devised the "necessary restraints." The rescinding of the permission on July 12, despite Ryan's offer to "present a piece for the benefit of the city," may be taken as evidence of difficulty, not of failure.

Evidence that Ryan mollified the City Fathers is found in contemporary newspapers. His announcement of the opening of Richmond's "New Theatre" appeared in the *Virginia Gazette, and Weekly Advertiser* on Saturday, June 5, 1784; it was repeated in the next issue, on June 12; and the same advertisement appeared in the *Virginia Gazette, or, the American Advertiser* of the same date. The advertisement is dated June 3, 1784, the date of the Common Hall's first mention of Ryan's "application." It states:

Dennis Ryan's most humble respects await the ladies and gentlemen of Richmond; begs leave to inform them that on Monday June 21st, 1784; the New Theatre will be opened by the American Company of Comedians, with the tragedy of *Douglas*, and the musical entertainment of the *Padlock*. He hopes his endeavours to render a rational, instructive and entertaining species of amusement, worthy of their patronage, will meet their general approbation; to merit which will be the highest of his ambition.

Unfortunately, there are no details of the "New Theatre." Whether Ryan built it, renovated it, or merely occupied it is unknown. But we may reasonably assume that his "American Company of Comedians" opened their Richmond season on Monday, June 21, 1784.

Further evidence of the identity of the Dennis Ryan Company may be deduced from the earliest known specimen of a Richmond playbill. It is mutilated, only the lower part remaining:

A Favorite Song by Mrs. Lewis.
To which (by desire) will be added a Farce, Called *The Cheats of Scapin*.

Scapin	By Mr. Wall
Gripe	By Mr. Lewis

DENNIS RYAN's

MOST humble refpects await the LADIES and GENTLEMEN of Richmond; begs leave to inform them, that on Monday June 21ft, 1784, the NEW THEATRE will be opened by the

AMERICAN COMPANY OF
COMEDIANS,

With the TRAGEDY of

DOUGLASS,

AND

THE MUSICAL ENTERTAINMENT
OF THE
PADLOCK.

He hopes his endeavours to render a rational, inftructive and entertaining fpecies of amufement, worthy their patronage, will meet their general approbation; to merit which will be the higheft of his ambition.
J U N E 3, **1784.**

Dennis Ryan's first announcement, from the *Virginia Gazette, and Weekly Advertiser*, June 5, 1784. (Courtesy the Library of The College of William and Mary in Virginia.)

Lower half of a play-bill for a performance given in Richmond in 1785. This is the earliest known specimen of a Richmond play-bill.

A FAVORITE SONG BY Mrs. LEWIS.

To which [by desire] will be added a FARCE, called

The CHEATS of SCAPIN.

SCAPIN,	BY	Mr. WALL;
GRIPE,		Mr. LEWIS;
LEANDER,	BY	Mr. SMITH;
CLARA,	BY	Mrs. SMITH,

End of the Farce a much admired Epilogue, in Character of an Old Woman.

N. B. TICKETS may be had at Mr. FORMICOLA's TAVERN, Mr. ANDERSON's TAVERN, and at Mr. SMITH's lodgings, at the BIRD in HAND TAVERN, at ONE DOLLAR each and no distinction of price.

. That Ladies and Gentlemen who are disposed to befriend Mr. Smith, may not be deterred from coming, they may be assured, that every precaution is taken for the safety of the house, and Peace Officers are appointed to keep good order outside.

Good MUSIC is engaged.

Richmond's first playbill, the Dennis Ryan Company, 1784. (Courtesy Virginia State Library.)

| Leander | By Mr. Smith |
| Clara | By Mrs. Smith |

End of the Farce a much admired Epilogue, in character of an Old Woman.

N.B. Tickets may be had at Mr. Formicola's Tavern, Mr. Anderson's Tavern, and at Mr. Smith's lodging; at the Bird in Hand Tavern, at One Dollar Each and no distinction of price.

That Ladies and Gentlemen who are disposed to befriend Mr. Smith, may not be deterred from coming, they may be assured, that every precaution is taken for the safety of the house, and Peace officers are appointed to keep good order.

Good Music is engaged.[7]

The custom of the time was to distribute playbills. This was undoubtedly one of many circulated throughout the city. It is not confirmed by a newspaper advertisement, but it is definitely a Richmond playbill. The three taverns mentioned were well-known Richmond taverns of the 1780s. According to custom, tickets were to be had of the player for whose benefit the performance was given, in this case, Mr. Smith, whose lodging place was evidently well known, since it is not named; I assume that it was not one of the three taverns. Mordecai tells us that "The oldest public house was *'the Bird in Hand'* on Main Street, at the foot of Church hill." Anderson's Tavern is identified along with Byrd's Warehouse by Mary Newton Stanard as among the "forty or fifty buildings in the heart of the town" destroyed by fire in 1787.[8]

The Cheats of Scapin was translated by Thomas Otway from *Fourberies de Scapin* by Molière. It was first acted at the Theatre Royal in Dorset Garden in December 1676. Seilhamer says: "The farce had been introduced to the American stage by the military Thespians in New York. The scene was laid at Dover, but it was little more than a translation of Molière's *Fourberies de Scapin*."[9] There are records of its performance in Baltimore on April 15, 1783, in Annapolis on April 23, 1783, and in New York on June 28, 1783, all by the Dennis Ryan Company. Seilhamer gives the cast for the Baltimore performance.

Gripe	Mr. Heard
Thrifty	Mr. Davids
Octavian	Mr. Church
Leander	Mr. Tilyard
Shift	Mr. Lewis

Sly	Mr. Atherton
Scapin	Mr. Wall
Lucia	Mrs. Elm
Clara	Mrs. Potter

George C. D. Odell gives the cast for the New York performance on June 28:

Gripe	Mr. Heard
Scapin	Mr. Wall
Thrifty	Mr. Davids
Octavian	Mr. Atherton
Leander	Mr. Brown
Shift	Mr. Lewis
Lucia	Mrs. Garrison
Clara	Mrs. Potter

Heard, Wall, Davids, Lewis, and Mrs. Potter played the same roles. Atherton, Brown, and Mrs. Garrison were replaced by Church, Tilyard, and Mrs. Elm. The role of Sly does not appear in the New York cast.[10]

Of these players, Wall, who played Scapin in Annapolis, New York, and Richmond, had been co-manager of the Wall and Lindsay Company, which was playing in Baltimore in 1782 when Mr. and Mrs. Dennis Ryan joined it. Ryan took over as manager in February 1783; Wall continued to play leading roles. Lewis played with this company in New York in June 1783; and Mrs. Smith joined the company in New York on July 12, 1783, making her debut in the title role of *Jane Shore*. Since Ryan's company is rather closely accounted for in Baltimore, Annapolis, and New York during all of 1783, I conclude that the performance which the earliest known Richmond playbill announces was by the Dennis Ryan Company during 1784.

Ryan's next extant advertisement appears on Saturday, November 27, 1784. It is headed "By Permission," which means that the theatre is being operated with the approval of the authorities. Evidently Ryan had paid the taxes and met the other conditions imposed by City Hall. He announced: "At the Theatre, on Monday Evening, the 29th of November, will be presented, a tragedy, called *The Roman Father*." The only character named is "Horatius (the Roman Father)," played by Godwin. The play concluded with "New Grand Transparent Scenery, and the entrance of Publius into Rome, accompanied with a Grand Procession, and singing by Mrs. Hyde, and Miss Wall." The afterpiece was "a Farce (never performed here) called *Tony Lumpkin in Town*." Disappointment comes in the last line: "Characters will be expressed in the Bills of the Day."[11]

One later advertisement from this season survives. It announced: "At the Theatre in Richmond, This Evening, Saturday, the 11th of December, 1784, will be presented a Comedy (never performed here) called the *Miser*." The only character named is Lovegold "(The Miser)," played by Godwin. There was singing by Mrs. Hyde and Miss Wall, probably between the play and the afterpiece, which was "a Farce (never performed here) called *A Trip to Scotland*." For cast of characters we are again referred to "the Bills of the Day."[12]

The following entry, in the records of the Common Hall, dated December 13, 1784, closes out the season: "Ordered that the Mayor be requested to notify to Mr. Ryan Manager of the Theatre in this City, that unless he render an account of the number of plays which he has performed within the same since his last Settlement and pay the tax arising thereon, that the permission granted him by a former Hall for performing in the City be suspended until such payment be made, and that in future a like settlement be made Weekly."[13]

The account book of John Marshall provides corroborative evidence that the Richmond theatre was active in 1784. For the twelve years he lived in Richmond (1783–95), Marshall kept meticulous accounts of his expenditures. We may be reasonably certain that Captain Marshall and Colonel James Monroe saw the Dennis Ryan Company on June 26, 1784, for Marshall entered in his accounts for that day: "Colo. Monroe & self at the play 1/10." Since the most expensive box seats were priced at eight shillings in 1785, this outlay of thirty shillings may indicate a theatre party. Marshall was, we know, fond of good company, and at this time was establishing himself both at the Richmond bar and in Richmond society. Perhaps some of the thirty shillings went for refreshment. On July 2 he spent twelve shillings on the theatre, which perhaps were for two box seats at six shillings each. Expenditures of thirteen shillings on July 3 and fifteen on July 13 also would have occurred during Ryan's first season. Entries of ten shillings on October 26 and six on December 2 indicate either that Ryan's company played in Richmond from June to December, or (a reasonable alternative) that there was a second season which extended at least from October 26 to December 2.[14]

Regrettably, Marshall never mentions a play by title or a player by name, nor is there any comment on the merits of any production. His account book does, however, corroborate newspaper advertisements of theatrical activity in Richmond between 1784 and 1794.

I conclude this account of Richmond's first theatre season with brief comments on the plays and the players. Parenthesized dates after titles refer to the day of performance as established previously in the chapter.[15]

Douglas (June 21, 1784), a tragedy by John Home, had been first acted in Edinburgh in 1756. It was acted at Covent Garden in 1757, in both New York and Philadelphia in 1759, and in Charleston in 1764. Records of several later performances in Richmond attest its popularity. *The Padlock*, by Isaac Bickerstaffe, with music by Charles Dibdin, had been first acted at Drury Lane on October 3, 1768. Its American premiere followed hard upon, at the John Street Theatre in New York on May 29, 1769. It was acted in Philadelphia the same year. There are records of several later performances in Richmond.

For *The Cheats of Scapin* (date conjectural) see above, pp. 4-7.

The Roman Father (November 29, 1784), a popular tragedy by William Whitehead, was based upon Corneille's *Horace*. It had its premiere at Drury Lane on February 24, 1750, and was acted in Philadelphia in 1767, New York in 1768, and Charleston in 1774. The Dennis Ryan Company presented it in Baltimore on April 11, 1783, and in Charleston on March 28, 1785. *Tony Lumpkin in Town*, a farce by John O'Keeffe, was first acted at the Second Haymarket on July 2, 1778. This Richmond performance is apparently its American premiere. It was produced by Godwin in Charleston on March 28, 1788. There is no record of its performance in Philadelphia.

The Miser (December 11, 1784), a comedy by Henry Fielding, was first acted at Drury Lane in 1733. It was acted in Philadelphia on February 9, 1767, and New York on March 14, 1768. A company managed by Godwin produced it in Charleston on January 5,

1787. *A Trip to Scotland*, a farce by William Whitehead, was first acted at Drury Lane in 1770. It was acted in Philadelphia in 1778, New York in 1779, and Charleston in 1794.

From the extant records we have the names of nine players: Godwin, Lewis, Ryan, Smith, Wall, Mrs. Hyde, Mrs. Lewis, Mrs. Smith, and Miss Wall. Almost certainly there were others whose names are lost. A year earlier in New York, Ryan's company had consisted of eleven men, five women, and Master Ryan. Neither Godwin, Mrs. Hyde, nor Miss Wall was named then. When Ryan produced *The Roman Father* in Baltimore in 1783, the following cast was named:

Publius Horatius	Mr. Ryan
Tullus Hostilius	Mr. Lewis
Valerius	Mr. Smith
Horatius	Mr. Heard
Horatia	Mrs. Ryan
Valeria	Mrs. Elm

Of the three players named in the advertisement of November 27, Miss Wall was the daughter of player parents, both of whom had acted with Hallam and Henry's Old American Company. She made her debut as the Duke of York in *Richard III* in Baltimore on January 15, 1782, with the Wall and Lindsay Company, with her father as Richard and her mother as Queen Elizabeth. She played minor roles. The management of this company was taken over by Dennis Ryan in February 1783.

Mrs. Hyde made her debut with Ryan's company as Hecate in *Macbeth* on October 11, 1783, in New York. She played Polly in *The Beggar's Opera*, Rosetta in *Love in a Village*, and Lady Sneerwell in *School for Scandal* with this company. She returned to Richmond with West and Bignall in 1790.

William Godwin had a long and important career on the American stage. He made his debut in Philadelphia in 1766. Then, leaving the Old American Company, he became one of the leaders of the New American Company, also called the "K" Company. He played in Annapolis in 1769. During the Revolution he rejoined the Old American Company in Jamaica and played with them there. In 1785 he opened the first theatre in Savannah. In 1786 he built Harmony Hall in Charleston, where he played two seasons, ending March 28, 1787. He played in Philadelphia in 1792, and in 1793 opened a new theatre in Baltimore. He was in Charleston again in 1795. He returned to Richmond in 1791.

SECOND SEASON
Dennis Ryan Company (?)
November 1785

How long the Dennis Ryan Company stayed in Richmond we do not know. I hazard that they played through the Christmas season. They were in Charleston in March 1785 and left May 7 on the schooner *Play-Actor*. Whether the company returned to Richmond we also do not know. Possibly some other company came to Richmond in 1785, but I suspect that Ryan's troupe returned; certainly the following entry in the Common Hall records dated November 14, 1785, indicates theatrical activity at that time: "Resolved that the Mayor be requested to inform the Managers of the playhouse that they must decline all representation of plays in this City unless they will let their seats on the following terms, to wit: each side Box to be numbered and to issue not more than twelve tickets for each Box at 8s. each, front Box 6s., pitt 4s."[16]

Whether the boxes were numbered as directed by the Hall or whether the Hall again reversed itself is uncertain from the following entry three days later, November 17: "It was agreed unanimously by those who were present, that Mr. Mayor be requested to inform the managers of the Theatre that they shall be permitted to continue their plays in this City, upon the same terms as usual."[17] The significance of these entries is their statement that there was in Richmond at this time a "playhouse," or "Theatre," a building with side boxes, front boxes, and "pitt." A building so equipped may be taken as evidence of some considerable theatrical activity.

This theatre may have been the wooden house in the rear of Rose's Brig, of which Mordecai had heard. Mordecai, however, briefly passes over this theatre (probably Dennis Ryan's) for what he considers the first regular theatre in Richmond, which was the well-known academy of Alexander Quesnay. On the basis of the

Common Hall records, however, it seems reasonable to assume that Quesnay's academy became the second regular theatre opened in Richmond. The first, I believe, was the one in which Dennis Ryan's Company of Comedians performed in 1784.

The company, characterized by Odell as "not particularly strong," included (besides Mr. and Mrs. Ryan and their son) Heard, Lewis, Wall, Davids, Brown, Walker, Roussell, Atherton, Jones, Coffy, Mrs. Garrison, Mrs. Potter, Mrs. Parsons, Mrs. Smith, Mrs. Fitzgerald. With the exception of Mrs. Fitzgerald, who left the company in New York, we may assume that these were members of the company that Ryan brought to Richmond. During their New York season they acted typical eighteenth-century fare, including *The Grecian Daughter, The Lying Valet, The Fatal Discovery, The Cheats of Scapin, The West Indian, The Fair Penitent, She Stoops to Conquer, Jane Shore, George Barnwell, Isabella, Douglas, Richard III, The Recruiting Officer, Macbeth, High Life below Stairs.*[18] These plays were probably acted in Richmond as in New York. Although both plays and players are conjectural, there seems to be reasonable evidence to hypothecate a theatrical season in Richmond in November 1785. It may have been Ryan's last season. He died in Baltimore in January 1786.

THIRD SEASON
Hallam and Henry Company
October 1786

Chronicle.   We know more about Richmond's second theatre, which began as an academy in 1785. Of this academy and its use as a theatre, Mordecai writes:

The site chosen by M. Quesnay and on which he erected his Academy is the square on which the Monumental Church and the Medical College now stand, the grounds extending from those lower points up Broad and Marshall to 12th street. The Academy stood nearly on the spot where the Carleton house stands. . . .

The extensive square, with the Academy-building on it, became the property of West and Bignal, or some other English actors, who managed the theatres in all Southern States. They converted the

Academy into one, and here the tragic and comic muses first excited the tears and smiles—in an edifice devoted to them—of a Richmond audience.[19]

An advertisement for August 6, 1785, announced Quesnay's academy, quoting tuition fees for instruction in drawing, fencing, dancing, languages, and music. Quesnay stated that "the school will positively be opened on the 26th instant" and that his intention was to hold school three days each week in Richmond and three in Petersburg until he could "induce the inhabitants of one of those places to fix his Academy." Again on Saturday, September 24, Quesnay advertised the "Richmond Academy," stating that "the different Schools of the Academy are at present attended by Mr. Quesnay next door to Capt. Mitchells, opposite the Bridge." He scheduled "Drawing, French, Music, &c" in the forenoon, dancing in the afternoon.[20]

Not until the following spring was there mention of a theatre. Quesnay's academy had, apparently, outgrown the schoolhouse "next door to Capt. Mitchells," and a new building was projected. The *Virginia Gazette, or, the American Advertiser* on Wednesday, May 17, 1786, printed more than a column on the academy, mostly Quesnay's address to his subscribers in which he informed them that "a delightful situation containing near 3 acres, and bordering on the Main street upon Shockoe hill, being already purchased for the buildings and garden, and the subscriptions at this time exceeding 1,000£" assured a successful opening by the beginning of next winter. In this address Quesnay proposed six trustees, among whose duties would be "to limit and direct the number, and arrangement of balls, concerts, theatrical and other public entertainments." In the last paragraph of his address, he said, "As one chief encouragement to the Masters who shall be employed by M. Quesnay in the Academy, must flow from the public entertainments to be promoted therein, the price of teaching from time to time, will greatly depend on the success of such entertainments, and the public favor that is extended to them."

Below Quesnay's address is published the minutes of the meeting at which the address was delivered. Trustees were appointed, and Benjamin Lewis was authorized to contract for the building. It was decided that possession be immediately given Quesnay "of the land purchased of Dr. Turpin by John Harvie for the use of the said Academy."

On Wednesday, August 30, the *Virginia Gazette and Independent Chronicle* carried a half-column advertisement of the academy. Quesnay set the date of opening on September 4 and printed details of rules, curricula, and the like. In the second paragraph, he stated: "As the Hall of the Academy will be for a short time occupied by Messrs. Hallam and Henry, as a Theatre, during their residence in this City, the Scholars shall be attended to as usual in the same private House now occupied for that Purpose. And the same Decorum will be kept, until the wings of the Academy shall be built, in Order that the Scholars have no Communication with the Theatre—and to keep that Decency requisite for such a public School." The notice is dated Richmond, August 28, and signed "A. M. Quesnay."

The news columns of the same issue carried the following item: "We are well informed, that the Old American Company of Comedians, (under the direction of Messrs. Hallam and Henry) which has performed with such eclat at New York, has obtained permission to perform in this City next October, when a spacious Theatre on Shockhoe-hill, will be built for their reception, by Messrs. Booker and Bell." This "spacious Theatre on Shockhoe-hill" was evidently Quesnay's academy.

Again on Wednesday, September 13, Quesnay advertised his academy. His advertisement concluded with the following notice: "N.B. The Academy-Hall being intended to be occupied occasionally as a Theatre seems to astonish some persons; but they are requested to look over the Subscription and Resolves, and they will see that it always was intended as such, as an Encouragement to the Masters to help supporting them genteely, in Case their respective Schools should not answer constantly the Purpose."[21]

Richmond was either ignorant or naive if it did not suspect Quesnay of intending to establish a theatre. A similar plan had already encountered, and been defeated by, piety in Philadelphia.[22] Evidently Quesnay succeeded in Richmond with the same academy-theatre scheme in which he had been thwarted in Philadelphia.

In his brief account of the theatre in Richmond, Seilhamer says that Hallam and Henry entered into articles with Mr. Quesnay for the privilege of giving theatrical entertainments in the hall of his Academy for four years, not to exceed two months in the year, the season to begin with the first day of the Richmond races. . . . Quesnay assumed the entire cost of the building, which was new and was calculated to contain sixteen hundred people, but he afterwards complained that some persons had charged that his Academy had been forgotten for the theatre. Hallam and Henry agreed for their part that the performances of the Old American Company in Virginia should be confined to Richmond. The theatre, erected in pursuance of this agreement, was opened with *School for Scandal* October 10th, 1786. No list of performances has been preserved beyond the fact that the bill for the 19th comprised *Alexander the Great* and *The Poor Soldier.*[23]

Seilhamer's statements are probably correct, though I believe his date for the performance of *Alexander the Great* and *The Poor Soldier* is incorrect, unless there were two identical performances, one on October 19, another on October 30, which I doubt.

More important, there is evidence that Seilhamer's date for the opening of the theatre is wrong. The *Virginia Gazette, or, the American Advertiser* for October 18, 1786, prints the following news:

Richmond, Oct. 18

Monday last was the day appointed for the meeting of the Honorable General Assembly, but very few members are as yet arrived.

Yesterday the Richmond Races began, when the Purse was won with ease in two heats, by Col. Sim's bay horse, the Ace of Spades.

Last evening the New Theatre under the management of Hallam & Henry was opened.

The three items are related. Any theatre manager would naturally schedule performances during sessions of the legislature and the races. Richmond was crowded for the legislature, and in festive mood for the races. I suspect that many of the same persons might have been seen at the legislature in the morning, at the races in the afternoon, and attending the theatre in the evening. Hallam and Henry were certainly shrewd enough to take advantage of the occasion. Indeed, Seilhamer says that the contract specified opening the theatre on the first day of the races.

This brief item definitely establishes the opening date as October 17 rather than October 10. We can only regret that no paper printed an account of the opening, which must have been an event of considerable social and cultural display. I hazard a curtain speech by Quesnay and the recitation of an ode by Hallam.

The Hallam and Henry Company played in Richmond during the autumn of 1786. Only one contemporary advertisement, dated Saturday, October 28, exists from their season: "Theatre: Monday Evening, *Alexander the Great; or, the Rival Queens,* and the *Poor Soldier.*" Monday was October 30. The same issue carried this further theatrical notice: "Theatre: The Public are respectfully informed the Subscriber will attend every Monday Morning from 8 to 10 o'clock, at his Office in the house on Shockhoe-hill, lately occupied by Mr. Dixon, to pay any demands against the Old American Company." The notice is dated Richmond, October 20, and signed "John Henry."[24]

The Old American Company of Lewis Hallam and John Henry was the best-known company of actors in eighteenth-century America. It played all the theatrical centers of the colonies, and later of the early Republic. The New American Company was an offshoot of the Old. It was also called the "K" company. The scant records from the Richmond newspapers are supplemented by Arthur Hornblow:

Hallam and Henry, on closing their John Street Theatre season in New York, August 2, 1786, went to Baltimore, where a new theatre had been erected on Philpot's Hill. The season was very brief, ending September 12, Sheridan's two comedies "The School for Scandal" and "The Rivals" being features of the repertoire. Following this engagement the company went to Richmond, Virginia, where the new theatre had been erected by Alexander Quesnay, and opened there on October 10, 1786, with "The School for Scandal," subsequent bills being "Alexander the Great" and "The Poor Soldier." The Richmond season closed late in the fall of 1786.[25]

Since the production of *Alexander the Great* and *The Poor Soldier* is corroborated by the newspaper advertisement, it seems reasonable to assume that the season was opened with *The School for Scandal,* although both Hornblow and Seilhamer give the wrong date.

Two items from contemporary Richmond newspapers are interesting as indications of public opinion in relation to the thea-

tre. On September 20, the *Virginia Independent Chronicle* carried
an article on the hot political issue of paper currency:

> Is it not astonishing that any man in his sober senses, should
> presume to oppose the excessive clamour of *certain descriptions
> of men for a paper currency,*—when we find, that bets are running
> only from 1 to 15 guineas, *that no more than £600* will be taken
> by Messrs. Hallam and Henry, on the three first nights of opening
> their Theatre in the new Church—new Academy I mean—in this
> city, the ensuing October—and, that the Company after a stay of
> *six weeks,* will not take more than £1500 clear money out of the
> State?

The writer's satire is obvious; the source of his theatrical information is unknown.

Whether Hallam and Henry left the state with £1,500 clear
money after a season of six weeks is an interesting speculation;
but after they were gone Alexander Quesnay felt obliged to explain again the actors' use of the academy. His advertisement on
November 22 includes the following explanation, the apologetic
tone of which indicates an attempt to placate opposition or to
mollify criticism:

> Although it has been always understood, that theatrical
> Amusements should be set on foot occasionally in the Academy,
> nevertheless, the respect M. Quesnay has for his Subscribers, will,
> and as he wishes to please them generally, makes him lament the
> necessity in which he is obliged to make Use of this Privilege,
> which occasion some Persons to imagine the Academy was for-
> gotten, for the Theatre.
>
> If M. Quesnay had Property enough of his own, he would think
> it more honorable to spend it in the Support of his Academy and
> set apart the Theatre: But if it should be considered impartially,
> and without Prejudice, that he has already spent 1200£ of his own,
> (above the subscription for the Building) that he must procure all
> kind of Instruments and give a great Salary and Encouragement to
> able Masters—that he has no other Funds to pay the Building, and
> support the Scheme, but the Income of his Labor and Industry—
> It cannot be expected that above all, in the beginning, the Scholars
> alone could defray such an Expence, without being prejudicial to
> them—Therefore it must appear to every impartial Person that if
> theatrical Amusements could be carried on so decently, as not to
> interfere with the Schools, that the profits arising from them, can-
> not be employed in a better Use. At the same Time, in M.

Quesnay's hands, it will be a means of giving Credit to the Indents, Certificates, and Civil-List; his Intention is, (if possible) to receive them at the Theatre, at Current Price, as well as Country Produce— such a mode as could only be adopted by an inhabitant.[26]

The reference to "Indents, Certificates, and Civil-List" indicates concern for the currency, while acceptance of country produce at the box office would establish a barter theatre in Richmond about a century and a half before a similar solution to a similar financial difficulty was found in Abingdon.

On March 8, 1787, the *Virginia Gazette, and Weekly Advertiser* published a column of "airs from the favorite Comic Opera of the *Poor Soldier.*" The airs were continued in the issues of March 15, 22, and 29. Apparently they were favorably received, for on May 17 the *Gazette* advertised as "just published: *The Poor Soldier,* a Comic Opera, in two acts." Advertisements of the play ran in the paper for several months. Richmond should have been familiar with the play by the time the *Gazette* carried this announcement on September 20, 1787: "The Theatre at Baltimore, was opened on the 27th ult. by The Old American Company of Comedians, under the direction of Messrs. Hallam and Henry, with the tragedy of the *Gamester,* and the Comic Opera of the *Poor Soldier.*"

The plays. Sheridan's *The School for Scandal* (October 17, 1786), one of the most famous plays of the English stage, had its premiere at Drury Lane on May 8, 1777. Odell assumes "with some degree of confidence" that it was first performed in New York on April 15, 1782, by soldier-actors during the military occupation of the city. He records its first New York production by professional actors on December 12, 1785, with John Henry as Sir Peter Teazle. Pollock assumes that it was first acted in Philadelphia by the Hallam and Henry Company in the summer of 1787: "There is little risk in assuming that *The School for Scandal* was produced during the season (for the first time in the city), though the tale advertised was '*The Pernicious Vice of Scandal.*'" Willis records its first performance in Charleston on April 6, 1793, by the West and Bignall Company. It seems that the play had its American premiere in New York by amateurs. Seilhamer says that its first American performance by professionals was in Baltimore on February 3, 1784, by the Dennis Ryan Company. There is record of one later performance in Richmond during this century.[27]

The Poor Soldier (October 30, 1786), a musical farce by John O'Keeffe, had been first acted at Covent Garden in 1783. It was acted in New York on December 2, 1785, and in Philadelphia on January 22, 1787. It was one of the most popular afterpieces in the early nineteenth-century American theatre and was acted frequently in Richmond. *Alexander the Great, or the Rival Queens*, a tragedy by Nathaniel Lee, had been first acted at Drury Lane in 1677. Its first performance in America had been in Philadelphia on December 30, 1768. It was first produced in New York at the John Street Theatre on February 24, 1769. "Famous for its acting roles, filled with occasional flashes of rhetorical splendor, appealing to the women because of its passionate interpretation of love, and to the men by its martial and manly parts, *The Rival Queens* held the boards as long as the tradition of declamatory eloquence survived in the theatre."[28] It was acted in Richmond again on October 9, 1811, on July 9, 1819, and in Charleston as late as 1835. Odell quotes an advertisement for the New York presentation on July 3, 1786: "In act second the TRIUMPHAL ENTRY of Alexander into Babylon, with a display of Armorial Trophies, Spoils, Ensigns, &c. descriptive of his Conquest.—The procession will close with a GRAND TRIUMPHAL CAR, after the manner of the ancient Macedonians. In act fourth, a GRAND BANQUET, in which will be introduced the song of "Thou like the Glorious Sun," from the Opera of Artaxerxes. With new Scenery, illuminations, &c,&c."[29] Could we assume that the Richmond production was of comparable magnificence?

Other plays in the repertoire of the company at this time included *As You Like It, Hamlet, Richard III, The Tempest, The Merchant of Venice, Catharine and Petruchio, Venice Preserved, Douglas, Jane Shore, High Life below Stairs, The Gamester, The West Indian, The Lying Valet, The Padlock,* and *The Critic,* all of which were produced during the New York season between November 21, 1785, and August 2, 1786. Since this list is typical of conventional eighteenth-century billing, we might reasonably suppose that these were the plays acted in Richmond during the season of 1786.

The players.   At this time the Hallam and Henry Company was the strongest in America, containing an adequate number of able actors. For names see Appendix 2. The members of the company most probably played in Richmond the roles they had previously played in New York, although we must again depend upon conjecture in the absence of playbills and newspaper advertisements.

FOURTH SEASON
William Verling Company (?)
November–December 1787

Chronicle.   There was one more season during the decade. On October 10, 1787, this tidbit of stylistic whimsy appeared in the *Virginia Independent Chronicle:* "We hear from Petersburg that the New-Emissioned Company of Comedians, under the old Veteran V-s, shortly intend to shew new and old faces in a new style at the Old Theatre in this City.—And however strange it may appear—'tis said they are chiefly from Old and New England and e'en part of the Old and New American Company of Comedians."

Hugh F. Rankin assumes that the "V" stands for William Verling, who was truly an "old Veteran" of the American stage.[30] Twenty years before, he had played the leading role of Beverly in *The Gamester* on March 6, and taken a benefit on March 20, 1766, in Charleston. He had been a member of the Virginia Company of Comedians at Williamsburg in 1768 and of the New American Company at Annapolis in 1769, playing leading roles with both companies.[31] Of the actors who appeared during this season in Richmond (we have names of twelve), none was with Verling in any of these places. Of contemporary actors whose names begin with *V*, Verling is perhaps as likely as any. Could "V-s" be a misprint for "V-g"?

The Richmond season evidently opened between October 10 and November 8, 1787, when the first advertisement appeared:

BY PERMISSION
On Monday evening next at the New Theatre, Shockhoe Hill, will be performed for the benefit of Mrs. Smallwood, Shakespeare's

Historical Play, call'd *King Henry the 4th* with the Humours of
Sir John Falstaff.
To which will be added *Miss in Her Teens, or The Medley of
Lovers*.
Comic Songs &c. &c. As will be expressed in the bills of the Day.
Box 4 s. 6 d.—Pitt 3 s.—Tickets to be had at Mr. Nicolson's
Printing Office, Mr. Anderson's tavern, the office of the Theatre,
and of Mrs. Smallwood.[32]

Henry IV seems a poor choice for Mrs. Smallwood. Usually a
benefit performance found the beneficiary in a favorite role, likely
a title role or a starring role; I doubt that Mrs. Smallwood played
Falstaff!

"Monday evening next" was the twelfth of November. There
may have been earlier performances, since benefits usually came
toward the close of the season. Even at times when we may reasonably expect to find theatrical advertisements, they do not appear,
and at times we must depend upon incomplete files of early
newspapers. The "bills of the Day" have not survived.

One week later, on Thursday, November 15, the *Virginia
Gazette, and Weekly Advertiser* carried another theatrical notice:
"At the New Theatre on Shockhoe Hill, on Saturday evening next,
Nov. 17, 1787, will be presented the Comedy of the *Recruiting
Officer*. To which will be added a dramatic satire, called *Lethe; or
Aesop in the Shades*." Tickets were to be had as before except for
Mrs. Smallwood. The performance on November 17 was advertised
"for the purpose of finishing the Academy." By "finishing" is
meant, I presume, adding the two wings that Quesnay had mentioned earlier. The main hall of the academy was being used by
the players, who may have paid, or helped to pay, for their use of
the building by this benefit.

The next advertisement which has been located appeared on
November 21:

BY PERMISSION

At the New Theatre, on Shockhoe Hill, this Evening, Wednesday,
Nov. 21, 1787, will be presented Shakespeare's celebrated Comedy
of the *Merchant of Venice*.
To which will be added a Farce, call'd *The Vintner Trick'd; or,
The White Fox Chas'd*.
No person on any account can be admitted behind the Scenes.—

Vivat Respublica[33]

In the advertisements of this season only one name, Mrs. Smallwood, has been mentioned as a member of the company. Later advertisements, however, enable us to identify what was probably the entire acting strength of the company. This one named three actors:

BY PERMISSION

At the New Theatre, Shockhoe Hill, on Friday Evening, Nov. 30th, 1787, will be presented the Tragedy of *Romeo and Juliet.*
In Act 2d, a Masquerade and Dance
End of the 4th Act, a Funeral Procession, and Solemn Dirge.
The Vocal Parts by Mrs. Giffard, Mr. Kidd, and Mr. Wells.
To which will be added a Farce call'd *The Citizen.*

This advertisement informs us also that "doors will be opened at half past five, and the performance begin precisely at half past 6 o'clock."[34] Presumably these hours were kept through the season, since no others are mentioned in other notices.

There is record of only one other performance this season. The *Virginia Gazette, and Weekly Advertiser* of December 6 carried an advertisement of the program for Friday, December 7, "the last night but one of the Company's Performing in this City." The performance was for the benefit of Mr. Bisset, with the following explanation: "The Company of Comedians respectfully inform the Public that the above benefit is given Mr. Bisset for the generous assistance rendered them by him." Mr. Bisset was a member of the acting troupe, but what "generous assistance" other than acting he rendered the company we do not know. This advertisement names the members of the troupe: "At the New Theatre Shockhoe Hill on Friday Evening, December the 7th, 1787, will be Presented the *Beggar's Opera* the characters by Mr. Kidd, Mr. Lewis, Mr. Welles, Mr. Lake, Mr. Bisset, Mr. Parsons, Mr. Rankin (being his first appearance on this stage) Mrs. Gifford, Miss Gordon, Mrs. Smallwood, Mrs. Parsons, and Polly by Mrs. Rankin (late Mrs. Remington), being her first appearance on the stage of this city, these two years." Afterpiece for the evening was "Macklin's celebrated Farce of *Love A-La-Mode,*" which was offered "by Particular desire." The advertisement gives the following cast of characters:

Sir Archy Macsarcasm (a Scotchman)	Mr. Bisset
Squire Groom (a Newmarket Jockey)	Mr. Welles

Beau Mordecai (an English Jew)	Mr. Lake
Sir Theodore Goodchild	Mr. Lewis
Servant	Mr. Parsons
Sir Callaghan O'Brallaghan (an Irishman)	Mr. Kidd
Charlotte	Miss Gordon

The evening was enlivened by "singing by Mr. Bisset, and Mr. Welles" between the pieces, and "the Comic Song of 'Four-and-twenty fidlers all in a Row'" by Mr. Bisset after the farce to conclude the evening. Tickets were on sale "at Mr. Nicolson's Printing office, at Mr. Rawlin's tavern, at Mr. Trower's tavern of Mr. Bisset, and at the Theatre." Prices were four shillings sixpence for boxes, three shillings for the "Pitt." We are again informed that "doors will be opened at half past five, and the performance begin precisely at half past 6 o'clock," and that "no person on any account can be admitted behind the scenes." The advertisement concludes with a resounding "VIVAT RESPUBLICA!"

Since the advertisement of December 7 identified this evening as the "last night but one," we may hypothecate one more, the last of the season. With equal probability we may hypothecate other performances in addition to the five of which records exist. It is probable that a one-month season, opening early in November and closing early in December, was played. We have records of performances on Monday, Wednesday, Friday, and Saturday. If we assume four performances each week for a month, we assume thirty-two plays acted on sixteen nights. We have ten titles: *Henry IV, Miss in Her Teens, The Recruiting Officer, Lethe, The Merchant of Venice, Trick upon Trick, Romeo and Juliet, The Citizen, The Beggar's Opera,* and *Love a-la-Mode.*[35]

If we accept Seilhamer's statement that Hallam and Henry "entered into articles with Mr. Quesnay" for four years and if we assume that they took a clear profit of £1,500 after a season of six weeks in 1786, we may wonder why they did not play out their contract from 1786 to 1790. There are several considerations. Most important, I suspect, was resentment against Quesnay's academy being used as a theatre. Quesnay evidently fell into disfavor with some of his subscribers, who were willing to support an academy but not a theatre, and who perhaps felt that they had been tricked into supporting the theatre. It is possible that the contract was canceled by disgruntled academy subscribers. Quesnay's grandiose plans for the academy were never realized; he gave up and returned to France. The use of the academy building as a theatre in 1786 was probably an important factor in the failure of the academy itself.

There was a disastrous fire in 1787, which, though it did not destroy the theatre, burned a large section of the city. In 1788 the theatre was occupied by the Virginia Constitutional Convention. Finally, the Hallam and Henry Company was busy in New York and Philadelphia during these years. At any rate, they did not return to play out their contract. The next significant development was the arrival of West and Bignall in 1790.

The plays. *Henry IV* (November 12, 1787) was acted in Richmond twice in 1811. *Miss in Her Teens*, a farce by David Garrick, was first acted at Covent Garden in 1747. It was acted in New York in 1751, and in Philadelphia in 1754. There are records of two performances in Richmond in 1804 and four in 1806.

George Farquhar's *Recruiting Officer* (November 17, 1787) was one of the most popular plays of the eighteenth-century American stage. It was performed in New York, Charleston, and Philadelphia, but we have a record of only this one performance in Richmond. *Lethe*, a dramatic satire by Garrick, also appears only this once in the Richmond records. It had been acted in New York in 1751 and in Philadelphia in 1759.

The Merchant of Venice (November 21, 1787) had been acted in New York in 1768 and in Philadelphia in 1776. It was acted again in Richmond in 1793 and in 1811. *The Vintner Trick'd* had been acted in Charleston on October 31, 1786, where it was advertised as a farce. *Trick upon Trick*, identified by Odell as a Harlequin pantomime, had been acted in New York on August 23, 1783. *Trick upon Trick, or the White Fox Chas'd*, which was acted in Richmond on July 23, 1791, was described as a "comedy in two acts." It seems probable, however, that these were all the same piece. Designations of afterpieces were not always accurate. Apparently this was one of the many Harlequin pantomimes which served as popular afterpieces everywhere.

Romeo and Juliet (November 30, 1787) was popular on the

eighteenth-century American stage. It was acted in New York as early as 1754 and in Philadelphia in 1759. It was acted again in Richmond on December 31, 1795, when it was advertised "as altered by Garrick." Almost certainly Garrick's version was acted in Richmond in 1787. *The Citizen*, a farce by Arthur Murphy, was first acted at Drury Lane in 1761. It was acted in New York in 1768 and in Philadelphia in 1766. It was acted again in Richmond in 1791.

The Beggar's Opera (December 7, 1787) as performed in Richmond was probably the "alteration of Gay's ballad opera" by Edward Thompson, which had been first acted at Covent Garden on November 8, 1777, although the play in earlier form had been acted in New York in 1750 and in Philadelphia in 1759.[36] *Love a-la-Mode*, a farce by Charles Macklin, had been first acted at Drury Lane in 1759. It was acted in both New York and Philadelphia in 1768.

The players.   From the repetition of names in the bill of December 7, I estimate the acting strength of this company at seven men and five women, plus manager Verling. In addition to William Verling (assuming he was manager), others are recorded in other American theatres. Mrs. Remington had probably been a member of the Hallam and Henry Company which opened the new theatre in Richmond on October 17, 1786. She came from the Theatre Royal in Dublin and made her American debut as Mrs. Malaprop in New York on June 23, 1786. Evidently she married Mr. Rankin some time between July 1786 and November 1787. Lewis and Mrs. Parsons had been members of the Dennis Ryan Company which played in Richmond in 1784. Bisset played in Philadelphia in 1792 and New York in 1793. Mrs. Gifford played in New York in 1787. Mr. and Mrs. Rankin played in Philadelphia in 1791, and she played in New York in 1791, '92, and '93. Benefits for Bisset and Mrs. Smallwood during this season indicate that they played leading roles or perhaps performed some additional service such as painting scenery.

Hiatus
1788–1789

There are no records of theatrical activity in 1788 or 1789. During these two years entertainment in Richmond was scarce. On April 2, 1788, the city was informed of a camel "lately imported from Asia," which was on view at Mr. Adams's Livery Stable for the space of ten or twelve days at the price of one shilling sixpence. On August 21, 1788, R. Villiers advertised an "Eidophusikon, or Moveing Pictures . . . at the old Theatre in this city." The "old Theatre" I take to be the theatre in which Dennis Ryan performed in 1784, not the new theatre which Hallam and Henry opened in 1786. Evidently both survived the fire of 1787. Villiers advertised that "the Theatre is already decorated, and fitted up, for the above occasion." Although the exhibition had to be postponed because of the indisposition of the artist (Villiers had the "dumb ague") and the badness of the weather, we may pause briefly to acclaim this precursor of D. W. Griffith and Walt Disney. After the "Moveing Pictures," the only entertainment we find advertised is "a Wild Beast called A Moose to be seen at Mr. Marsierson's opposite The Courthouse." The price of admission was one shilling each, children fourpence.[37]

One final flare of dramatic interest rounds out the decade. The *Virginia Gazette and Independent Chronicle* for October 25, 1788, carried, under a New York dateline of June 2, 1788, and a Richmond dateline of October 11, 1788, the following announcement:

Proposals, For Printing by Subscription, The Contrast, A Comedy, Written by Major Tyler.

Mr. Wignal who has been favored by Major Tyler, with this opportunity of presenting to the Public the first Dramatic Production of a Citizen of the United States, in which the Characters and Scenes are entirely American, respectfully solicits the patronage and assistance that are necessary to enable him to print and embellish this Book, in a form suitable to its intrinsic merit. A performance so interesting to the national feelings and so honorable to American genius and literature, will naturally recommend itself to general attention, and command in the closet a confirmation of that applause which it has already received on the stage: The Editor, therefore can only upon this occasion evince his respect for the Author by the manner of introducing it to the Public; and, to render that as perfect as possible, he proposes the following Conditions.

First. That the Comedy shall be printed in large octavo, with an elegant type, upon superfine paper.

Secondly. That the most interesting scene in the Comedy shall be prefixed in an engraving, executed by an American Artist.

Thirdly. The Price to each Subscriber to be Half a Dollar.

Subscriptions taken in at the Store of Messrs. Warrington and Keene, merchants Richmond, who will be answerable to such Ladies and Gentlemen who please to honor this Performance with their names, for its being duly delivered to them.

The Contrast was published by Prichard and Hall in Philadelphia in 1790. Wignell, who created the role of Jonathan, was responsible for securing the subscriptions. The list was headed by "the President of the United States." So the decade ends on a new note of nationalism.

During the 1780s we can identify three companies of players in Richmond; of these the strongest was undoubtedly the Hallam and Henry Company, which opened the new theatre in the fall of 1786. We can reasonably establish four seasons: June–December 1784; November 1785; October 1786; November–December 1787. We have one playbill. Careful search of extant Richmond newspapers has revealed only eleven theatrical notices, three in 1784, one in 1785, two in 1786, five in 1787. Early histories of the American theatre contain slight information; contemporary research (especially Odell, Pollock, and Willis) is valuable for checking and comparing records. This present study indicates considerable theatrical activity, of which few and scattered records remain.

CHAPTER II

1790–1794

FIFTH SEASON
West and Bignall Company
August 1790–January 1791

Chronicle.   In 1790 Richmond had a population of 3,761. Compared with Charleston (16,359), Philadelphia (28,522), and New York (33,131), Richmond was small; but compared with Petersburg (2,828), Norfolk (2,959), and Alexandria (2,748), it was the metropolis of Virginia. More important, it was the capital city, where the legislature met, and where the political life of the state centered. Richmond was inheriting from Williamsburg, along with political leadership, the social and cultural leadership of the state. Overlooking the city from Shockoe Hill stood the Capitol, and near it was the theatre.

Seilhamer discusses the Virginia Company, going at some length into a controversy over the merits of the new company organized by West and Bignall in relation to the older company managed by Hallam and Henry.[1] I shall not continue the controversy; suffice it that the Virginia Company was by some regarded as the best in America, by others as second best. Just when they came to Richmond is unknown, but Seilhamer says that they gave *The Evening Brush* in August 1790, "the announcements being made by handbills." No handbill survives, and I have located no newspaper corroboration of the performance, which may have been West and Bignall's first in Richmond.

I have located only one other performance of *The Evening Brush:* in Charleston on May 6, 1793, by the West and Bignall Company for the benefit of Manager West. Willis gives these details:

The Celebrated Pasticcio (as performed in London upwards of 300 nights with distinguished applause) called "The Evening Brush for Rubbing off the Rust of Care." Among a variety of laughable characters too extensive to be enumerated, will be introduced the following:—Spluttering Actors, Tragedy Taylors, Bell-wethers in Buskins—Boglers in blank verse—Wooden actors, Ghosts without their lessons, Yorkshire Jockeys, Lullaby Jinglers, Theatrical Candidates, Tragedy Pipers, Tragedy Bruisers, Butchers of Blank verse—

Parish Clerks, Readers without their Eyes,—Foote's Hamlet, Clown, and Church Warden. The Irish School Master and Pupil, The Actor and Scotch Pedler.
In the course of the Pasticcio the following Original Songs—
"Haste Away to the Brush," Mr. West,
Shakespeare's "Seven Ages," Mr. Bignall.
"The Siege of Troy, or the Classical Ballenamora"
   by Mr. West.
"Paddy Bull's Expedition," Mr. Bignall
The whole to conclude with "The Golden Days of Good
   Queen Bess." by Mr. West.
(This Pasticcio was originally performed in America by
   Messrs. West and Bignall with the greatest success.)[2]

I assume that "originally performed in America" refers to its American premiere in Richmond in August 1790 and that the two performances were closely similar.

Seilhamer continues: "How long this company remained at Richmond it is impossible to say, as the performances were seldom advertised in the newspapers." There are, however, records which indicate that they stayed well into January 1791.

On September 16, 1790, the Common Hall received

a petition of West and Bignall setting forth, that with the permission of the Hall, they intend to establish theatrical amusements in this City, and praying that an exclusive privilege may be granted them for that purpose, Resolved that the Mayor with the Recorder and eldest Alderman be appointed to confer with the petitioners upon their Application, and that they be authorized on the part of the Hall to make such contract with the petitioners, touching the subject of their petition as to them shall seem most conducive to the interests of the City.[3]

Evidently a satisfactory contract was made, for on October 18 the West and Bignall Company was acting in the theatre. The *Virginia Gazette, and General Advertiser* for Wednesday, October 13, announced for Monday the eighteenth at the "Theatre on Shockoe Hill (never performed here) the Comedy *Know Your Own Mind; or The Rover Reclaimed* (as written by Arthur Murphy Esq.)." The theatre had probably opened some time earlier (perhaps in August), but this is the first advertisement I have located for this season. Doors opened at six and the performance began at seven o'clock. Admission was six shillings, box; four shillings sixpence, pit; and three shillings, gallery. The advertisement stated: "No

BY THE VIRGINIA COMPANY.

✿✿✿✿✿✿✿✿✿✿✿✿

At the THEATRE, *on* SHOCKŒ-HILL, *on* MON-
DAY EVENING, *the* 18th *of* October, 1790,
will be presented (never perform'd here) the
CELEBRATED COMEDY OF

Know your own Mind;
O R,

The Rover Reclaimed.

(As wrtiten by ARTHUR MURPHY, Efq.)

Millamour (the Rover)	Mr. *Bignall*;
Old Bygrove,	Mr. *Lewis*;
Malvil,	Mr. *Biddle*;
Sir Harry Lovewit,	Mr. *Richards*;
Sir John Millamour,	Mr. *Tobine*;
Captain Bygrove,	Mr. *Walpole*;
Charles,	Mr. *Diddep*;
And Dafhwould,	Mr. *Weft.*
Lady Bell,	Mrs. *Weft*;
Lady Jane,	Mrs. *Hide*;
Mrs. Bromley,	Mrs. *Lewis*;
Madam La-Raige,	Mifs *Wade*;
And Mifs Neville,	Mrs. *Bignall.*

End of the Play, a Hunting Song, by Mrs. HIDE.

To which will be added, *a celebrated*
COMIC OPERA—*called,*

The FARMER;
O R,

The World's ups and downs.

(Written by JOHN O'KEEFE, Efq;) and perform'd
at the Theatre Royal Covent-Garden, upwards
of two hundred nights with univerfal applaufe.

Old Blackberry, (the Farmer)	Mr. *Biddle*;
Captain Valentine,	Mr. *Weft*;
Rundy, (the Plough Boy)	Mr. *Lewis*;
Lawyer Fairly,	Mr. *Walpole*;
Colonel Dormant,	Mr. *Richards*;
Councillor Flummery,	Mr. *Tobine*;
Stubble,	Mr. *Diddep*;
And Jemmy Jump, (the Macaroni	
Stay Maker)	Mr. *Bignall*;
Louifa,	Mrs. *Hide*;
Molly Maybufh,	Mifs *Wade*;
Land Lady,	Mrs. *Davids*;
And Betty Blackberry, (alias Mifs	
Eliza Timbertop)	Mrs. *Bignall*;

Doors to be open at fix, and begin precifely at
feven o'clock.

Admittance, Box 6/.—Pit 4/6.—Gallery 3/.
No Money will be received at the Door.
Tickets to he had at the Poft-Office, the Eagle
Tavern, Mr. Scott's, and at the Theatre, where
places for the Boxes may be taken.

West and Bignall Company advertisement, from the *Virginia Gazette, and General Advertiser*, October 13, 1790. (Courtesy Library of Congress.)

Money will be received at the Door." Tickets were on sale at the post office, the Eagle Tavern, Mr. Scott's (probably the actors' boarding house), and "at the theatre, where places for the Boxes may be taken."

A complete cast of characters for *Know Your Own Mind* was included in the advertisement, featuring Bignall as Millamour (the Rover), West as Dashwould, Mrs. West as Lady Bell, and Mrs. Bignall as Miss Neville:

Millamour (the Rover)	Mr. Bignall
Old Bygrove	Mr. Lewis
Malvil	Mr. Biddle
Sir Harry Lovewit	Mr. Richards
Sir John Millamour	Mr. Tobine
Captain Bygrove	Mr. Walpole
Charles	Mr. Diddep
Dashwould	Mr. West
Lady Bell	Mrs. West
Lady Jane	Mrs. Hide
Mrs. Bromley	Mrs. Lewis
Madam La-Raige	Miss Wade
Miss Neville	Mrs. Bignall

Between play and afterpiece Mrs. Hide sang "a Hunting Song." Afterpiece was "the Comic Opera *The Farmer; or, The World's Ups and Downs* (written by John O'Keefe Esq.)." Again Mr. and Mrs. Bignall played featured roles, he as Jemmy Jump (the Macaroni Stay Maker), and she as Betty Blackberry (alias Miss Eliza Timbertop):

Old Blackberry (the Farmer)	Mr. Biddle
Captain Valentine	Mr. West
Rundy (the Plough Boy)	Mr. Lewis
Lawyer Fairly	Mr. Walpole
Colonel Dormant	Mr. Richards
Councillor Flummery	Mr. Tobine
Stubble	Mr. Diddep
Jemmy Jump (the Macaroni Stay Maker)	Mr. Bignall
Louisa	Mrs. Hide
Molly Maybush	Miss Wade
Land Lady	Mrs. Davids
Betty Blackberry (alias Miss Eliza Timbertop)	Mrs. Bignall

The next record of performance was on Wednesday, October 27, when *Venice Preserved* and *The Poor Soldier* were advertised for the twenty-eighth. The only player named was Mrs. Bignall, who played Patrick (the Poor Soldier). I assume that she was irresistible in this "breeches part," and that she played to a full house.

The same newspaper that advertised *Venice Preserved* and *The Poor Soldier* carried this interesting item from West and Bignall:

> Messrs. West & Bignall, viewing with regret the imperfect state of Dramatic Exhibition in this part of the World, are determined from motives of duty as well as that of interest, to exert themselves in the service of their generous patrons and the public at large, by Augmenting their Company with Characters of real merit. Well knowing that persons of that description only can render the stage useful and respectable; in which, above all others, the human genius has opportunities of displaying itself in the most agreeable, the most engaging light, and perhaps to the greatest advantage. For in this profession it is that all the powers of eloquence, all the variety of expression of which action or language are capable, and all the graces of delivery, are peculiarly requisite; and in no other school are virtue and good manners more emphatically enforced or vice and folly more effectually put out of countenance.
>
> In order to put their resolution in force they now offer very liberal salaries to young Gentlemen of figure and education, who may incline to make the stage their profession. Every attention shall be paid to the Cultivation of dawning merit.
>
> Note. —A letter addressed to Messrs. West & Bignall, Managers of the Virginia Company, will be punctually attended to.[4]

West and Bignall were already recruiting actors for what was later to become the largest company in America. The advertisement of October 13 had named thirteen actors, including several experienced and able performers. Later advertisements add five names, making a company of eighteen. In all, there were eleven men and six women; Master Davids brings the total to eighteen. There were several changes when the company played its next season in Richmond in the fall of 1791.

There is no record of performance between October 28, 1790, and January 5, 1791. The advertisement of October 27 indicates that the company was acting in Richmond. It is possible that the company went to Petersburg (only twenty miles away) for a few weeks; it is equally probable that they continued their season in Richmond without benefit of newspaper advertisements. Perhaps handbills were cheaper. But the newspapers have been better preserved.

The next record of theatrical production appeared on January 5, 1791, when was advertised for Friday, January 7, "the Comedy *The Busy Body* written by Mrs. Centlivre, with alterations and additions by David Garrick Esq." The afterpiece for the evening was "Dibdin's Musical Farce of *The Padlock*." Complete casts were given for both plays. Bignall played the two featured roles, Marplot in *The Busy Body* and Mungo in *The Padlock:*

The Busy Body

Marplot (the Busy Body)	Mr. Bignall
Sir Jealous Traffick	Mr. West
Sir Francis Gripe	Mr. Richards
Charles	A Gentleman for his Amusement
Whisper	Mr. Whipple
Sir George Airy	Mr. Hallam
Miranda	Mrs. West
Isabinda	Miss Wade
Scentwell	Mrs. Davids
Patch	Mrs. Bignall

The Padlock

Don Diego	Mr. West
Leander	Mr. Richards
First Scholar	Mr. Hallam
Second Scholar	Mr. Whipple
Mungo	Mr. Bignall
Ursula	Mrs. Davids
Leonora	Mrs. Bignall

The role of Charles in *The Busy Body* was played by "a Gentleman for his Amusement." Possibly he was a local amateur who had responded to the advertisement for new talent. Features of the evening's entertainment were the songs "To the Greenwood Gang with Me," "Lud Don't You Keep Teazing Me So," and "I Tremble at Twenty-Two," by Mrs. Bignall; and "The Grecian Fabulist," by Mr. Bignall.[5]

The last record of this season appeared on January 12, 1791, when was advertised "At the Theatre Richmond this Evening . . . Southern's Celebrated Tragedy of *Isabella; or The Fatal Marriage.*" The afterpiece was "A Farce call'd *The Citizen*." Complete casts were given for both plays:

Isabella

Villeroy	Mr. Hallam
Carlos	A Gentleman for his
	Amusement
Count Baldwin	Mr. Richards
Sampson	Mr. West
Pedro	Mr. Solomon
Child	Master Davids
Bellford	Mr. Whipple
Biron	Mr. Bignall
Nurse	Mrs. Davids
Isabella	Mrs. West

The Citizen

Young Philpot	Mr. Bignall
Young Wilding	Mr. Hallam
Old Philpot	Mr. Richards
Beaufort	Mr. Solomon
Quilldrive	Mr. Whipple
Sir Jasper Wilding	Mr. West
Corinna	Miss Wade
Maria	Mrs. Bignall

Carlos was played by "a Gentleman for his Amusement." Was this the same gentleman who had appeared five days before, or were West and Bignall trying out several local candidates for membership in the company? The latter seems probable. The advertisement this date is headed "By the Virginia Company." The performance was "for the Benefit of Mr. Hallam."

Hallam richly rewarded his audience. Not only did he play Villeroy in *Isabella* and Young Wilding in *The Citizen;* between the plays he performed "an Awkward Hornpipe, in character of a Dwarf Three feet high," and he concluded the evening "with an Epilogue, and a flying leap through a hogshead of Blazing Fire." There was also "singing by Mr. and Mrs. Solomon" and "Lash to the Helm" by Mr. Solomon. Could anyone ask more for three shillings (boxes, 6s.)?[6]

During this season there are newspaper records of four performances by the Virginia Company. Eight plays are named, with casts given for six. Of these eight plays, five, *Isabella, The Busy Body, Venice Preserved, The Farmer,* and *Know Your Own Mind,* were acted in Richmond for the first time. Three, *Isabella,*

Know Your Own Mind, and *The Farmer,* were acted for the first time in America. To these we may add *The Evening Brush* as probable.

The plays. *Know Your Own Mind* (October 18, 1790), by Arthur Murphy, had been first acted at Covent Garden on February 22, 1777, and was published in 1778. It was acted in Charleston on February 14, 1793, by the West and Bignall Company. Although there were many changes in the company, Mr. and Mrs. West and Mr. and Mrs. Bignall all appeared in the same roles they played in Richmond. *Know Your Own Mind* was acted in New York on April 24, 1795, and in Philadelphia on May 4, 1795. Presumably, this Richmond performance was the first American production of the play. *The Farmer,* by John O'Keeffe, had been first acted at Covent Garden on October 31, 1787, and was published in 1788. It was acted in Philadelphia on November 16, 1792. Willis records a performance in Charleston on February 15, 1793, in which Mr. and Mrs. Bignall again played Jemmy Jumps and Betty Blackberry. Three days later, on February 18, 1793, *The Farmer* was presented at the John Street Theatre in New York. It seems, therefore, that this also was an American premiere.

Venice Preserved (October 28, 1790), a tragedy by Thomas Otway, had been first acted at Dorset Garden on February 9, 1681/82. One of the most popular plays on the American stage, it had been acted in New York as early as 1752, Philadelphia in 1767, and Charleston in 1782. There are many records of performances in Richmond in later years. *The Poor Soldier* had been previously acted in Richmond on October 30, 1786, as afterpiece to *Alexander the Great.* It also was a particular favorite of American audiences.

The Busy Body (January 7, 1791), by Susannah Centlivre, was first acted at Drury Lane in 1709. Its American premiere was at Williamsburg in 1736. It was acted in both New York and Philadelphia in 1768, and in Charleston in 1774. It was not an outstanding play either in dramatic merit or stage history, although there are records of several later performances in Richmond. *The Padlock* was acted in Richmond on June 21, 1784, as afterpiece to *Douglas* on the opening night of Dennis Ryan's "New Theatre."

Thomas Southerne's *The Fatal Marriage, or the Innocent Adultery* (January 12, 1791) had been first acted at Drury Lane in 1694. It was revised by Garrick as *Isabella, or the Fatal Marriage* and acted at Drury Lane in 1757. The version acted in Richmond was almost certainly Garrick's. *Isabella* was acted in Philadelphia on February 18, 1791. It was acted in Charleston by the West and Bignall Company on November 5, 1794. This performance in Richmond was evidently its American premiere.

The players.   Several of this company can be identified on other stages in eighteenth-century America. Charles Biddle had played with the Hallam and Henry Company in New York in 1785 and 1787 and evidently had been well received. The New York *Daily Advertiser* on June 8, 1787, carried this puff: "Biddle in honest Colin [in *The Fashionable Lover*] operated most powerfully upon the sensibility of the spectators. . . . Mr. Biddle has not yet had a *benefit*, and a pity it is, that an Actor of his ability should want encouragement. Would the generous citizens of New York, who are friends to elegant and rational entertainments, and who have seen Mr. Biddle in the characters of Father *Luke,* Father *Paul,* Colin M'Leod, and others, be backward to patronize him? I think not." Biddle played Jessamy in the New York production of *The Contrast* on June 10, 1789, with Lewis Hallam as Colonel Manly. He was with this company, the Old American Company, when it played in Philadelphia in 1790. He died in Richmond in 1791.

Lewis had played with the Dennis Ryan Company in New York in 1783; he was in Richmond with Ryan in 1784. He played at Ricketts's Circus at Philadelphia in 1799. Odell mentions him in New York in later years. The Hallam who took a benefit on January 12 was Mirvin, son of Lewis, the third generation on the American stage.

Solomon was with the Hallam and Henry Company in Philadelphia in November 1794 and went on with the company to New York for the season of 1794-95. Mrs. Solomon and Miss Solomon were also with the company. The name appears with and without the final *s.*

Richards was actually Richard Crosby, a younger son of British nobility who adventured for several years on the American stage with the Hallam and Henry Company. He played in Philadelphia in 1794 and made his New York debut as Barbarossa on December 28, 1793. Odell prints his picture and gives interesting details about his person and background.

Most important were, of course, West and Bignall themselves; the fullest treatment of both is by Susanne K. Sherman:

Thomas Wade West was forty-five years old when he landed in Philadelphia in 1790. With him were his wife Margaretta, his children, and his son-in-law and future partner, John Bignall. He brought to Lewis Hallam, Jr., Manager of the Old American Company, a letter of introduction from his sister, Mrs. Mattocks, a well-known English actress. Hallam welcomed the actors, assuring Mr. and Mrs. West and Mr. and Mrs. Bignall places in his company; but he offered them only two guineas a week, and he would not guarantee that they would ever be permitted to play the parts for which they felt themselves best qualified. These parts had already been claimed by the established members of the company—if not by the managers themselves. It was not a promising prospect, but there was no other manager in the United States who could offer them more.

Of the four actors, it was probably Thomas Wade West who decided that they should refuse Hallam's offer and form a company of their own with which to tour the South. As an actor, he was probably worth no more than the two guineas and the parts offered him; but it was he who had the vision, the executive ability and the money which were necessary to gather together and maintain a first class company of actors, superior to the Old American Company which at that time served Philadelphia and New York.

The company of West and Bignall, which was to lay the foundations for twenty-two years of uninterrupted theatre of such exceptionally fine quality, was formed before the actors departed from Philadelphia; for one of the comedians of the Old American Company left the management of Hallam and Henry to join it. This newly-formed company, although smaller than it would ever be again, already gave promise of the high quality which was to characterize it. Thomas Wade West was an experienced and adequate actor with a good voice for the comic songs which were so popular as entr'acte entertainments. His wife Margaretta excelled in tragic parts. His daughter Ann West Bignall was young and inexperienced, but she was pretty and blessed with a good singing voice, and she doubtless gave promise of the incomparable actress she was to become. Charles Biddle, a useful actor, adept at portraying Scotsmen on stage, was so valued by Hallam and Henry that they complained, through the newspaper, that he had been lured away from them. The star of the new company, however, was John Bignall. He was probably still under thirty. Playing in England under the name of Mr. Moneypenny, he had been characterized as a young adventurer. He was a versatile actor who could, and often did, take the leading roles in both the tragedy and the farce of one evening's entertainment; but the rare quality which set him above all the other actors was a warmth which he could project beyond the footlights—a warmth which made the audience who laughed at him as he played the dunderhead, the yokel and the fool, love him.[7]

The success of the Wests and Bignalls in Richmond is attested, perhaps even exaggerated, by a poem of about a hundred lines appearing in the *Virginia Gazette, and General Advertiser* on Wednesday, November 24, 1790. The poem praises Adams, Franklin, Washington, Jefferson, Science, Philosophy, Literature. It concludes:

> The Theatre demands our praise supreme;
> Ah! may my song be equal to my theme.
> And hark! a second Siddons charms each part;
> Nature in her is clos' by link'd with Art.
> The name of West should every tongue employ;
> She comes to give us pain, which leads to joy.
> Nor less his merit claims the muses Art,
> Whose talents are imprinted on each heart.
> The husband's vocal powers attention gain.
> Soft as the accent of Thalias' strain.
> *Bignall! thy frame was meant the stage to grace;
> Easy thy mein and beautiful thy face.
> The comic muse to thee has liberal been;
> And thou canst well repay her in each scene.
> Bignall like Edwin never fails to shine,
> Great are his powers in each scenic line;
> Like him in humour gains our just applause,
> And ranks thee foremost in the comic cause.
> Since thus, O Richmond! merit you befriend
> May ev'ry choicest bliss on thee attend!
> And none to thee this tribute should refuse;
> Dear to the Arts, to Commerce and the muse.
>
>   Philo-Theatricus
>
> *Mrs.

I cannot refrain from making here, on behalf of Augustine Davis, publisher of the *Gazette, and General Advertiser*, the obvious and appropriate remark: carrying such a puff, the issue of November 24 carried no theatrical advertisement. Ingratitude, thy name is West and Bignall!

SIXTH SEASON
Godwin and Company
July 1791

Chronicle. The next record of activity in the theatre appeared in the *Virginia Gazette, and Public Advertiser* for July 2, 1791, when was advertised "By Permission, on Monday Evening, July 4, *Douglas*, with an elegant set of new Scenes, adapted to the Play, designed by Mr. Hodgson and Mr. Busselot." Afterpiece was "a Pantomime Entertainment, *Harlequin Restored; or The Miller Deceived*." Doors opened at 7, and the performance began at 7:45. Admission was six shillings, box; four and sixpence, pit; and three shillings, gallery. Tickets were "to be had at the Post Office, at Mr. Wolfe's Store, and at the Office of the Theatre." The notice concluded: "Mr. Godwin respectfully informs his Friends and the Public in general that the above Exhibition has been preparing several weeks past—and they may rest assured that all possible Endeavour to merit Encouragement shall be exerted—having in constant View—'We that live to please must please to live.' Long Live The President."

We have had *"Vivat Respublica."* Now "Long Live the President" echoes the "Long Live the King" of colonial days. Godwin himself bridges the gap between the old colonies and the new states.

The next performance was advertised on July 9:

Mr. Godwin & Co. respectfully begs leave to return their grateful thanks, for the honor and applause conferred on them last Monday evening 4th July.

The motive of Mr. Godwin's performing at this time, being to do justice to some worthy citizens of this City, to whom he is particularly obliged, induces him thus publicly to solicit the assistance of any young Gentleman who may have a taste for Theatrical Amusement.

Plays advertised for Tuesday, July 12, were *The Revenge* and "the Pantomime Entertainment, *Harlequin Restored; or, The*

Miller Deceived," the same afterpiece as on July 4. *The Revenge* was staged "with additional scenery and decorations," but apparently without the lavish stage effects of *Harlequin Restored,* which included not only "new Songs by Mrs. Busselot" but the following fascinating attractions:

In the 1st part of the Pantomime, a double Hornpipe, by Mr. Godwin and Mrs. Busselot, in character of Harlequin and Columbine.

In the second part a view of the late Bastile in Paris, previous to its being destroyed by the *National new-inspired Sons of Liberty!* In which scene, Harlequin will leap into a Cannon, from which he will be fired by the Clown.

Several alterations and improvements will be made in the pantomime.[8]

There is record of one more performance by Godwin. On July 23 the *Virginia Gazette, and Public Advertiser* announced for "This evening *Summer Amusement, or The Comic Mirror,* Garrick's contrasted Medley of Lovers—a Comedy in two acts." To this was added "a Comedy in two acts, (never performed here) called *Trick Upon Trick, or The White Fox Chas'd."* The third piece of the evening was "a Pantomimical Entertainment of *Harlequin delivered from the Chymist's Magic Bottle by Fire."*

Between pieces Mrs. Busselot sang "Bonny Jemmy, O" and "The Card Invites." The notice stated that tickets were on sale "at the Eagle Tavern, at this Office [the Newspaper office], at Mr. Wolfe's Store, at Mr. Woodworth's Grocery Store, and at the Office of the Theatre." Prices were as before. In conclusion, "Mr. Godwin respectfully gives Notice, that the above Performance being to defray sundry Demands against the Theatre, cannot give tickets on his private Account."

During what was probably a brief season—these three performances are, I suspect, all—Godwin performed six plays: *Douglas, The Revenge, Summer Amusement, Trick upon Trick, Harlequin Restored,* and *Harlequin Delivered,* two of which, *Trick upon Trick* and *Douglas,* had been previously acted in Richmond.

The plays. Harlequin Restored, or the Miller Deceived (July 4, 1791) is not listed in any of the histories of the American theatre which I have examined. It may have been the same as *Harlequin*

Restored, or the Country Revels (Drury Lane, 1732). The title indicates merely another variation on the popular Harlequin theme; there were many, all more or less similar, depending largely upon dancing, acrobatics, and special stage effects for their audience appeal. The storming of the Bastille is, however, unique among the Harlequin pantomimes I know. A strolling player must have a fertile fancy.

The Revenge (July 12, 1791), a tragedy by Edward Young, was first acted at Drury Lane in 1721. It was acted in Philadelphia in 1767 and New York in 1780. *Douglas* was the tragedy with which Dennis Ryan opened the "New Theatre" in Richmond on June 21, 1784, with, I suspect, Godwin in the title role.

Summer Amusement, or the Comic Mirror (July 23, 1791), advertised as "Garrick's contrasted Medley of Lovers, a Comedy in two acts," I cannot find attributed to Garrick by any authority other than Godwin. I suspect that its real author was Godwin, who sought by using Garrick's name to enhance the box office appeal of his piece. Whatever it was, it was probably the same as *The Comic Mirror, or All the World's a Stage,* which Godwin acted in Charleston on December 5, 1786. Although advertised as "never performed here," *Trick upon Trick, or the White Fox Chased* was almost certainly the same Harlequin pantomime which had been acted in Richmond in 1787. The pantomime of *Harlequin Delivered from the Chymist's Magic Bottle by Fire* I have been unable to find elsewhere. It was doubtless a combination of Harlequin's usual merry pranks with stage tricks devised by Godwin.

The players.   Obviously, Godwin himself was most of the troupe. He was assisted by Hodgson, who was probably stage manager, and by Mr. and Mrs. Charles Busselot. Busselot evidently shared with Hodgson the duties of staging, while Mrs. Busselot sang and danced with Godwin. The advertisement of July 9 indicates that they may have been assisted by local amateurs. A strolling troupe of four players was adequate for Harlequin pantomimes, but they must either have had other actors not named in the newspaper notices or else enlisted local talent in supporting roles for the production of *Douglas* and *The Revenge.*

SEVENTH SEASON
West and Bignall Company
October–December 1791

Chronicle. After playing in Fredericksburg in August and September, the company returned to Richmond. The first notice of the season appeared Wednesday, October 19, 1791, when was advertised for "this date the Comedy *The Foundling; or Virtue Its Own Reward*," with the afterpiece of "the Comic Opera *Rosina; or, Love in a Cottage.*" Complete casts were given for both plays:

The Foundling

Young Belmont	Mr. Hallam
Sir Charles Raymond	Mr. J. Kenna
Sir Roger Belmont	Mr. West
Col. Raymond	Mr. Cleland
Villiard	Mr. Andrews
Footman	Mr. Riffetts
Faddle	Mr. Bignall
Rosetta	Mrs. West
Fidelia (the Foundling)	Mrs. Bignall

Rosina

Mr. Belville	Mr. Hallam
Capt. Belville	Mr. Courtenay
Rustic	Mr. J. Kenna
Mortough O'Blarney	Mr. Andrews
Teddy O'Wallaghan	Mr. Riffetts
William	Mr. Bignall, Jun.
Rosina	Mrs. Decker
Dorcas	Mrs. Davids
Phoebe	Mrs. Bignall

The advertisement stated that this was the first appearance "on this stage" of Cleland, who played Colonel Raymond in *The Foundling. Rosina*, however, offered even more histrionic novelty. In it appeared Courtenay as Captain Belville, "his first appearance on any stage," Bignall, Jr., as William, and Mrs. Decker as Rosina for the first time on this stage. The public was also informed that "Mr. Riley and Mrs. Johnson, from the Theatre Royal, Liverpool, will shortly make their appearance in two principal characters."

Admission was the same as last season; but what had then been gallery at three shillings had now become "Upper Boxes" at four shillings sixpence. Cynicism leads me to suspect that the additional one shilling six bought only the more elegant designation. Naturally one expects to pay more for an "Upper Box" than for a seat in the gallery. But the theatre may have been remodeled since the last season; it probably needed it. Doors opened at six and the performance began at 6:30; tickets were on sale at the post office, Mr. Wolfe's store, and the office of the theatre; there was "no admittance behind the scenes."[9]

The next performance featured another play by the Reverend Moore. It was *The Gamester; or, False Friend*, which was advertised for Thursday, October 27. Afterpiece was *The Farmer; or, the World's Ups and Downs*. Complete casts were given for both plays, featuring Bignall as Beverly and Mrs. West as Mrs. Beverly in *The Gamester*, with Bignall as Jemmy Jumps and Mrs. Bignall as Betty Blackberry in *The Farmer*. Reilly danced a hornpipe between pieces:

The Gamester

Beverly (the Gamester)	Mr. Bignall
Lewson	Mr. Hallam
Jarvis	Mr. Reilly
Bates	Mr. Cleland
Dawson	Mr. Andrews
Waiter	Master West
Stukely (the False Friend)	Mr. J. Kenna
Charlotte	Mrs. Bignall
Lucy	Mrs. Davids
Mrs. Beverley	Mrs. West

The Farmer

Capt. Valentine	Mr. Courtenay
Farmer Blackberry	Mr. J. Kenna
Rundy	Mr. Bignall, Jun.
Col. Dormant	Mr. Andrews
Waiter	Master West
Fairly	Mr. Riffetts
Jemmy Jumps (the Macaroni Stay Maker)	Mr. Bignall
Molly Maybush	Mrs. Decker
Louisa	Mrs. J. Kenna
Betty Black Berry	Mrs. Bignall[10]

In the *Virginia Gazette, and Public Advertiser* for Saturday, November 5, "The Virginia Company" announced "By Authority" in the "Theatre Richmond" on "This Evening the Comedy *The Busy Body.*" Afterpiece was *The Midnight Hour; or, War of Wits.* Complete casts were announced for both plays, with Bignall as Marplot, Mrs. West as Miranda, and Hallam as Sir George Airy in *The Busy Body.* Hallam also played the Marquis in *The Midnight Hour,* with Mrs. Bignall as Flora. Mrs. Decker sang "a Hunting Song" between pieces:

The Busy Body

Marplot (the Busy Body)	Mr. Bignall
Sir Francis Gripe	Mr. J. Kenna
Sir Jealous Traffick	Mr. Riley
Charles	Mr. Andrews
Whisper	Mr. Courtenay
Butler	Mr. Cleland
John	Mr. Riffetts
Sir George Airy	Mr. Hallam
Satch	Mrs. Bignall
Isabinda	Mrs. J. Kenna
Scentwell	Mrs. Davids
Miranda	Mrs. West

The Midnight Hour

Gen. Don Guzman	Mr. J. Kenna
Sebastian	Mr. J. Bignall
Matthias	Mr. West
Ambrose	Mr. Riley
Nicholas	Mr. Bignall
The Marquis	Mr. Hallam
Julia	Mrs. Decker
The Duenna	Mrs. Johnson
Flora	Mrs. Bignall

The next record of performance was on November 12, when was announced for "This Evening the Comedy (never performed here) *The Father; or American Shandyism* (written by a Citizen of the United States)." Afterpiece was again *The Farmer.* Complete casts were given for both plays. *The Father* featured Bignall as Dr. Quiesent and Mrs. Bignall as Susanna:

Col. Duncan	Mr. J. Kenna
Mr. Racket	Mr. Courtenay

Banter	Mr. Cleland
Captain Haller	Mr. Hallam
Cartridge	Mr. West
Captain Campley	Mr. Andrews
Jacob	Mr. Riffetts
Doctor Quiesent	Mr. Bignall
Mrs. Granade	Mrs. Johnson
Mrs. Racket	Mrs. Decker
Miss Felton	Mrs. J. Kenna
Susanna	Mrs. Bignall[11]

Cast of *The Farmer* was the same as on October 27. Betty, previously "Blackberry" and "Black Berry," was now "Blackbury." The eighteenth century was not afflicted with orthographic meticulosity. Again Mrs. Decker sang between pieces. This is the first recorded appearance of Mrs. Johnson. I assume that she joined the company some time between October 19 and November 12.

On Wednesday, November 16, was announced for "This date" *The Gamester* and *Rosina*. Cast of *The Gamester* was the same as on October 27, except that the waiter, played then by Master West, was now played by Riffetts. Cast of *Rosina* was identical with that advertised for October 19. The only extra feature of the program on November 16 was a song, "High Mettled Racer," by Courtenay between pieces.[12]

The *Virginia Gazette and Weekly Advertiser* for December 16 contains nearly a whole column describing "the Inimitable Piece" which is to be staged "This Evening (Friday)." The piece was the "celebrated Comedy, written by Shakespear, and altered by Dryden, called *The Tempest, or The Inchanted Island*." "Never Performed Here," it was presented "with proper Scenery, Machinery, Dresses, Music, Dances and Decorations."

A full cast of fifteen actors was named, headed by Kenna as Prospero. Bignall, Jr., played Caliban and doubled as Neptune:

Prospero (the banished Duke of Milan)	Mr. Kenna
Ferdinand (Prince of Savoy)	Mr. Cleland
Alonzo (the Usurping Duke)	Mr. Riffitts
Antonio } His Privy Counsellors	{ Mr. Andrews
Gonzalez }	{ Mr. Reilly
Caliban (a Monster of the Isle)	Mr. Bignall, Jun.
Hypolito (a Youth who never saw a Woman)	Mr. Courtney
Mustatio } Sailors	{ Mr. Hallam
Ventoso }	{ Mr. Andrews

West and Bignall Company advertisement, from the *Virginia Gazette, and Weekly Advertiser*, December 16, 1791. (Courtesy Virginia Historical Society.)

Stephano (Master of the Ship)	Mr. West
And Trincalo (the Drunken Boatswain)	Mr. Bignall
Dorinda } Girls who never saw a Man	{ Mrs. West
Miranda	{ Mrs. Decker
Ariel (an Airy Spirit with Songs)	Mrs. Bignall
And Amphitrite	Mrs. Johnson

Staging was spectacular:

The opening discovers a troubled Horizon and Tempestuous Sea, where the Usurper's Vessel is tossed a considerable time in sight, and gives signal of an approaching storm, amidst repeated claps of Thunder, Lightning, Hail, Rain, &c. and being dashed on a Chain of Rocks, (which both sides of the stage strikingly represent) and at the same instant, a dreadful shower of fire, pouring from the distempered Elements, the crew gives signals of distress, the Waves and Winds rise to an affecting degree, and the vessel sinks in full view of the audience. The Scene altogether forming a most awful, but perfect picture of A SHIP WRECK, This Hurricane (which is supposed to be raised by Magic) ceases, a delightful prospect of the Inchanted Island appears, also of the Enchanter's Dwelling,—here the business of the Play commences; and through the course of it (which abounds with Poetic Beauties) is represented the strange being CALIBAN, a Monster of the Isle, dressed from Nature, and agreeable to the Author's fancy of the wonderful and truly original Character.

Act II was enlivened by "a Dance of Daemons, bearing flaming torches," in which Hallam, Bignall, Sheldon, and West appeared as "Singing Devils."

In Act III

the spirit ARIEL invisible to FERDINAND leads him in Enchantment; and by proper Songs Music, &c. (composed by that learned and excellent Master Dr. PURCELL), brings the Prince to the Cave of PROSPERO; where his sudden passion for the Magician's Daughter, MIRANDA, and his friendship for the Infant Heir of MANTUA, (whose simplicity in the end raises the Jealousy of FERDINAND) joined to the virtuous loves of the two young Females for the two Princes, which being wrong understood by each party, introduces a Scene truly natural and entertaining, till damped by the untimely fall of HYPOLITO whose life is nevertheless still preserved by the interposition of Magic, which likewise terminates the whole in A VIEW OF A CALM SEA, On which NEPTUNE and AMPHITRITE appear in a Shell Chariot, drawn by Sea-Horses. NEPTUNE, Mr. Bignall, Jun. AMPHITRITE Mrs. Johnson. The Piece concludes with the Spirit ARIEL'S appearing in A CHARIOT OF CLOUDS.

Afterpiece was the farce *Three Weeks after Marriage, or What We Must All Come To*, in which Bignall played Sir Charles Racket and Mrs. West played Lady Racket:

Sir Charles Racket	Mr. Bignall
Woodley	Mr. Cleland
Lovelace	Mr. Bignall, Jun.
And Old Drugget	Mr. Kenna
Demity	Mrs. Bignall
Mrs. Drugget	Mrs. Johnson
Nancy	Mrs. Decker
And Lady Racket	Mrs. West

The *Virginia Gazette, and General Advertiser* for Wednesday, December 21, announced for "This date a Comedy *He Would Be A Soldier*," with the afterpiece of *The Romp, or Love in a City*. Complete casts were given, featuring Bignall as Caleb "with a Song" in *He Would Be a Soldier* and Mrs. Bignall as Priscilla Tomboy in *The Romp*.

He Would Be a Soldier

Colonel Talbot	Mr. J. Kenna
Captain Crevelt	Mr. Hallam
Sir Oliver Oldstock	Mr. Reilly
Count Pierpoint	Mr. Cleland
Mandeville	Mr. Courtenay
Wilkins	Mr. Andrews
Amber	Mr. West
Johnson	Mr. Bignall, Jun.
Caleb	Mr. Bignall
Lady Oldstock	Mrs. Johnson
Harriet	Mrs. Decker
Mrs. Wilkins	Mrs. Bignall
Betty	Mrs. Kenna
Nancy	Mrs. Davids
Charlotte	Mrs. West

The Romp

Wattey Cockney	Mr. Bignall
Captain Sightly	Mr. Hallam
Old Cockney	Mr. Reilly
Old Barnacle	Mr. J. Kenna

Penelope	Mrs. Decker
Miss La Blond	Mrs. Kenna
Priscilla Tomboy (the Romp)	Mrs. Bignall

Between pieces there was a song by Mrs. Bignall and "(by desire)" "Lash'd to the Helm" by Courtenay. The evening was concluded with "Paddy Bull's Expedition" by Bignall. The performance was for the benefit of Cleland. Tickets were on sale as usual and by "Mr. Cleland at Mr. Roussell's." Roussell was a dancing teacher; Cleland evidently boarded in Roussell's house. Actors sometimes put up at the public houses; sometimes they boarded in private houses during the season.

The *Virginia Gazette, and Weekly Advertiser* for Friday, December 23, advertised Courtenay's benefit for "This Evening . . . with the celebrated Comedy of *She Stoops to Conquer, or The Mistakes of a Night* (written by Doctor Goldsmith)." Complete cast was given:

Young Marlow	Mr. Bignall
Hardcastle	Mr. Reilly
Hastings	Mr. Hallam
Sir Charles Marlow	Mr. Andrews
Diggory	Mr. Bignall, Jun.
Cymon	Mr. Courtney
Roger	Mr. Riffetts
Jeremy	Mr. Cleland
Tony Lumpkin (with songs)	Mr. Kenna
Mrs. Hardcastle	Mrs. Johnson
Miss Neville	Mrs. Decker
Betty	Mrs. Davids
Miss Hardcastle	Mrs. West

Afterpiece was the "Musical Entertainment (never performed here) called *The Rival Candidates, or The Borough Election*," with the following cast:

Byron	Mr. Courtney
General Worry	Mr. Kenna
Sir Harry Muff	Mr. Hallam
First Gardener	Mr. Bignall, Jun.
Second Gardener	Mr. Andrews
Third Gardener	Mr. Reilly
Spy	Mr. Bignall
Narcissa	Mrs. Decker
Jenny	Mrs. Bignall

Between pieces Courtenay sang, in character and by particular desire, the favorite song of "Major Andre's Lamentation" and the admired song of "Jene Scai Quoi." I assume that the fractured French was for comic effect. There was also a song (no title given) by Mrs. Bignall.

There is one more record of a performance during this season: a playbill. The bill—or, rather, a fragment of it—begins ". . . and Mrs. Davids," and announces a benefit shared by some unknown player and Mrs. Davids:

> . . . and Mrs. Davids. With the greatest Respect they beg leave to acquaint the Ladies and Gentlemen of Richmond and its Vicinity, that their Benefit is fixed for Friday Evening, December 30, 1791, and humbly Solicits their Patronage on the occasion. Will be presented the celebrated Tragedy, of *Isabella or The Fatal Marriage.*

Villeroy	Mr. Hallam
Carlos	Mr. Kenna
Count Baldwin	Mr. Andrews
Belford	Mr. Courtenay
Pedro	Mr. Riffetts
Sampson	Mr. Reilly
Child	Master Davids
and Biron	Mr. Bignall
Nurse	Mrs. Johnson
and Isabella	Mrs. West[13]

Including this lone playbill, we have records of nine performances during this season, the first on October 19, the last on December 30, 1791. Almost certainly there were others. Performances are spaced so as to indicate a continuous season from October through December. There are records of performances on Wednesday, Thursday, Friday, and Saturday. I surmise that the company played a three-month season, acting three or four times each week, a hypothetical total of more than thirty performances. Eight newspaper notices and a fragment of a playbill are thin gleanings from what was probably a rich season.

There are records of fourteen plays: *The Busy Body, The Farmer, The Father, The Foundling, The Gamester, He Would Be a Soldier, Isabella, The Midnight Hour, The Rival Candidates, The Romp, Rosina, She Stoops to Conquer, The Tempest,* and *Three Weeks after Marriage,* two of which, *The Midnight Hour* and *The Romp,* are recorded as American premieres.

The handbill dated December 30 is the last record of this season. When the season ended we do not know. I guess that it did not run long after this date and that the company left Richmond early in 1792 to play elsewhere.

The plays. *The Foundling* (October 19, 1791), by Edward Moore, was brought out at Drury Lane in 1747/48. It was acted in New York in 1788, Philadelphia in 1810, and by the West and Bignall Company in Charleston in 1793. It was not a particularly successful play and was acted only this once in Richmond. *Rosina*, a comic opera by Frances Brooke, with music by William Shield, had been first acted at Covent Garden in 1782. It was acted in New York in 1786 and Philadelphia in 1787. There are records of several later performances in Richmond.

The Gamester (October 27, 1791), by Edward Moore, had its premiere at Drury Lane in 1753; its immediate success is attested by performance in both New York and Philadelphia in 1754. A dramatic sermon against the evils of gambling, it probably helped to appease the prejudice of respectable people against profane stage shows. At any rate, it held the stage through the nineteenth century.

The Midnight Hour; or, War of Wits (November 5, 1791), a farce by Elizabeth Inchbald, was first acted at Covent Garden in 1787 and was published the same year. This performance in Richmond was apparently its American premiere. It is recorded in New York, Philadelphia, and Charleston in 1794.

The Father (November 12, 1791), by William Dunlap, is, I believe, the first play by an American author acted on the Richmond stage. It had its premiere at the John Street Theatre in New York on September 7, 1789, and was acted in Philadelphia in 1790. It was acted by the West and Bignall Company in Charleston in 1793, where it was advertised as having been performed in Pennsylvania and Virginia. There is record of only this one performance in Richmond.

Advertised as "altered by Dryden," this version of *The Tempest* (December 16, 1791) was almost certainly the Dryden-Davenant adaptation, with music by Purcell, which held the stage in England and America for more than a century. Davenant invented Hypolito and gave Miranda a sister, Dorinda, both listed in the cast; he also

West and Bignall Company playbill, December 30, 1791. (Courtesy Virginia State Library.)

gave Caliban a sister, Sycorax, and Ariel a sweetheart, Milcha, who are not listed. Odell says that the Dryden-Davenant version of *The Tempest* was acted in New York in 1773. It was probably this version (called an "opera") which was acted in Philadelphia in 1787. The Richmond version was undoubtedly the one acted by the West and Bignall Company in Charleston on April 20, 1793. This is the only record of a performance of *The Tempest* in Richmond before 1800. *Three Weeks after Marriage*, a farce by Arthur Murphy, was brought out at Covent Garden in 1776. It was acted in New York in 1780, Philadelphia in 1791, and Charleston on May 3, 1793, by the West and Bignall Company. This is the only record of its performance in Richmond before 1800.

He Would Be a Soldier (December 21, 1791), a comedy by Frederick Pilon, was first acted at Covent Garden in 1786. Its American premiere was in New York on June 22, 1789. It was acted in Philadelphia in 1792, and Charleston in 1794. *The Romp, or Love in a City,* a musical farce altered by T. A. Lloyd from Isaac Bickerstaffe's *Love in the City*, with music by Charles Dibdin, had its premiere at Covent Garden in 1778 and was published in 1786. It was acted in Philadelphia on October 22, 1792, in New York on February 6, 1793, and in Charleston by the West and Bignall Company on February 13, 1793. This performance in Richmond seems to be its first recorded performance in America. It was a popular stage success, and the role of Priscilla Tomboy was for a long time a favorite of the leading comediennes of the American stage.

Goldsmith's famous comedy *She Stoops to Conquer* (December 23, 1791) was first acted at Covent Garden on March 15, 1773. It was acted in New York on August 2, 1773, Charleston, January 15, 1774, and Philadelphia, June 23, 1788. *The Rival Candidates* is not recorded in Charleston; it was acted in Philadelphia on June 13, 1791, and in New York on May 8, 1793, "as performed in Philadelphia with universal applause." Odell identifies it as an "opera in two acts." I am unable to establish authorship, although the subtitle indicates English origin. I doubt any relation to Col. Robert Munford's *The Candidates: or, the Humours of a Virginia Election,* published in Petersburg in 1798. Political satire has never depended upon literary sources.

The players. The company was the same one that had played in Richmond in 1790. It was managed by West and Bignall and called itself the Virginia Company. Bignall played leading roles in both comedy and tragedy; Mrs. Bignall was the leading lady in comedy, and Mrs. West in tragedy. There were perhaps twenty players in the company. There had been changes since the previous season. Only the Bignalls, the Wests, Mrs. Davids, and Hallam remained. They were, of course, the leading players; the supporting players were all newcomers to the troupe.

The Kenna family consisted of Mr. and Mrs. Kenna, their daughter, Miss Kenna, and their son and his wife, Mr. and Mrs. J. Kenna. All were actors, and all but Miss Kenna appeared this season. They were in Philadelphia in the spring of 1791; apparently they came from there to Richmond for this season and continued to play with the West and Bignall Company. They had been with the Hallam and Henry Company in New York in 1786. Odell tells much of their careers on the New York stage.

Master Davids appeared in concerts in New York during several later years. Riley made what seems to be his American debut in Harmony Hall, Philadelphia, on November 7, 1789. Mrs. Decker appeared in Philadelphia at Ricketts's Circus in December 1799.

The most interesting new actor during this season was Mrs. Johnson, "from the Theatre Royal, Liverpool," who had been advertised on October 19 to make her appearance shortly in a principal character. Her name appeared in the cast of characters advertised on November 5, 1791, when she played Mrs. Granade in Dunlap's *The Father* and on December 21 as Lady Oldstock in *He Would Be a Soldier.* She was also listed in the Richmond playbill of December 30, 1791, when she played the Nurse in *Isabella.*

Mrs. Johnson made her New York debut with the Hallam and Hodgkinson Company on February 10, 1796, as Lady Townley in *The Provoked Husband.* The *Daily Advertiser* elaborated her "distinguished talents which cannot fail to render her the favourite of the public." The article continued:

Her person, elegant and graceful; her countenance pleasing, animated, and peculiarly expressive of those lively emotions which she so powerfully excites; chaste and spirited in her manner; her action easy and proper; her pronunciation correct, distinct and clear. Such is the faint outline of those qualities which with taste and judgment, has enabled her to reach the true point of nature, without *stepping* over that just limit which Hamlet recommends to his players.[14]

She played with Cooper at the Park Street Theatre in 1798, appearing as Rosalind in *As You Like It* on January 29, opening night of the season.

She returned to England but was back in New York on November 17, 1802, when "her first appearance was a great success. Mrs. Johnson had become a highly finished representative of ladies of fashion, and of what are known as high comedy heroines. Probably no better actress in this line has ever appeared in America."[15] Odell has much to say about her New York career. She played leads for several years in New York's best productions, making her last appearance on April 25, 1817. It seems that one of America's most famous actresses made her American debut in Richmond.

EIGHTH SEASON
West and Bignall Company
August–December 1792

Chronicle. In the Epilogue that concludes his *History of the American Theatre,* Seilhamer regrets "the abrupt and in some respects inconclusive close of this volume," and specifies four omitted chapters: "Before me lies the MS of chapters telling the story of Bignall and West's company in the south, 1792-7."[16] To my knowledge this manuscript material is not extant. It would have been invaluable had it been published. I fear that, like the playbills, it is lost. This season, however, has much to add to the story of West and Bignall in Richmond.

Too often we have been uncertain of opening and closing dates; this time we can be definite. The *Virginia Gazette, and General Advertiser* of Wednesday, August 1, 1792, carried this notice of the opening: "West and Bignall with the greatest respect, inform the ladies and gentlemen of Richmond, and its vicinity, the Theatre will open This Evening, August 1st, 1792." The plays were

"O'Keefe's new comedy *Wild Oats; or, The Strolling Gentleman*" and "a Farce (never performed here) *The Pannel; or Mask'd Apparition.*" Complete casts were given:

Wild Oats

Rover	Mr. Bignall
Harry	Mr. Courtnay
John Dory	Mr. J. Kenna
Emphriam Smooth	Mr. Sully
Sim	Mr. M. Sully
Banks	Mr. Hallam
Midge	Mr. T. West
Trap	Mr. J. Bignall
Gammon	Mr. Andrews
Zachariah	Mr. Riffetts
Sir George Thunder	Mr. Hamilton
Amelia	Mrs. Sully
Jane	Miss Sully
Lady Amaranth	Mrs. West

The Pannel

Don Guzman	Mr. Kenna
Don Carlos	Mr. Courtnay
Don Ferdinand	Mr. J. Bignall
Don Pedro	Mr. Andrews
Lazarillo	Mr. Sully
Octavio	Mr. Riffits
Muskato	Mr. Bignall
Donna Aurora	Mrs. Decker
Donna Marcella	Mrs. Kenna
Leonarda	Mrs. Sully
Beatrice	Mrs. Bignall

New players mentioned in the advertisement were Sully and M. Sully "from the Royal Circus, Edinburgh, being their first appearance on this stage," and Hamilton "from the Theatre Royal, Dublin, being his first appearance on this stage." Hamilton played Sir George Thunder and M. Sully played Sim in *Wild Oats*. Sully played Ephraim Smooth in *Wild Oats* and Lazarillo in *The Pannel*; he also recited "Tar for All Weathers" between the plays. Mrs. Sully played Amelia in *Wild Oats* and Leonarda in *The Pannel*.

The advertisement stated that the doors opened at six and the curtain rose at 7:30. Tickets were on sale at the post office,

Pritchard's bookstore, and the office of the theatre. Admission was the same as last season.

The next record of performance appeared on Wednesday, August 29, which announced for "Tomorrow a Comic Opera *The Maid of The Mill*" and "also a Farce *The Widow's Vow; or, Second Thoughts Are Best.*" *The Maid of the Mill* featured Bignall as Ralph "(the Miller's Son)" and Mrs. Bignall as Patty "(the Maid of the Mill)." Appearing also were Sully as Farmer Giles, Mrs. Sully as Lady Sycamore, and Miss Sully as Theodosia. *The Widow's Vow* was also replete with Sullys; Mrs. Sully played Inis, Miss Sully, Flora, and Miss E. Sully, Ursula. "Miss Sully" was Charlotte, the eldest, and the "E." identifies the second daughter, Elizabeth. Mr. Sully sang a song between pieces:

The Maid of the Mill

Lord Aimworth	Mr. J. Kenna
Sir Harry Sycamore	Mr. Hamilton
Farmer Giles	Mr. Sully
Fairfield	Mr. Andrews
Mervin	Mr. Courtnay
Gypsies	Messrs. Riffetts,
	J. Bignall, &c.
Ralph (the Miller's Son)	Mr. Bignall
Fanny (a Gypsy)	Mrs. Decker
Lady Sycamore	Mrs. Sully
Theodosia	Miss Sully
Patty (the Maid of the Mill)	Mrs. Bignall

The Widow's Vow

Don Antonio	Mr. J. Kenna
The Marquis	Mr. Hallam
Carlos	Mr. Andrews
Jerome	Mr. Bignall
The Countess	Mrs. West
Isabella	Mrs. Kenna
Inis	Mrs. Sully
Ursula	Miss E. Sully
Flora	Miss Sully[17]

The *Virginia Gazette, and General Advertiser* of Wednesday, September 5, announced for "Tomorrow a new Tragedy *The Sorrows of Werter; or, The Disconsolate Lovers,*" with the after-piece of "*Shakespeare's Jubilee*" written by Mr. Garrick and

Performed with Universal applause." The cast of *Werter* only was given, featuring Bignall as Werter, with Mrs. West as Charlotte:

The Sorrows of Werter

Werter	Mr. Bignall
Sebastian	Mr. Courtney
Leuthrop	Mr. Hamilton
Paulina	Mr. Hallam
Bartrand	Mr. J. Bignall
Albert	Mr. J. Kenna
Laura	Mrs. Decker
Charlotte	Mrs. West

Act III included songs by Mrs. Decker as Laura and by Courtenay as Sebastian. The advertisement went on to laud the literary and the moral merits of *Werter*: "Who has not heard of Werter's Sorrows? . . . A Tale so popular and full of Merit engaged our Author's attention, nor has his Pen done injustice to the beautiful original. . . . The Scenes wrought up with commanding force . . . Language nervous and highly polished—in that Nature—Pathetic Sentiments—all unite to recommend Werter to public notice; while the dreadful light in which Self-murder is held to View, gives a salutary lesson to desponding Misery."

About this time competition reared its program in the Eagle Tavern. The *Virginia Gazette, and General Advertiser* for September 12, contains no theatrical notice. It does contain, however, notice of a "Musical Performance" at the Eagle Tavern "this evening." The music was "composed by Mr. Taylor, Music Professor lately arrived from London." The entertainment was in three parts: first "An Interlude *The Constant Lass; or, The Sailor's Frolic*, Consisting of dialogues, songs, duets, etc, by Mr. Taylor and his pupil Miss Huntley late of Covent Garden." Part two consisted of "Comic and Pastoral Songs by Mr. Taylor and Miss Huntley," and the final part was "a Burletta in one act, *The Quack, or The Doctor in Petticoats.*" The performance began at 7:30, and tickets were to be had at the Eagle Tavern.

The next theatrical notice appeared on Monday, October 1, announcing for Tuesday, October 2, "a New Play *Such Things Are: or The Christian Sultan*," with the afterpiece of *Ways and Means, or A Trip to Dover*, "a Comedy in 3 acts written by Mr. Coleman Junr." No casts were given. Instead of advertising casts of characters, the notice featured the talents of the male Sullys as a finale to the evening's performance: "The Whole to conclude with several surprising feats of activity in Lofty Tumbling, by Mr. Sully Junior (who was justly the admiration of Britain; —assisted by Master Sully). Clown to the Performance, Mr. Sully, sen."[18] The three were, I presume, Matthew Sully, Matthew, Jr., and either Chester or Thomas (age nine).

On Thursday, October 4, The *Virginia Gazette, and General Advertiser* announced for "This Evening the Rev. Mr. Homes Tragedy of *Douglas; or The Noble Shepherd.*" Afterpiece was *The Romp; or Love in a City.* Casts were given for both plays. In *Douglas* Bignall played the title role, with Mrs. West as Lady Randolph. In *The Romp* leading roles were played by Bignall as Watty Cockney and Mrs. Bignall as Priscilla Tomboy:

Douglas

Norval (Douglas)	Mr. Bignall
Lord Randolph	Mr. J. Kenna
Glenalvan	Mr. Hallam
Officers	Messrs. Courtnay,
	Riffets, Andrew
Old Norval	Mr. Hamilton
Anna	Mrs. Kenna
Lady Randolph	Mrs. West

The Romp

Watty Cockney	Mr. Bignall
Captain Sightly	Mr. Hallam
Old Cockney	Mr. Riffets
Richard	Mr. Andrews
Old Barnacle	Mr. J. Kenna
Miss La Blond	Mrs. J. Kenna
Penelope	Miss E. Sully
Priscilla Tomboy (the Romp)	Mrs. Bignall

The *Virginia Gazette: and Richmond Daily Advertiser* for October 6, announced: "This evening the celebrated Comic Opera (never presented in America) called, *The Woodman,*" with the afterpiece of *Appearance Is against Them.* Cast was given for *The Woodman* only. It was replete with Sullys: Sully as Medley, M. Sully as Bob, Mrs. Sully as Miss Di Clacket, Miss Sully as Miss Emily, and Miss E. Sully as Kitty Maple:

The Woodman

Fairlop (the Woodman)	Mr. J. Kenna
Sir Walter Waring,	
(the Justice of Peace)	Mr. Hamilton
Medley (his Clerk)	Mr. Sully
Bob (the Miller)	Mr. M. Sully
Mr. Wilford	Mr. Courtney
Filbert (the Gardener)	Mr. J. Bignall
Capt. O'Donnel	Mr. Bignall
Miss Emily	Miss Sully
Miss DiClacket	Mrs. Sully
Polly	Miss West
Bridget	Mrs. J. Kenna
Kitty Maple	Miss E. Sully
Dorothy Fairlop	Mrs. Bignall
Female Archers, Woodmen, &c.	

The play was staged "with the Original Overture, Songs, Duets, Chorusses" as well as "New Dresses and Decorations." This must have been one of the major productions of the season. The advertisement stated: "This admired piece is the production of the Rev. Mr. Bate Dudley, (author of the *Flitch of Bacon*, *Rival Candidates*, and several Dramatic pieces now in the highest estimation), and has been represented upwards of 100 nights at Covent Garden, with the most unbounded applause." There were two slight changes in the house. Doors still opened at six, but curtain time had been moved up from 7:30 to "precisely at seven o'clock," and "Mr. Dixon's printing-office" had been added to the ticket offices.

On Monday, October 8, was announced for "This evening the celebrated Comedy (written by Mrs. Cowley) called, *More Ways Than One: or, A New Way to Catch Hearts*." Afterpiece was "the Musical Entertainment (written by the celebrated Allan Ramsay) of *The Gentle Shepherd; or, Patie and Roger*." Casts were given for both plays:

More Ways than One

Bellair	Mr. Hallam
Evergreen	Mr. Hamilton
Doctor Freelove	Mr. J. Kenna
Carlton	Mr. Courtney
Le Gont	Mr. Sully

David	Mr. Sully, jun.
Lawyer's Clerk	Mr. Riffetts
Stranger	Mr. Bignall, jun.
Doctor's Servant	Mr. Andrews
Sir Marvel Mushroom	Mr. Bignall
Miss Archer	Mrs. West
Miss Juvenill	Mrs. J. Kenna
Mrs. Johnson	Miss Davids
Arabella	Mrs. Bignall

The Gentle Shepherd

Patie, (the Gentle Shepherd)	Mr. M. Sully
Sir William Worthy	Mr. J. Kenna
Glaud	Mr. Sully
Simon	Mr. Andrews
Roger	Mr. Courtney
Bauldy	Mr. Hamilton
Jenny	Miss E. Sully
Mause	Mrs. Sully
Madge	Mrs. Davids
Peggy	Miss Sully

The Gentle Shepherd was staged "with the Original Overtures, Songs, Duets, Chorusses, Reels, &c. &c."[19] Its production brought out most of the Sully family: Young Matthew in the title role as "Patie, (the Gentle Shepherd)," his father as Glaud, his mother as Mause, his sister Elizabeth as Jenny, and his sister Charlotte as Peggy.

Next performance was the following evening, Tuesday, October 9: "This evening the tragedy of *Isabella; or The Fatal Marriage*," with the afterpiece of *"Harlequin Statue: or The Spirit of Fancy."* Casts were given for both pieces; *Isabella* as follows:

Biron	Mr. Bignall
Carlos	Mr. J. Kenna
Count Baldwin	Mr. Hamilton
Belford	Mr. Courtney
Sampson	Mr. J. Bignall
Pedro	Mr. Riffetts
Isabella's Child	Master Sully
Villeroy	Mr. Hallam
Nurse	Mrs. Davids
Isabella	Mrs. West

The Harlequin pantomime was apparently an all-Sully production in which the father played the clown, young Matthew played Harlequin, and Elizabeth played Columbine. The advertisement gave elaborate details of the pantomime:

. . . invented, Songs, &c. by the managers of the Royal Circus, London, where it was performed upwards of thirty nights successively with the greatest tokens of approbation—the scenery, machinery tricks and deceptions executed by Mr. Schoulty.

A statuary yard, filled with beautiful Images. The melancholy Columbine, occasioned by her love for the Statue of Harlequin, is excellently relieved by the ascension of Ariel, in A Chariot of Clouds, who Animates Harlequin, when many picturesque attitudes by him are exhibited. —After many complicated [word illegible] Harlequin leaps through rocks. The Pantaloon and Lover attempting to pursue are prevented, by violent Flashes of Lighting, A Monkey meets the clown, and a most laughable scene takes place. A scene of a Miliner's Shop is then presented, through which Harlequin takes a leap seven feet high—the Clown wishing to amuse himself puts on an elegant hat, which is changed by Harlequin to a Balloon, and takes the clown up with it—after which will be represented the celebrated scene of the Death and Re-Animation of Harlequin by the Airy Spirit. Who again escapes with Columbine to a beautiful view of the Eagle Tavern, which by the magic sword of Harlequin is transformed to a striking representation of the front of the Capitol of Richmond; through which Harlequin makes his escape through a leap fourteen feet high. The whole to conclude with a view of beautiful water works; and the elegant dance of Double Allemonde.[20]

In the *Virginia Gazette: and Richmond Daily Advertiser* for the next day, October 10, "The Virginia Company" advertised "By Authority" for "this evening a Comic Opera (never performed here but once) called *Robin Hood: or Sherwood Forest*." The play was announced with the following fanfare: "Robin Hood and his merry archers have often been represented on the stage—the Biographia Dramatica gives an account of six pieces in which this celebrated Out-Law was the Hero, exclusive of the Sad Shepherd, written by Ben Johnson, but none ever met the success of Leonard M'Nally's, which is presented to the amateurs of the drama as a singular treat, it has been performed in both London and Virginia, with the most flattering bursts of applause for upwards of three hundred nights."

Again, I direct suspicion toward the accuracy of newspaper puffs. It is, however, quite likely that *Robin Hood* had been acted previously in Richmond. I suspect that this was the second production of *Robin Hood* for this season. Complete cast was given:

Men Resident in the Forest

Robin Hood, (capt. of Out-Laws)	Mr. J. Kenna
Scarlet, (a principal Out-Law)	Mr. M. Sully
Allen-A-Dale, (Shepherd)	Mr. Bignall, jun.
Bowman, (an Out-Law)	Mr. Andrews
Out-Laws and Archers	Messrs. Riffetts, Andrews, &c.
Little John, (R. Hood's friend)	Mr. Sully

Men Visitors to the Forest

Baron Fitzherbert, (disguised as Friar Tuck)	Mr. Hamilton
Edwin, (the Hermit of the dale)	Mr. Courtney
Rutekin, (an itinerant tinker)	Mr. Bignall

Women Resident in the Forest

Stella (a shepherdess)	Mrs. Kenna
Lasses	Ladies of the company

Women Not Resident in the Forest

Angelina, (a Pilgrim)	Miss E. Sully
Annette, (her tiny foot page)	Miss Sully
Clorinda, (huntress of Titbury)	Mrs. Bignall

The afterpiece of the evening was "Mrs. Cowley's laughable farce of *Who's The Dupe?*" with the following cast:

Old Doiley	Mr. J. Kenna
Granger	Mr. Hallam
Sandford	Mr. J. Bignall
Servant	Mr. Andrews
Gradus	Mr. Sully
Miss Doiley	Mrs. Decker
Charlotte	Mrs. Sully

On October 11 "The Virginia Company" advertised "By Authority" for "This evening, a Comedy called *The Wonder: or a Woman keeps a Secret* . . . to which will be added, O'Keefe's laughable farce of *The Agreeable Surprise*." Complete casts were given:

The Wonder!

Don Felix	Mr. Bignall
Colonel Britton	Mr. Hallam
Lissardo	Mr. Sully
Frederick	Mr. Andrews
Don Pedro	Mr. J. Kenna
Don Lopez	Mr. Riffetts
Alguazile	Mr. Courtney
Vasquez	Mr. J. Bignall
Gibby, (a Highlander)	Mr. Hamilton
Violante	Mrs. West
Isabella	Mrs. Decker
Iris	Mrs. J. Kenna
Flora	Mrs. Bignall

The Agreeable Surprise

Sir Felix Friendly	Mr. Hamilton
Compton	Mr. J. Bignall
Eugene	Mr. Courtney
Thomas	Mr. Bignall
John	Mr. Sully
Cudden	Mr. M. Sully
Farmer Stump	Mr. Riffetts
Chicane	Mr. Andrews
Lingo	Mr. J. Kenna
Laura	Mrs. Decker
Fringe	Mrs. Kenna
Mrs. Cheshire	Mrs. Davids
Cowslip	Mrs. Bignall

Courtenay sang a song between the pieces, and the evening concluded "with several new and surprising Feats of Activity by Mr. M. Sully (who was justly the Admiration of Britain) assisted by Mr. Sully, sen. and Mas. Sully."[21]

Again "By Authority" "The Virginia Company" announced on October 12, for "Tomorrow October 13 . . . the dramatic piece *A School for Soldiers: or, The Deserter*," with the afterpiece of "O'Keefe's comic opera *The Farmer: or, The World's Ups and Downs.*" Full casts were given for both plays. Bignall played Bellamy "(the deserter)," and J. Bignall played Colonel Valentine in *A School for Soldiers*. In *The Farmer*, Bignall played his usual role of Jemmy Jumps, but Betty Blackberry, the female lead previously played by Mrs. Bignall, was played by Miss Sully. Mrs.

Bignall did not appear in the billing, but four members of the Sully family did; they were, besides Miss Sully, M. Sully as Captain Valentine, Mrs. Sully as Mrs. Mildmay in *A School for Soldiers*, and Master Sully as the waiter in *The Farmer*:

A School for Soldiers

Bellamy, (the deserter)	Mr. Bignall
Mr. Hector	Mr. Hamilton
Captain Valentine	Mr. Sully
Colonel Valentine	Mr. J. Bignall
Frederick	Mr. Andrews
Major Bellamy	Mr. J. Kenna
Clara	Mrs. West
Mrs. Mildmay	Mrs. Sully

The Farmer

Blackberry, (the farmer)	Mr. Hamilton
Captain Valentine	Mr. Courtney
Colonel Cormant	Mr. Andrews
Rundy	Mr. J. Bignall
Waiter	Master Sully
Counsellor Flummery	Mr. Hallam
Jemmy Jumps (the macaroni stay-maker)	Mr. Bignall
Molly Maybush	Mrs. Decker
Louisa	Mrs. J. Kenna
Landlady	Mrs. Davids
Betty Blackberry	Miss Sully

The staging of *A School for Soldiers* was impressively described:

Scene the Last, the Field, Procession to the Execution. Pioneers. Drum muffled, and Fife. A coffin, carried on a tressel by four soldiers. Regimental Band, playing the dead march in Saul. Colonel. Battalion, who divide to the right and left, and rest on their arms.

chaplain   major at
the left   Bellamy   his right
                    Soldiers to execute the sentence[22]

This run of seven performances from Thursday, October 4, through Saturday, October 18, is the longest and most satisfactory consecutive record we have had. Such performances were probably usual during this season, but they are difficult to document. What we have had to hypothecate in previous seasons (and must again) we can here establish.

Along with newspaper advertisements and handbills, a source of valuable information about the theatre should be contemporary letters and diaries of early citizens or visitors to Richmond. The search for such has been almost completely unrewarding. There is, to my knowledge, no diary or journal extant in which some Richmonder wrote about his visits to the theatre. We have John Marshall's account book, but the young lawyer's record of theatre attendance is more concerned with expenditures for tickets than with comments on the plays. While wishing vainly for some Richmond Pepys or Boswell, I can offer scant mention of the theatre in letters of this period. On November 10, 1792, William Munford wrote from Richmond, "The players are in town, and I intend to get them to bring a farce of my father's writing upon the stage this winter."[23]

William's father was Col. Robert Munford, whose *Collection of Plays and Poems* was published at Petersburg in 1798. Besides some conventional eighteenth-century verse, the volume contains two plays, *The Candidates* and *The Patriots*, both lively satires of contemporary politics. The two plays were almost certainly intended for the stage; yet despite the son's efforts, there is no record of the production of either play. Both lay dormant for a century and a half, but have recently been edited and republished.[24] Both, I think, deserved production, but were perhaps denied the stage because of the very qualities that give them interest and value to us today: realistic low comedy, biting political satire, and timely interest in civil liberties.

Munford's letter is the only evidence we have that the theatre was open during the month of November. We have had similar hiatuses in previous seasons, due sometimes to incomplete newspaper files, sometimes to absence of theatrical notices from extant papers. It seems reasonable to assume that the theatre continued during such periods. It may be equally reasonable to conjecture that the company traveled to Petersburg or Norfolk. The last recorded performance was on October 13; the next is on December 5, 1792, when the *Virginia Gazette, and General Advertiser* announced for "This evening A New Comedy (never performed in America) *The Road to Ruin; or, School for Gamesters*, as performed at Covent Garden upwards of 100 nights." Afterpiece was "a comic opera (never performed in America) *No Song No Supper;*

or, The Lawyer in a Sack." Complete casts were given for both plays. We have seen several Sullys on the stage, and it has generally been supposed that Lawrence, portrait painter and eldest son, did not act; yet in this advertisement the role of Jacob is clearly filled by "L. Sully." That this is not a misprint is indicated by the appearance of the other members of the family in other roles in the same play. Matthew Sully (the father) played Mr. Silky, Matthew, Jr., played Harry Dornton, Mrs. Sully played the Widow Warren, Miss Charlotte Sully played Jenny, and Miss Elizabeth Sully played the Mantuamaker. Bignall played Squire Goldfinch, and Mrs. Bignall, Sophia. In *No Song, No Supper* five Sullys (all but Lawrence) appeared for their second roles of the evening. A big night for the Sully family!

The Road to Ruin

Squire Goldfinch	Mr. Bignall
Harry Dornton	Mr. M. Sully
Mr. Sulky	Mr. J. Kenna
Mr. Silky	Mr. Sully
Mr. Milford	Mr. Courtney
Mr. Smith	Mr. Andrews
Hosier	Mr. J. Bignall
Jacob	Mr. L. Sully
Tennis Marker	Mr. Riffetts
Old Dornton	Mr. Hamilton
The Widow Warren	Mrs. Sully
Jenny	Miss Sully
Mrs. Ledger	Mrs. Decker
Milliner	Mrs. J. Kenna
Mantuamaker	Miss E. Sully
Sophia	Mrs. Bignall

No Song, No Supper

Farmer Crop	Mr. J. Kenna
Frederick	Mr. Courtney
Lawyer Endless	Mr. Sully
William	Mr. M. Sully
Thomas	Mr. Andrews
Robin	Mr. Bignall
Dorothy Crop	Mrs. Decker
Louisa	Miss Sully
Nelly	Miss E. Sully
Deborah	Mrs. Sully
Margaretta	Mrs. Bignall

This was a particularly large evening in other respects. It was Bignall's benefit. Between the pieces there was a song by Mrs. Decker, and another song, "No Indeed, Not I," by Mrs. Bignall. The evening concluded with a double allemande and Scotch reel.

One week later there was announced for Wednesday, December 12, "a Comedy (never performed here but once) *Know Your Own Mind; or The Capricious Lover* written by Arthur Murphy, Esq." The afterpiece, *No Song, No Supper*, was repeated with identical cast of characters. In *Know Your Own Mind*, Bignall played Millamour and Mrs. Bignall, Miss Neville:

Mr. Millamour	Mr. Bignall
Old Bigrove	Mr. Hamilton
Malville	Mr. Courtney
Sir Harry Lovewit	Mr. Sully
Captain Bigrove	Mr. M. Sully
Sir John Millamour	Mr. Andrews
Charles	Mr. Hallam
Robert	Mr. Riffetts
Dashwood	Mr. J. Kenna
Miss Neville	Mrs. Bignall
Mrs. Bromley	Mrs. Decker
Lady Jane	Mrs. J. Kenna
Madam La Rogue	Miss Sully
Lady Bell	Mrs. West

The performance was for the benefit of Mrs. Decker, who played Mrs. Bromley in *Know Your Own Mind*, Dorothy Crop in *No Song, No Supper*, and sang "a Favourite Hunting Song" between the two. Additional specialties between pieces were "Dish of All Sorts" by Bignall, "The Dwarf Dance" by Hallam, and "a Favourite Song of 'Jack the Guinea Pig'" by Courtenay. The evening concluded with "a Hornpipe by Sully, Jun."[25]

The last advertisement of the season appeared on December 29. It announced that

on Monday Evening, Dec. 31, will be presented the favorite Comedy written by David Garrick and George Coleman, *The Clan-Destine Marriage.*

Between the Play and Farce, a favorite Burletta (as performed at Sadler's Wells upwards of 30 nights) written by Holcroft, called *April Day; or The Frenchman Outwitted.*

To which will be added, O'Keefe's celebrated Farce (never performed in America) of *Modern Antiques, or, The Merry Mourn-*

ers as performed at Covent Garden upwards of 100 nights with distinguished applause.

No roles were included in the advertisement. Admission was advertised as "boxes six shillings, pit, four shillings and sixpence, upper boxes, four shillings and sixpence." Doors opened at 5:30, and the curtain rose "precisely at half past six o'clock." Tickets were on sale "at the Post Office, at Mr. Carey's Printing Office, and at the Office of the Theatre."

At the end of the second act of *The Clandestine Marriage* the audience was favored with " 'When first I slipt my Leading Strings,' a favourite Song from the Woodman, by Miss Harriet Sully—Three years of Age." There was also " 'Thomas be quiet & let me alone,' a comic song, by Mrs. Bignall." The program concluded with "Ground & Lofty Tumbling, by the Messieurs Sully's." That the performance was "for the Benefit of Mrs. West," wife of one of the managers of the company and sister of the senior Sully, probably made it a special effort; also, it was "Positively the last Night this Season." [26]

This season is easily the richest on record up to this time. We have announcements of both opening and closing dates, August 1 and December 31; we have reliable information about the house, records of fourteen evenings, and the American debut of the Sully family.

From what must have been a distinguished repertoire there are records of twenty-eight different plays, among them ten American premieres: *Wild Oats, The Pannel, The Sorrows of Werter, Shakespeare's Jubilee, Such Things Are, Ways and Means, The Woodman, Robin Hood, The Road to Ruin,* and *Modern Antiques.* In addition there were two plays, *Appearance Is against Them* and *April Day,* not previously known to have been acted in America.

Performances are recorded on every night of the week (Sunday excepted) through five months. It is, however, unlikely that six performances were given weekly during this time. Three would be a more likely figure. If the company played three nights a week from August 1 to December 31, there would have been something like sixty performances during the season, although we can authenticate only fourteen from extant newspapers. We can, however, hypothecate a brilliant season, one of the most spectacular in any eighteenth-century American theatre. One detail is lacking to glad-den the historian's heart: there is no record of American authorship; the plays that delighted these Richmond audiences were all British imports. If only Colonel Munford's satire might have been pro-duced on Shockoe Hill! It had its premiere on January 18, 1949, in Phi Beta Kappa Hall at The College of William and Mary, Williamsburg, Virginia.[27]

We can assume that the theatre was well attended, and I believe we can predicate a financially successful season. The company went straight to Charleston, where they opened the new theatre on Monday, February 11, 1793. They played a successful season, closing on May 31 for Mrs. West's benefit. On June 3 they sailed in the *Swift Packet*, Captain Thompson, for Norfolk. Sherman says they played there in July and August; they did not open in Richmond until September 20.

The plays.   *Wild Oats* (August 1, 1792), a comedy by John O'Keeffe, was first acted at Covent Garden on April 16, 1791, and was published during the year. It was acted in New York, Charles-ton, and Philadelphia in 1793, on March 18, May 1, and July 20, respectively. The Charleston production was by the West and Bignall Company. Apparently this performance in Richmond on August 1, 1792, was its American premiere.

The Pannel (August 1, 1792), a farce which J. P. Kemble altered from Isaac Bickerstaffe, was first acted at Drury Lane on Novem-ber 28, 1788, and was published in 1789. There is no record of its performance in Philadelphia. It was acted in New York at the John Street Theatre on May 31, 1797. On February 24, 1794, it was acted in Charleston by the West and Bignall Company. Ap-parently, this also was an American premiere.

The Maid of the Mill (August 30, 1792), a comic opera by Isaac Bickerstaffe, was brought out at Covent Garden in 1765 and was acted in both Philadelphia and New York in 1769. *The Widow's Vow*, a farce by Elizabeth Inchbald, was first acted at the Second Haymarket on June 20, 1786. Its American premiere was less than a year later at the John Street Theatre in New York on March 23, 1787; it was acted in Philadelphia in 1788. This is the only record of its performance in Richmond.

The Sorrows of Werter (called *Werter* in Philadelphia and *Werter and Charlotte* in New York) (September 6, 1792) was a tragedy by Frederick Reynolds, first acted at Bath on November 25, 1785, and published in 1786. It was acted in New York on May 9, 1796, and in Philadelphia on April 10, 1797. This Richmond performance of September 6, 1792, was apparently its American premiere. *Shakespeare's Jubilee* (also called *Shakespeare's Garland*) was first performed at Drury Lane on October 14, 1769. A collection of ballads, catches, and glees arranged by David Garrick with music by Charles Dibdin, it was published in 1769. It was acted in Charleston on May 31, 1763, by the West and Bignall Company. Its first performance in Philadelphia was on June 1, 1795, and in New York on May 18, 1801. This date, September 6, 1792, seems to mark two American premieres in Richmond.

Such Things Are, or *the Christian Sultan* (October 2, 1792), a drama by Elizabeth Inchbald, was first acted at Covent Garden on February 10, 1787. It was published in 1788. It is recorded in Charleston, New York, and Philadelphia in 1793, on February 18, May 13, and July 5, respectively. This performance in Richmond on October 2, 1792, is apparently its American premiere. Unfortunately the cast was not published. Nor was the cast advertised when the play was acted in Charleston by the West and Bignall Company. The Charleston audience, however, was favored by this additional piece of information about "*The Christian Sultan*": "This much admired play by Mrs. Inchbald is superior to any piece she has yet wrote, and to the best modern comedies. The character of the philanthropic Howard (for whom so many societies all over the world are named today) the widow speaks his charities—the orphan lisps his bounties, and the rough, fierce Indian melts in tears to bless him." *Ways and Means*, a comedy by George Colman, the younger, was first acted at the Second Haymarket on October 7, 1788, and was published the same year. It was acted in Philadelphia, New York, and Charleston in 1793, on January 9, March 6, and May 17, respectively. This performance in Richmond, antedating the Philadelphia performance by about three months, is recorded as another American premiere.

The Woodman (October 6, 1792) was advertised as "never presented in America," but such newspaper notices must be regarded with suspicion. Apparently, however, this one was correct. *The Woodman* was acted in Charleston by the West and Bignall Company on May 13, 1793, when it was advertised as the second performance in America. It was acted in Philadelphia on June 18, 1794, but did not reach New York until February 6, 1818. A comic opera by Henry Bate (alias Bate Dudley) with music by William Shield, it had been first acted at Covent Garden on February 26, 1719, and was published in that year. This performance of *Appearance Is against Them*, a farce by Elizabeth Inchbald, is the only record which I have been able to locate of its production in America. It was first acted at Covent Garden on October 22, 1765, and was published in 1785.

The Gentle Shepherd (October 8, 1792), by Allan Ramsay, was acted in Philadelphia on February 4, 1791, and in New York on June 5, 1791. *More Ways than One*, a comedy by Hannah Cowley, was first acted at Covent Garden in 1783. It was acted in New York in 1786, in Philadelphia in 1790, and in Charleston in 1794 by the West and Bignall Company.

Harlequin Statue (October 9, 1792) is recorded in New York in 1766 and in Philadelphia in 1795. The three productions were probably similar. I suspect that the Sullys presented the equivalent of *Harlequin Statue* in Charleston. The description given here illustrates the *commedia dell'arte* form of these pantomimes in which the stock characters of Harlequin, Columbine, and the clown performed stock scenes combined with such ingenious novelties as the imagination of the dancers and the skill of the stage manager could contrive. Especially interesting is the local adaptation of scene in which Harlequin's magic sword transforms the Eagle Tavern into the Virginia State Capitol. Such adaptability doubtless helps to account for Harlequin's ubiquity and longevity.

Robin Hood (October 10, 1792), a comic opera by Leonard MacNally, with music by William Shield, was first produced at Covent Garden on April 17, 1784, and was published the same year. It was acted in Charleston on February 16, 1793, by the West and Bignall Company; in Philadelphia on March 10, 1794; and in New York on April 30, 1794. This performance (perhaps the second in Richmond) is the first record of its performance in America. *Who's the Dupe?*, a farce by Hannah Cowley, was brought out at Drury Lane on April 10, 1779. It was acted in New York in 1780, in Philadelphia in 1790, and in Charleston in 1806. This is the only record of its performance in Richmond.

The Wonder (October 11, 1792), a comedy by Susannah Centlivre, had its premiere at Drury Lane in 1714. First acted in Philadelphia in 1766, and in New York in 1768, it held the American stage through most of the nineteenth century. *The Agreeable Surprise*, a comic opera by John O'Keeffe, with music by Samuel Arnold, was brought out at the Haymarket in 1781. It was first produced in New York in 1785 and in Philadelphia in 1787. It too was long a favorite of American audiences.

A School for Soldiers (October 13, 1792) was almost certainly the version done by John Henry while the Hallam and Henry Company was in Jamaica in 1783. An earlier version by Charles Dibdin titled *The Deserter* had been acted at Drury Lane in 1773. Henry's version was acted in New York in 1788 and in Philadelphia in 1790. It was acted in Charleston in 1793 by the West and Bignall Company with an almost identical description of the last scene, but with the addition of "at the end of Act 3, 'The Tobacco Box or Soldier's Pledge of Love,' a favorite dialogue by Mr. West and Mrs. Bignall." The Richmond announcement did not advertise this extra romantic attraction.

No Song, No Supper (December 5, 1792), a comic opera by Prince Hoare, was brought out at Drury Lane on April 16, 1790. Its American premiere was at Philadelphia on November 30, 1792, five days before this performance in Richmond. It was first acted in New York on February 15, 1793. One of the most popular plays of this period, it held the stage well into the nineteenth century. There are frequent records of later performances in Richmond. *The Road to Ruin*, a comedy by Thomas Holcroft, was first produced at Covent Garden on February 18, 1792, and was published within the year, probably shortly after its production. This performance in Richmond, less than ten months later, is the play's American premiere. It was acted in Philadelphia only five days later, on December 10; it reached New York on February 8, 1793, and was acted in Charleston on April 19, 1793, by the West and Bignall Company. It was a successful play, holding on well into the nineteenth century.

The Clandestine Marriage (December 31, 1792), a comedy by David Garrick and the elder Colman, was brought out at Drury Lane in 1766; it was acted in both New York and Philadelphia in 1767. This is the only record of its performance in Richmond. *April Day, or the Frenchman Outwitted* appears to have been the burletta by Kane O'Hara, first acted at the Haymarket in 1777 and published in the same year. This is the only record I have found of its production in America. *Modern Antiques, or the Merry Mourners*, a farce by John O'Keeffe, had its premiere at Covent Garden in 1791 and was published in 1792. This performance was apparently its American premiere. It was acted in Philadelphia in 1794 and in both Charleston and New York in 1795. A popular afterpiece, it was acted in Richmond several times during the first part of the nineteenth century.

The players. The Sullys were one of the famous families of American theatrical history. After their Richmond debut they adorned and enlivened both stage and ring in Charleston, Philadelphia, New York, and other cities. "Sully" was Matthew Sully; "M. Sully" was Matthew Sully, Jr.; "Mrs. Sully" was wife of one and mother of the other. Mr. Sully's sister Margaret was the wife of Thomas Wade West. There were several other members of the family, most of whom seem to have appeared on the Richmond stage this season. I have difficulty keeping them straight, especially when designations in the programs are incomplete. There were nine children: Lawrence, Matthew, Chester, and Thomas; Charlotte, Elizabeth, Julia, Jane, and Harriet. I imagine little Sullys peering from the wings as their elders trod the boards or flew through the air with agility and grace, while the youngest fell asleep backstage. I hope there was a governess, but I fear there was not. I put Mrs. Sully down as a gallant lady and a great trouper.

Eola Willis tells us that the Sully family came originally from the English village of Long Crendon, that Matthew attended theological seminary as preparation for the Anglican clergy, but became enamored of Sarah Chester, whom he left the seminary to marry, and, disinherited, forsook the Church for the stage. Susanne K. Sherman tells us that his real name was O'Sullivan, and that he was the nephew of Sir John O'Sullivan, who served as aide-de-camp to

Bonnie Prince Charlie in the Battle of Culloden. We are reminded, however, that his descendants were more important than his ancestors.

The West and Bignall Company was probably at its strongest during this season. It included, according to newspaper records, thirteen men and nine women, as well as the ample supply of Sully child-actors. Leading roles were usually played by Mr. and Mrs. Bignall, or Mr. and Mrs. Sully; there was strong supporting talent in Courtenay, J. Kenna, Matthew Sully, Hallam, J. Bignall, Andrews, Riffits, and Hamilton among the men; while Mrs. West, Mrs. Decker, Mrs. Kenna, Mrs. J. Kenna, Mrs. Davids, and Mrs. Sully all played important roles. Manager West and Miss West appeared in minor parts. We have recorded the only known stage appearance of Lawrence Sully. According to the custom of the time, the eldest daughter was "Miss Sully"; this was Charlotte; "Miss E. Sully" was Elizabeth. The "Miss Sully" who appeared with "Miss E. Sully" as "her tiny foot page" in *Robin Hood* on October 10 was probably Harriet, three years old, who sang "When First I Slipt My Leading Strings" on December 31. The "Master Sully" who appeared as Isabella's child in the production of *Isabella, or the Fatal Marriage* was either Chester or Thomas. One advertisement mentions "Sully, Jun." and "Bignall, Jun.," whom I take to be Matthew Sully and J. Bignall. Schoultz is identified as stage manager. The company was rich with talent in music, dancing, acrobatics, as well as in acting, being strongest, I believe, in the comic line.

According to Willis, the company that arrived in Charleston from Richmond consisted of Mrs. West, Mr. and Mrs. Bignall, Mr. and Mrs. Kedey, Mr. and Mrs. Decker, Mr. and Mrs. Sheldon, Miss Sully, Miss E. Sully, Miss H. West, Mr. J. Bignall, Mr. Kenna, Mr. Courtenay, Mr. West, Jr., Mr. Andrews, Mr. Riffits, M. Gollier, and M. Lacot.

NINTH SEASON

Curtis and Company

August 1793

Chronicle.   In the summer of 1791 a group of strolling players, "Mr. Godwin & Co.," had entertained Richmond audiences. During the summer of 1793 another group from the fringes of theatrical history appeared. I draw several inferences from Curtis's advertisement in the *Virginia Gazette, and Weekly Advertiser* of Friday, August 16, 1793:

BY PERMISSION

For the Last Time in this city, will be performed at the New Theatre, at the back of the Capitol, on Saturday Evening, August 17th, at half-past 7 o'clock, by the celebrated Mr. Curtis & his company, A great variety of Feats of Activity (Superior to any yet seen here) on the Tight Rope, also, Tumbling. Likewise will be performed, Many curious Equilibriums on the Slack Rope.

The whole will be concluded with the celebrated Pantomime of the Cobler from Paris. Particulars will be expressed in the Bills of the day.

N.B. The doors will be opened at six o'clock—Tickets to be had at the Theatre, or at Mr. Curtis's lodging room at Mr. Stevenson's brick house on Shockoe Hill— Boxes four shillings, and six pence, Gallery three shillings, Pit three shillings.

If any person wishes to purchase a Stage Waggon and three Horses and the Theatre where Mr. Curtis performed, will please to apply to him at the theatre.

First, from the "Stage Waggon and three Horses" I infer that Curtis had been traveling, though where he came from or where he went I can only guess: Baltimore, Petersburg, Fredericksburg? He does not appear in histories of the legitimate stage. From his program, he was obviously a mountebank. Who else, or how many, comprised his "company" is unknown. I hazard Mrs. Curtis, Miss Curtis, Master Curtis.

His "New Theatre" was evidently not the one in which the West and Bignall Company performed. Evidence of Curtis's theatre and his declining fortunes I derive from an official notice in the *Virginia Gazette, and General Advertiser* of Wednesday, August 21:

Will be sold by auction, at the vendue-office, to-morrow at 11 O'clock, The New Theatre on Shockhoe Hill, lately built by Mr. Curtis, which cost him upwards of £140—Possession to be given on Tuesday next. Also a Stage Waggon with harness compleat, and three draft horses.

M. Vandewall, V.M.

I deduce that Curtis and Company arrived in Richmond in his Stage Waggon drawn by three horses; that they first performed on the wagon; that he then built a theatre costing £140, in which performances, consisting mostly of acrobatics and pantomimes, were given during the summer of 1793. His declining fortunes I deduce from his attempt to sell his wagon and horses one week before Vendue Master Vandewall sold him out, wagon, horses, and theatre, at public auction on Thursday, August 22. Exit another strolling player.

What happened to Curtis and Company? Let us hope the sale of his theatre brought enough to enable Curtis to pay off his creditors, buy back his wagon and horses, and drive off to other audiences and better luck elsewhere. What happened to his theatre? I doubt that we shall ever know.

Richmond had other diversions. On Wednesday, September 11, the "Dancing School of Louis Roussell" was advertised to open on the twenty-third, with "a Special Night School for Gentlemen" to open on the twenty-fifth. Roussell thanked the "Ladies and gentlemen of Richmond" for the "liberal encouragement" they had given him "these four years past."[28] Other advertisements appeared during 1793, '94 and '95. He was probably the same Roussell who had played in New York in 1783 with the Dennis Ryan Company which came to Richmond in 1784. I assume that he acted with Ryan in Richmond and either stayed on or returned later to teach dancing.

TENTH SEASON
West and Bignall Company
September–December 1793

Chronicle.   It may have been the arrival of West and Bignall that prompted the following notice in the *Virginia Gazette, and Rich-*

mond and Manchester Advertiser for June 27, 1793: "The Subscribers to the House on Shockoe Hill, built by Alexander Quesnay for an Academy, or their representatives, are requested to meet at Mr. Moss' Tavern on Saturday next at Ten o'clock, on business which will be then communicated. Richmond, June 25, 1793."

That West and Bignall were in Richmond in July is attested by the following notice:

THEATRE

TWENTY POUNDS REWARD

Whereas some persons, maliciously inclined, have frequently broke open and feloniously taken from the Theatre on Shockoe Hill, upwards of 400 yards of painted canvass, one mahagony dressing table, six chairs, a pair of brass knockers from the stage doors, one pair of cast iron kitchen dogs, three setts of fire irons, and several other articles not yet recollected, and otherwise (through wanton wickedness) much damaged the house.

We promise whoever may give information sufficient to bring the depredators to punishment, shall receive the above reward.

Richmond July 23, 1793   West and Bignall[29]

The theatre that had been robbed was, of course, Quesnay's theatre, in which West and Bignall had performed, not the theatre which Curtis built. Whether the stolen articles were recovered is unknown, but the damage to the house was evidently repaired. On September 19 this notice appeared:

BY AUTHORITY

RICHMOND THEATRE

West and Bignall, with the greatest respect, inform the Ladies and Gentlemen of Richmond, Manchester &c. the Theatre will positively open on Friday Evening, the 20th September, 1793— When will be presented the favorite Comedy (never performed here) of the *School for Wives; or, The Faithful Irishman.*

Afterpiece was "the Comic Opera *Rosina; or Love in a Cottage* with the original overture." Full casts were given for both pieces:

School for Wives

Belville	Mr. Edgar
General Savage	Mr. Hamilton
Lawyer Torrington	Mr. J. Kenna

Leeson	Mr. I. Bignall
Captain Savage	Mr. M. Sully
Wolfe	Mr. Sully
Leech	Mr. West
Crow	Mr. Kedey
Servant	Mr. Riffetts
Conolly (the Faithful Irishman)	Mr. Bignall
Mrs. Belville	Mrs. Edgar
Lady Rachel Mildew	Mrs. Gray
Mrs. Tempest	Mrs. Kedey
Miss Leeson	Miss Sully
Miss Walsingham	Mrs. Bignall

Rosina

Belville	Mr. J. Kenna
Captain Belville	Mr. M. Sully
Rustic	Mr. I. Bignall
First Irishman	Mr. Hamilton
Second Irishman	Mr. Riffetts
William	Mr. Bignall
Rosina	Mrs. Gray
Dorcas	Mrs. Edgar
Phoebe	Mrs. Bignall

Doors opened at six and the curtain rose "precisely at 7 o'clock." Tickets were on sale "at the Post-office, the Eagle Tavern, and at the Office of the Theatre." The role of Belville in *School for Wives* was played by Mr. Edgar "from the Theatre Royal, Covent Garden, being his first appearance on this stage"; and Mrs. Belville was played by Mrs. Edgar, "her first appearance on this stage." The advertisement stated further: "The Scenery designed and executed by the celebrated artist, Mons. Audin, from the Opera-House, Paris."[30]

Under the heading "By Authority," "The Virginia Company" advertised on October 24 for "This Evening . . . the celebrated Comedy of *The Young Quaker* (written by O'Keefe, author of *The Poor Soldier* &c.)" Complete cast was given:

Sadboy (the Young Quaker)	Mr. Edgar
Chronicle	Mr. J. Kenna
Captain Ambush	Mr. Hallam
Spatterdash	Mr. M. Sully
Shadrach	Mr. I. Bignall

Old Sadboy	Mr. Kedey
Malachy	Mr. Riffetts
Twig	Mr. Sully
Goliah	Master C. Sully
Clod	Mr. Bignall
Araminta	Mrs. Chambers
Lady Rounceval	Mrs. Edgar
Mrs. Millefleur	Mrs. Kedey
Pink	Miss Sully
Judith	Mrs. Gray
Diana Primrose	Mrs. Bignall

Afterpiece was "the celebrated Comic Opera of *The Flitch of Bacon, or, The Custom of Dunmow Priory* (Written by the Reverend Bate Dudley, author of *The Woodman* &c.) The music by Mr. Shields." Complete cast was given:

Major Benbow	Mr. J. Kenna
Captain Wilson	Mr. Chambers
Captain Greville	Mr. Sully
Justice Benbow	Mr. Hamilton
Ned	Mr. I. Bignall
Kilderkin	Mr. Kedey
Putty	Mr. Riffetts
Tipple	Mr. Bignall
Eliza	Mrs. Chambers

Mrs. Decker sang between pieces. Tickets were on sale at the same places, and prices were given: boxes, six shillings; pit and upper boxes, four shillings sixpence.[31]

A similar advertisement on November 7 announced for "This Evening (Thursday) . . . the celebrated Comic Opera, composed by Sig. Storace, call'd *The Haunted Tower; or, Baron of Oakland*, as performed at Drury Lane, with distinguished applause." Cast was given:

Baron of Oakland	Mr. Hamilton
Lord Wm. (under the assumed title of Sir Pallimede)	Mr. Chambers
Lord De Courey	Mr. Murray
Robert	Mr. Clifford
Hugo	Mr. Kedey
Lewis	Mr. Sully
Charles	Mr. M. Sully
Martin	Mr. I. Bignall

Edward	Mr. Bignall
Lady Elinor De Coury	Mrs. Chambers
Cecily	Miss Sully
Maud	Mrs. Gray
Adela (under the assumed	
title of Lady Elinor)	Mrs. Bignall

Servants, Huntsmen, Cooks, & Fishermen, by
Supernumeraries, and the rest of the Company.

The following scenes, "painted by Monss. Audin," were exhibited: "Rocks and a Tempestuous Sea — Maud's Cottage — Adela's Cottage — An Antique Apartment in the Haunted Tower — A Kitchen, with an Ox Roasting — A beautiful outside view of the Haunted Tower, &c.&c." At the end of the first act Clifford sang "The Heaving of the Lead, or the Deep Nine," and between pieces he sang "Washington's Council Forever, Huzza!"

Afterpiece was *Love a-la-Mode; or the Humours of the Turf*, with the following cast:

Squire Groom	Mr. Henderson, from London
	(being his first appearance
	in America)
Sir Archy Macsarcasm	Mr. Hamilton
Beau Mordecai	Mr. I. Bignall
Sir Theodore Goodchild	Mr. J. Kenna
Sir Callaghan O'Brallaghan	
(with a song)	Mr. Bignall
Charlotte	Miss Sully[32]

The next notice of the season is found in the *Virginia Gazette, and Richmond and Manchester Advertiser* for November 11. The copy which I examined is mutilated, but I think it can be emended. My emendations are bracketed:

BY AUT[HORITY]

THE VIRGIN[IA COMPANY]

This Evenin[g Monday November 11]
will b[e presented]
The co[medy of The]
West [Indian]

Belcour (the West Indian,	[Mr. Chambers]
Mr. Stockwell,	[Mr. J. Kenna]
Captain Dudley,	[Mr. Riffets]

Charles Dudley,	[Mr. I. Bignall]
Stukely,	[Mr. Sully]
Fulmer	Mr. Kedey
Varland	Mr. Hamilton
Major O'Flaherty,	Mr. Bignall
Louisa (daughter to	
Capt. Dudley)	Miss Sully
Lady Rusport	Mrs. Gray
Mrs. Fulmer	Mrs. Kedey
Lucy	Mrs. Murray
Charlotte Rusport	Mrs. Edgar

Midas

Immortals

Jupiter	Mr. I. Bignall
Bacchus	Mr. Riffetts
Mars	Mr. Kedey
Apollo	Mr. Chambers
Juno	Miss Sully

Mortals

Midas	Mr. Hamilton
Sileno	Mr. Bignall
Daemetas	Mr. Sully
Pan	Mr. J. Kenna
Nysa	Mrs. Chambers
Daphne	Mrs. Decker
Mysis	Mrs. Edgar

On November 28 was advertised for "Tomorrow Evening . . . a Musical Comedy, Never performed in America, written by the celebrated Mrs. Cowley, authoress of *The Belles Stratagem*, &c.&c. called *A Day in Turkey, or The Russian Slaves.*" Complete cast was given:

TURKS

Ibrahim (the Grand Signior)	Mr. J. Kenna
Mustapha	Mr. Sully
Azim (a slave driver)	Mr. Hamilton
Muley	Mr. I. Bignall
Ismael	Mr. Hallam
Hafez	Mr. Riffetts
Melider	Mr. Greenwood
Selim (with a song)	Mr. Chambers
Lauretta	Mrs. Edgar

Selima	Mrs. Kedey
Basca	Miss Sully
Fatima	Mrs. Chambers

FRENCH

A la Greque (with a song)	Mr. Bignall

RUSSIANS

Count Orloff	Mr. Edgar
Peter Petronitz	Mr. M. Sully
Old Petronitz	Mr. Kedey
Paulina Petronitz (with a song)	Mrs. Bignall
Alexina	Mrs. West

The advertisement listed the following scenes "painted by M. Audin—The Gardens of the Bassa, decorated with palms, fountains, &c. in the Eastern Stile. A Grand Canopy. A Wide Court, with several unfinished Buildings." Afterpiece was "the Comic Opera of *The Quaker, or, May Day Dower*," with the following cast:

Steady (the Quaker)	Mr. Hamilton
Solomon	Mr. Bignall
Farmer Easy	Mr. Riffetts
Lads and Lasses by the rest of the Company	
Lubin	Mr. Chambers
Floretta	Mrs. Edgar
Cicily	Mrs. Gray
Gillian	Mrs. Chambers[33]

Next notice appeared on Friday, December 6:

BY AUTHORITY

THE VIRGINIA COMPANY

Mr. & Mrs. Kedey

Respectfully inform the Ladies & Gentlemen of Richmond, Manchester, &c. their Benefit is fixed for This Evening, December 6, 1793 when will be presented Shakespeare's Celebrated Comedy of *The Merchant of Venice; or, The Inexorable Jew.*

The afterpiece was "a Farce, never performed here, called the *True Born Irishman; or The Irish Fine Lady* written by Charles Maclin, author of *The Man of the World, Love A-La-Mode,* &c. &c." Complete casts were given for both plays:

The Merchant of Venice

Antonio (the Merchant of Venice)	Mr. Edgar
Bassanio	Mr. Marriott
Graciano	Mr. Bignall
Lorenzo, (with Songs)	Mr. Chambers
Launcelot	Mr. Sully
Salarino	Mr. Kedey
Salanio	Mr. Riffetts
Tubal	Mr. J. Bignall
Gobbo	Mr. Henderson
Balthazar	Mr. Greenwood
Shylock (the Jew)	Mr. J. Kenna
Jessica	Mrs. Chambers
Narissa	Mrs. Henderson
Portia	Mrs. Marriott

True Born Irishman

Murrough O'Dogherty	Mr. Hamilton
Councellor Hamilton	Mr. Henderson
Major Gamble	Mr. Kedey
John	Mr. Riffetts
Williams	Mr. Greenwood
James	Mr. Murray
Count Mushroom	Mr. Chambers
Kitty Farrell	Miss Sully
Lady Kinnegad	Mrs. Chambers
Lady Bob Frightful	Mrs. Gray
Mrs. Gazette	Mrs. Murray
Mrs. Diggerty (the Irish Fine Lady)	Mrs. Kedey

Kedey played Salarino, a small role for a benefit performance. He also played Major Gamble in *The True Born Irishman*, in which Mrs. Kedey played the featured role of "Mrs. Diggerty (the Irish Fine Lady)." Between pieces Chambers sang "Stand to Your Guns," and Henderson sang "Murder in Irish." Tickets were on sale "at the Post Office, the Eagle Tavern, at the Office of the Theatre, and of Mr. and Mrs. Kedey, at Mrs. Ghovares's, on Shockoe Hill."[34]

On Monday following, December 9, the *Virginia Gazette, and Richmond and Manchester Advertiser* announced for "This evening the Comedy *Wild Oats; or The Strolling Gentlemen.*" *Rosina* was again the afterpiece. When it had been presented on September 20, opening night of the season, leading roles of Belville and Rosina had been filled by J. Kenna and Mrs. Gray. For this performance they were taken by Mr. and Mrs. Chambers. Mrs. Chambers also played Jane in *Wild Oats*. Bignall took the featured role of Rover in *Wild Oats* and played William in *Rosina*. Complete casts were given for both pieces:

Wild Oats

Rover	Mr. Bignall
John Dory	Mr. J. Kenna
Harry Thunder	Mr. Hallam
Sim	Mr. Sully
Banks	Mr. Kedey
Midge	Mr. Greenwood
Gammon	Mr. Edgar
Zachariah	Mr. Riffetts
Ephraim Smooth	Mr. Henderson
Sir George Thunder	Mr. Hamilton
Lady Amaranth	Mrs. Henderson
Amelia	Mrs. Kedey
Jane	Mrs. Chambers

Rosina

Belville	Mr. Chambers
Capt. Belville	Mr. Sully
William	Mr. Bignall
Rustic	Mr. J. Kenna
First Irishman	Mr. Hamilton
Second Irishman	Mr. Riffetts
Phoebe	Mrs. Henderson
Dorcas	Mrs. Edgar
Rosina	Mrs. Chambers

This performance was for the benefit of Mrs. Hallam and Mr. and Mrs. Henderson. Between pieces Edgar recited "Bucks Have at You All." At the end of the first act of *Rosina* Mrs. Henderson sang "The Poor Little Gypsey." The evening concluded with "an occasional address to the Ladies and Gentlemen of Richmond, Manchester, &c. by Mrs. Henderson."

On Thursday, December 12, the benefit of Mr. and Mrs. Marriott was announced for "Tomorrow Evening . . . [when] will be performed, the celebrated Tragedy called *The Orphan, or Unhappy*

Marriage" with Mr. and Mrs. Marriott in the leading roles of Castalio and Monimia (the orphan). Afterpiece was *High Life below Stairs*, with "(by particular desire)" a mock minuet by Edgar and Hallam in the second act. No cast was given for either play. Between pieces Marriott presented a "Gallimaufry, or Thespian Regalia, consisting of the following Entertainments, 1st, A Description of the Follies and Fashions of the Times. 2nd, A Description of the Furor Dramaticer. 3rd, Retaliation exploded. 4th, Lying serviceable in some Cases." The evening concluded with "Surprising Feats of Activity, By Mr. M. Sully, Mr. L. Sully, and Masters C. and T. Sully."[35] Those would have been Matthew, Jr., Lawrence, Chester, and Thomas.

"Positively the Last Night" of the season was advertised for "This Evening" on December 16. It was Mrs. West's benefit. The evening opened with "a celebrated Comedy (never performed here) called *The Jealous Wife.*" Then came a song, "The Contented Shepherd," by Clifford, and "a Song" (no title given) by Henderson. The feature of the evening and of the season was "the Grand Serious Pantomime (under the immediate direction of Mr. M. Sully) of *The Death of Captain Cook, In the Island of O Wy Hee, in the Pacific Ocean.*"

Cast was given as follows:

Captain Cook (of the Resolution)	Mr. Bignall
His First Lieutenant	Mr. J. Bignall
His Midshipman	Mr. Henderson
His Sailors	Mr. Greenwood, &c.
His Soldiers	Supernumeraries

Indians

Tereoboo (King of O-Wy-Hee)	Mr. Hamilton
Perea (the favorite lover of Emai)	Mr. Chambers
Warriors, Messrs, Murry, Riffets, and supernumeraries	
And Koah (the revengeful lover of Emai)	Mr. M. Sully
Emai (the King's daughter)	Miss Sully

Female Islanders, Mrs. Edgar, Mrs. Chambers, Mrs. Marriott, Mrs. Henderson, Mrs. Kedey, Mrs. Murry, Mrs. Gray, Mrs. J. Kenna, Miss J. Sully.

If this did not cause expectation to rise on tiptoe, certainly Richmond must have roused when it read on:

In Act first, the Method of Courtship and Marriage Ceremony in the Island of O-Wy-Hee. Manners of a single Combat with Battle-Axes.

In Act second, the Arrival of Captain Cook in the ship Resolution, his reception by the King and Warriors of O-Wy-Hee. A War Dance by the Natives.

Their Preparations for War and Manners of Sacrifice, with an exact representation of the death of Captain Cook, by the Warriors.

Act Third, the Funeral Ceremonies made use of at O-Wy-Hee, with a Procession of the Natives and English to the Monument of Captain Cook, with Military Honors.

The Whole to conclude with an Awful Representation of a Burning Mountain.

It should have been superfluous to add that such an extravaganza included "Original Music, Marches, Dances, Decorations, &c.&c."[36]

This was the last night of the season. The company opened in Charleston on January 22, 1794.

During this season, which opened on September 20 and closed on December 16, we have nine newspaper advertisements, announcing seventeen different plays (*Rosina* was repeated), of which thirteen were acted for the first time in Richmond: *A Day in Turkey, The Death of Captain Cook, The Flitch of Bacon, The Haunted Tower, High Life below Stairs, The Jealous Wife, Midas, The Orphan, The Quaker, The School for Wives, The True Born Irishman, The West Indian, The Young Quaker.* We record the American premiere of *The Young Quaker* and the only American performance of *A Day in Turkey.* Compared with previous seasons, this one seems slight. Newspaper records are not preserved. Explanation of the extraordinary number of American premieres in the previous season is that the Sully family had just arrived from England. Richmond had first look at the Sully repertoire.

Toward the end of this season Co-manager Bignall became the subject of a detailed and extended piece of criticism, the longest and most important we have had. Titled "Hold the Mirror Up to Nature," it is addressed to Augustine Davis, editor of the *Virginia Gazette, and General Advertiser,* in which it appeared under date of December 14, 1793:

As in all civilized and wise governments, the stage has been constantly nourished and protected, so will it ever be found the best school of morality and virtue, that human wisdom can constitute, whilst it is wisely conducted and confined by proper regulations and restrictions. The mind of man is not capable of receiving an entertainment at once so delightful and rational as the striking representation of a well written play will afford him. —A good moral Comedy abounding with characters drawn from nature, delineated in chaste language with lively wit and just satire, where the actors neither out-step the modesty of nature, nor come tardy off in representing her affords the most delicious treat that art and ingenuity can offer to the human mind. Our native tongue has produced innumerable excellent plays, both in Tragedy and Comedy, from which abundant stock an infinite variety of entertainment for the public, may be readily brought forward. Human nature requires and demands as much variety to gratify the mind, as an epicurean expects and devours to satiate his intolerable longing for high flavoured dishes, and choice viands; it therefore becomes the business of a manager to vary his entertainments so, that the public desire be not palled by too frequent repetitions of the same thing. In performing this task, he must perpetually be attentive to his avocation, or the finest wit and aided by the soundest judgment will fail to procure him success. He should not only perfectly understand every minutiae behind the scenes; but himself should be a good actor, that from his own feelings, he may better judge of others acting. He should be perfectly well stored with all dramatic authors, and have judgment to determine on their various merits; and above all things his studies should make him fully acquainted with the habits, the temper and manners of those whom his exhibitions are intended to please. These requisites are so essentially necessary in every manager of a public Theatre, that without them he cannot, with the best company, continue to be long successful let his auditory at first be ever so play-mad. Without variety to whet the appetite, this mania will presently cloy and cure itself.

Where dramatic exhibitions are offered to the public, the magistracy there residing can authorize, restrain or encourage the performances; it is therefore highly incumbent on every manager to select such pieces for public representation that at once will divert the mind and charm the auditory insensibly, as it were, into the practice of morality and virtue. As the stage was, or ought to have been, instituted for these purposes, whenever it deviates from them, the magistrate will severely reprehend the manager in the first instance, and should he prove incorrigible, will wholly suppress his performances: For the peoples morals are not to be corrupted to fill the purse of any individual or set of men. By holding up the mirror shew vice and folly their native ugliness and deformity, and virtue her beauteous and lovely features. By seeing the fictitious distresses of others, pourtrayed in strong colours, our minds are softened, humanized and prepared to alleviate the real misfortunes of our fellow-creatures. For ends like these theatric representations should be encouraged, because, in spite of our own coarse and obstinate natures, they force us into acts of kindness and brotherly love—they show us the loveliness of virtue and morality—and they lead us into the practice of humanity and charity to all men—thus becoming able assistants to the pulpit.

I have been led into the foregoing observations by the conduct of Mr. Bignall, as manager of and actor on our Richmond Theatre: As much knowledge, good sense, and sound judgment is so absolutely necessary to execute the office of manager with propriety, I will say nothing more on that subject to Mr. Bignall. But it being in the power of any man possessed of the following qualities to make a decent stage performer, I beg leave to recite them and then to offer a few observations on Mr. Bignall's playing. To become a decent player on such a Theatre as ours it only requires a tolerable good person, voice and ear, a small share of ability and a little common sense. If to these requisites be added a modest confidence in the knowledge that you possess them—they are enough to make a middling good player. In the first place a decent person gracefully managed, is as essential to a stage player, as a friendly letter of recommendation is to a man in a strange foreign country. Each introduces the individual to the party they wish to see and their own conduct must do the rest. A clear voice modulated by a good ear will enable you to speak well in public; and possessing ability enough to understand your author's meaning, common sense will assist you to deliver it properly, whilst a modest conviction that you possess these requisites will enable you to display them to advantage, without recurring to the hard necessity of foisting into the text words that dont belong to it. Last night and Wednesday evening, you astonished me, Mr. Bignall, more than ever I was amazed by an actor on the stage. Either my ears deceived me exceedingly, in almost to every sentence you added an oath, or something like it. I hope I was mistaken; but if not, I entreat you, both as a man and an actor, to break the practice of such an horrid custom. You cannot think, I am sure you cannot, Mr. Bignall, suppose that the inhabitants of Richmond, delight in blasphemy. If you have acquired a habit of using a word which sounds so much like swearing that those who hear, suppose you actually utter an oath, set about breaking yourself of it directly, or you may come before an audience, less inclined to favour you than that of Richmond. Before I finish, allow me to advise you not to be too solicitous for applause: By asking for it *on* the stage, you defeat your own purpose. A contorted countenance, and distorted body may draw a plaudit from the ignorant vulgar; but men of sense will shake their heads. Imitate nature in every thing you act, speak what your author has written and no more, then you will succeed here and shall be assured to receive the plaudits of your friend.

Thespis

Here is illustrated the typical eighteenth-century justification of the theatre as rational entertainment, conducive to moral conduct through adducing examples of both virtue and folly for the edification of the audience. "Thespis," whoever he was, stands closer to the Age of Reason, which lay behind him, than to the Romantic Revolution, which was incipient at the time. He writes more like Dr. Johnson than Coleridge; and he probably represents accurately the attitudes of the Richmond audience for which he speaks.

So large and strong a company as this one must have played a brilliant season. We can establish opening and closing dates; we know there was a season of about three months. In three months (March, April, May) in Charleston between these two Richmond seasons the company played thirty-six evenings. It should be reasonable to assume about thirty performances in Richmond during this present season.

Lest we lament the sparseness of these records, let us reconsider the barren years that lie behind and cast an apprehensive glance ahead.

The plays. *The School for Wives, or the Faithful Irishman* (September 20, 1793), a comedy by Hugh Kelly, was brought out at Drury Lane on December 11, 1773. It was acted in both New York and Philadelphia in 1788. This is the only record of its performance in Richmond.

The Young Quaker (October 24, 1793), a comedy in five acts by John O'Keeffe, was brought out at the Haymarket on July 26, 1783. It was acted in Charleston on February 10, New York, May 12, and Philadelphia, September 26, 1794. Apparently this Richmond performance was its American premiere. *The Flitch of Bacon*, a farce by Henry Bate, was brought out at the Haymarket on August 17, 1778. It was acted in New York on October 30, 1781, Philadelphia, February 3, 1787, and Charleston, April 19, 1793.

The Haunted Tower (November 7, 1793), a comic opera by James Cobb with music by Stephen Storace, was brought out at

Drury Lane on November 24, 1789. It was acted in Charleston on April 24, 1793, Philadelphia, December 2, 1794, and New York, January 9, 1795.

The West Indian (November 11, 1793), a comedy by Richard Cumberland, was first presented at Drury Lane on January 19, 1771. It was acted in Philadelphia in 1772, and in New York in 1773. There are records of several later performances in Richmond. *Midas*, a burletta by Kane O'Hara, was first produced in Dublin in 1762. It was played at Covent Garden in 1764, in Philadelphia in 1769, in New York in 1773. It was paired with *The West Indian* in Charleston on April 25, 1774.

A Day in Turkey (November 29, 1793), a comic opera by Hannah Cowley, had its premiere at Covent Garden on December 3, 1791. I have found no record of its performance in any other American theatre. *The Quaker, or, May Day Dower*, a comic opera with words and music by Charles Dibdin, was first acted at Drury Lane on October 7, 1777. It was acted in Charleston on February 14, 1793, Philadelphia, October 6, 1794, and New York, December 23, 1794.

The True Born Irishman, or the Irish Fine Lady (December 6, 1793), a farce by Charles Macklin, had been brought out at the Crow Street Theatre, Dublin, on May 14, 1762. It was acted in New York in 1787, in Philadelphia in 1788, and in Charleston in 1794. This is the only record of its performance in Richmond.

The Orphan (December 13, 1793), a tragedy by Thomas Otway, was first acted at Dorset Gardens in 1680. It was mentioned in Charleston on January 24, 1734/35, in what Willis calls "the earliest theatrical notice of Carolina." It was acted in New York on March 27, 1750, and in Philadelphia on January 9, 1770. *High Life below Stairs*, a farce in two acts by James Townley, was first acted at Drury Lane on October 31, 1759, when it was attributed to Garrick. It was acted in Philadelphia on January 26, 1767, New York, February 8, 1768, and Charleston, December 22, 1773.

The Death of Captain Cook (also called *Captain Cook*) (December 16, 1793), a "Historical Pantomime," was presented in the John Street Theatre, New York, on May 31, 1793. It was, I suspect, brought from there to Richmond by one of the new actors recruited by West and Bignall for this season. I have been unable to identify the author or to establish publication. I suspect that, like many pantomimes, it was worked up by the company, probably from contemporary news accounts. Cook had been murdered in 1779. Willis does not record its production in Charleston, but it was given in Philadelphia in 1796. *The Jealous Wife*, a comedy by George Colman, the elder, was brought out at Drury Lane in 1761. It was acted in Charleston in 1764, Philadelphia in 1767, and New York in 1769. There are records of several later performances in Richmond.

The players. Names in advertised casts indicate that the company had been considerably enlarged. It had apprently lost Mrs. Sully, Mrs. Davids, Andrews, and Courtenay. It had added Mr. and Mrs. Edgar, Mr. and Mrs. Marriott, Mr. and Mrs. Kedey, Mr. and Mrs. Murray, Mr. and Mrs. Henderson, Mrs. Gray, Chambers, Clifford, and Greenwood. Mrs. Chambers of this season was Miss Sully (Charlotte) of the previous season (They were married in Charleston on May 30, 1793.) Chambers's forte was musical comedy. He had played at the Haymarket before coming to America. In all, there were eighteen men, the two Sully boys (Chester and Thomas), and eleven women, plus Miss Sully (Elizabeth) and little Julia Sully, who appeared in *The Death of Captain Cook*. Hallam was still in the company, playing regularly through the season. Considerable strength had been added, but the loss of Mrs. Sully must have been felt. Lawrence Sully appeared once.

Mr. and Mrs. Marriott "from the Theatre Royal Edinburgh" appeared in Philadelphia with the Hallam and Henry Company on September 20, 1794. From Philadelphia they went on to New York, where they appeared with the Hallam and Hodgkinson Company in December 1794. Odell says that Marriott was supposed to fill Henry's shoes, but the shoes were too big for him. He played Pierre in *Venice Preserved* on December 18 but was a failure in the role. Mrs. Marriott played Arabella in *Such Things Are* on December 20, and also failed.

Mrs. Gray had played in New York with the Hallam and Henry Company in 1791-92. Chambers played Belville in *Rosina* in Philadelphia on October 24, 1792. Kedey was in Philadelphia on March 13, 1792, when he played Romeo and appeared also as Compton in the afterpiece, *The Agreeable Surprise*. Pollock thinks that he made his Philadelphia debut as Zanga in *The Revenge* on

February 25, 1792. Both Mr. and Mrs. Kedey played in Philadelphia in what Seilhamer called the "K" Company.

Names of three male Bignalls appear in the casts: Mr. Bignall, whose name was John, was the co-manager; there were two more, identified as "I." and "J.," who were, I think, brother Isaac and son John, Jr. The most important actor was co-manager Bignall, who played both leading and supporting roles throughout the season.

Hiatus

1794

We have no record of a theatrical season in 1794. Toward the end of 1793 Rosainville, "Master Fire Worker," advertised an exhibition of "Fire Works" at the "New-Theatre near the Capitol, on Friday evening the 29th instant (November)." He gave a list of eleven spectacles to be presented, plus a grand finale.[37] I assume that this "New-Theatre near the Capitol" was the one recently built by Curtis for £140, not the one in which West and Bignall were playing.

Again on December 6 Rosainville advertised his fireworks. He announced a special exhibition in honor of Washington's birthday on February 11, and "his Theatre being too small to exhibit largely, he will open a subscription to perform publicly."[38] Subscriptions were taken "at the Eagle Tavern." Another advertisement on January 3, 1794, in the *Virginia Gazette & Richmond Chronicle* announced that subscriptions for the Washington's birthday exhibition were to be not less than six shillings and that the fireworks would show the "Surrender of Cornwallis at Little York, a descriptive View of the French Fleet," and other patriotic scenes.

Throughout 1794 there were scattered notices of entertainment. On May 22 Ricketts announced the erection of "a Commodius Circus" on the green opposite Hyland's Tavern. Opening night was Saturday, May 25, with equestrian performances to commence at 5:30 P.M., "Adm. Box 6 shillings, Pitt 4 shillings 6 pence."[39] Ricketts had performed equestrian feats in the Charleston Circus in February.

On June 13, 1794, was advertised the "Last Night But One" of the circus. Ricketts performed equestrian prodigies, and "Master Ricketts [rode] on his head in full speed on one horse." There was also "the Taylor riding to Brentford, or Johnny Gilpins Journey on a Road Horse."[40] From Richmond, Ricketts went on to Philadelphia where he established an amphitheatre.

Odell calls Ricketts "incomparably the greatest circusman of his time; the finest rider New York had seen. He came originally from London and reached New York by way of Philadelphia, where he had already established a circus."[41] Pollock tells of his career in Philadelphia, and Willis in Charleston. When Ricketts opened his "New Circus" in New York on March 16, 1797, Mr. and Mrs. Chambers (the former Charlotte Sully) and "Miss Sully, a pupil of Chambers," made their first appearance in New York. Sully, Sr., and Master Sully played as clown and acrobat at Ricketts's Circus in New York in September 1795. They appeared frequently with Ricketts in Philadelphia.

The Mrs. Decker who advertised "a Concert of Vocal & Instrumental Music at the Eagle Tavern on Tuesday July 1" was probably the same Mrs. Decker who had appeared with the West and Bignall Company. There was a ball after the concert. Tickets at four and sixpence were on sale at the Eagle Tavern and of Mrs. Decker on Shockoe Hill.

The following notice, appearing on August 28, 1794, attests, I trust, financial difficulty for Mr. Ball rather than for the Richmond theatre: "To be Sold, Two Negro Shoemakers, who are good workmen, and of an unexceptionable character.—also—A Subscription Share in the Playhouse. For terms apply to Henry Ball."[42] I scarcely know what it attests for the two shoemakers. It ran again on October 2 and 6, indicating, I infer, a slow market for shoemakers and playhouse shares.

On November 21, 1794, the *Virginia Gazette & Richmond Chronicle* carried a whole column advertisement of Signor Falconi, who exhibited "Philosophical Experiments," including "an Indian figure with bow and arrow who shoots." There was also magic, a hornpipe, and a scene of a "Storm at Sea & Ship in Distress." This was in "the Theatre," Curtis's theatre, I assume, not West and Bignall's.

Signor Falconi had been in New York on June 26, 1787, when he exhibited "Natural Philosophical Experiments," including "a

Sympathetic Wind-Mill" and other marvels. On July 2 he displayed "a Head of solid Gold, of the size of a Walnut, shut up Hermetically, in a Chrystal Vessel, and which will answer by Signs, every Question." Again on July 9 he made a "Sallad" grow two inches in five minutes while holding it in his hand, and on July 21 he exhibited a "Magic Swan."[43] Richmonders, I assume, gaped at these wonders as did New Yorkers.

In April 1807 Le Sieur Falconi was in New Orleans exhibiting "physical and mathematical recreations, a galvanic machine and hydraulic experiments." Roger McCutcheon wrote of the presentation: "Perhaps finding the scientific appeal of his performances not entirely suited to the disposition of the New Orleans public, he announced the addition of a quick-change dancer, a young girl, 'who, while she is dancing, will change her costume so promptly that the audience will be unable to perceive it. She will appear as a luminous body surrounded by shadows of great natural grandeur for three or four minutes.' "[44] New York and Richmond theatregoers apparently had been satisfied to get their science without sex. Alas!

Also in Curtis's theatre, I assume, was a grand exhibition on Tuesday, December 16, of "Fire Works by Rosainville," who took half a column to elaborate details of the spectacle. He assured the public that there was no danger, as he was accustomed to performing fireworks in theatres, "in Petersburg at Armistead's Tavern; at Norfolk in the Old Theatre, the 11th of February."[45] Does this mean that Rosainville's subscription project for Washington's birthday in Richmond on February 11 failed to come off?

On such a note we come to the middle of the decade. The most brilliant season was in 1792; there was another of perhaps comparable excellence in 1793, but records are lacking. The last year was a thin one with no record of legitimate theatre. The next season of theatrical significance opened on October 12, 1795.

CHAPTER III

1795–1799

ELEVENTH SEASON

West and Bignall Company

October 1795–January 1796

Chronicle.   The West and Bignall Company closed their season in Charleston on May 7, 1795. After playing a summer season in Norfolk, the company, with several changes, returned to Richmond, probably in September, for they were performing in October. The first record of performance appeared in the *Richmond and Manchester Advertiser* of October 10, which announced for Monday, October 12, the "Comic opera (never performed here)" of *Cymon and Sylvia; or the Enchantress* by "Mr. Garrick." Afterpiece was the "French Dancing Ballet, *The Bird Catcher; or, The Lasses Frolic.*" Casts were given:

Cymon and Sylvia

Merlin	Mr. Marriott
Linco (the Merry Shepherd)	Mr. West
Justice Dorus	Mr. Nelson
Damon	Mr. Bignall
Strephon	Mr. Jones
Dorilas	Mr. Munto
Paelemon	Mr. Grey
Cymon	Mr. J. West
Sylvia	Mrs. J. West
Urganda	Mrs. Decker
Dorcas	Mrs. Grey
First Shepherdess	Miss West
Second Shepherdess	Mrs. Kenna
Fatima	Mrs. West

The Bird Catcher

The Bird Catcher	Mr. Placide
Colin	Mr. Latte
Hunters	Messrs. Jones, Bignall, Grey, &c.
Rosetta	Mrs. Placide

Although not announced as such, this may have been the opening night of the season. According to the advertisement,

Nelson "from the Theatre New York" made his first Richmond appearance as Justice Dorus in *Cymon and Sylvia*; J. West made his first appearance as Cymon; and Mrs. Placide played Rosetta in *The Bird Catcher*, "being her first appearance in Virginia." It may also have been the first appearance of Placide, who played the bird catcher. Entertainment between pieces consisted of "Dancing on the Tight Rope by the celebrated Mons. Placide from Paris, who will dance a Hornpipe, and play on the violin in many different attitudes on the Rope." There was also a song, "The Plowman or Lucky Escapes," by Nelson. The evening concluded with "the minuet de la cour, and the Gavotte by Mons. and Madame Placide."

Next record of performance appeared on Thursday, October 15: "This date a tragedy not performed here these four years *Venice Preserved; or, A Plot Discovered*." Afterpiece was a "New Ballet Pantomime Comic (never performed here) composed by Mr. Francisquy, *The Two Hunters and the Milk Maid, or, The Death of the Bear*." Casts were given:

Venice Preserved

Jaffier	Mr. Edgar
Renault	Mr. West
Priuli	Mr. Nelson
Bedamer	Mr. J. West
Duke of Venice	Mr. Bignall
Captain of the Guard	Mr. Munto
Spinosa	Mr. Jones
Elliot	Mr. Gray
Theodore	Mr. Latte
Piere	Mr. Marriott
Belvidera	Mrs. West

The Two Hunters and the Milk Maid

Guillot	Mr. Francisquy
Colas	Mr. Dubois
An Attorney	Mr. Val
Perrette (the Milk maid)	Mrs. Val[1]

Two first appearances were announced: Edgar as Jaffier in *Venice Preserved* and Francisquy "from the Opera House Paris" as Guillot in *The Two Hunters*. Edgar's appearance is of particular interest. He had been manager of his own company in Charleston and had vehemently denied a rumor that he would join the West and Bignall Company:

Theatre, Church Street, November 28th, 1794.
    Mr. Edgar the new manager of this theatre complains of a maliciously circulated report that he had solicited a return to Mr. West's Company. He publicly declares, to the disgrace of the author of this report, that he had never dreamed of such return although having in his possession a letter soliciting it.[2]

What negotiations went on between West and Edgar, we shall never know; perhaps West did attempt to combine Edgar's company with his after Bignall's death. Edgar had signed up the Sully family, who had been with West and Bignall in Richmond in 1792. At any rate, here is Edgar, less than a year after he had all but challenged to a duel the author of such vile rumor, playing with the West and Bignall Company. Or was it now the "West and Edgar" Company? Mrs. West played opposite Edgar as Belvidera. Edgar continued to play leading roles during this season.

    On Saturday, October 24, was advertised for "This Date the Comic opera (for the first time here) *The Children in the Wood*; as lately performed at London, Dublin, &c." Afterpiece was "a Burlesque Comic Pantomime (never performed here) *Harlequin Doctor; or The Power of Magic.*" Casts were given:

The Children in the Wood

Sir Rowland	Mr. Marriot
Lord Alford	Mr. Bignall
Apathy	Mr. Nelson
Gabriel	Mr. T. West
Oliver	Mr. Munto
1st Ruffian	Mr. Jones
2nd Ruffian	Mr. Latte
Servant	Mr. Gray
Walter	Mr. J. West
Helen	Mrs. Decker
Winifred	Mrs. Gray
Josephine	Mrs. J. West
Boy { Children in	Master West
Girl { the Wood	Master Gray

Harlequin Doctor

Harlequin	Mr. Francisquy
Old Man	Mr. Latte

Majician	Mr. Nelson
Miller	Mr. Bignall
Waiter	Mr. Jones
Pierot (the clown)	Mr. Placide
Columbine	Mrs. Placide
Lads and Lasses	Messrs. Bignall, Gray,
	T. West, Duport,
	Mrs. Decker, Mrs.
	Gray, Mrs. Kenna,
	and Miss West.

The Children in the Wood included four Wests. *Harlequin Doctor* featured Francisquy as Harlequin, with Mr. and Mrs. Placide as Pierot and Columbine. Between pieces there was "a Song" by J. West, and "a Hornpipe" by Master Duport. The evening concluded with a "new country Dance." Doors opened at six, with curtain at seven. Tickets were to be had "at the post-office, Eagle Tavern, & Office of the Theatre." Prices were: "Box 6 Shillings, Pit and Upper Boxes 4 Shillings and Sixpence." The advertisement concluded: "N.B. No Person can be admitted behind the Scenes."[3]

On Tuesday, October 27, the *Richmond Chronicle* announced for "This date a Piece in two acts, *All The World's a Stage, or The Butler in Buskins.*" It was followed by "a New Pantomime, intermix't with Dances, *The Old Soldier; and The Two Thieves.*" The evening concluded with a third piece, "the Comic opera *No Song, No Supper; or The Lawyer in a Sack.*" Casts were given:

All the World's a Stage

Sir Gilbert Pumpkin	Mr. Nelson
Harry Stukeley	Mr. Edgar
Charles Stanley	Mr. Bignall
Cymon	Mr. J. West
Wat	Mr. Jones
John	Mr. Latte
William	Master West
Hostler	Mr. Gray
Diggory Duckling	Mr. T. West
Miss Bridget Pumpkin	Mrs. Gray
Miss Kitty Sprightly	Mrs. J. West

The Old Soldier

The Old Soldier	Mr. Placide
Lord of the Manor	Mr. Val

A Clown	Mr. Bignall
The Two Thieves	Messrs. Latte & T. West
And Lucas	Mr. Francisquy
The Milk Maid	Mrs. J. West
Margot (Mother of Colette)	Mrs. Gray
And Colette	Mrs. Placide

No Song, No Supper

Crop	Mr. Nelson
Frederic	Mr. Munto
Lawyer Endless	Mr. Edgar
William	Mr. Bignall
Thomas	Mr. Jones
And Robin	Mr. J. West
Dorothy Crop	Mrs. Gray
Louisa	Miss West
Nelly	Mrs. Decker
Margaretta	Mrs. J. West

All the World's a Stage included four Wests: Master West, T. West, Mr. and Mrs. J. West. Placide played the title role in *The Old Soldier*, with Mrs. Placide as Colette, and Bignall as clown. In *No Song, No Supper* there were three Wests: Mr. and Mrs. J. West and Miss West.

The Richmond performance of *The Old Soldier* included "Un Pas de Deux by Mons. Francisquy and Madame Placide—Un Pas Seul by Master Duport, and a fight with Pistols and Broad Swords, by the Old Soldier and The Two Thieves." We are also told that "this Pantomime is taken from a true History which happened within ten years, in a Forest four leagues from Paris. An old Veteran who is dismissed from his Regiment, on his way to Paris, delivers a young Girl from the hands of Two Thieves, and kills them."

The next record of performance appeared on October 29. It was headed "By authority" and announced for "Thursday evening October 29, 1795, a Comedy (never performed here) *The Jew, or, Benevolent Hebrew* written by Richard Cumberland Esqe. Author of the *School for Scandal, Fashionable Lovers, Natural Son, Brothers, West-Indian* &c." Afterpiece was "a Ballet Pantomime, Composed by Mr. Francisquy, *Three Quakers, or The Dutch Coffee House*." Casts were given:

The Jew

Sir Stephen Bertram	Mr. Munto
Frederick (his son)	Mr. J. West
Charles Ratcliff	Mr. Marriott
Jaba (the Jew's man)	Mr. T. West
Saunders	Mr. Bignall
Waiters	Messrs. Jones, Latte, & Gray
And Sheva (the Jew)	Mr. Edgar
Mrs. Ratcliff	Mrs. Decker
Mrs. Goodison	Mrs. Kenna
Dorcas (the Jew's servant)	Mrs. Gray
And Elizabeth Ratcliff	Mrs. J. West

Three Quakers

Mr. Vanderweek	Mr. Placide
Lover	Mr. Francisquy
The Three Quakers	Messrs. Val, Francisquy, Placide
And Mrs. Vanderweek	Mrs. Placide

Richard Sheridan, who had caricatured Richard Cumberland as Sir Fretful Plagiary in *The Critic* in 1779, would have been interested to read that Cumberland was the author of *The School for Scandal.* Cumberland's Jew was played by Edgar, with T. West as Jaba "(the Jew's man)." Mr. and Mrs. Placide played Mr. and Mrs. Vanderweek in *The Three Quakers*, with Francisquy as the Lover; both Placide and Francisquy doubled as Quakers. Between pieces there was "a Song" by J. West and "a Hornpipe (in wooden shoes)" by Master Duport. *The Three Quakers* included "un pas seul" by Placide, and concluded with "a Double Comic Allemande" by Val, Francisquy, Placide, and Mrs. Placide.[4]

The *Richmond and Manchester Advertiser* for Saturday, October 31, contained no notice of a theatrical performance, but later critical and controversial articles establish the performance on this date of *The Farm House* with Edgar as Modely and Mrs. West as Aura. Neither Edgar, who acted in it, nor "Thespis," who criticized Edgar's performance, thought much of it. More of this later.

The one extant copy of the *Richmond Chronicle* for Tuesday, November 3, 1795, is mutilated; only the bottom part of the theatre advertisement remains. It begins: "To which will be added, an entire new Pantomime (never performed here) called *Harlequin Baloniste; or Pierot in the Clouds.*" We do not know what *Harlequin Baloniste* was added to, but there is much about the pantomime, including quite a large cast:

Harlequin	Mr. Francisquy
Lover	Mr. J. West
Old Man	Mr. Nelson
Peasant	Mr. Val
Hair Dresser	Mr. Latte
Reapers	Messrs. Marriot, Bignall, T. West, Jones, Gray, &c.
And Pierot (the Clown)	Mr. Placide
Enchantress	Mrs. Gray
Millener	Mrs. J. West
Gleaners	Mrs. Decker, Mrs. Kenna Miss West, &c.
And Columbine	Mrs. Placide

The piece was advertised with "New Scenery, Machinery decorations &c," and included "the Laughable Scene of the Bear, The Magic Chamber, The Surprising Candlesticks, and a Superb View of the Palace of Cupid."

On Saturday, November 7, was advertised for "This date a Tragedy (never performed here) *The Earl of Warwick; or Margaret of Anjou* written by the celebrated Dr. Benjamin Franklin." It was followed by "the grand Serious Pantomime of *The Death of Captain Cook in the Island of O-Why-Hee, in the Pacific Ocean.*" Both casts were given:

The Earl of Warwick

Edward	Mr. J. West
Earl of Suffolk	Mr. Marriott
Earl of Pembroke	Mr. Bignall
Lord Hastings	Mr. Jones
Duke of Buckingham	Mr. Nelson
Duke of Clarence	Mr. Munto
Lord of the Council	Mr. Latte
And Earl of Warwick	Mr. Edgar
Lady Eliza Gray	Mrs. J. West
Lady Clifford	Mrs. Gray
And Margaret of Anjou	Mrs. West

Captain Cook

Capt. Cook (of the Resolution)	Mr. Edgar
His Lieutenant	Mr. Marriot
His Midshipman	Master West
His Sailors and Mariners	By Supernumeraries
Terroboo (King of O-Why-Hee)	Mr. Val
Peerea (the favorite Lover of Emai)	Mr. Francisquy
Priest	Mr. Munto
Warriors	Messrs. J. West, T. West, Bignall, Nelson, Jones, Gray, Latte, Duport, &c.
And Koah (the Revengeful Lover of Emai)	Mr. Placide
Emai	Mrs. Placide
Female Islanders	Mrs. West, Mrs. J. West, Mrs. Gray, Mrs. Decker, Mrs. Kenna, &c.

Edgar played the title role in *The Earl of Warwick*, with Mrs. West as Margaret of Anjou. He also played the title role in *Captain Cook*, in which Mrs. Placide played the romantic lead of Emai "(the King's Daughter)" opposite Placide as Koah "(the Revengeful Lover of Emai)."[5]

The advertisement included a summary of the action similar to that given for the previous performance in Richmond on December 16, 1793, but specifying that the "Grand War Dance By the Natives" was danced by Messrs. Placide, T. West, Francisquy, Bignall and Latte; and that the "single combat with Battle axes" was between Peerea (Francisquy) and Koah (Placide). This summary concluded with the burial of Captain Cook "with Military Honors," omitting the "awful Representation of a Burning Mountain" which concluded the presentation in 1793. I perceive a concession to the difficulty, or perhaps expense, of spectacular stage effects.

The *Richmond and Manchester Advertiser* of November 7 contained no notice of a performance in the theatre on that date, but there was a long letter addressed to "Mr. Pleasants" (Samuel Pleasants, editor), the most revealing piece of theatrical criticism to be located thus far:

The Theatre when judiciously managed, may be regarded as a school of moral instruction and of rational amusement.—Good taste in selecting, and skill in performing the different pieces, are however, indispensibly necessary to the attainment of these desired ends. Being myself an admirer of the exhibitions on the stage, I have generally attended the representations in this city, since the present season commenced. It is with regret that I feel myself in some measure under the necessity of remarking, that the managers of the Richmond Theatre, have displayed but little judgment in selecting, and have paid still less attention to the performance of those pieces which have been presented to the public. Neither amusement or instruction are the consequences of visiting this Theatre. The pieces selected for representation have been generally destitute of humour or of moral sentiment, and are merely calculated to seduce the public mind by the fascinating charms of theatrical entertainments. It would, however, be the source of some satisfaction to the audience if the different actors, were strenuous in their exertions to please. But their neglect on this score, has risen to an intolerable height. In several instances an actor has made his appearance with a book in his hand, and some of the performers have even ventured on the stage when in a state of perfect intoxication. Nothing but the extreme liberality of the audience, would tolerate such abuses of public favor. But the more unpardonable breach of duty consists in their inattention to qualify themselves even to repeat their different parts.

The prompter may be heard in every part of the house, and the indulgence of the audience frequently rewards the player with a plaudit instead of an hiss for this neglect. It will be unnecessary to particularize the instances in which these breaches of duty have happened, they are numerous and frequent. But I cannot conclude without making some remarks on the performance of Saturday evening. The play itself [wants] interest and the conduct of the principal actor, seemed but to increase the general langor. Mrs. West in Aura, was alone worthy of approbation, but Mr. Edgar did injustice even to the character of Modely. Unable to repeat his part, he frequently supplied it with something low and fulsome, when he was at too great a distance from the prompter.

Conduct of this kind is reprehensible in any man who ventures to appear on the stage, but it becomes unpardonable when it is the result of inattention rather than of incapacity. The Actor alluded to possesses talents which would at least entitle him to comparative approbation, if they were properly exerted. But the public favor which has hitherto attended him, will be forfeited, without some vigorous exertions to re-establish his theatrical reputation, which is rapidly on the decline. These remarks are not of a selfish nature, they are facts of public notoriety, and the general voice of the city which is raised in support of them will entitle them to the considerations of the managers of the theatre.

Thespis

"Thespis" was a popular nom de plume for theatre critics. I have no idea who this "Thespis" was, but I suspect his criticism was warranted. That he hit his target is attested by Edgar's reply, which appeared on November 12:

To the Editor of the Richmond and Manchester Advertiser:
Sir,
As a public performer, anxious for the good opinion of the town, I cannot help taking some notice of the remarks made by Thespis, in your paper of Saturday last.
I am not about to deny one tittle of what he has said with respect to the demerits of the performance of the Farm House; it deserved, in my opinion, more censure, than the audience, or even Mr. Thespis has given it.
I could wish (if Thespis is not one of the Theatre) he would make some enquiry into the cause of those imperfections which have so frequently destroyed the effect of our performances. I think he would then be less severe on Some of us poor devils (called actors) and by accusing of those, really in fault, perhaps, reform the Theatre.
I hope I am not lessened (as Mr. Thespis asserts) in the opinion of the Town—for, since my first appearance in it (about two years ago) I have been in continual employment in my profession, and have paid every attention to the duties of it, and should suppose myself more capable of pleasing my auditors Now than at that period.
It must be known to Mr. Thespis, I have lately recovered from a very alarming illness—consequently cannot possess those requisites to please, were I in perfect health—and was, on the night I so unfortunately subjected myself to his malicious critique, obliged to appear without a rehearsal and violently indisposed: I have only to observe, if I fail in my endeavours to please, it is from a deficiency of talent, and not want of attention or cheerful disposition to conciliate the regard of a public, to whom I have been particularly obliged, and whose distinguished favors, I shall ever most gratefully remember.

H. Edgar

Despite Edgar's protestation of his "alarming illness," I suspect that his drunken appearance in a role for which he was admittedly unprepared may indicate some friction between Edgar as leading man and West as manager. They had been at swords' points in Charleston a year before.

Meanwhile, despite the controversy, the plays went on. The *Richmond Chronicle* of Tuesday, November 10, advertised for

"This evening *The Beaux Stratagem: or, The Humours of the Litchfield Landlord.*" Afterpiece was the "Burlesque Comic Pantomime *Harlequin Doctor; or Power of Magic.*" Casts were given:

The Beaux Stratagem

Archer	Mr. Edgar
Aimwell	Mr. J. West
Boniface	Mr. Marriott
Sir Charles Freeman	Mr. Bignall
Gibbet	Mr. T. West
Foiguard	Mr. Jones
Sullen	Mr. Munto
Hounslow	Mr. Nelson
Bagshot	Mr. Gray
And Scrub	Mr. West
Mrs. Sullen	Mrs. West
Dorinda	Mrs. Moore
Lady Bountiful	Mrs. Gray
Gipsey	Mrs. Decker
And Cherry	Mrs. J. West

Harlequin Doctor

Harlequin	Mr. Francisquy
Old Man	Mr. Latte
Majician	Mr. Nelson
Miller	Mr. Bignall
Waiter	Mr. Jones
Pierot (the clown)	Mr. Placide
Columbine	Mrs. Placide
Lads and Lasses	Messrs. Bignall, Gray, T. West, Duport, Mrs. Decker, Mrs. Gray, Mrs. Kenna, and Miss West

Mrs. Moore played Dorinda in *The Beaux Stratagem*, "being her first appearance on this stage." Edgar was sufficiently recovered (or sobered) to take the leading role of Archer, and apparently any ill feeling between him and Manager West was at least patched up, since five Wests appeared: Mr. West, Mrs. West, T. West, J. West, and Mrs. J. West. Miss West did not appear. In *Harlequin Doctor*, Francisquy and Mr. and Mrs. Placide played their usual roles of Harlequin, Pierrot, and Columbine. Entertainment between pieces consisted of "a Hornpipe" by Master Duport (the wooden shoes were not mentioned) and "a Favorite Song" by J. West. The evening concluded with a "New Country Dance."

The next record of performance was one week later, on Tuesday, November 17: "This date a Piece, *The Midnight Hour; or War of Wits*," with the following cast:

Marquis	Mr. J. West
Nicholas	Mr. T. West
Sebastian	Mr. Bignall
Mathias	Mr. Jones
Ambrose	Mr. Munto
And the General Don Guzman	Mr. Marriot
Julia	Mrs. Decker
Cicily	Mrs. Gray
And Flora	Mrs. J. West

Afterpiece was *Captain Cook*, with a few additions to the cast as advertised for November 7. Jones played the Captain's Midshipman; J. West, W. West, Bignall, Munto, Gray, Latte, and Duport appeared as warriors; and Mrs. Moore was added to the cast of "Female Islanders." The role of the priest was not included, nor was the description of spectacular stage effects. Edgar was sufficiently recovered to appear in the title role. J. West sang "a Song" between the pieces.[6]

On Saturday, November 21, was advertised for "This date a Ballet Pantomime *The Three Quakers*." It was followed by "the Musical Farce (not performed here these three years) *The Romp; or Love in a City*." Third piece of the program was the "Favorite Pantomime (never performed here) *La Belle Dorothee*."

The role of Landlady in *The Three Quakers* was played by Mrs. Val, "being her first appearance." The pantomime concluded with "a Double Comic Allemande by Mr. Val, Mr. Francisquy, Mrs. Placide, and Mrs. Val," the three Quakers, and the landlady. Mrs. J. West played Priscilla Tomboy in *The Romp*, with J. West as Watty Cockney, Munto as Captain Sightley, Jones as Cockney, and Nelson as Old Barnacle. Mrs. Decker played Penelope, and Mrs. Gray, Miss La Blond. *La Belle Dorothee* taxed the manpower of the company: twenty names were listed:

Latremouille (the French General and Husband to Dorothee)	Mr. Francisquy

Antoine (an Old Soldier in the service Latremouille)	Mr. Placide
The Archbishop of Milan (Uncle of Dorothee)	Mr. Val
An Officer (being received Knight)	Mr. Bignall
Page	Master West
Herald at Arms	Mr. Nelson
Knights	Messrs. J. West, T. West Marriott, Jones, Munto, Latte, &c.
A Serjeant (who executed the orders of the Archbishop)	Mr. T. West
Beno [*illegible*] (Son of Latremouille and Dorothee)	Master Gray
And Sacregorgon (Commander of the troops of the Archbishop)	Mr. Placide
Nurse	Mrs. Gray
Ladies of Orleans	Mrs. Decker, Mrs. Kenna, Mrs. Moore, Mrs. Val, and Miss West
And Dorothee	Mrs. Placide[7]

On Tuesday, November 24, the *Richmond Chronicle* advertised for "This date Shakespeare's comedy *As You Like It; or Love in a Forest.*" Afterpiece was the "Grand Serious Domestic Pantomime Tale *La Foret Noire, or Maternal Affection,*" which was presented "with New Scenery, Decorations &c." Complete casts were given for both plays:

As You Like It

Orlando	Mr. Edgar
Jaquis	Mr. Marriott
Adam	Mr. Nelson
Amiens (with Oliver, Songs)	Mr. J. West
Bannish'd Duke	Mr. Bignall
Duke Frederick	Mr. Munto
Le Beau William }	Mr. T. West
Corin	Mr. Jones
Foresters	Messrs. Gray, Latte, &c.
And Touchstone	Mr. West
Celia	Mrs. Moore
Phoeby	Mrs. Decker
Audry	Mrs. Gray
And Rosalind	Mrs. J. West

La Foret Noire

Geronte (Father of Lucille)	Mr. Val
Pince (a Finnical Abbe, & intended Husband of Lucille)	Mr. J. West
Adolphe (Child of Lanzedan & Lucille)	Master Gray
Frontin ⎰ Servants to ⎱	Mr. Latte
Pasquin ⎱ Geront ⎰	Mr. Munto
And Lanzedan (an Officer)	Mr. Francisquy
Marton	Mrs. Gray
And Lucille (Privately Married to Lanzedan)	Mrs. Placide

Banditti

Le Terreur (Captain of the Banditti)	Mr. Placide
San Quartier (Lieutenant)	Mr. Bignall
Robert	Mr. T. West
And Banditti	Messrs. West, Marriott, Nelson, W. West, Gray, Jones, Munto, Latte, &c.

On Friday, December 5, was advertised for "This date the comedy *A Wonder A Woman Keeps A Secret*," which was followed by the "Grand Pantomime Ballet, *The Maid's Revenge; or The Enraged Musician.*" The program concluded with *The Spoiled Child.* Casts were given for all three plays:

A Wonder a Woman Keeps a Secret

Don Felix	Mr. J. West
Colonel Briton	Mr. Edgar
Don Lophez	Mr. Jones
Frederic	Mr. T. West
Gibby	Mr. Marriott
Don Pedro	Mr. West
Alguzile	Mr. Munto
Vasquez	Master West
Servant	Mr. Gray
And Lissardo	Mr. Bignall
Donna Violante	Mrs. West
Donna Isabella	Mrs. Decker
Inis	Mrs. Moore
And Flora	Mrs. J. West

The Maid's Revenge

Wood Cutters	Messrs. Val & Duport
Lucas (the Musician)	Mr. Placide
Colas (a Shepherd)	Mr. Francisquy
A Country Innkeeper	Mr. Latte
Shepherds and Shepherdesses	Messrs. Bignall, Jones, Munto,
	T. West, Mrs. Kenna,
	Mrs. Gray, Mrs. Decker,
	&c.

The Spoiled Child

Little Pickle (the Spoil'd Child)	Mrs. J. West
Old Pickle	Mr. Jones
John	Mr. Bignall
Thomas	Mr. Gray
William	Mr. Latte
And Tag (an Author)	Mr. J. West
Miss Pickle	Mrs. Gray
Maria	Mrs. Kenna
Margery	Mrs. Decker
And Susan	Mrs. Moore[8]

On December 23 there was given for the benefit of Mr. and Mrs. Val the "Comic Opera *The Maid of the Mill*" and "a Grand Pantomime (never performed here) *American Independence, or The Fourth of July 1776*." No cast for either piece was given. The clue to the scattered newspaper advertisements is, however, here: "Particulars expressed in the bills of the day."[9]

On December 30 the *Richmond and Manchester Advertiser* announced for Thursday, December 31, "(for the first time these three years) Shakespeare's celebrated Tragedy, As altered by Garrick, of *Romeo & Juliet*." Afterpiece was "the Farce (never performed here) *A Trip to Scotland, or, The Road to Matrimony* in which will be described the very humorous scenes of *Gretna Green*." Between the tragedy and the farce there was "a Dramatic Piece in one act (first time) *All in Good Humour*."

This was evidently an elaborate program for New Year's Eve. *Romeo and Juliet* included "in Act First, A Grand Masquerade A la mode Paris, under the direction of Mons. Francisquy. In course of which the minuet Delacour, by Mons. Francisquy and Madame Placide. Un Pas Seul in Character of A Shepherd, by Master Duport. And the Masquerade will conclude with the favor-

ite Alemande by Mons. Francisquy, Madame Placide, and Madame
Val." Act four included "a Solemn Dirge and Funeral Procession
of Juliet to the Monument of the Capulets, to be conducted by
Mons. Placide."

There was also "in the Course of the evening, for the first time
here, A Tripple Hornpipe and Scotch Reel, by Madame Placide,
Mons. Francisquy, and Master Duport." Edgar contributed "a
Serio Comic dessertation on Taxation or the Minister in the Sudds,
as spoken by him on the Bath, Liverpool and London Theatres."
A Trip to Scotland concluded the evening with "the Favorite Gar-
land Dance by the Characters with the kind assistance of Mons.
Placide and Mons. Francisquy."

Casts were given for all three plays. Edgar played Romeo to
Mrs. J. West's Juliet, and Mrs. Edgar appeared as the Nurse, her
first recorded appearance of the season. In *A Trip to Scotland*,
Mrs. Placide played Cupid "(in Character and habit of a postilion)"
—a breeches part—and Mrs. J. West played her third female lead
of the evening as Miss Griskin:

Romeo and Juliet

Romeo	Mr. Edgar
Friar Lawrence	Mr. Nelson
Benvolio	Mr. Bignall
Capulet	Mr. Sully
Paris	Mr. T. West
Prince	Mr. Jones
Tybalt	Mr. Munto
Page	Master Gray
And Mecutio	Mr. J. West
The Parts of the Nurse and Peter by Mons. Placide and Mrs. Edgar	
Lady Capulet	Mrs. Gray
And Juliet	Mrs. J. West

All in Good Humour

Squire Hairbrain	Mr. J. West
Robin	Mr. T. West
Crop	Mr. Bignall
Bellamy	Mr. Munto
And Chagrin	Mr. Jones
Dorothy	Mrs. Edgar
Mrs. Chagrin	Mrs. Gray
And Sophia	Mrs. J. West

A Trip to Scotland

The Part of Cupid (in character and habit of a postilion)	Mrs. Placide
Jemmy Twinkle	Mr. J. West
Griskin	Mr. Jones
Sotherton	Mr. Bignall
Chamberlain	Mr. Munto
Mrs. Filligree	Mrs. Edgar
Miss Flack	Mrs. Gray
Landlady	Mrs. Moore
Betty	Mrs. Nelson
And Miss Griskin	Mrs. J. West

There is record of one more performance this season. On Wednesday, January 6, 1796, the *Virginia Gazette, and General Advertiser* announced for "This evening a Comic Opera (never performed here) *Lionel & Clarissa; or School for Fathers.*" There was also "a new Pantomime (never performed here) *The Wood Cutters; or Militia Man.*" The evening concluded with "a musical Farce (not performed here this season) *The Farmer; or The World's Ups and Downs.*" This was J. West's benefit. The brief advertisement included no details of casts or staging.

Assuming that the season opened on October 12, 1795, and closed on, or soon after, January 6, 1796, we have a three-month season, during which there should have been thirty-six performances (three per week for twelve weeks). We have record of sixteen. The largest number of any previous season is fourteen. Thirty-two different plays are recorded, twenty-two of which are not previously recorded in Richmond. There were no American premieres. The repertoire was heavy with pantomime, ballet, and operetta, although *Venice Preserved* and *Romeo and Juliet* add the weight of tragedy.

The company was a mixture of actors from the West and Bignall Company (the Virginia Company of 1792) and the company that Edgar had managed in Charleston during the winter of 1794-95. To these were added several talented musicians and dancers from "The French Theatre" of Charleston: Mr. and Mrs. Placide, Mr. and Mrs. Francisquy, Mr. and Mrs. Val. From advertised casts, I count a company of thirty-two performers, including eighteen men and ten women, plus four children. Throughout the season, male leads were played by Edgar, female leads by Mrs. J. West.

The company probably left Richmond soon after January 6; they opened in Charleston on February 15.

The plays.   *Cymon and Sylvia* (October 12, 1795) (called *Cymon* by Nicoll), a comic opera by David Garrick, was brought out at Drury Lane in 1767. It was acted in New York and Philadelphia in 1773, and in Charleston in 1774. The "Dancing Ballet" of *The Bird Catcher* was performed in New York and Philadelphia in 1792 and in Charleston on April 12, 1794, with Mrs. Placide as Rosetta.

The Two Hunters and the Milk Maid (October 15, 1795) was first acted at Charleston on July 12, 1794. It was acted in New York on March 3, 1796. Odell calls it a "grand Pantomime Dance in one act, composed by Mr. Francisquy."[10] I found no record of its performance elsewhere.

Harlequin Doctor (October 24, 1795), probably composed by Francisquy, had been performed in Charleston on April 29, 1794; it was performed in New York in 1804. *The Children in the Wood*, a comic opera by Thomas Morton, was brought out at the Haymarket in 1793. It was acted in New York and Philadelphia in 1794 and in Charleston in 1798. The advertisement includes this description of the piece:

The historical fact, on which the above beautiful Drama is founded, has for centuries past employed the pens of some of our most celebrated writers—tis here faithfully handed down with all of its original purity, nor has the modern writer robbed it of its native simplicity though in its theatrical dress the incidents and situation are rendered more animated and affecting.
The catastrophe is somewhat altered in order to give Innocence its triumphs and Villainy its punishment—thus Sentiment, morality and Comic Humour have their charms. The airs are happily selected and the musical composition perhaps unrivalled, etc.

All the World's a Stage (October 27, 1795), a two-act farce by Isaac Jackman, had its premiere at Drury Lane in 1777. It was acted in New York in 1782, Charleston in 1786, and Philadelphia in 1790. *The Old Soldier and the Two Thieves*, most probably another dance pantomime by Francisquy, had been performed in New York and Philadelphia in 1792 and Charleston in 1794.

The Jew (October 29, 1795), a comedy by Richard Cumberland, had its premiere at Drury Lane on May 8, 1794. It was acted in Philadelphia on February 11, New York February 25, and Charleston April 20, 1795. Francisquy's ballet pantomime *The Three Quakers* had been presented in Charleston on December 13, 1794. I have found no record of performance elsewhere.

The Farm House (October 31, 1795), a farce by J. P. Kemble, had its premiere at Drury Lane in 1789. Kemble's play was altered or adapted by Royall Tyler,[11] and it was probably Tyler's adaptation which was acted in Richmond, in Philadelphia on March 4, 1795, New York May 9, 1795, and Boston May 6, 1796.

Harlequin Baloniste (November 3, 1795) was probably another ballet pantomime by Francisquy, who took the leading role. It had been presented by the Placides (who played Pierrot and Columbine) in New York on May 3, 1792, and Philadelphia June 20, 1792.

The tragedy of *The Earl of Warwick* (November 7, 1795) was written, not by "the celebrated Dr. Benjamin Franklin," but by the less celebrated Dr. Thomas Francklin, and was first acted at Drury Lane in 1766. It was acted in Philadelphia in 1791 and New York in 1796.

George Farquhar's *The Beaux Stratagem* (November 10, 1795), one of the most popular eighteenth-century comedies, dates from 1707. First record of performance in America was at Williamsburg in 1736. It was acted in New York in 1739, Philadelphia 1769, and Charleston 1786.

La Belle Dorothee (November 21, 1795) was, I suspect, another pantomime, or ballet, by Francisquy, who took the leading role. It was presented in Charleston on May 27, 1794, and in Philadelphia on July 11, 1797.

La Foret Noire (November 24, 1795) was probably another ballet by Francisquy, who appeared in it. It was first presented in Philadelphia on April 26, 1794, then in New York on March 20, 1795, and Charleston on February 24, 1796. *As You Like It* was first recorded in New York on July 14, 1786, in Philadelphia on May 30, 1794, and in Charleston on February 1, 1797. The subtitle indicates that this was the adaptation by Charles Johnson.

The Maid's Revenge (December 5, 1795) was probably another ballet by Francisquy, who appeared in it. I have located no record of its performance elsewhere. *The Spoiled Child* was a farce in two acts, probably by Isaac Bickerstaffe. It had its premiere at Drury Lane in 1790 and was acted in New York, Philadelphia, and Charleston in 1794. *A Wonder a Woman Keeps a Secret* was first performed in Richmond under its proper title: *The Wonder: A Woman Keeps a Secret* on October 11, 1792.

American Independence (December 23, 1795), a pantomime in three acts, had been presented in Charleston on July 30, 1794, by Val. Willis attributes it to Placide, who probably appeared in this production. I suspect that Val, Francisquy, and Placide all contributed to and appeared in it.

All in Good Humour (December 31, 1795), a one-act farce by W. C. Oulton, had been brought out at the Haymarket on July 7, 1792. It was presented in Charleston on January 2, 1795, by Edgar. It reached New York in 1797 and Philadelphia in 1798.

Lionel and Clarissa (January 6, 1796), a comic opera by Isaac Bickerstaffe, with music by Charles Dibdin, had been brought out at Covent Garden in 1768. It was acted in Philadelphia in 1772, and in Charleston and New York in 1794. *The Wood Cutters* was probably the same pantomime presented in Charleston on May 15, 1794, and brought from there to Richmond by members of this company.

The players.   Nelson, "from the theatre New York," had played there with the Hallam and Hodgkinson Company in 1794-95. A critic writing in the *American Minerva* of January 3, 1795, said that he "is not brot forward as his merit as a singer and an actor deserves." Possibly this was because he "labours under every inconvenience that a violent rheumatism can inflict."[12] He was in Philadelphia from September to December 1794, evidently going from there to New York to join Hallam and Hodgkinson. He was not a featured performer in Richmond.

Munto was with Nelson in Philadelphia between September and December 1794; he evidently went with Nelson to New York to join the Hallam and Hodgkinson Company. Dunlap says that on December 15, 1794, at the John Street Theatre production of *Love in a Village* he was "brought forward in Eustace, but was merely tolerable."[13] This was most probably the role he played

Benjamin H. Latrobe's sketch of Richmond, 1796. (Courtesy Valentine Museum.) The theatre is on Shockoe Hill, to the right of the Capitol in this sketch.

in the Richmond production of *Love in a Village* on December 26. Throughout this season he appeared in supporting and minor parts.

Mr. and Mrs. Marriott were in Philadelphia during this same season of September–December 1794. They too apparently went from Philadelphia to New York to join Hallam and Hodgkinson. Marriott was presented in New York on December 18 as Pierre in *Venice Preserved* and apparently was not a success in so large a role. Odell says that he "was expected to take some of the roles vacated by John Henry, but Henry's shoes were large to fill." [14] Mrs. Marriott, who played with her husband in New York, was not with him in Richmond.

Jones was in Philadelphia between October 1796 and February 1797. He was in New York with the Sollee Company, appearing as Lissardo in *The Wonder* on August 18, 1797, when he was presented as "Mr. Jones, from the theatres royal Weymouth, Exeter, Cheltenham, Salisbury &c. likewise from the city theatre Charleston, South Carolina, and last from Boston, being his first appearance on this stage." [15] He too played minor roles in Richmond.

Latte was one of the members of the French Company in Charleston who joined West and Edgar; in Charleston he was Latté. Although they are not mentioned by Willis, I assume that Dubois and Duport were with the same company in Charleston and that Duport was the father of the little dancer.

Co-manager John Bignall had died in Charleston on August 11, 1794. The "Bignall" who played this season was the J. Bignall of the previous season; evidently he dropped the initial after his father's death. After her husband's death, Mrs. Bignall, daughter of Manager West, assumed managerial responsibilities, and the company continued as the West and Bignall Company. Some time before the opening of this season she became Mrs. J. West, under which name she continued to play leading roles. Eight Wests are named in bills of this season: "West" was Manager Thomas Wade West; "Mrs. West" was his wife, the former Margaret Sully; "Mrs. J. West" was their daughter Ann, the former Mrs. John Bignall; "J. West," her husband, was, I think, the James West who had played in New York in 1793; one other was probably the "West, jun." who had played with him there, whether "T.," "W.," or "Master" I do not know. I am confident, however, that neither

"T." nor "W." of the Richmond bills identified Manager T. W. West; I suspect that "T." (sometimes "Tom") was his son, perhaps Thomas Wade West, Jr.; I identify "Miss West" as Harriet West, who married Isaac Bignall. The Sullys, the Wests, and the Bignalls were prolific; there was frequent intermarriage; records are incomplete; my identifications are sometimes positive, sometimes conjectural.

TWELFTH SEASON
West and Bignall Company
November 1796–January 1797

Chronicle.   Traveling by sea between Richmond and Charleston, the actors passed the seaport city of Norfolk, and as they sailed upriver to Richmond at the falls of the James, they passed Petersburg, which was at this time almost as big as Richmond. Quite probably they stopped to play both cities. The *Norfolk Herald* of October 1, 1796, advertised for that date in the "New Theatre" *Speculation* and *The Lying Valet* performed by the same company which played in Richmond on November 24. Sherman says they played in Norfolk between July and October.

There was, however, other entertainment in Richmond. The *Virginia Argus* of November 22, 1796, advertised an exhibition of the "Execution of the late King and Queen of France, Louis XVI and Antoinetta." The exhibition showed "details of execution including head dropping in a basket." This edifying spectacle was on view from 9 A.M. to 9 P.M. at the Exchange Coffee House at the foot of the bridge. The price was only two shillings threepence.

First advertisement of the theatre appeared on November 23, 1796, announcing for Thursday, November 24, "a favorite Play *School for Soldiers; or The Deserter.*" Afterpiece was "the Farce (never performed here) *The Irishman in London.*" Between pieces "a comical Ditty 'Poor Old Woman of Eighty'" was sung by Turnbull. Both casts were given:

School for Soldiers

Bellamy	Mr. Green
Captain Valentine	Mr. Bartlett

Mr. Hector	Mr. Turnbull
Colonel Valentine	Mr. Morton
Frederick	Mr. Copeland
Servant	Mr. T. West
Major Bellamy	Mr. Prigmore
Clara	Mrs. West
Mrs. Mildmay	Mrs. Turnbull

The Irishman in London

Mr. Frost	Mr. Turnbull
Edward	Mr. T. West
Collooney	Mr. Morton
Capt. Seymore	Mr. Bartlet
Cymon	Mr. West
Servant	Mr. Copeland
Murtoch Deleaney	Mr. Green
Louisa	Mrs. Graupner
Cubba	Miss West
Caroline	Mrs. Shaw[16]

In *School for Soldiers* the leading role of Bellamy (the deserter) was played by Green, a newcomer, who also played Murtoch Deleaney in the farce. Although no first appearances were advertised, there were many new performers; indeed, the company had changed greatly since its last appearance. The only familiar names among the two casts were the Wests: Mr. and Mrs. West, T. West, and Miss West. Newcomers to the company were Bartlet, Copeland, Green, Morton, Prigmore, Mr. and Mrs. Turnbull, Mrs. Graupner, and Mrs. Shaw. Absence of "his first appearance on this stage" following any of these new names leads me to assume that this was not the opening night of the season. I conclude that this is merely the first extant announcement and that the season opened earlier, probably between the first and the middle of November.

On Wednesday, November 30, was announced for "This date a Comedy *Wild Oats; or, The Strolling Gentleman*," with Green in the leading role of Rover. Afterpiece was the "Grand Spectacle *Don Juan; or the Libertine Destroyed*," which was staged "with a variety of New Scenery, Machinery, Dresses, and Decorations. The Fireworks prepared by Mr. T. West." Don Juan was played by Mr. Douvillier, and Donna Anna by Mrs. Douvillier, both new to

Richmond. Act II was enlivened by "a Fandango" by Mrs. Douvillier. Casts were given for both plays:

Wild Oats

Rover	Mr. Green
Harry	Mr. Bartlet
John Dory	Mr. T. West
Ephraim Smooth	Mr. Prigmore
Banks	Mr. Heeley
Gammon	Mr. Morton
Sim	Mr. Fitzgerald
Zachariah	Mr. Copeland
John	Mr. Shaw
Sir George Thunder	Mr. Turnbull
Lady Amaranth	Mrs. Shaw
Amelia	Mrs. Turnbull
Jane	Mrs. Graupner

Don Juan

Don Juan	Mr. Douvillier
Commandant	Mr. Prigmore
Don Ferdinand (the Lover)	Mr. Bartlet
Scaramouch	Mr. T. West
Donna Anna	Mrs. Douvillier
Fisher Women	Mrs. Green and Mrs. Graupner
Ladies	By the Ladies of the Company[17]

I trust the juxtaposition of *Wild Oats* and *Don Juan* appealed to the Richmond audience as it does to me, permitting us to contemplate the same theme treated first as comedy then as tragedy. The fireworks prepared by T. West occurred at the end of *Don Juan*, when the libertine was "bound in chains by the furies and thrown into the flames of the fiery abyss" to conclude "one of the finest morals and grandest spectacles that ever was exhibited at any Theatre."[18]

On Wednesday, December 7, the *Virginia Gazette, and General Advertiser* announced for "This evening the comedy (never performed here) *Every one Has His Fault* (written by Mrs. Inchbald)." Afterpiece was "the farce *The Village Lawyer*." Between pieces there was "a Song" by Bartlet. Green played leading roles in both:

Sir Robert Ramble in *Every One Has His Fault*, and Scout (the lawyer) in *The Village Lawyer*. Casts were given:

Every One Has His Fault

Sir Robert Ramble	Mr. Green
Lord Norland	Mr. Heely
Harmony	Mr. Turnbull
Captain Irwin	Mr. Fitzgerald
Mr. Placid	Mr. Bartlet
Hammond	Mr. Morton
Edward	Master Shaw
Servant	Mr. Copeland
Mr. Solus	Mr. Prigmore
Lady Elenor Irwin	Mrs. West
Miss Woobourn	Mrs. Graupner
Miss Spinster	Mrs. Turnbull
Mrs. Placid	Mrs. Shaw

The Village Lawyer

Scout (the Lawyer)	Mr. Green
Snarle	Mr. Turnbull
Charles	Mr. Bartlet
Mittimus	Mr. Morton
Countryman	Mr. Fitzgerald
Constable	Mr. Copeland
Sheep Face	Mr. Prigmore
Kate	Mrs. Graupner
Mrs. Scout	Mrs. Turnbull

For the first time this season the advertisement informed the ladies and gentlemen of Richmond and environs that tickets were to be had at the post office and at the office of the theatre. Doors opened at five, with curtain at six. The most interesting detail specified "Days of Performance" as Monday, Wednesday, and Friday. We know, therefore, that there were three performances each week. So far we have records of three performances in three weeks.

The next record of performance is one week later, on Wednesday, December 14: "This evening the comedy (not performed here these six years) *A Bold Stroke for a wife; or, Guardians Outwitted.*" If this play had been performed in Richmond six years earlier, it would have been between October 1790 and January 1791, when the West and Bignall Company was active. There are, however, records of only four performances and eight plays from this season, and *A Bold Stroke for a Wife* is not among them. This is the first recorded Richmond performance. The leading role of Colonel Fainall (given in the cast of characters as Fainwell) was played by Green, Obadiah Prim, the Quaker guardian, by Turnbull, and his ward, Ann Lovely, by Mrs. Shaw. The true Quaker, the real Simon Pure (whence our expression) was played by Fitzgerald. Between pieces there was "a song, 'Dibdon's Sailor's Life,'" by Mr. West. Cast as advertised was:

Colonel Fainwell	Mr. Green
Sir Philip Modelove	Mr. Bartlet
Perewinkle	Mr. Prigmore
Tradelove	Mr. Moreton
Freeman	Mr. Heely
Sackbut	Mr. T. West
Simon Pure	Mr. Fitzgerald
Obadiah Prim	Mr. Turnbull
Mrs. Prim	Mrs. Turnbull
Betty	Mrs. Graupner
Mask'd Lady	Miss West
Ann Lovely	Mrs. Shaw

Afterpiece was "a Grand Spectacle *Oscar and Malvina; or the Hall of Fingal* (from the Poems of Ossian) with the original Airs, Duets, choruses, &c, as performed at Covent Garden Theatre upwards of fifty successive nights, and at the Circus Edinburgh." The advertisement further stated that "the Manners, Characters, and Incidents [were] taken from the Poems of Ossian, translated by the late James M'Pherson, Esq." Mr. and Mrs. Douvillier played the leading roles of Oscar and Malvina. Cast as advertised was:

Fingal (Chief of the ancient Caledonians)	Mr. Turnbull
Oscar (his Grand-Son, betrothed to Malvina)	Mr. Douvillier
Morven ⎰ Attendant Squires ⎱	Mr. T. West
Draco ⎱ on Carrol ⎰	An Amateur
Durmouth 'Squire to Oscar	Mr. Heely
Pedlar (going to harvest home)	Mr. Prigmore
Carrol (A neighboring chief, in love	
with Malvina)	Mr. Green
Malvina	Mrs. Douvillier
Bards, Vassals (Male and Female)	
Piper, attendants, Soldiers, Peasants, &c.	

The scenery was "entirely new, painted for the purpose." "Spectacles Incidental to the Piece" were enumerated in detail:

The Feast of Shells, Celebrated in Hall of Fingal
The Ancient Broadsword Combat
The Cavern in which Morven Bleeds himself upon Malvina's Scarf, to make Carrol believe he has murdered her
View of the Great Mountains, and the March of Carrol's Soldiers down them.
The Leap of Oscar, from the Turret of a prodigious high Tower, into the arms of his Soldiers
The Conflagration of Carrol's Camp, by the Troops of Oscar
The Death of Carrol, who is stabbed upon a Bridge by Malvina
View of Loch-Lomond by Moon Light[19]

Ossian was the legendary Gaelic warrior and bard, the son of Fingal, supposed to have lived in the third century. James Macpherson published his *Fingal*, an "ancient epic poem in six books," in 1762.

On December 20 there was advertised for Wednesday, December 21, "a comedy (never performed here) called *The Rage; or, A Picture of Present Manners*." Afterpiece was *The Critic; or a Tragedy Rehearsed*, in which Green took the leading role of Puff. Casts were given:

The Rage

Sir Paul Perpetual	Mr. Prigmore
Flush	Mr. Turnbull
Darnley	Mr. Heely
Sir George Gauntlet	Mr. Bartlet
Hon. Mr. Savage	Mr. T. West
Ready	Mr. Morton
Gingham	Mr. Green
Lady Sarah Savage	Mrs. Shaw
Clara	Mrs. Green
Mrs. Darnley	Mrs. West

The Critic

Puff	Mr. Green
Sneer	Mr. Prigmore
Sir Fretful Plagiary	Mr. Turnbull
Dangle	Mr. Morton

The Italian family with the mock Italian Trio by,
Mr. Bartlet, Mrs. Green and Miss West

Mrs. Dangle	Mrs. Turnbull

Characters in the Tragedy

Lord Burleigh	Mr. West
Governor of Tilbury Fort	Mr. Fitzgerald
Earl of Leicester	Mr. Turnbull
Sir Walter Raleigh	Mr. Heely
Sir Christopher Hatton	Mr. Copeland
Beef Eater	Mr. Bartlet
Don Ferolo Whiskerandos	Mr. T. West
Tilburina	Mrs. Shaw
1st Niece	Mrs. Green
2nd Niece	Miss West
Confidant	Mrs. Turnbull

This was Green's benefit, and there were several specialties. Between pieces Mrs. Green sang "a Hunting Song," and *The Critic* concluded with a "Grand Sea-Fight, attack upon Tilbury Fort and destruction of the Armada. The fireworks by Mons. Rosainville." Tickets were on sale "at the Post-office, at the office of the Theatre, at Messrs. Pritchard and Davidson's book-store, and of Mr. Green, at Mr. Watson's." Boxes were six shillings, "Pit and upper Boxes," four and six. Doors opened at five, "the Curtain to rise precisely at six o'clock." Mrs. Shaw announced her benefit for Friday, December 23.[20]

On Friday, December 23, the *Virginia Argus*, advertised for "This evening the Tragedy *George Barnwell, or The London Apprentice*" with Green in the title role, and Mrs. Green as Maria. Barnwell's seducer, the heartless courtesan Millwood, was played by Mrs. Shaw. Afterpiece was "the comic opera *Peeping Tom of Coventry*," in which Peeping Tom was played by Prigmore, with Miss West as Lady Godiva. The role of Emma was played by Mrs. Fitzgerald, "her first appearance on the stage." Prigmore as Peeping Tom sang "The Little Farthing Rush Light." Between the tragedy and the farce was "a new Pantomime interlude *Rural Rumpus or the Humours of a Country Wak[e]*" in which was introduced "a Race in Sacks for a Gold Laced Hat." Between pieces Bartlet sang "The Song of American Commerce and Freedom." The following casts were given:

George Barnwell

George Barnwell	Mr. Green
Trueman	Mr. Bartlet
Uncle	Mr. Heely
Blunt	Mr. Moreton
Jailor	Mr. Copeland
Thoroughgood	Mr. Turnbull
Millwood	Mrs. Shaw
Lucy	Mrs. Turnbull
Maria	Mrs. Green

Peeping Tom of Coventry

Peeping Tom	Mr. Prigmore
Harold	Mr. Bartlet
Crazy	Mr. Fitzgerald
Count Louis	Mr. Morton
Count Mercia	Mr. Heely
Mayor of Coventry	Mr. Turnbull
Maud	Mrs. Green
Mayoress	Mrs. Turnbull
Lady Godiva	Miss West
Emma	Mrs. Fitzgerald

This same issue of the *Argus* advertised for Monday, December 26, "the Comic opera *Love in a Village*" and "the farce *Barnaby Brittle, or a Wife at Her Wits End.*" No casts were given. It was Mrs. Turnbull's benefit and there were special attractions: "Between pieces a Comic Song 'The learned Pig' by Mrs. Turnbull" and "An Ode to Columbus," written by Turnbull and performed by "Bartlet, as the Genius of America, Turnbull, as a Philosophic Patriot, and Prigmore as an American Hero." I fear (alas!) that Turnbull's Ode is lost to American literature.

The next record of performance was on December 27, when was advertised for Wednesday, December 28, 1796, "Shakespeares admired tragedy of *Romeo and Juliet*" and "The Comic opera *No Song No Supper.*" No casts were given, but the advertisement featured special stage effects in *Romeo and Juliet*:

In Act First a Grand Masquerade
In Act Fifth Juliet's Funeral Procession to the Monument of the
    Capulets with a Solemn Dirge the vocal parts by Mrs. Green,
    Miss West, Mr. Bartlet, Mr. Turnbull, and Mr. Prigmore
Order of Procession

Six boys bearing lighted torches, two Banners, Six Mourners, Six
Girls, bearing Garlands of Flowers, two Banners, vocal parts
of the Dirge, two Banners, Friar Lawrence, The Bier, Capulet
and Lady Capulet, Chief Mourners

This was Prigmore's benefit. Between pieces he rendered "a
Description of the Destruction of the Bastille, in the character of
a Sailor." I cannot tell whether this was a dramatic recitation or a
song. A further note in connection with Prigmore's benefit is of
special interest: "Mr. Prigmore presents his respects to the Ladies
and Gentlemen of this city and vicinity, and informs them that he
has provided Stoves to warm the house for that night."[21] This was,
of course, the middle of winter, and the theatre had been open
since November. Evidently, there had been no heat before Prigmore provided stoves. Evidently, also, it was a good idea; the next
advertisement stated: "There will be stoves provided." I hazard
that once installed they stayed for the rest of the season.

On December 28, 1796, was advertised for "Friday next
December 30 the Comedy (never performed here) *Notoriety*,
written by Reynolds, author of *The Dramatist, How to Grow
Rich* &c." Afterpiece was "The Musical Entertainment *The Son-
In-Law.*" This was Bartlet's benefit. Special attractions consisted
of "a New Song" by Bartlet, "a Comic Song" by Turnbull, and
"a New Ballet, *The French Vauxhall Gardens*," performed between
pieces. No casts were given.[22]

On December 30 the *Virginia Argus* advertised for "Monday,
January 2, 1797, a Tragedy (never performed here) *The Robbers*
(translated from the German of Mr. Schiller)." Afterpiece was "a
New Pantomime (never performed here) *The Devil Upon Two
Sticks, or Columbine Invisible.*" Casts were given:

The Robbers

Maximillian, Count de Moor	Mr. Turnbull
Francis de Moor	Mr. Prigmore
Herman	Mr. Morton
Peter	Master Shaw
Commissary	Mr. Bartlet
Switzer	Mr. T. West
Roller	An Amateur
Speigelberg	Mr. Fitzgerald
Schusterla	Mr. Heely

Grinam	Mr. Copeland
Razman	Mrs. Turnbull
Robbers	Supernumaries
Charles de Moor (Capt. of Robbers)	Mr. Green

The Devil upon Two Sticks

Harlequin	Mr. T. West
Devil Upon two sticks	Master Shaw
Cassander (father of Columbine)	Mr. Turnbull
Lover	Mr. Bartlet
Capt. of Artillery	Mr. Prigmore
Soldiers	Messrs. Copeland, Morton, Fitzgerald, &c.
Pastry Cook	Mr. Heely
Clown	An Amateur
Shepherdesses	Miss West, Mrs. Turnbull & Mrs. Fitzgerald
Columbine	Mrs. Green

In the pantomime Prigmore played Captain of Artillery, with a song, "Let Fame Sound the Trumpet." Between pieces there was "a Song" by Mrs. Green.

The announcement included not only casts but stage effects. In the fifth act of *The Robbers* there was "an attack upon the Castle by the Robbers who set fire to it and carry off Francis de Moor. In the course of said act Old de Moor is rescued from a dark tower in which he had been confined by Francis de Moor, and himself thrown into it." In the Harlequin pantomime "will be introduced a variety of Tricks and Changes, particularly the favorite Dying and Skeleton Scenes, the Sedan Chair and Bridge, Harlequin shot from a Cannon &c, &c, &c. To Conclude with a March and Dance by the Characters."

On January 3, there was advertised for Wednesday, January 4, "a comedy *The Road to Ruin*" and a "musical entertainment *The Romp*," for Mrs. Green's benefit. The performance was, however, postponed "on account of the weather" to Friday, January 6, when Mrs. Green appeared as Sophia in *The Road to Ruin* and as Priscilla Tomboy in *The Romp*. Casts were given for both plays:

The Road to Ruin

| Mr. Dornton | Mr. Turnbull |
| Harry Dornton | Mr. Prigmore |

Mr. Sulky	Mr. Morton
Mr. Silky	Mr. T. West
Goldfinch	Mr. Green
Milford	Mr. Bartlet
Mr. Smith	Mr. Copeland
Jacob	Mr. Sully
Widow Warren	Mrs. Shaw
Sophia	Mrs. Green
Mrs. Ledger	Mrs. Turnbull
Millener	Mrs. Fitzgerald

The Romp

Old Barnacle	Mr. Turnbull
Cockney	Mr. Heely
Captain Sightly	Mr. Bartlet
Watty Cockney	Mr. Prigmore
Miss Penelope	Mrs. Fitzgerald
Miss La Blond	Miss West
Priscilla Tomboy (the Romp)	Mrs. Green

Between them was a ballet, "*The Sailor's Landlady, or Jack in Distress,*" in which Jack was played by Prigmore, Ben Block "(with a Song)" by Bartlet, and the Landlady by Mrs. Turnbull. Tickets were to be had "at the Post Office, at Messrs. Pritchard and Davidson's bookstore, of Mrs. Green, and at the Office of the Theatre."[23]

On January 6 the *Virginia Argus* advertised for Monday, January 9, "the tragedy of *The Widow of Mallabar*" and "the pantomime *The Foreign War.*" No casts were given. This was the benefit of Mrs. West, and "the last night of performing this season."

The season began some time between October 13, 1796, when the company was in Norfolk, and November 24, their first recorded performance in Richmond. It ended on January 9, 1797.

The theatre was occupied soon after. On February 17 Salenka advertised "a great variety of entertainments in the theatre on Saturday, February 18." The feature of Salenka's entertainment was "a Learned Dog"; Salenka himself sang, performed sleight-of-hand tricks, and concluded the evening with "a German Hornpipe." Prices were four shillings, six for boxes, three shillings for the pit.[24]

On the same day was advertised, under the direction of Shaw, a concert "consisting of vocal and instrumental performances such as can be procured in Richmond and Petersburg." The concert was to be followed by a ball. The most interesting part of the announcement concerns the whereabouts of the actors: "The great part of the performers being at present in Petersburg," the Richmond public was requested to subscribe soon to assure getting them back for the concert. Evidently subscriptions were forthcoming, for the *Virginia Argus* of February 24 carried a big advertisement giving the program of the concert, including the "Facetious History of John Gilpin" recited by Green.

If we assume that the company opened in Richmond near the beginning of November, they played a season of about two months; and if they played three nights each week (as advertised), there should have been at least twenty-four performances. We have records of twelve performances and twenty-seven plays, twenty-one of which were new to Richmond. We have casts for sixteen plays, a total of twenty-one actors, twelve men and seven women, plus Miss West and Master Shaw.

The company probably left Richmond soon after January 9. Sherman says they opened a new theatre in Petersburg on Wednesday, January 18, with *The Dramatist* and *The Irishman in London.* The season included *School for Scandal, Macbeth*, and some lavish pantomime productions. They played in Norfolk during the summer.

The plays. *The Irishman in London* (November 24, 1796), a farce by William Macready, had its premiere at Covent Garden in 1792 and was acted in both New York and Philadelphia in 1793.

Don Juan (November 30, 1796), a pantomime ballet by Carlo Delpini, with music by Gluck, was brought out by Garrick at Drury Lane in 1790. It was presented in Philadelphia in 1792, New York in 1793, and Charleston in 1794.

Every One Has His Fault (December 7, 1796), a comedy by Elizabeth Inchbald, was brought out at Covent Garden in 1793. It was acted in New York and Philadelphia in 1794, and Charleston in 1795. *The Village Lawyer*, a farce by William Macready, had its premiere at the Haymarket in 1787. It was acted in Philadelphia in 1794 and New York in 1795.

A Bold Stroke for a Wife (December 14, 1796), a comedy by Susannah Centlivre, had been brought out in 1717. It was first acted in New York in 1750, in Charleston in 1754, and in Philadelphia in 1767. The pantomime *Oscar and Malvina* is an adaptation of the Ossianic epic by James Byrne. It was first performed at Covent Garden in 1791. Its American premiere was in Philadelphia on December 3, 1796, just eleven days before this Richmond production. It was presented in Charleston three times during March 1799, Baltimore in 1812, and New York in 1823.

The Rage (December 21, 1796), a comedy by Frederick Reynolds, had its premiere at Covent Garden on October 23, 1794, and was acted in both New York and Philadelphia in 1795. *The Critic*, a burlesque in two acts by R. B. Sheridan, had its premiere at Drury Lane on October 30, 1779. It was acted in New York in 1786 and Philadelphia in 1790.

George Barnwell (December 23, 1796), George Lillo's famous domestic drama in which for the first time commonplace commercial life was made the subject of tragedy, was brought out at Drury Lane in 1731. It was acted in New York in 1753, Charleston in 1754, and Philadelphia in 1759. *Peeping Tom*, a comic opera by John O'Keeffe, with music by Samuel Arnold, had its premiere at the Haymarket on September 6, 1784. Its American premiere was in Charleston, by the West and Bignall Company on February 21, 1794. It was acted in Philadelphia on April 27, 1794, and New York on September 6, 1797. The pantomime interlude *Rural Rumpus* was apparently a slapstick diversion devised by the company for the occasion. It was probably similar to *Rural Waggish Tricks* (Charleston, 1794), *Rural Revels* (Philadelphia, 1795) and *Rural Merriment* (Philadelphia, 1796).

Love in a Village (December 26, 1796), a comic opera by Isaac Bickerstaffe, was brought out at Covent Garden in 1762. It was acted in Charleston in 1766, Philadelphia in 1767, and New York in 1768. *Barnaby Brittle*, a farce adapted anonymously from Thomas Betterton's *The Amorous Wife*, was brought out at Covent Garden in 1781. Its American premiere was in Charleston on March 26, 1794, by the West and Bignall Company. It was acted in Philadelphia on May 16, 1796, and New York on September 13, 1797.

Notoriety, or a Dash at the Day (December 30, 1796), a comedy by Frederick Reynolds, had its premiere at Covent Garden on November 5, 1791, and was acted in both New York and Philadelphia in 1793. *The Son-in-Law*, a musical farce by John O'Keeffe, with music by Samuel Arnold, was brought out at the Haymarket in 1779. It was acted in Philadelphia in 1794 and New York in 1796. *French Vauxhall Gardens* was apparently a ballet devised by the company for the occasion. I found no record of it elsewhere.

There were several translations and adaptations of Schiller's *The Robbers* (January 2, 1797). This was probably the same version acted by the West and Bignall Company in Charleston in 1796; it may also have been the same version acted in New York in 1795 and Philadelphia in 1799. Quinn attributes a version to John Howard Payne, but is uncertain as to date and place of performance. *The Devil upon Two Sticks* was, I think, not the comedy by Samuel Foote, scenes from which were presented by Godwin in Charleston on November 24, 1786, followed by a Harlequin pantomime. This Richmond production was definitely a Harlequin pantomime. It was advertised as "Taken from le Diable Boiteux of le Sage," which may have indicated a source or a suggestion. Mostly it was, I suspect, the product of the imagination and ingenuity of the company, as Harlequin pantomimes usually were.

Jack in Distress (January 4, 1797) was apparently a ballet prepared by the company for the occasion. It was recorded in Charleston on January 27, 1809.

I have found no other performance of *The Foreign War* (January 9, 1797). I assume that it was a patriotic pantomime devised by the company for the occasion. Quinn has much to say about *The Widow of Malabar*:

From the point of view of literary merit, the romantic plays with a tragic impulse are the most significant. The earliest of these is *The Widow of Malabar*, by David Humphreys, produced by the American Company on May 7, 1790, during their visit to Philadelphia, at the old Southwark Theatre, and repeated next season in Philadelphia and New York. It was played as late as 1798 by Wignell's company in Baltimore for Wood's debut. It is based on *La Veueve de Malabar*, by Le Mierre, produced in 1779 and revived with great success ten years later. David Humphreys (1753-1818) was aide-de-camp to Washington, received the captured British standards at Yorktown, and became Minister to Portugal and to Spain. He mentions more than one projected comedy in his letters, and he published one, *The Yankey in England*, in 1815. *The Widow of Malabar*, the only play of his to be performed by professional actors, is a romantic drama, laid in India, and is based upon the custom of widows immolating themselves upon a funeral pyre. Lanissa, the widow, is saved by the French general Monteban, who captures the city. The play is respectably dull. The best lines are in the Epilogue, written apparently by John Trumbull, and spoken by Mrs. Henry.

> "Am I to blame, if this dear life to save
> I lik'd a lover better than a grave;
> And held, retreating from my funeral urn,
> 'Twas better far to marry than to burn?' "[25]

The Widow of Malabar seems to be the third important play by American dramatists to be performed in Richmond, the other two being William Dunlap's *The Father*, on November 12, 1791, and Royall Tyler's *The Farm House*, on October 31, 1795. There were probably others of which record is lost.

The players. One male member of the Sully family (which one I do not know) played with this company. There is only one record of his appearance during the season: as Jacob in *The Road to Ruin* on January 6. According to Pollock, the Sullys (Mr., Jr., Master and Miss) were in Philadelphia at this time.[26] Mr. Sully played the leading roles at the Philadelphia Circus during October and November. There were four Wests: Manager Thomas Wade, Mrs. West, T. West, and Miss West. Leading roles were played by Green, a newcomer, and by Mr. and Mrs. Douvillier, also newcomers.

Willis tells of the company in Charleston from February 15 to June 1, 1796, naming Sully, Sr., T. West, Copeland, and Douvillier (spelled Douvilliers), with West as manager. In Richmond these actors were joined by fourteen newcomers: Mr. and Mrs. Green, Bartlet, Heely, Morton, Mr. and Mrs. Turnbull, Mr. and Mrs. Fitzgerald, Prigmore, Mrs. Shaw and Master Shaw, Mrs. Graupner, and Mrs. Douvillier, almost an entire new company. Although they played in Richmond, Norfolk, and Petersburg, they no longer advertised as the Virginia Company.

Prigmore, who joined the company this season, was evidently the actor recorded by Pollock in Philadelphia off and on in 1792, '93, '94, '96, and '97.[27] Actors are notoriously peripatetic. Odell says that he was imported by Henry for the New York season of 1793, calls him "a conceited fellow," and quotes Dunlap as saying that he "with grimace, antiquated wigs, painted wrinkles and nose, became a favorite for a time of the gods and the groundlings."[28] He played with the Hallam and Hodgkinson Company in New York between 1793 and 1796.

Mrs. Graupner made her first appearance with Sollee's Charleston company as Melinda in *The Recruiting Officer* on April 7, 1796; she was with this company in New York, playing Isobella in *The Wonder* on August 18, 1797, when she was announced as "from the theatre royal Drury Lane, being her first appearance here."[29]

The Douvilliers were in Philadelphia in 1797-98; and Mrs. Shaw was there in 1794-95 and '96, although Master Shaw was not mentioned.[30]

Green appeared in Philadelphia with the Wignell and Reinagle Company at the Chestnut Street Theatre, playing Sanguino in *The Castle of Andalusia* on opening night, February 17, 1794. He was in Philadelphia in 1794, '95, and '96. On June 24, 1796, he married Miss Williams, who had played in Philadelphia with the same company during the same years.[31] They became popular favorites in Richmond during the first decade of the next century.

Although Morton was twice spelled Moreton, I do not think that this was the famous John Pollard Moreton of the Philadelphia and New York stages.

THIRTEENTH SEASON

West and Bignall Company

Autumn 1797–January 1798

Chronicle. The company evidently returned to Richmond in the autumn of 1797, although I have located only one newspaper advertisement from the season. On Wednesday, November 8, the *Virginia Gazette, and General Advertiser* announced for "This Evening . . . Shakespeare's celebrated Comedy of *As You Like It; or Love in a Forest* . . . to which will be added, the Musical Farce of *The Farmer; or, The World's Ups and Downs.*" Between pieces was a "Song by Mr. J. West." The advertisement was headed "By Authority." No casts were given, but the appearance of J. West identifies the West and Bignall Company.

We have observed that files of Richmond newspapers from these years are scattered and incomplete. Further, we are certain that there were performances that were not advertised. Nevertheless, newspaper advertisements constitute practically our sole source of recorded performances. We come now to the rare instance in which we can authenticate performance from another source.

Benjamin Henry Latrobe, generally considered the father of architecture in America, sailed from England in March 1796, landed at Norfolk, and made his way to Richmond, which was to be his home for two years. He was immediately accepted into Richmond society and visited at the plantation homes of such notables as the Randolphs and the Washingtons. His biographer, Talbot Hamlin, tells us that he quickly formed friendships among the players of the West and Bignall Company, most of whom were English; "for him they had a basic congeniality as artists."[32] Hamlin quotes from Latrobe's journal of January 17: "began a Comedy the idea of which was suggested in Mr. Jone's phaeton on my trip with him to Hansen, but had lain dormant till my desire to serve Mrs. Green, the excellent comedian, & the more excellent man revived it. . . . Though I finished it in 26 hours, the necessary trouble of making fair copies & writing out the parts was very great & this is my first free day, on which I could think of my old habits of journalizing."[33]

The Apology was performed on Saturday evening, January 27, 1798, with the following cast:

Vaucamil	Mr. Turnbull
Bob Vaucamil	Mr. Tom West
Twoshoes	Mr. Sully
Simon Care	Mr. Lathy
Louisa	Mrs. J. West
Skunk, a newspaper editor	Mr. Green

According to Hamlin, "Mrs. Green, Mrs. Turnbull, and Bignall also had parts, but they are not specified. The Prologue (which was written but a few hours before the play went on) was spoken to great applause by Mr. Green who also recited an 'apology' at the the end. The afterpiece was *Octavian*."

Following Latrobe's journal, Hamlin goes on to hint at a hitherto unknown West-Green jealousy and to reveal conspicuous flaws in the acting of the play:

Apparently the performance was worse than indifferent; Latrobe was bitterly disappointed in it and in his journal suggests that the Wests' jealousy of the Greens may have had something to do with its flaws. Some of the actors did not know their parts and improvised absurdly. Several were wooden and stiff; some spoke their parts automatically without any apparent understanding of the words. In the last act Sully did not get his cue from Bignall, who had forgotten his part, and, writes Latrobe, "Sully, not receiving his cue, & being unused to act, & very bashful,—having moreover a cold which made him hoarse as a raven—was so embarrassed that not a word was spoken for so many minutes that the whole play ended there, nobody knew how or why.—In Simon Care's last speech Lathy was so hampered by the word *municipal* that the rest of his speech was drowned in the laughter caused by his embarrassment. Mrs. J. West in Louisa was very correct."[34]

The *Apology* does not survive. There is no record of its performance elsewhere. Hamlin mentions "a legend" that it was later acted successfully in Philadelphia, where Latrobe went when he left Richmond, but there is no record of such a performance, and from the nature of the play, I suspect that it would have been unwelcome in that stronghold of the Federalists. Even in Richmond it provoked controversy: "*The Apology* was largely a satire on the Federalists, especially Hamilton and Cobbett, who were undoubtedly lampooned as 'Vaucamil' and as 'Skunk, a newspaper editor.' Then, too, there was adultery in the plot and perhaps some rather outspoken language, though at the end sin was punished and virtue triumphed. But the political implications aroused the Richmond Federalists to a storm of objections, and a violent newspaper controversy followed."[35]

Altogether, we have here a remarkable wealth of detail: an unknown play by a famous American, including source and composition, a unique performance, criticism of poor acting, and response to the play in the community, response that established *The Apology* as effective political satire. Had the play survived it would be a rare example of contemporary political satire on the American stage.

In addition to *The Apology*, we have, out of Latrobe's journal, record of two other plays: *Octavian*, on January 27, and *Richard III*, on January 30. Hamlin writes: "On Monday, bad weather prevented any performance; on Tuesday, West played one of his most popular parts, Richard III."[36]

Since this was Mrs. Green's benefit, we expect "the more excellent man," her husband, to appear in a featured role. I think he played Octavian in *The Mountaineers* on this occasion. My assumption is strengthened by the fact that when *The Mountaineers* was next presented in Richmond (March 19, 1804) Green played Octavian. I suspect that Mrs. Green played Agnes, the heroine, on her benefit night.

The Latrobe-West association produced at this time plans for what would have been the finest theatre in the United States, details of which are given in Appendix 1.

This was in many respects a remarkable season; most remarkable, however, was its close, details of which are reconstructed by Susanne K. Sherman:

By the end of 1797, Thomas Wade West had six theatres either in operation or under construction. He brought the year's work to a close with a season in Richmond. The theatre there, the wooden structure on Shockoe Hill, was the poorest of the six. Designed by a soldier-dancing master for an Academy of Arts and Sciences, it was over-large, inconvenient, a fire hazard, and easy prey to thieves and vandals. The thieves had proved to be such a problem that Thomas Wade West found it advisable to keep the company's stock of costumes at his own lodgings and to take to the theatre each day only those dresses needed for the evening's performance.

The Richmond season extended into January of 1798. While the actors played three nights a week, they rehearsed constantly, as usual, for new plays. The scene designer and the painters who assisted West were busy constructing "all new scenes and machines" for a production with which to open the Norfolk season. By the twenty-third of January, the company was in the midst of the benefit performances with which each season closed, performances from which the proceeds went to the actor or actress in whose name the entertainment had been given. The new scenery for the Norfolk season was finished. It was rolled and stacked near the stage door ready to be loaded onto the ship which would take it down the James to the theatre for which it had been designed. Mrs. Greene's benefit was over and although the *Apology*, the original farce which brought the evening's entertainment to a close, had offended at least one staunch Federalist, it had doubtless pleased the Jeffersonian democrats who were in the majority

Benjamin H. Latrobe's sketch of the West and Bignall properties room, 1797, from the title page of Latrobe's plans for a theatre, assembly rooms, hotel. (Courtesy Library of Congress.)

in Richmond. The audience had departed in good humor, and the actors had removed their costumes and make-up and returned to the homes where they boarded. Thomas Wade West had taken the costumes home with him.

It was then that the fire started. Before the alarm was spread, the building was doomed. With its flue-like walls, the best fire department could not have saved it. In Richmond, there was no fire department. As one inhabitant complained in the newspaper, people went to their doors when they heard the call of "Fire"; but if they saw no flames, they concluded that the alarm was false and returned to their chairs. However, on the night of January 23, 1798, the comedians who, for the most part, lodged within sight of the theatre, answered the alarm with an alacrity born of self-interest. Entering the raging inferno, some of them succeeded in rescuing the new scenery which had been designed for the opening of the Norfolk season. Nothing else was saved. The building was completely razed, and the scenery, machinery, and stage properties were lost. The newspaper estimated the loss at three thousand pounds.[37]

The date given, January 23, is, I think, incorrect. Hamlin gives January 27 (Saturday) as the date of the performance of Latrobe's *Apology*; following Latrobe's journal, he specifies no performance on Monday (January 29), and *Richard III* on Tuesday (January 30), with the fire after *Richard III*. On any date, it was catastrophe for the theatre in Richmond.

The plays.   Although Hamlin italicizes *Octavian*, indicating that it was the title of the play produced as afterpiece to *The Apology* (January 27, 1798), I think that Octavian was the featured role, rather than the title. The play was most probably *The Mountaineers*, an opera by George Colman, the younger, with music by Samuel Arnold, which had been brought out at the Haymarket on August 3, 1793. It was acted in New York, Philadelphia, and Charleston in 1796, its American premiere being in Charleston on March 15. Willis says: " 'The Mountaineers,' the new comic opera just arrived in Charleston, was one of Colman's greatest favorites, and all the leading actors of the day vied with one another in their delineations of the Mad-Lover, *Octavian*" (Willis's italics).[38]

The *Richard III* which West acted (January 30, 1798) was undoubtedly Colley Cibber's alteration, which had been first acted at Drury Lane in 1700, and which held the stage for the next two centuries as one of the favorite combinations of declamatory tragedy and stage spectacle. It was presented in New York in 1750, Philadelphia in 1759, and Charleston in 1774. There are many records of later performances in Richmond, but only this one before 1800.

The players. The "Tom West" of this season was evidently the T. West of the previous season, not Thomas Wade West, who played Richard III the night of the fire. Only Lathy was new to the company.

FOURTEENTH SEASON
West and Bignall Company
December 1798–April 1799

Chronicle. Susanne K. Sherman assures us that despite a loss that would have ruined most theatre managers of the time, Thomas Wade West "continued to employ forty to fifty people and to produce new and elaborate entertainments. He kept the remaining theatres functioning and continued the construction of the new building in Alexandria. He continued to pay taxes in five cities, to drive a horse and chair, and to live with his silver, paintings and pier glasses in the style befitting a gentleman."[39] During most of 1798 the West and Bignall Company played in other Virginia cities. They were probably in Richmond before December, but there is no record of performance before then.

For this season theatre advertisements are few. There is no long run of consecutive advertisements with casts and descriptions of stage effects. I assume that bills of the day were distributed, but none survives. We make do with what we have, brief and abstract though it be.

The first advertisement of the season, which appeared Friday, December 14, 1798, was headed "Richmond Temporary Theatre— Market Hall." It stated that no money would be taken at the doors; tickets were on sale at "Prichard and Davidson's Book Store, Office of the *Examiner*, and of Mr. Mann at the Ticket

Office under the Hall." Doors opened at five, with performance at six. Admission was one dollar. Before 1795 prices had been in shillings and pence. The price is revealing because there is no mention of boxes, gallery, or pit. Market Hall must have been a poor substitute for the academy theatre, dilapidated though it may have been.

Plays for the evening were "A New Comedy (never performed here) *A Cure For The Heart-Ache,*" and *The Poor Soldier.* Casts were given:

A Cure for the Heart-Ache

Sir Herbert Stanley	Mr. Taylor
Charles Stanley	Mr. J. West
Vortex	Mr. Bignall
Old Rapid	Mr. Sully
Young Rapid	Mr. Green
Frank Oatland	Mr. T. West
Farmer Oatland	Mr. Watts
Bronze	Mr. Radcliffe
Heartley	Mr. M'Kinzie
Landlord	Mr. Tubbs
Servant	Mr. Williams
Ellen Vortex	Mrs. Bignall
Miss Vortex	Mrs. Decker
Jessy Oatland	Mrs. J. West

The Poor Soldier

Patrick (the Poor Soldier)	Mr. J. West
Captain Fitzroy	Mr. Radcliffe
Father Luke	Mr. Bignall
Bagatelle	Mr. Watts
Dermot	Mr. Sully, jun.
Darby	Mr. Green
Norah	Miss Arnold
Kathleen	Mrs. J. West

The Poor Soldier was preceded by "an occasional Prologue by Mr. Green." To the familiar names, this advertisement added the following new ones: Mrs. Decker, M'Kenzie, Radcliffe, Taylor, Tubbs, Watts, and Williams. Notable is the first acting role of Miss Arnold, who played Norah in *The Poor Soldier.*[40]

Under the heading "Richmond Temporary Theatre—Market Hall," the Richmond *Examiner* for December 20, 1798, announced that "on Friday Evening, Dec. 21, 1798, will be presented the favorite comedy (never performed here) of *Wives As They Were, and Maids as they Are.*" Cast was given:

Sir William Dorrillon	Mr. Green
Mr. Bronzley	Mr. T. West
Lord Priory	Mr. Bignall
Sir George Evelyn	Mr. J. West
Mr. Norberry	Mr. Taylor
Oliver	Mr. M'Kenzie
Nabson	Mr. Radcliffe
Servant	Mr. Watts
Lady Mary Raffle	Mrs. West
Lady Priory	Mrs. Green
Housekeeper	Mrs. Watts
Betty	Mrs. Bignall
Miss Dorrillon	Mrs. J. West

Afterpiece was *The Flitch of Bacon,* with the following cast:

Captain Greville	Mr. J. West
Major Benbow	Mr. Sully
Justice Benbow	Mr. M'Kenzie
Captain Wilson	Mr. Tubbs
Ned	Mr. Bignall
Putty	Mr. Taylor
Kilderkin	Mr. Radcliffe
Tipple	Mr. Sully, jun.
Eliza	Mrs. J. West

Mr. Tubbs and Miss Arnold performed a comic dance between pieces.

The next advertisement appeared Monday, December 24, announcing for "This Evening A New Comedy *A Cure for the Heart-ache,*" with "the musical Farce (never performed here) *Bannian Day; or The Attorney Ousted*" as afterpiece. The performance was in the "Temporary Theatre in Market Hall," and the same details of tickets, price of admission, and time of opening were given. The "Printing office of Samuel Pleasants, Jr." was added to places where tickets were available. I assume that Pleasants, editor of the *Virginia Argus*, printed the company's handbills.

Casts were given for both pieces, with *A Cure for the Heart-ache* unchanged from December 14.

Bannian Day

Jack Hawser	Mr. West
Batch (a baker)	Mr. Bignall
Bobby Notice (a Lawyer)	Mr. J. West
Old Goodwill	Mr. Sully
Lieutenant Goodwill	Mr. Radcliffe
Captain Macgallahee	Mr. Green
David	Mr. Taylor
Servant	Mr. Watts
Bailiff	Mr. M'Kinzie
Polly	Mrs. J. West
Mrs. Goodwill	Mrs. Green

"An occasional Prologue" (probably the same as on December 14) was spoken before the play by Green; between pieces there was "a Patriotic Song 'Hail Columbia' by J. West & Company."[41]

The *Virginia Argus* of December 25 announced for "Wednesday December 26 an Historic Tragedy (never performed here) *Bunker Hill or, The Death of General Warren* written by John Burke, late of Trinity College, Dublin, and performed at the Theatres of Boston and New York, for 14 nights with unbounded applause. To which will be added (for the second time) a new comic opera *Bannian Day; or The Attorney Ousted*." Performance was in the "Temporary Theatre, City Hall," which I assume to be the same as "Temporary Theatre, Market Hall."

No casts were given. We may assume that *Bannian Day* was acted by the same cast as on December 24, and since this was its second performance we assume that the theatre was dark on Christmas night. During this season, plays were given, I think, on Mondays, Wednesdays, and Fridays.

Bunker Hill was something special. The advertisement offered a summary of the action, preceded by these noble and nationalistic sentiments:

A nobler theme than this to grace the stage
Where can we find in all th' Historic page?
Of Rome's and Cato's fall, the world has rung,
Why not Columbia's rising fame be sung?

Interestingly, the announcement of *Bunker Hill* in Charleston on January 8, 1798, had been identical, beginning with the same puff about performances in Boston and New York, and ending with the same quatrain.[42]

I think I know who was responsible both for the announcement and for bringing the play to Richmond. In Charleston the role of Governor Gage was played by "Mr. McKenzie," who was, I assume, the same actor who as "Mr. M'Kinzie" played Heartley in *A Cure for the Heart-ache* and Bailiff in *Bannian Day* in Richmond on December 24. After the closing of the Charleston season on March 31 he left the Sollee Company and joined the West and Bignall Company, bringing with him, I assume, a copy of the play and a newspaper clipping of its Charleston production. He probably played Governor Gage in Richmond.

Quinn says that *"Bunker Hill* may have been the first play in which battle scenes of the Revolution were actually put upon the stage."[43]

This advertisement tells us just what those scenes were:

A view of the American Camp—in Act I a view of Bunker Hill, &c.

Act II commences with the confusion caused among the English troops—In Act IV the embarkation of the British troops—Act V opens with the Battle on the Hill—the English are obliged to retreat three times, advance, and are again beat back; when gen Warren addresses his Soldiers.

Gen Warren mortally wounded—the whole to conclude with A Grand Funeral Procession, with an Elegy over the Bier of Gen Warren, by Mrs. Green, Mrs. Decker, and Mr. J. West.

Quinn considers John Daly Burk "the most interesting" among early American writers of tragedy: "Although not a native, since he was born in Ireland about 1776, his dramatic career is entirely American. He came to this country when he was twenty, and was an editor by profession and a stormy petrel at all times. [He] first attracted attention by his *Bunker Hill."*[44]

Under the heading "Richmond Temporary Theatre—City Hall," the *Virginia Argus* on January 18 announced for "Saturday January 19 a favorite Comedy *The Jew; or Benevolent Hebrew."* Afterpiece was "the Musical Farce *The Quaker; or May Day Dower."* The advertisement gave no casts, no description of scenery, no specialties between pieces.

The next advertisement, which appeared Tuesday, January 22, was equally brief. It announced for "this date the Comedy _The School for Scandal_" and the "Musical Farce (never performed here) _The Adopted Child_." Again there were no casts, no stage effects, no specialties. We are told what we already know: admission was one dollar; no money was taken at the doors, which opened at 5, with performance at 6.[45]

On January 29 was announced for "Wednesday January 30 A Tragedy _The Gamester; or False Friend_." Afterpiece was "The Musical Romance _Cymon and Sylvia, or, the Justice Trapped_." No casts were given; "a Pas Seul by Miss Gillespie" provided the only name; the only detail of scenery was in _Cymon and Sylvia_, "a View of the Black Tower;" and of staging, "the Piece to conclude with an Arcadian Procession, to the nuptials of Cymon and Sylvia with a Grand Garland Dance."[46]

On February 5 there was advertised for "Thursday February 7 a Comedy interspersed with songs _The Battle of Hexham; or Days of Old_ (written by George Coleman, Esq. Author of _Inkle and Yarico_." Afterpiece was the "musical farce _The Devil to Pay; or the Wives Metamorphosed_." No casts were given, but between pieces there was "a double hornpipe by Miss Gillespie and Mr. Sully junior." There was also an adequate puff, written probably by Manager West:

The story of this favorite Play being taken from a remarkable occurrence in history renders it more particularly interesting. Dramatic productions founded merely on fabulous or ideal circumstances, excite the admiration of the Public only in proportion to the happy invention of the Author, or the excellence of his execution. But where historical facts are the leading features of a performance and the facts masterly treated, the Audience becomes doubly gratified: Such has been the effect of this charming piece.

The comic Characters of the Play possess a quaintness and simplicity strictly accordant, and in many instances, equal to the humorous Clowns of the immortal Shakespeare.

The affecting story of Gondibert and Adeline forms the most beautiful episode in the whole Arcania of the drama—and we think it no flattery to premise, that the piece wants but to be seen to be admired.[47]

On February 12 was advertised for "Wednesday February 13, the comedy (not performed here these five years) *A Bold Stroke for a Husband*." Afterpiece was "a new pantomime entertainment *The Weird Sisters; or—The Birth of Harlequin*." No casts were given. Between pieces Miss Gillespie performed "a Hornpipe in the character of a Sailor." The Harlequin pantomime included "several comic Changes, Tricks, and Leaps. The whole to conclude with a dance by the characters and a Hornpipe by Miss Gillespie"—her second of the evening.[48] The only performer mentioned by name was Miss Gillespie, but I assume that Sully played the clown in the pantomime and that he was largely responsible for the piece, which, I suspect, came to him through Mrs. Placide, who played Columbine in the New York production of *The Birth of Harlequin* on April 27, 1792. The same pantomime was given in Philadelphia on June 27, 1797, Sully's benefit.

On Friday, February 15, the *Virginia Argus* announced for "this date the Comedy (never performed here) *He Would be a Soldier*," with "the musical farce *No Song No Supper; or—The Lawyer in the Sack*" as afterpiece. No casts were given and no stage effects mentioned, but entertainment between pieces consisted of a hornpipe by Miss Gillespie and a "Comic Song" by Mr. Sully, Jr.

Reliability of newspaper notices is denigrated in the "(never performed here)" ascribed to *He Would Be a Soldier*, which had been performed in Richmond seven years before by the West and Bignall Company with both West and Bignall in the cast.

Next record of performance appeared February 22: "entertainments planned for this evening are postponed until Saturday February 23." The entertainments, which were presumably performed on the twenty-third were the "Historical Play *The Surrender of Calais*, with a Ballet Dance called the *French Vauxhall Gardens*, and the Musical Farce of *The Padlock*." The performance was for the benefit of Mr. and Mrs. Decker. No casts and no details were given.[49]

On Tuesday, March 5, there was announced for "this date the Comedy *The Beaux Stratagem*." Afterpiece was the same ballet presented on February 23, "The *French Vauxhall Gardens; or Folly of the Times*." No casts were given. This was the benefit of the senior Sully, who between the play and the ballet rendered "a Comic Song, Money is Your Friend." There were also "New and surprising Feats of Activity by Mr. Sully Jr.—with the Comic Exhibitions of Mr. Sully, sen. in the character of a Clown." Miss Gillespie danced a hornpipe, and the ballet concluded "with a Country Dance by the Characters."[50]

The *Virginia Argus* of March 8 advertised for "Saturday March 9 the Comedy (never performed here) written by Shakespeare—*The Merry Wives of Windsor; or Falstaff in the Buck Basket.*" Afterpiece was the farce *All in Good Humour*, and between the two was "an interlude called *Jack in Distress; or The Generous American Tar.*" No casts were given. This was the benefit of M'Kinzie and Radcliffe, who provided a special feature: "In the course of the evening's amusements, Mr. Gasper Arnaud, Professor of the noble and useful art of Defence, (having kindly offered his assistance to Mr. M'Kinzie & Mr. Radcliffe) will display the advantages resulting from a knowledge of Fencing, by several Examples."

The next record of performance was Tuesday, March 12: "This date the comedy *The Dramatist; or —Stop Him Who Can,*" with *The Romp* as afterpiece. This was the benefit of Mrs. J. West, who was featured as Priscilla Tomboy in *The Romp.* No others in either cast were named. Tickets were to be had as usual and "of Mrs. J. West at Mrs. Liles." Between pieces there was a song by Mr. J. West, and "Ground and Lofty Tumbling by Mr. Sully, Jr." with "clown by Mr. Sully." The evening concluded with "a Ballet Dance called *The Merry Girl and the Two Quakers.*"[51]

On March 15 was advertised for "Saturday March 16 (never performed but once in Virginia) a favorite comedy *The Will; or School for Daughters.*" Afterpiece was "a favorite Ballet called *The Wapping Landlady, or— Jack in Distress.*" No casts were given. This was the benefit of Sully, Jr., and tickets were to be had "as usual and of Mr. Sully, jr. at Mrs. Lile's." There were several specialties. Between the play and the ballet Mrs. Green sang "a Hunting Song called Tantivy," and after the ballet Mrs. J. West sang "a Comic Song called No indeed not I." There were also "Surprising Feats of Activity" by Sully, Jr., with clown by Sully, Sr., and second clown by Williams, "the whole to conclude with Goldsmith's Harlequin Epilogue, in Character by Mr. Sully Jr. who will take a Flying Leap through a Hogshead of Fireworks."[52]

The *Virginia Argus* of Tuesday, March 19, announced for "This date the Comic Opera *Lionel & Clarissa,*" with "an interesting Tale

told in action *La Foret Noire; or The Natural Child"* as afterpiece.
This was Mrs. Green's benefit, with "Tickets as usual & of Mrs.
Green at Raphael's Tavern." No casts were given, and the only
specialty announced was Mrs. Green's: "In the course of the opera
(by particular desire) Mrs. Green will introduce the Soldier tir'd
of Wars Alarms." The evening concluded with "a Commic Ballet
Dance, called *Shelty's Frolic.*"

There was evidently a performance on Friday, March 22, but
we know neither the plays nor the players. Our only information
is this notice: "Mr. Mann respectfully informs the ladies and
gentlemen of Richmond, Manchester and their vicinities, that the
Entertainments intended for last evening, were on account of the
inclemency of the weather, postponed till this evening, Friday,
March 22d."[53] At the beginning of the season it was announced
that tickets were to be had of Mr. Mann at the theatre. I assume
that he was business manager or agent for the company; he was
not a player.

The next record of performance announced for "Monday
March 25 a Comedy (not performed here these 5 years), *The
Belle's Stratagem; or Way to Win Him,"* with the afterpiece of
"the Farce (never performed here) *A Trip to Scotland, or Cupid
turned Postilion."* Between pieces was "a Comic Ballet (never performed here) *The Mechanic Society; or, Devil Among the Tailors."*
This was the benefit of Miss Gillespie, who might be expected to
perform some featured specialty, but if she did it was not advertised. No casts were given.[54]

The *Virginia Argus* of Friday, March 29, informed the public
that on account of the indisposition of Mr. Green, the program
for last evening was postponed to this evening. The program consisted of the comedy *The Way to Get Married* and "the grand
serious spectacle of *Don Juan."* It was J. West's benefit, and
tickets were to be had, "as usual and of Mr. J. West at Mrs. Lile's."
Don Juan was "under the direction of Mr. T. West." No casts were
given.

On April 2 there was advertised for "Wednesday April 3 A
Tragedy (never performed here but once) *The Maid of Normandy,
or The Death of the Queen of France,"* with the afterpiece of
"the grand serious pantomime of *The Death of Captain Cook in
the Island of O-why-Hee in the Pacific Ocean."* No casts were

given. Between pieces Mr. Sully sang "an Irish Song Paddy O'Blarney." Possibly because this was the benefit of Mrs. West, the wife of Manager West, the advertisement included descriptions of stage effects for both plays. The staging of *Captain Cook* was almost identical to previous descriptions, the piece having been produced in Richmond once in 1793 and twice in 1795. *The Maid of Normandy* was also staged impressively:

> In Act 4th, the Trial of the Queen of France by
> the Revolutionary Tribunal
> The Dungeon of the Conciergerie
> The Procession to the Scaffold

Officer		Serjeant
	Soldiers two and two	
	Guards	
Robespierre	Queen of France	Chaplin
	Guards	
	Soldiers two and two	
	Scene last	

The stage exhibits the scaffold and the Guillotine.[55]

Benefits were held toward the end of the season; we have records of the following: February 23, Mr. and Mrs. Decker; March 5, Sully, Sr.; March 8, M'Kinzie and Radcliffe; March 12, Mrs. J. West; March 16, Sully, Jr.; March 19, Mrs. Green; March 25, Miss Gillespie; March 29, J. West; April 3, Mrs. West; a total of nine benefits for eleven actors. There were probably others of which record is lost. There had, however, been disappointments; the advertisement of Friday, April 12, in the *Virginia Argus* reads:

TEMPORARY THEATRE–CITY HALL

The Manager of the Theatre having considered that from the severity of the season several of the performers have failed in their nights advertised for their Benefits, has been induced to give up the house for their use; and in consequence, the patronage of the public is solicited for a few evenings, on which every exertion will be used to render the entertainments worthy [of] Attention.

The advertisement then announced for "Saturday, April 13, A Comedy in four acts *The Deserter: or The School for Soldiers*," with "the Musical Entertainment of *The Prize; or— 2, 5, 3, 8*" as afterpiece. No casts were given, nor was any benefit announced.

There was, however, between the play and the farce "Ground and Lofty Tumbling by Mr. Sully Jun.—Clown, Mr. Sully."

The next advertisement, headed "Temporary Theatre—City Hall," appeared April 16. It announced for "Wednesday April 17 a Comedy (never performed here) *Fashionable Levities; or, The World as It Goes.*" Afterpiece was *The Prize.* No casts were given. Between pieces there was the same ground and lofty tumbling by the younger Sully, with his father as clown. One interesting note was added: we are told that the "Days of Playing" this week are Wednesday, Thursday, Friday, and Saturday.[56]

The next record of performance was Friday, April 19. Again headed "Temporary Theatre—City Hall," it advertised for "This date a Play *The Child of Nature; or The Happy Discovery.*" Afterpiece was "the Grand Serious Pantomime of *The Death of Captain Cook in the Island of O-Why-Hee, in the Pacific Ocean,*" which was advertised "with the original music, Marches, Dances, Decorations &c." There was a long description of setting and action, identical with that given for April 3. Between pieces there were songs (no titles given) by Miss Gillespie and Sully, Jr., but no casts were advertised.[57]

This is the last record of performance of the season. I suspect that the season ended either with this performance or soon after, since the manager's announcement of April 12 indicated that the season was supposed to end then. For this season there is no definite date of either opening or closing. There is, however, much of interest.

During a season of approximately seventeen weeks, there are records of twenty-three performances. If we assume three performances a week, there should be fifty. We have records of performances on every day of the week, though I doubt that there were six performances during any week. I suspect that we have records of less than half of this season. Nevertheless, it is the largest season to date, including tragedy, history, drama, comedy, farce, opera, pantomime, ballet. There are records of four plays not known to have been acted in America: *Bannian Day, The Maid of Normandy, The Mechanic Society,* and *Fashionable Levities.* There is one notable play of American authorship: *Bunker Hill,* acted on December 26, 1798. Among forty-one different pieces, twenty-three were new to Richmond.

During this season, we rely mainly on one newspaper, and advertisements are uncommonly brief. At the beginning of the season there were two advertisements, one in the *Virginia Argus*, one in the *Examiner*, with full casts of characters. Through the rest of the season, advertisements did not list casts. Some mention specialties such as songs, dances, and acrobatics; some give descriptions of scenery and action, but generally they are disappointingly short.

The plays. *A Cure for the Heart-ache* (December 14, 1798), a comedy by Thomas Morton, had its premiere at Covent Garden in January 1797. It was acted in New York and Charleston in November of the same year, and in Philadelphia on January 1, 1798.

Wives as They Were (December 21, 1798), a comedy by Elizabeth Inchbald, was brought out at Covent Garden on March 4, 1797. It was acted in New York on October 13, Charleston, November 25, and Philadelphia, December 13 of the same year. It held the stage well into the nineteenth century.

Bannian Day (December 24, 1798), a musical farce by George Brewer, with music by Samuel Arnold, was first acted at the Haymarket on June 11, 1796. There is no record of its performance elsewhere in America.

Bunker Hill (December 26, 1798), a historical tragedy by the American playwright John Daly Burk, was first produced at the Boston Haymarket on February 17, 1797. It was acted in New York on September 8, 1797, and in Charleston on January 8, 1798, but did not reach Philadelphia until 1813.

The Adopted Child (January 22, 1799), a musical farce by Samuel Birch, had its premiere at Drury Lane in 1795. It was acted in New York in 1796 and Philadelphia in 1797. Especially interesting is its performance in Charleston on November 27, 1797, when Miss Arnold played the title role; I assume she appeared in the same role in Richmond.

The Battle of Hexham (February 7, 1799), a comedy by George Colman, the younger, with music by Samuel Arnold, was brought out at the Haymarket in 1789. It was acted in New York and Philadelphia in 1794, and in Charleston by the West and Bignall Company on October 24, 1794, when the same puff was published. *The Devil to Pay*, a musical farce by Charles Coffey, had its

premiere at Drury Lane in 1731. It was acted in Charleston in
1735, New York in 1750, and Philadelphia in 1766.

A Bold Stroke for a Husband (February 13, 1799), a comedy
by Mrs. Hannah Cowley, was brought out at Covent Garden in
1783. It was acted in New York on May 19, 1794, and Philadelphia
on October 13, 1794. Its American premiere was apparently in
Charleston on April 28, 1794, by the West and Bignall Company.
It may, however, have been performed in Richmond (as the adver-
tisement stated) by this company, which played there between
September 20 and December 16, 1793. If so, record of another
American premiere is lost. *The Weird Sisters, or the Birth of Harle-
quin* was almost certainly the same pantomime as *The Birth of
Harlequin* performed in New York on April 27, 1792 with Mrs.
Placide as Columbine, and *The Weird Sisters, or the Adoption of
Harlequin* performed in Philadelphia on June 27, 1797, for Sully's
benefit. It was evidently contrived by this company, but strangely
there is no record of its performance in Charleston.

The Surrender of Calais (February 23, 1799), a romantic drama
by George Colman, the younger, had its premiere at the Haymarket
on July 30, 1791. It was acted in New York and Philadelphia in
1794. Its American premiere was apparently in Charleston on
April 29, 1793, when it was presented by the West and Bignall
Company for Bignall's benefit.

The Merry Wives of Windsor (March 9, 1799) was first recorded
in America in Philadelphia in 1770. It was acted in New York in
1789 and Charleston in 1798.

The Dramatist (March 12, 1799), a comedy by Frederick
Reynolds, was brought out at Covent Garden in 1789. Its American premiere was in Philadelphia on May 26, 1791. It was acted in
New York and Charleston in 1793. *The Merry Girl* was performed
in New York on April 29, 1795, and in Philadelphia on June 10,
1796, but is not recorded in Charleston.

The Will (March 16, 1799) was a comedy by Frederick Reynolds
which had been brought out at Drury Lane in 1797. Its popularity
is attested by performances in Charleston, Philadelphia, and New
York in 1798, its American premiere being in Charleston on January 12, twelve days before its performance in Philadelphia. Possibly
it had been performed once before in Virginia, as advertised, but
I cannot confirm the newspaper assertion.

Shelty's Frolic (March 19, 1799), advertised as a "Commic Ballet Dance," was probably not the same as *The Highland Reel*, a "comic opera" (March 17, 1804) in which the featured role was Shelty the piper; nor was it the same as William Dunlap's *Shelty's Travels*, performed in New York on April 24, 1794.

The Belle's Stratagem (March 25, 1799) may have been previously acted in Richmond, as the advertisement stated, but this is the first record of its performance. A comedy by Hannah Cowley, it had its premiere at Covent Garden in 1780 and its American premiere in Charleston on December 8, 1781. It was acted in New York in 1786 and Philadelphia in 1790. *The Mechanic Society* is not recorded elsewhere, and this is the only record of its performance in Richmond.

The Way to Get Married (March 29, 1799), a comedy by Thomas Morton, had its premiere at Covent Garden in 1796 and was acted in New York and Philadelphia in 1797.

The Maid of Normandy (April 3, 1799), a tragedy by Edmund John Eyre, was first acted at Wolverhampton in 1794. This is the only record of its performance in America.

The Deserter (April 13, 1799) was probably the same as *The School for Soldiers*. Nicoll says that "Sedaine's *Le Deserteur* (1769) was adapted by Charles Dibdin as *The Deserter* (Drury Lane, 1773) and by Henry as *The School for Soldiers* (Jamaica, 1783)."[58] Since two previous performances (October 13, 1792, and November 24, 1796) by the West and Bignall Company had used the title *School for Soldiers*, I assume that this was the same play and that it was Henry's, not Dibdin's. I consider it unlikely that two different versions of the same play would have been used by the same company. *The Prize*, a musical farce by Prince Hoare, had its premiere at the Haymarket on March 11, 1793, and its American premiere in Philadelphia on May 26, 1794. It was acted in Charleston in 1795 and New York in 1797.

Fashionable Levities (April 17, 1799), a comedy by Leonard MacNally, was brought out at Covent Garden in 1785. This is the only record of its performance in America.

The Child of Nature (April 19, 1799), a drama in four acts by Elizabeth Inchbald, had its premiere at Covent Garden on November 28, 1788. It was acted in Philadelphia and New York in 1793.

The players.   We have names of twenty-one actors, many of whom were new to this company. M'Kinzie, Tubbs, and Miss Arnold had played with the Sollee Company in Charleston before resigning to come to Richmond with West and Bignall. I suspect that the Taylor who played Sir Herbert Stanley in *A Cure for the Heart-ache* on December 14 and 24, 1798, was the same Taylor who made his debut in Charleston on February 11, 1799. Radcliffe may have been the same as the Radcliff who played in Philadelphia in December 1799. Pollock suspects that he may be the Ratcliff (also spelled Ratlief) who played there in 1791. The Mrs. Bignall of this season was, I think, the wife of John Bignall, Jr., son of Mrs. J. West, who was the Mrs. Bignall of former seasons. Five Wests appeared: Mr. and Mrs. Thomas Wade, T., J., and Mrs. J. Both Matthew Sully and Matthew, Jr., appeared.

The most interesting new player of this season was Miss Arnold, who performed a comic dance with Mr. Tubbs between pieces on December 21, 1798. Elizabeth Arnold had come to this country in 1796 with her mother, an accomplished actor, and Mr. Tubbs, who soon became her stepfather. Her first role was Biddy Bellair in *Miss in Her Teens*, which she played on November 25, 1796, in Portland, Maine, at the age of nine. She played Maria in *The Spoiled Child* in New York on August 18, 1797, then went with her mother to Charleston, where she appeared frequently during the season of 1797-98. She played leading roles in Philadelphia, New York, and other cities,, first as Miss Arnold, then as Mrs. Charles Hopkins, and last as Mrs. David Poe. She was playing in Richmond in 1811 at the time of her death, and her two children, Edgar and Rosalie, were taken into Richmond homes. Despite her distinguished career in the theatre, she is remembered as the mother of Edgar Allan Poe.

Interlude

Radcliffe and M'Kinzie

April 1799

M'Kinzie of Richmond was almost certainly the McKenzie of Charleston who in 1798 resigned, with others, from the Sollee

Company and joined West and Bignall. At the beginning of this season he played Heartley in *A Cure for the Heart-ache* and Bailiff in *Bannian Day*, both minor roles. Radcliffe played Bronze in *A Cure for the Heart-ache*, Captain Fitzroy in *The Poor Soldier*, and Lieutenant Goodwill in *Bannian Day*, all minor roles. These are their only notices during the season.

We hear from them with a vengeance, however, toward the end of the season. The *Virginia Argus* of March 29, 1799, carried this notice:

TO THE PUBLIC

In consequence of being informed, you have had a misrepresentation of the causes, which obliged us NOT to perform on Monday evening, for the benefit of Miss Gillespie (our names being inserted in the bills of the day) and fearing we might suffer in your good opinions, from a false statement industriously circulated, in order to impress your minds with an unfavorable idea of our Conduct on this occasion—We conceive it, therefore, our duty to vindicate our actions; conscious of the justice of our proceedings.—Briefly, the Manager's ill treatment of us, was the cause of our nonappearance—'twas not the fault of our own inclination, as has been reported.—The Circumstances of the affair in question, we defer till another opportunity.

Charles Lace Radcliffe
Daniel M'Kinzie

Richmond, March 28, 1799

Obviously, it was a quarrel between the two actors and the management. Lacking management's statement, we shall probably never know who said or did what to whom. I suspect that Radcliffe and M'Kinzie's published statement was in response to a curtain announcement on Monday evening, when, their names having appeared in the bills of that day, they failed to appear. Miss Gillespie's benefit, at which they failed to appear, was on March 25, the plays, *The Belle's Stratagem* and *A Trip to Scotland*.

Manager West probably suspended Radcliffe and M'Kinzie and fined them a week's pay. Then, after their audacity in publishing their charge of "the Manager's ill treatment," he fired them forthwith. They say as much in their next notice, which appeared on Friday, April 5:

NEW TEMPORARY THEATRE
In the Eagle Tavern Assembly Room
The subscribers have been discharged from the old Theatre at a
moment's warning, and placed in very disagreeable circumstances,
have received the very generous offer, by a Society of young
Gentlemen, to perform a Play, Farce &c for their Benefit—In
consequence of which they respectfully beg leave to inform the
Ladies and Gentlemen of Richmond, Manchester and their vicinities, that on Tuesday next the 9th inst. will be presented the
Celebrated Tragedy of *Venice Preserv'd; or A Plot Discovered.* To
which will be added the admired Farce of *Love A-La-Mode; or,
The Humors of the Turf,* with other Entertainments as will be
expressed in the Bills.
    Solicitors of your patronage we will endeavor, in conjunction
with the Society, to render the Evening's amusements as agreeable
as possible.

Charles Lace Radcliffe
Daniel M'Kinzie[59]

April 3d, 1799

The Assembly Room of the Eagle Tavern was adequate for
concerts and balls; it could be fitted up for plays. Radcliffe and
M'Kinzie were not modest; *Venice Preserv'd* was an ambitious
undertaking. *Love a-la-Mode* and the "other entertainments" were
less demanding. The farce, which had been acted in Richmond in
1787, required only seven actors, but the tragedy, as acted by
West and Bignall in 1795, required eleven. Assuming that Radcliffe
and M'Kinzie played leads in both, they still needed nine actors.
These evidently came from the "Society of young Gentlemen"; I
wish we knew who they were. They were probably listed in "the
Bills," which, as usual, have not survived.
    The performances must have been reasonably successful, though
receipts were perhaps smaller than hoped for. At any rate, there
was a second performance a week later. A notice on Tuesday,
April 16, 1799, announced:

Messrs. Radcliffe & M'Kinzie Impressed with the liveliest sense of
gratitude for the public patronage experienced by them on Tuesday evening last, at their infant Theatre—Respectfully beg leave to
inform the Ladies and Gentlemen of Richmond, Manchester, and
their vicinities, that the gentlemen of the Society, (having considered the receipts of the first night's performance Only Adequate
to the expenses unavoidably incurred in consequence of fitting up

the Theatre, &c) have with unbounded generosity, offered to assist in Another attempt to obtain a repetition of public favor.

Venice Preserv'd was repeated. Afterpiece was changed to "the admired farce of *The Ghost; or Dead Man Alive*." Between pieces was "a Ballet Dance *The Two Quakers; or the Merry Girl*" and the popular dramatic recitation of "Bucks Have at Ye All." No names were given. Admission was one dollar, with children under twelve at half price.

Tickets at Prichard & Davidson's Book Store, Printing Office of S. Pleasants jr. Mr. Davis' Printing Office, Office of *The Examiner*, of Radcliffe & M'Kinzie at Mr. Deggogue's, & on evening of performance at the Eagle Tavern.
The Theatre is neatly fitted up with new Scenery, &c. painted for the purpose.
Doors open at 6. Performance at 7.
Vivat Respublica.[60]

The Two Quakers had been presented by the West and Bignall Company on March 12; I assume that Radcliffe and M'Kinzie repeated their roles in this production. *The Ghost*, a farce of unknown authorship, had its premiere in Dublin in 1767. It was acted in New York in 1785, Charleston in 1786, and Philadelphia in 1798.

These two performances were apparently all of the Radcliffe and M'Kinzie rebellion. I assume that they left Richmond soon afterward.

FIFTEENTH SEASON
West and Bignall Company
October 1799

Chronicle. The West and Bignall Company ended their season in April. I doubt that the full company returned in October, although it may have been some of them (who had advertised as the Virginia Company in 1791, '92, and '93) who placed the following advertisement on Friday, October 11, 1799: "The Public are respectfully [informed], that The Virginia Company of Comedians Intend performing for the Race-Week, at the Eagle Tavern, To Commence on Monday evening October 14th, 1799, with a favourite Comedy, Farce and Entertainments, as will be expressed in the bills of the day."[61]

Whatever bills they distributed are lost; I have located no further advertisements. There was, I assume, a short season. Who performed, what plays were produced, and with what success. I do not know. The Eagle Tavern was a poor substitute for a theatre. Did Radcliffe and M'Kinzie organize a new company?

In concluding, I note an advertisement of November 5 of "a Beautiful African Lion to be seen at Mr. Bowler's Tavern" for a quarter of a dollar, children half price; "also a curiosity, The Learned Pig" for the same price.[62] On Tuesday, December 3, "Mr. Warrell, Principal Dancer from the Theatres Philadelphia and Baltimore" respectfully informed the ladies and gentlemen of Richmond that he was opening a dancing school.[63] We end on a mixed note: an African Lion, a learned pig, and a dancing master.

Perhaps the company moved in April from Richmond to Alexandria. Sherman says that Manager West was there in the summer of 1799, superintending the construction of his new theatre and living temporarily in the unfinished building. Her account of what happened on July 28 follows:

Awaking between the hours of three and four in the morning, he went into the theatre and stood where he could look down on the stage. What he saw, filled him with alarm. From somewhere on the dark stage, rays of light shone on the scenery. The memory of the Richmond fire was all too fresh in his mind. He rushed to the carpenter's gallery to get a better view of the source of that light. In his haste, in the darkness, with all his attention focused on the stage below, he tripped over one of the ceiling joists and crashed to the stage below. He lived only a few minutes after his fall, but those minutes were enough to assure him that his theatre was not to be consumed by fire so soon.

He was buried on the following morning with all the honors of a Masonic funeral. The "procession was attended by a vast concourse of respectable citizens" and the "dramatic performers also paid their tribute of respect." A stone was placed over the grave bearing the inscription:

To the Memory
of
T. W. West
Who Departed this Life July 28th 1799
Age 54 years

The stone still stands. It is beside the path which leads from Christ Church to the parish house. It is a large stone and the inscription is clear enough for the passer-by to read at a glance; but no one remembers. No one stops before the stone to ponder: here lies a gentleman who built five theatres in nine years; here lies an actor who played the grave digger in *Hamlet* from Baltimore to Savanah; here lies the man who brought the artists Lawrence and Thomas Sully, to this country—their uncle; here lies a Mason, Brother to George Washington, buried the same year by the same men with the same rites; here lies a great executive who lived and died before "the executive" gained the prestige he now enjoys; here lies the manager of the Virginia Company, the South Carolina Company, who for nine years maintained the best theatrical company in these newly-formed United States.[64]

The West and Bignall Company was never to be the same again. The end of Thomas Wade West marks the end of an era in theatrical history. Curtain.

CHAPTER IV

1800–1805

Hiatus, 1800–1802

In 1800 Richmond had a population of 5,737, a gain of two thousand since the census of 1790. By 1800 there was a substantial bridge across the James connecting Richmond and Manchester, river traffic was thriving, Broad Street extended several blocks west beyond the site of the theatre, and Mr. Jefferson's new Capitol dominated the city from Shockoe Hill. Indisputably the metropolis of Virginia, Richmond alone among leading cities of the state had no theatre.

At the turn of the century, the Richmond theatre suffered three serious setbacks: the burning of the theatre on January 30, 1798; failure of plans for the new Latrobe theatre proposed in 1798; and the death of Manager Thomas Wade West on July 28, 1799. Of these, the last was probably the greatest. At the age of fifty-four West was the established veteran of the Virginia circuit, operating theatres in Richmond, Petersburg, Norfolk, Fredericksburg, and Alexandria. For a decade he had provided Richmond with what Susanne K. Sherman considered "the best theatrical company in these newly-formed United States."[1] His death was followed by a hiatus which lasted for three years.

During this period there was, so far as I can determine, no legitimate theatre in Richmond. There were, however, many indications of continuing interest and frequent advertisements of public entertainments. On February 11, 1800, the *Virginia Argus* advertised "for Sale at this Printing Office" *Female Patriotism, or The Death of Joan D'Arc*, identified as "an Historic Play in V Acts, by John Burk—author of *Bunker Hill, Prince of Sufa* and other Dramatic Pieces." *Female Patriotism*, which Quinn considers Burk's masterpiece, was produced at the Park Theatre in New York in April, 1798;[2] there is no record of its performance in Richmond; *Bunker Hill* had been acted in Richmond in 1796.

The *Virginia Federalist* of April 26 carried an advertisement of a concert in the Eagle Tavern by Mr. Salter, a blind musician, "assisted by his Son 13 & daughter 10." Tickets were one dollar. There was dancing after the concert.

"The Dramatic Works of Baron Kotzebue" was advertised for sale "at William Pritchard's Book Store" in the *Federalist* of May 14. Three translations from Kotzebue were produced in the Richmond theatre during 1803 and 1804.

On October 24 James and Thomas Warrell announced in the *Virginia Argus* the opening of their "Dancing Academy" on November 5 at 10 A.M. There was also "for convenience of gentlemen an Evening School" at 6 P.M.

The Sully family was prominent on the Richmond stage for more than a decade. One of the sons, Laurence, became an artist instead of an actor. In the *Argus* of October 27, 1801, L. Sully, "Miniature and Fancy Painter," announced the opening of a "Drawing School" at his dwelling provided sufficient pupils apply before the first Monday in November.

Of especial interest is the announcement in the *Examiner* of November 4, 1800, that "Mr. Sully, Sen. having retired from theatrical Pursuits is induced by the solicitations of many of his friends to publish the Memoirs of his Life," described as "occurring in England, France, Ireland, Scotland, and lastly in Virginia and Charleston South Carolina in America." Price was one dollar by subscription. Evidently subscriptions were inadequate; the book was never published. Efforts to locate the manuscript in Richmond and Charleston have been fruitless.

On February 24, 1801, the Richmond Company, including M. Sully, C. Sully, Green, Davis, and Bignall, advertised in the *Norfolk Herald* a performance in the Norfolk theatre of *Secrets Worth Knowing* and *The Farmer*. Later advertisements announced performances of *The Mountaineers, The Gamester, The Romp, Barnaby Brittle,* and other plays that the company had acted in Richmond. This Norfolk season closed on July 7 with the benefit of J. West. Here is evidence that, despite the death of Thomas Wade West, the company continued. It acted, not only in Norfolk, but in the theatres that West had built in Alexandria, Fredericksburg, and Petersburg. There was no theatre in Richmond.

Again on March 16, 1802, the same company advertised in the Norfolk *Epitome of the Times* a performance of *The Village Law-*

yer and *Pizarro*, "written by Augustus Von Kotzebue, and adapted
to the English Stage by R. B. Sheridan Esq."

The *Argus* of Friday, March 27, 1801, carried an advertisement
of "*Plays and Poems* by the late Col. Robert Munford of Mecklen-
burg Co. lately published and for sale at S. Pleasants Printing
office, Richmond." Price was seventy-five cents. The advertisement
was repeated in several later issues. Although Colonel Munford's
son William had tried to get one of his father's plays produced in
Richmond in 1792 (see chapter 2), there is no record of a performance.

On May 1, 1802, "G. Green, M.D." announced in the *Argus* a
"Lecture on Electricity with Experiments" at the Free-Mason's
Hall on Thursday, May 6. There was also "Concise Definition of
the Historical Creation of the World in seven distinct periods, illus-
strated with Figures; and calculated to promote useful knowledge."
Tickets were "half a Dollar."

Also for a "half-dollar" Richmonders viewed in the Eagle Tavern
wax figures by Mr. Davenport, including George Washington,
Thomas Jefferson, and Mrs. Siddons.[3]

During the spring and summer of 1802 there were frequent
advertisements of Hay Market Gardens and Vauxhall Garden, both
popular places of amusement. On April 28 it was announced that
"the Hay Market Gardens in this City, are open for the Season."
Several "improvements" were advertised, including an "elegant
organ imported from London." There were frequent exhibits of
fire and water works, and amusements included "riding in the
Flying Gigs, Semivertical Coaches, etc." There was also a "Ball
Room."[4] On Wednesday, May 19, it was announced that "Mr.
Derieux has just arrived from Norfolk with a grand preparation of
Fire Works which he proposes to exhibit at the Hay Market Gar-
den on Friday evening next."[5]

Competition was announced in the *Argus* of May 12, 1802,
which carried an advertisement of Vauxhall Garden, "which has
been fitted out as a Pleasure Garden and will be splendidly illuminated with colored lights every Monday, Thursday, and Saturday.
Visitors will be entertained with a Band of Music and refreshments
of all sorts will be served." The garden was open every night; admission of half a dollar was charged on nights of illumination.

The closest approach to real theatre was probably at the Hay Market Gardens, which announced on May 19, 1801, that the gardens were open for the season: "The buildings that surround the Gallery are extensive enough to contain an audience of at least one thousand persons and admirably calculated for a Summer Theatre." The advertisement concluded: "Liberal encouragement will be given to good Vocal, Violin, Clarinet, Horn and Bassoon performers; a good set of players; Rope and Wire Dancers, or Equestrian Performers."[6] There is, however, no record that plays were performed.

During these years the company continued to play in the other theatres that Thomas Wade West had built in Virginia. Arthur Hobson Quinn's biography of Edgar Allan Poe traces the theatrical careers of the poet's parents.[7] Both Mr. and Mrs. Hopkins played with what Quinn calls "Green's Virginia Company" in Alexandria between July 25 and September 16, 1802. This was a part of the old West and Bignall Company, later the Placide and Green Company, which played Richmond between 1790 and 1812. Mrs. Hopkins, the former Elizabeth Arnold, later Mrs. Poe, appeared frequently in Richmond. She died there in 1811. Both Mr. Hopkins and Mr. Poe played in Richmond.

The best account of Mrs. West's management of the company after her husband's death is by Susanne K. Sherman, who from incomplete newspaper records follows theatrical activities in Richmond, Norfolk, Petersburg, and Fredericksburg during these years.[8] Assisted by Green, Mrs. West held the company together until her death in Norfolk on June 6, 1810. By any standard, in any place, at any time, Margaret Sully West was a woman of remarkable character and extraordinary professional ability. She is notable as one of the important figures in the history of the American theatre.

SIXTEENTH SEASON
West and Bignall Company
August–October 1802

Chronicle. The three-year hiatus ended on August 14, 1802. The last previous record of legitimate theatre in Richmond was in

October 1799, when the Virginia Company of Comedians played in the Eagle Tavern. After the burning of the theatre in 1798, the West and Bignall Company played in "Temporary Theatre—Market Hall" from December 1798 to April 1799. Market Hall was evidently more satisfactory than the Eagle Tavern, for it was to Market Hall that the company returned.

On Saturday, August 14, 1802, the *Virginia Argus* announced: "By Authority—Market Theatre—Richmond." "By Authority" indicates, as we have seen, that the company had the approval of the city authorities. It may indicate the opening of a new season. Plays were a comedy, *The Apprentice*; a farce, *A Preparation for a Cruize, or the Jovial Tars*; and a pantomime, *Harlequin's Shipwreck, or the Wizard of the Rocks*. No casts were given. The Harlequin pantomime consisted of "a variety of tricks and escapes, viz. The Magic Bottle and Enchanted Jug in which will be introduced The Skeleton Scene, taken from the celebrated Pantomime of Doctor Faustus." The evening concluded with "the much admired song of American Commerce and Freedom by Mr. J. West." The same song had been sung in the Richmond theatre by Bartlet on December 23, 1796.

The advertisement stated prices: boxes were one dollar, and gallery four shillings, sixpence, with "children half price." Tickets were on sale at the office of the theatre and at the Eagle Tavern. Doors opened at 6:30, with performances at 7:30, "no money taken at the doors." Just how Market Hall had been refurnished as a theatre we do not know, but "boxes" and "gallery" indicate serious effort toward a tolerable temporary theatre.

There is no further theatre notice until October. It seems reasonable to assume that the company continued to play during August and September, perhaps three performances a week, but no record exists. The Richmond season may have been interrupted by a visit to another Virginia city. The next advertisement appeared October 2, announcing for "This date the Comedy in five acts (never performed here) *The Poor Gentleman* by Coleman the Younger." There was also a "farce by O'Keefe *The Prisoner at Large, or the Happy Release*." Between the two was "a Song by J. West." No casts were given. The only other name mentioned is "Mr. M'Kenzie," whose benefit was this date.[9] M'Kenzie had left the company in the spring of 1799 after a quarrel with Manager West. I assume that he returned some time after West's death.

The significant item of this advertisement appears in capitals below the usual information about tickets and time of opening: "No People of Colour Admitted." To my knowledge, this is the first announcement of its kind for the Richmond theatre. Whether "people of colour" had been admitted previously (perhaps in a segregated section of the house) or whether there had always been some sort of gentleman's agreement on a lily-white audience, we can only surmise. Hoole states that "no admittance for People of Colour in any part of the House" was a fixed rule in Charleston at this time.[10]

The next advertisement appeared one week later, on Saturday, October 9. It announced for "This evening the comedy *The Poor Gentleman*" and "the Entertainment *The Liar*." No casts were given. Again there was "between pieces A Song by Mr. West." This performance was "for the benefit of the Poor."[11] Since benefits usually came toward the end of a season, I suspect that this season may have ended soon after.

This is the last record of performance of this season. Certainly there were others of which no record exists. I surmise that the company played from the middle of August to the middle of October, a season of perhaps eight weeks. There should have been three performances a week, perhaps twenty-four in all; we have record of only three, but all six plays were new to Richmond.

Only two names, West and M'Kenzie, are preserved. They establish this as at least a part of the old Richmond Company (the Virginia Company of Comedians) previously managed by Thomas Wade West. The company, including M'Kenzie, Sully, Martin, Perkins, Comer, and Hopkins, played *George Barnwell* in Petersburg on November 20.[12] Sherman says they played in Petersburg during December. They were back in Richmond in January 1803.

The plays. *The Apprentice* (August 14, 1802), a farce by Arthur Murphy, had its premiere at Drury Lane on January 2, 1756, and its American premiere in Philadelphia on May 4, 1767. It was acted in New York in 1768 and Charleston in 1774. A pantomime called *Harlequin Shipwrecked* was staged in Philadelphia in 1791.

I found no other record of *A Preparation for a Cruize*, which I assume to have been a rollicking farce concocted by the company.

The Poor Gentleman (October 2, 1802), a comedy in five acts by George Colman, the younger, was brought out at Covent Garden on February 1, 1801. Its American premiere was in New York on January 2, 1802. It was acted in Charleston on March 3, 1802, and Philadelphia on March 15, 1811. *The Prisoner at Large*, a farce by John O'Keeffe, had its premiere at the Haymarket in 1788 and its American premiere in New York on November 28, 1789. It was acted in Philadelphia on February 3, 1790, and Charleston, May 15, 1793.

The Liar (October 9, 1802), a two-act farce by Samuel Foote, was first acted at Covent Garden in 1762. It was acted in New York on January 30, 1777, Philadelphia, May 1, 1788, and Charleston, April 25, 1800.

SEVENTEENTH SEASON
West and Bignall Company
January 1803

Chronicle.   We know that the West and Bignall Company played in Petersburg in November 1802. Just when they returned to Richmond we do not know. Advertisements in both the *Virginia Argus* and the *Examiner* of Wednesday, January 5, 1803, announce that "tomorrow evening will be presented the celebrated tragedy of *Pizarro, or Spaniards in Peru*, with entertainments." The *Argus* informs us further that *Pizarro* was "written by Augustus Von Kotzebue, and adapted to the English Stage by R. B. Sheridan, Esq." It also adds the "new opera *The Rival Soldiers, or Sprigs of Laurel*" to the program. *Pizarro* was staged with "new Scenery, Dresses, Music and Decorations." The new scenery was "painted by Mr. Jones." Admission was one dollar; tickets were to be had at the office of the theatre; doors opened at five with performance at six.

The next advertisement appeared on Saturday, January 15: "Theatre: This evening will be presented the much admired Drama of the *Stranger*, with entertainments."[13] That is all. "Entertainments" presumably included an afterpiece and music between the pieces.

One week later, on Saturday, January 22, the *Examiner* carried this puff: "We learn that the Dramatic piece of *Oberon, or the Siege of Mexico*, written by Mr. Burke, author of *Bunker Hill*, is in rehearsal, and will be shortly brought forward for the benefit of Mrs. West, jun. This play was performed last season at Petersburg, to crowded houses, and received with distinguished and unbounded applause."

The following Wednesday both the *Examiner* and *Argus* carried advertisements of *Oberon*, the latter slightly fuller than the former. Headed "Temporary Theatre," it announced for "This evening, January 26, for the first time on this stage, the new Historical Drama, *Oberon; or The Siege of Mexico* written by J. D. Burke, author of *Bunker Hill*, &c." Afterpiece was "The Farce of *Sultan; or A Peep into the Seraglio*." No casts were given. The performance was "for the benefit of Mrs. West, jun'r . . . for Character, Scenery and other Entertainments, see the Bills." The program included "a Comic Dance" by Sully, "a Country Dance &c," and concluded with "a Comic Ballet Dance, called the Devil among the Taylors." Tickets were "to be had of Mrs. West, Jr. at the office of the Theatre"; doors opened at five o'clock with performance at six; and there was "no admittance behind the scenes." *Oberon* was produced "with New Scenery, Dresses, & Music, adapted to the piece," and staging included "in Act 2d, inside of the Temple of the Sun, Act 5th, the burning of the Spanish Camp." Clearly it was a major production.

This is the last advertisement of the season. In the same issue of the *Examiner* Mr. J. Rannie advertised ventriloquism, imitations of birds and beasts, a display of "Black Arts," and "Nimble Tumbling" at the Bell Tavern on Thursday, January 27. Admission was one dollar.

This season evidently opened early in January and extended into February. I hypothecate a season of about six weeks, with perhaps twenty performances. Records of only three survive, but they indicate that the company was offering first-rate fare: the latest works of the leading contemporary English and American playwrights. All five plays were new to Richmond. Only Mrs.

West, Jr., and Mrs. Sully are named performers, but this was undoubtedly the same company that had played in Richmond in 1802. From Richmond they went downriver to Norfolk, where they played from March 9 to July 13.[14]

The plays.   There were three English versions of August von Kotzebue's *Pizarro* (January 6, 1803): by R. B. Sheridan, William Dunlap, and Anne Plumptre, each in five acts. Odell says that Dunlap's version was acted at the Park Theatre in New York on March 26, 1800. Sheridan's version was first acted at Drury Lane on May 24, 1799. It was acted in Charleston on January 24, 1800. This Richmond performance was certainly Sheridan's version. The play was one of the most popular tragedies on the nineteenth-century American stage. *The Rival Soldiers*, a comic opera by John O'Keeffe, had its premiere at Covent Garden in 1793. Its American premiere was in Philadelphia on April 5, 1799.

The Stranger, or Misanthropy and Repentance (January 15, 1803) was a five-act drama by Kotzebue, adapted by Dunlap. It had its premiere at the Park Theatre in New York on December 10, 1798. It was acted in Charleston on March 13, 1799, and Philadelphia on April 1, 1799.

Quinn says that J. D. Burk's *Oberon* (January 26, 1803) was produced in Norfolk on March 23, 1803, and Odell records a performance in New York on June 5, 1805. There is no record of performance in Philadelphia or Charleston. Apparently the play had its premiere in Petersburg in November or December 1802 and was produced by the same company in Richmond in January and in Norfolk in March. We have records of only these three performances. A premiere in Petersburg seems likely since Burk was living there at this time. *The Sultan*, a farce by Isaac Bickerstaffe, was first acted at Drury Lane on December 12, 1775. It was acted in New York on May 3, Philadelphia, May 19, and Charleston, December 20, 1794.

The players.   "Sully" was probably Matthew Sully, Jr.; the senior Sully had retired in 1800. I cannot identify "Mrs. West, Jr." If Tom West was Thomas Wade West, Jr. (as I suspect), she would have been his wife.

Between Seasons

February–December 1803

On June 7 the *Norfolk Herald* advertised *Blue Beard* and *Prisoner at Large* with West, McKenzie, Bailey, Story, Comer—obviously the Richmond Company. Where they were between June and December I do not know; they were probably playing somewhere between Alexandria and Savannah; they did not return to Richmond until December.

There are, however, several items of theatrical interest in Richmond newspapers between seasons, the most important of which appeared in the *Examiner* on Saturday, February 5, 1803:

TO MASTER BUILDERS

A New Theatre is designed to be built on the lot of ground on Shockoe Hill where the old Theatre formerly stood, now the property of Mrs. West.

The funds necessary for the completion thereof, are raised partly by subscription and partly from the funds of the proprietor. Those disposed to undertake the Building, or a part thereof, are requested to send in their Proposals immediately to Mr. Meriwether Jones, who will show the plan, and from whom more particular information may be acquired.

N.B. The Subscription for the above building is still open.

The last previous effort to rebuild the theatre had failed in 1798. Evidently Mrs. West, having inherited the property from her husband, now intended to build a theatre to replace the temporary one in Market Hall, where the West and Bignall Company had been acting since the old theatre burned. Need for a new theatre in Richmond was obvious.

During 1803 there were various kinds of entertainment in several different places. Rannie the ventriloquist appeared again at the Bell Tavern on Saturday, April 23. There was "Grand & Ingenious Fireworks" at Hay Market Gardens on Saturday, June 25. On Thursday, July 21, Mr. Bernard presented "to the lovers of the Drama" at the Bell Tavern Assembly Room "the Dramatic olio, called *Variety, or The Feast of Reason.* In two acts, consisting of Comic Sketches, Songs, Stories, and Recitations, with additions and alterations." Admittance was one dollar. Two days later Mr. and Mrs. Hopkins and Mrs. Decker gave a program of songs and recitations in the same room.[14]

The Sullys were ubiquitous. On July 30 M. Sully advertised equestrian performances in Hay Market Gardens for next week, the circus there "being nearly completed." On August 24 he advertised equestrian performances and ground and lofty tumbling, "The Circus being completed with seats in the Upper and Lower Boxes." On September 14 Mrs. Sully advertised "a concert of Vocal & Instrumental Music at the Hay Market Gardens on Thursday September 15th. She will be assisted by several Gentlemen Amateurs of Richmond."[16]

Beginning Wednesday, October 26, an African Lion was exhibited at the Bell Tavern "every day (Sundays excepted)" for twenty-five cents. Prices which used to be shillings and pence are now given in dollars and cents.[17]

In the *Virginia Argus* of November 9 James Warrell advertised the opening of his Dancing Academy on Thursday, November 10, in a room over Mrs. Smith's opposite Lynch's Tavern on Main Street.

On November 16 a Mr. Story, "not long since from the London Theatre," passing through Richmond on his way to Charleston, advertised an "Entertainment of Music, recitation &c," and again on November 23 "a Musical and Dramatic Olio, assisted by Mr. & Mrs. Hopkins, Mr. M'Kenzie, and several Instrumental performers." On December 3 Mr. and Mrs. Cornillion, who had recently moved to Richmond, advertised to teach music, French, and drawing. They resided at Hay Market Gardens and provided music for entertainments there.[18]

The *Argus* of December 14 reported that "a new Historical Drama *Bethlem Gabor* by John D. Burk of Petersburg, author of *Bunker Hill, Prince of Sufa, Joan D'Arc, Oberon,* &c, &c, was performed the 2nd time in the Theatre in that town on Saturday evening last." Again on December 17 the *Argus* reported from Petersburg on the performance of *Bethlem Gabor, or the Manhating Palatine.* According to the *Petersburg Intelligencer,* the theatre was crowded and general satisfaction was evinced at the performance of this piece, which is acknowledged the author's best.

Quinn does not confirm this judgment of the play. He calls it a "wild melodrama laid in Transylvania, in which ventriloquism and mysterious mirrors are mingled in glorious unconcern with blood and tears." It was, Quinn says, performed in Petersburg by amateurs with the author in the title role, and was published in Petersburg in 1807 with a cast "which corresponds to the company at the Richmond theatre."[19] Although Quinn says that it was first produced in the Richmond theatre about 1803, I have found no record of its performance in contemporary Richmond newspapers.

EIGHTEENTH SEASON
West and Bignall Company
December 1803–April 1804

Chronicle.   The next season opened with this announcement in the *Virginia Gazette* on December 21, 1803:

RICHMOND THEATRE

The public are respectfully informed the Temporary Theatre, at Maj. Quarrier's will open this evening, Wednesday, December 21, 1803, with a celebrated Comedy, called *John Bull; or, An Englishman's Fire-Side* written by George Colman, Esq. Author of "Speed the Plough," "Poor Gentleman," "Heir at Law," &c. &c. and which has been received with more distinguished marks of approbation than any comedy since the "School for Scandal."

Afterpiece was "the Musical Entertainment of *Rosina*." Doors opened at five, and performance began "at 6 o'clock precisely." Tickets were to be had "at Mr. Pritchard's Book Store, at Mr. Davis's Printing Office, and at the Theatre. Admittance one Dollar." No casts were given.

Evidently the opening performance of *John Bull* was a success; it was announced again for Monday, December 26. This time the advertisement was headed "Richmond Temporary Theatre," and the afterpiece was changed to *The Poor Soldier*. No cast was given for *The Poor Soldier*, but a full cast was given for *John Bull*. It included several newcomers to the company, but some old familiar actors from the days of West and Bignall were still there:

Peregrine	Mr. Story
Sir Simon Roachdale	Mr. Clare
Frank Roachdale	Mr. Bailey
Lord Fitz Balaam	Mr. Barrymore
Hon. Tom Shuffleton	Mr. Sanfort
Job Thornberry	Mr. M'Kenzie
Dennis Brulgruddery (with Epilogue Song)	Mr. Green
Dan	Mr. West
Steward	Mr. Cane
John Burr	Mr. Martin
Lady Caroline Braymore	Mrs. Green
Mrs. Brulgruddery	Mrs. Lynch
Mary Thornberry	Mrs. West, Jun.[20]

Should any skeptic doubt that this Christmas performance was attended by an elegantly attired audience, I submit this item from the *Gazette* of Wednesday, December 28: "Found, at the Theatre, on Monday night last, a large Gold Sleeve Button, with the letters I.A.S. engraved on it. The owner may have it again by applying at this Office, and paying the expence of this advertisement." I assume that I. A. S. shook the gold sleeve-button off his dress uniform in vociferous applause.

The same issue announced for Friday, December 30, "a Celebrated Drama called, *The Point of Honor; or, The School for Soldiers.*" Afterpiece was "(for the first time here) The Comic Opera, in two acts, called, *The Turnpike Gate; or The World in a Village.*" *Point of Honor* included "a Grand Military Procession, with the regular order of Leading a Deserter to execution." No casts were given.

The next advertisement appeared on Saturday, December 31. Like most of the advertisements of this season, it was headed "Richmond Temporary Theatre." It announced for "This evening . . . a Comedy, from the German of Kotzebue, call'd *Indigence and Nobleness of Mind.*" Afterpiece was "the Musical Entertainment of *The Farmer.*" No casts or other details were given.[21]

Another performance of *John Bull* was advertised on Wednesday, January 18, 1804. Although no advertisements for January 1804 appear before this one, I estimate three or four performances a week. This performance of *John Bull* advertised the same cast as on December 26, except for Hopkins as Sir Simon Rochdale and Martin as Steward. Clare, who played Sir Simon in December, now appeared as John Burr. The rest of the advertisement is identical, except for change of afterpiece, which on January 18 was "(for the second time here) a favorite Musical Entertainment, called *The Sixty-third Letter*."[22]

On Saturday, January 21, the *Virginia Gazette* advertised for "This evening . . . the opera called *Inkle and Yarico; or the American Heroine*." Story played Inkle, and Mrs. Green, Yarico, the only actors named. Afterpiece was "the Farce of *Fortune's Frolick, or the True Use of Riches*," for which no cast was given.

The *Gazette* of Wednesday, February 1, advertised for "This evening a Comedy, *The School for Scandal*. To which will be added, (for the third time here) *The Tale of Mystery*, A Melo Drame." No casts or other details were given. Of particular interest is a brief item in the same issue:

WANTED

A person to contract for the digging and laying a foundation for a building, to be used as a Theatre, upon the lot opposite Mrs. Heron's, Shockoe Hill. Application to be made to Mr. Green, near Colonel Quarrier's.

Richmond, January 14th, 1804.

Here is evidence that progress was being made on the new theatre. The location was the same on which the old theatre had burned in 1798. The lot was owned by Mrs. West, widow of Manager West, who evidently made some arrangement with Green, who had for some time been leading actor in the company and who was at this time emerging as manager.

On Saturday, February 4, was advertised for "This Evening a Grand Romance *Blue Beard: or, Female Curiosity* to which will be added a Farce called, *The Midnight Hour; or A War of Wits*." No casts or other details were given.[23]

The next record of performance was Wednesday, February 8: "This evening a comedy *The School for Scandal*. Also the Grand Historical Pantomime of *The Death of Captain Cook*." Again, no casts and no details were given.[24] Both plays had been produced in Richmond before 1800.

On Saturday, February 11, was announced for Monday, February 13, "a celebrated Play *The West Indian* . . . to which will be added the Grand Romance of *Blue Beard or Female Curiosity.*" No cast was given for *Blue Beard*, but a full cast was given for *The West Indian*:

Stockwell	Mr. M'Kenzie
Belcour	Mr. Story
Captain Dudley	Mr. Clare
Charles Dudley	Mr. Bailey
Major O'Flaherty	Mr. Green
Stukely	Mr. Comer
Fulmer	Mr. Hopkins
Varland	Mr. West
Servant	Mr. Martin
Lady Rusport	Miss Melford
Charlotte Rusport	Mrs. West, Jun.
Louisa	Mrs. Green
Mrs. Fulmer	Mrs. Lynch
Lucy	Mrs. Story

No songs, dances, or other specialties were advertised.[25]

The *Gazette* of Wednesday, February 15, advertised for Thursday "a Favorite Comedy *The Cure for the Heart Ache*," with complete cast. Clark played Charles Stanley, "being his second appearance." No afterpiece was advertised; instead, the advertisement concluded: "(For the Farce, and other particulars, see bills of the day.)" This performance was advertised "for the Benefit of the Poor." I surmise that the terms of agreement between the company and the city authorities specified one such benefit each season.

The Cure for the Heart-Ache

Young Rapid	Mr. Green
Old Rapid	Mr. Hopkins
Vortex	Mr. Rutherford
Sir Hubert Stanley	Mr. M'Kenzie
Charles Stanley	Mr. Clark
Farmer Oatland	Mr. Comer
Bronze	Mr. Bailey
Heartly	Mr. Clare
Frank Oatland	Mr. West

Servants	Messrs. Santford,
	Martin and Barrymore
Ellen	Mrs. Green
Jesse	Mrs. West, Jun.
Miss Vortex	Miss Melford

On Saturday, February 18, was announced for "This evening for the last time this season the celebrated Romantic Drama *The Castle Spectre* . . . after which will be presented the Farce of *The Romp*." No specialties were announced, but complete casts were given for both pieces:

The Castle Spectre

Earl Osmond	Mr. M'Kenzie
Earl Reginald	Mr. Green
Earl Percy	Mr. Story
Kenric	Mr. Bailey
Father Philip	Mr. Hopkins
Hassan	Mr. Clark
Saib	Mr. Martin
Nunley	Mr. Clare
Alaric	Mr. Barrymore
Motley	Mr. Comer
Angela	Mrs. West, Jun.
Alice	Miss Melford
Evelina	Mrs. West

I note the appearance of Mrs. West as Evelina. Whether she had appeared previously, or how soon after her husband's death she resumed acting, I do not know.

The Romp

Young Cockney	Mr. Hopkins
Barnacle	Mr. M'Kenzie
Old Cockney	Mr. Clare
Captain Sightly	Mr. Bailey
Priscilla Tomboy	Mrs. Green
Penelope	Mrs. Story
Miss La Blond	Miss Melford[26]

The *Gazette* of Wednesday, February 22, announced for "This evening . . . the much admired Comedy, called *Speed the Plough*. To which will be added (for the second time here) the Grand

Pantomime, called *The Corsair.*" No casts or other details were
given.

On Saturday, February 25, was advertised for Monday,
"Shakespeare's celebrated Tragedy of *Hamlet.* Also the Musical
Farce *Flitch of Bacon.*" This was Green's benefit; presumably he
played Hamlet; no casts or other details were given, nor is there
any indication of the version or adaptation which was used.[27]

The next advertisement appeared on Wednesday, February 29:
"This evening (for the first time here) the celebrated Drama,
Rolla: or The Virgin of the Sun." Afterpiece was "the Farce *Miss
in Her Teens; or, A Medley of Lovers.*" No cast was given for
the farce, but *Rolla* was cast as follows:

Rolla	Mr. Green
Ataliba	Mr. Santford
High Priest of the Sun	Mr. Rutherford
Telasco	Mr. Clare
Zorai	Mr. Clark
Xairai	Mr. Comer
Chamberlain	Mr. Barrymore
Cora (the Virgin of the Sun)	Mrs. West, Jun.

This was Mrs. West's benefit, and Cora was a starring role.[28]

The *Gazette* of Saturday, March 3, advertised for Monday, "a
celebrated Comedy *John Bull; or, An Englishman's Fire-Side.*"
Afterpiece was "the Musical Entertainment *No Song No Supper;
or, The Lawyer in the Sack.*" The advertisement, which appeared
beside a three-fourth-column news story headed "Deplorable and
Distressing Fire!! Norfolk, February 25," announced that the proceeds of the performance were "for the use of the sufferers by the
Fire at Norfolk." The West and Bignall Company played in both
Richmond and Norfolk. No casts were given.

On Wednesday, March 7, was announced, "This evening, for the
first time in Virginia, the celebrated Comedy of *Hear Both Sides*
(written by Thomas Holcroft, author of "School for Arrogance,"
"Road to Ruin," &c. &c.)" Afterpiece was the "celebrated Farce,
(never performed here) called *Mrs. Wiggins.*" Complete casts were
given for both plays:

Hear Both Sides

Fairfax	Mr. M'Kenzie
Transit	Mr. Green
Headlong	Mr. Story
Melford	Mr. Clark
Sir Ralph Aspen	Mr. Hopkins
Steward	Mr. Rutherford
Quillet	Mr. Clare
Sir Luke Lostall	Mr. Bailey
Major Tennis	Mr. Santford
Gregory	Mr. West
Jones	Mr. Martin
Master of Hotel	Mr. Comer
Bailiff	Mr. Sully
Robert	Mr. Barrymore
Eliza	Mrs. Green
Caroline	Miss Melford

Mrs. Wiggins

Old Wiggins	Mr. M'Kenzie
Young Wiggins	Mr. Hopkins
Mr. O'Bubble	Mr. Green
Mr. Postop	Mr. Clare
Trim	Mr. Rutherford
1st Bailiff	Mr. Comer
2d Bailiff	Mr. Barrymore
1st Waiter	Mr. Santford
2d Waiter	Mr. Martin
Mrs. Chloe Wiggins	Miss Melford
Mrs. T. Wiggins	Mrs. Lynch

Between plays there was "a Comic Song—'What is Woman Like?' " by Hopkins and "a Song" by Story. This was M'Kenzie's benefit.[29]

A story in the *Virginia Argus* of March 7, on a celebration at the Bell Tavern on March 4, stated: "After dinner the following toasts were drank, accompanied by discharges of cannon from the Market Square, and appropriate music by the Band from the Theatre." March 4 was Sunday, and the theatre was dark. Just what sort of "Band," or orchestra, was playing in the theatre I do not know. Frequent comic operas and musical entertainments indicate an orchestra of several pieces. We have names of actors, but no names of musicians; even playbills did not list musicians.

The performance of Monday, March 12, was "for the Benefit of

Mr. Rutherford." Plays were "a Comedy," *Wild Oats, or the Strolling Gentleman* and a "favorite opera," *The Padlock*. No casts were given.[30]

On Wednesday, March 14, there was announced for "This evening Shakespeare's Tragedy of *Romeo and Juliet* . . . to which will be added, the favourite Farce of *Peeping Tom of Coventry*." No cast was given for *Peeping Tom*, but cast for *Romeo and Juliet* was complete:

Romeo	Mr. Green
Paris	Mr. Bailey
Capulet	Mr. Clare
Mercutio	Mr. Story
Benvolio	Mr. Rutherford
Tibalt	Mr. Clark
Friar Lawrence	Mr. M'Kenzie
Friar John	Mr. Martin
Balthasar	Mr. Barrymore
Apothecary	Mr. Hopkins
Peter	
Juliet	Mrs. West, Jun.
Lady Capulet	Mrs. Lynch
Nurse	Miss Melford

This was Miss Melford's benefit. Tickets were to be had "as usual and of Miss Melford at Col. Quarriers."[31]

With especial patriotic fanfare, the *Gazette* of Saturday, March 17, announced:

RICHMOND TEMPORARY THEATRE

This evening, the Comedy of *The Contrast, or The True American Son of Liberty*. (Written by a Citizen of the United States.) This Comedy has many claims to public patronage, independent of its intrinsic merits.—It is the first essay of American genius in the Dramatic art.

Afterpiece was "(for the first time this season) the admired Comic Opera of *The Highland Reel*." Specialties between pieces were "the favorite Song of 'No Indeed not I' by Mrs. West, Jun.," a "Song in character from the Comic Opera of the *Poor Soldier* by Mr. Bailey," and " 'Monsieur Tonson or the Humours of Tom King' by Mr. Green." This was Bailey's benefit, and tickets were to be had "as usual—and at the Swan Tavern (Manchester) and of Mr. Bailey, at Mr. E. Hallam's near the Capitol."

The same issue of the *Gazette* advertised for Monday, March 19, "a celebrated Play, interspersed with Songs &c *The Mountaineers.*" Leading roles of Octavian and Floranthe were played by Green and Mrs. West, Jr., the only characters named, and in the second act Story, Bailey, and Comer sang "Ye High-born Spanish Noblemen." Afterpiece was the "grand serious Pantomime," *Don Juan, or the Libertine Destroyed.* This was West's benefit.

The next advertisement appeared in the *Virginia Argus* of Wednesday, March 21. It announced for "This Evening a celebrated drama, altered from the French, called *The Point of Honor, or, The School for Soldiers.*" There was also "an interlude in one act *Sylvester Daggerwood, or The Actor in Distress.*" The evening concluded with "the musical Farce of *The Agreeable Surprise.*" This was Mrs. Hopkins's benefit. Entertainment included the following songs between pieces: "Ben Buckstay" by Story, "No Indeed Not I" by Mrs. West, Jr., and "Poor Old Woman of Eighty" by Hopkins, who also, in *Sylvester Daggerwood*, "will endeavor to explain 'What a Man is Like.'" Hopkins ended a big evening by playing the leading role of Lingo in *The Agreeable Surprise*, the only character named in the three plays.

The advertisement stated: "Tickets to be had as usual, and of Mrs. Hopkins, at Mr. Shields." Such announcements were usual for benefit nights. Evidently the actors boarded in several different houses around town: the Hopkinses and the Greens at Mr. Shield's, the Wests and Bailey at Mr. E. Hallam's, and Miss Melford at Colonel Quarrier's.

On Saturday, March 24, the *Gazette* stated that Monday, March 26, would be "the last night of performance, til Easter Holidays." Offerings were *Everyone Has His Fault* and *Tom Thumb the Great*, with, in the former, Green as Sir Robert Ramble, Mrs. Green as Miss Woodburn, and Miss Green as Edward. I have found no previous mention of Miss Green, yet the cast does not state that this is her first appearance; perhaps she made her debut earlier during the season. The title role of Tom Thumb was played by "Miss Decker, being her first appearance on this stage." This was Mrs. Decker's benefit. Between pieces Story sang "The sweet Little Girl That I Love," and Hopkins sang a "Comic Song." Cast of *Everyone Has His Fault* was given:

Lord Norland	Mr. Clare
Sir Robert Ramble	Mr. Green
Mr. Sollus	Mr. Hopkins
Mr. Placid	Mr. Bailey
Mr. Irwin	Mr. Story
Hammond	Mr. Comer
Porter	Mr. Barrymore
John	Mr. Santford
Edward	Miss Green
Lady Eleanor Irwin	Mrs. West
Mrs. Placid	Miss Melford
Miss Spinster	Mrs. Lynch
Miss Woodburn	Mrs. Green

The Mrs. West who played Lady Eleanor Irwin was not the Mrs. West, Jr., who had played Floranthe in *The Mountaineers* on March 19; this was the senior Mrs. West, widow of Thomas Wade West, former manager of this company. Mrs. West, Jr., was, I think, wife of Tom West, who may have been Thomas Wade West, Jr.

Both the *Argus* and the *Gazette* of March 24 carried the following notice:

At a meeting of the subscribers to the Richmond Theatre, held at the Eagle Tavern on Monday the 19th day of March, 1804, present, Eighteen Shares, by their Representatives.

John Marshall was chosen Chairman.

Resolved, That a committee be elected, to consist of five persons, who shall also be the Trustees of the company.

Resolved, That John William Green, James McCaw, William Cooke, Joseph Darmstadt, and John Foster, be appointed a Committee and Trustees, to have the powers which by the original terms of subscription are vested in the Committee and Trustees.

Resolved, That George Fisher be appointed Treasurer of the Company.

J. Marshall, Chairman

We have had evidence of John Marshall's interest in the theatre in earlier years. Now he appears in the leading role in efforts to build a new theatre. Here is also evidence of Green as manager, or responsible business agent for the company; he appears to have taken over leadership from the late Thomas Wade West.

Immediate action by the committee is published in the same two papers:

NEW THEATRE

Notice to Subscribers—The Committee appointed to superintend the building of the New Theatre, have directed that each subscriber pay, by the first day of April next, the sum of 50 dollars on each share, to their treasurer.

March 23d, 1804   Geo Fisher, Treasurer

Despite such aggressive actions, the new theatre was not opened for nearly two years. Whether delay was because of difficulties in financing or in construction I do not know.

On March 27, 1804, William T. Barry wrote from Petersburg describing a visit to Richmond:

The canal is a very grand work; the water is brought seven miles in it. I had not time to go up and see the locks. I visited the Theatre one evening, and was very much entertained with the performance. Some of the actors performed admirably, and all of them much better than any I ever saw before. The Theatre in Richmond is a very indifferent one; it is only a temporary thing; they are about to build a very elegant one. I was much pleased with Richmond and think it a very handsome place.[32]

Regrettably, he names neither the play he saw nor any of the actors who "performed admirably."

On Saturday, March 31, there was announced "the last night but two this season" for Monday, April 2, when "will be presented a Play, translated from the German of Kotzebue, called *The Stranger, or Misanthropy and Repentance.*" Afterpiece was "the Musical Entertainment of the *Children in the Wood.*" No casts were given. This was Mrs. Green's benefit. Between pieces she sang "Bright Chanticleer," and Miss Green gave "an occasional Epilogue."[33]

On Wednesday, April 4, was announced "the last night but one this season" with the "celebrated Play written by Kotzebue, author of *Pizarro, Stranger,* &c. called *Lover's Vows.*" Afterpiece was "the Musical Farce of *The Padlock.*" No casts were given. The performance was "for the Benefit of Mrs. Lynch, Messrs. Martin, Santford, and Barrymore," all of whom had been acting with the company throughout the season. I note particularly Barrymore, the first of his lustrous family on the American stage, who played minor roles throughout this season. There were several specialties: "an occasional Epilogue" by Miss Green, "Bright Chanticleer" by Mrs. Green, "The Moments Were Sad When My Love and I Parted" by Story, and "a Hornpipe by Mr. Santford, in Character of Harlequin, to conclude with a leap through a transparent Sive."[34]

Announcement of "The last night this Season" appeared in the *Gazette* on Saturday, April 7. Plays were "the celebrated Tragedy of *The Gamester*" and "*A Tale of Mystery*, a Melo Drame." Although this last performance was for the benefit of Mrs. West, widow of Manager West, no casts, specialties, or other details were advertised.

This season extends over three months. There are records of twenty-six performances and forty-four plays, of which twenty-one were new to Richmond. It was a strong company; fifteen men and six women are named, plus two girls. Repertoire included established masterpieces such as *School for Scandal, Hamlet, Romeo and Juliet,* as well as contemporary successes of the London stage such as *John Bull* and *Speed the Plough.* Two performances were apparently American premieres: *The Corsair,* some time before February 22, and *Sylvester Daggerwood* on March 21. That there were many musical afterpieces indicates vocal talent in the company. Spectacles such as *Captain Cook* and *Don Juan* made specially large demands upon stage facilities, which I suspect were minimal for such productions. Of especial interest during this season are efforts to build in Richmond the new theatre which was completed two years later.

I surmise that the company left Richmond soon after April 7, probably to play in Petersburg or Norfolk.

The plays.   *John Bull* (December 21, 1803) is generally considered the best work of the younger Colman. It had its premiere at Covent Garden on March 5, 1803, and before the year was out had been performed in three American theatres: New York, November 21, Charleston, November 23, and Richmond, December 21. It was popular on the American stage well into the nineteenth century.

Despite this subtitle, *The Point of Honor, or the School for Soldiers* (December 30, 1803), a drama in three acts by Charles Kemble, is a different play from *The School for Soldiers* by John Henry, first acted in Richmond in 1792. Both were adaptations from French originals, the former from Mercier, the latter from Sedaine. *The Point of Honor* had its premiere at the Haymarket in 1800 and its American premiere at Charleston on May 1, 1802. It was acted in New York in 1804 and Philadelphia in 1813. *The Turnpike Gate*, a comic opera in two acts by Thomas Knight, had its premiere at Covent Garden on November 14, 1799, and its American premiere in New York on June 8, 1801. It was acted in Charleston in 1802 and Philadelphia in 1814.

I have found no other record of Kotzebue's *Indigence and Nobleness of Mind* (December 31, 1803) on stage either in England or America.

The Sixty-third Letter (January 18, 1804), a farce by W. C. Oulton with music by Samuel Arnold, had its premiere at the Haymarket on July 28, 1802, and its American premiere in New York on November 30, 1803. It was produced in Charleston in 1820. Although advertised as "second time here," this is the only record of its performance in Richmond.

Inkle and Yarico (January 21, 1804), a comic opera by George Colman, the younger, had its premiere at the Haymarket in 1787 and its American premiere in New York in 1789. It was played in Philadelphia in 1790 and Charleston in 1801. *Fortune's Frolic*, a farce by John Till Allingham, was first acted at Covent Garden on May 25, 1799. It was acted in Charleston on March 16 and in New York on November 16, 1801.

The Tale of Mystery (February 1, 1804), a melodrama by Thomas Holcroft, had its premiere at Covent Garden on November 13, 1802. It was acted in New York on March 16 and in Charleston on May 3, 1803.

Blue Beard (February 4, 1804), a melodrama by the younger Colman, was brought out at Drury Lane in 1798. It was acted in Philadelphia in 1799, in Charleston in 1801, and in New York in 1802.

The Castle Spectre (February 18, 1804), a romantic drama by M. G. Lewis, was brought out at Drury Lane in 1797. It was acted in New York on June 1, 1798, and in Charleston on April 17, 1799, but did not reach Philadelphia until December 31, 1810.

Speed the Plough (February 22, 1804), a comedy by Thomas Morton, had its premiere at Covent Garden in February 1800 and its American premiere in New York in November of the same year. It was acted in Charleston in 1801 and in Philadelphia in 1810. The "Grand Pantomime" of *The Corsair* was, I suspect, the same as the pantomime by the same title recorded by James in Baltimore, Philadelphia, and Washington in 1814. It cannot have been Edwin C. Holland's blank verse dramatization of Byron's poem, which both Quinn and Hoole record in Charleston on February 18, 1818.

Although *Hamlet* (February 27, 1804) had been acted in Philadelphia in 1759, New York in 1761, and Charleston in 1773, this is the first record of its performance in Richmond. I surmise that there were earlier performances of which record is lost.

The original *Virgin of the Sun* (February 29, 1804) was by Kotzebue. Although there were translations by Frederick Reynolds and Anne Plumptre, this version was almost certainly the one by William Dunlap, which was acted in New York on March 12 and in Charleston on April 4, 1800.

Hear Both Sides (March 7, 1804), a comedy by Thomas Holcroft, had its premiere at Drury Lane on January 29, 1803, and its American premiere in Charleston on May 3, 1803. It was acted in New York the next day, May 4. I note that the cultural lag between the English stage and the American was often less than a year. *Mrs. Wiggins*, a farce by John Till Allingham, was first acted at the Haymarket on May 27, 1803, and first acted in America in New York on December 14, 1803.

The Contrast (March 17, 1804), described by Quinn as "the first native comedy to be produced by a professional company," was first acted at the John Street Theatre in New York on April 16, 1787. Its author, Royall Tyler, was born in Boston in 1757, served in the Revolution with the rank of major, practiced law in Maine and Massachusetts, and arrived in New York just one month before his play was produced. *The Contrast* was acted in Philadelphia on December 10, 1789, and was published there in 1790. It was acted in Charleston on February 25, 1793. Its chief comic character, the

Yankee Jonathan, was the prototype of the stage Yankee in later American comedy. Although no cast was given, I assume that the role was played by Green in Richmond. *The Highland Reel,* a comic opera by John O'Keeffe, had its premiere at Covent Garden in 1788 and its American premiere in Charleston on February 11, 1793. It was acted in New York and Philadelphia in 1794.

Sylvester Daggerwood (March 21, 1804), a farce in one act by the younger Colman, had its premiere at the Haymarket on July 16, 1790. It was first acted in New York on July 29, 1805, Charleston on March 6, 1807, and Philadelphia on April 5, 1811. Apparently this Richmond performance was its American premiere.

Tom Thumb the Great (March 24, 1804) as altered by Kane O'Hara was first acted at Covent Garden in 1780. The original burlesque opera by Henry Fielding was first acted in 1730, and was acted in New York as early as 1753, and Philadelphia in 1767. This performance was almost certainly O'Hara's version.

Lovers' Vows, or the Natural Son (April 4, 1804) was translated or adapted from Kotzebue's *Das Kind der Liebe* by Benjamin Thompson, Elizabeth Inchbald, John Howard Payne, Anne Plumptre, and William Dunlap. Dunlap's version was acted in New York and Philadelphia in 1799. Payne's version, a combination of Inchbald's (1798) and Thompson's (1800), was published in 1809. The version acted in Richmond was most probably Dunlap's.

The players. Was "Cane" an alternate spelling for "Cain"? Possibly this was the Alexander Cain who played in Philadelphia in 1799 and Richmond in 1811. "Martin" may have been the John Martin who played in Philadelphia during the 1790s. "Sully" was probably Matthew Sully, Jr. "Mrs. West, Jr." was not Mrs. J. West; I think she was the wife of Tom West, son of Thomas Wade West. I doubt that the "Bailey" who played regularly in supporting roles was the C. G. Bailey who was box keeper for this company in Charleston from 1804 to 1809; more likely, I think, C. G. Bailey would have been box keeper in Richmond. Clark, "from the Charleston theatre," played in New York in 1805, Comer in 1807, Rutherford in 1806, and Santford in 1808. I suspect that the "West" who appeared this season and several later seasons was

Tom West, perhaps Thomas Wade West, Jr., who dropped the identifying initial after his father's death in 1799.

Between Seasons

1804

In the absence of the actors, other entertainment was available. On April 18 the *Gazette* advertised:

SPORTS OF THE PIT

The Equestrian Circus at the Hay-Market Garden will be opened for the Sports of the Pit on Saturday next. A number of Cocks are collecting to furnish such as have not fowls of their own. Admittance as usual; the bearer of a Cock admitted gratis.

William Roberts

Of more immediate interest is the advertisement in the same paper of April 21:

RICHMOND TEMPORARY THEATRE

For the Benefit of the Free-School on Monday evening, April 23, 1804, will be presented, by a Company of Young Gentlemen of this city, the much admired Drama called *The Point of Honor.*
End of Play, A Hornpipe
Bagatelle's Song in character, by Mr. _____
A Song, by Mr. _____
A Song, by Mr. _____
To which will be added, A Humorous Farce, called *Love A-La Mode; or The Humours of the Turf.*

Admittance one Dollar. Tickets to be had at Mr. Pritchard's book-store, at the Bell Tavern, and at the office of the theatre.

Doors to be opened at 5, and curtain to rise at 7 o'clock. No admittance behind the scenes.
No person of colour admitted.

There were probably other amateur performances, but this is the best example we have. Moreover, it provoked the best piece of criticism we have found so far. The young gentlemen performed on Monday; promptly on Saturday, April 28, the *Gazette* published its evaluation:

"The hero is a youth—by fate designed
For culling simples—but his stage-struck mind,
No fate could rule—nor his indentures bind."

The Theatre has always been esteemed the proper school for correcting the little foibles and weaknesses of mankind, and no way is more likely to produce this effect than stage performances, where properly conducted. But no practice has also a greater tendency to promote dissipation, than theatrical representations, by characters unsuited for the purpose, or by youth habituated to other pursuits. While therefore, every encouragement and support ought to be given to able performances and performers; on the other hand, sporting clubs, and private theatrical parties, should be universally checked and discouraged.

It is therefore with sincere regret I observe, that the theatrical spirit, which ought to be confined to the description of characters which I have mentioned, has diffused itself among the young men of Richmond, who might have been much better employed than by exerting their talents in the art of mimickery. An entertainment of this kind was attempted last Monday evening, April 23, by a party of our youth, who in general acquitted themselves more to the satisfaction of the audience than was to be expected from a first attempt.

The Play which they selected, was certainly well adapted to the minds of Virginians. It was the *Point of Honor*. The Principal character, the Chevalier St. Franc, was performed by a young gentleman possessed of good theatrical address, and a correct delivery, but whose figure did not so perfectly correspond with the venerable and martial appearance of the Chevalier.

The character of Valcour was not performed with the same justness and feeling, but with a readiness and ease which merited the applause that was bestowed. The gentleman who performed Steinburg received the highest encomiums. The whole audience seemed astonished with the humor and address which he displayed in that character. He appeared to have studied and to have been intimately acquainted with the manners of some original Steinburg, who afforded him a model of decrepid stature, amorous old age, and deceitful cunning.

Durinnel, and the other characters, were also performed with considerable eclat and deserved approbation. The young gentleman who acted the part of Bertha, proved that the elegance of female manners was perfectly familiar to him, and that he was no stranger to the gentle softness and placidness of disposition so engaging in the beautiful fair.

The Farce was *Love A-La-Mode, or the Humors of the Turf*; a piece said to have been written by Macklin, the celebrated Comedian, for the express purpose of ridiculing the chieftain pride and poverty of the Scotish nation. The character of Sir Archy McSarcasm, which was intended to satyrize a Sir Archibald Grant of Grant, then notorious in London for servility and sychophancy of manners, was represented with much humor by Mr. L. who seemed to have a perfect conception of the farcical family consequence, which prevails among the lower nobility of Scotland, and which unfortunately continues the miserable appendage of several of their descendants who have crossed the Atlantic.

The Hibernian traits of Sir Callaghan O'Brallaghan were likewise well supported by Mr. Le M.— Between the Play and the Farce, a Hornpipe was danced by a young gentleman, who displayed great dexterity, agility and art. The Song of Bagatelle was done with character and humor by the gentleman who acted the part of Bertha.

These remarks I trust will not have the effect of exciting our theatrical youths to a repetition of their frolic; for, although on this occasion they perhaps may have surpassed expectation, yet they ought to remember their success and favorable reception proceeded more from the complaisance of the audience than from those rays of superior genius which fired the soul of Garrick, and blazed in the family of Kemble and Siddons.

Young men who have entered into respectable occupations in life, ought to have a proper regard for their characters, to prevent them from becoming the buffoons of the public; for however ingenious and laborious the profession of an actor may be, yet in all ages and in all countries, the gentlemen of the buskin have been regarded as connected with the lowest orders in society. It is however justice to remark, that the emoluments arising from the performance were designed for a laudable purpose.

A Friend to Youth

Whoever he was, this "Friend to Youth" was apparently well equipped for the office of theatre critic. Regrettably, he did not write regular criticism of the professional company. His article evidently stirred interest enough to draw from him this follow-up note, which appeared in the *Gazette* of Wednesday, May 2: "The author of the piece subscribed, A Friend to Youth, regards it necessary to inform the public, that the sentiments expressed by him relative to the character of the gentlemen of the Drama were not intended in any manner to reflect upon their profession, the merit of which he is highly sensible, but to benefit the youth of Richmond."

The young gentlemen were not discouraged; they persisted. On Wednesday, May 2, they acted *Speed the Plough* and *No Song, No Supper*, and on Monday, May 7, *Abaellino, the Great Bandit,* and *The Wedding Day.*[35]

This was an ambitious repertoire for amateurs. Of the six plays they produced, two, *Love a-la-Mode* and *No Song, No Supper*, were old favorites; two, *Point of Honor* and *Speed the Plough*, were contemporary successes; and two, *Abaellino, the Great Bandit* and *The Wedding Day*, are not previously recorded in Richmond.

The "Sports of the Pit" continued at the Hay Market on "Whitsun Monday and Tuesday," and on Friday, May 25, a "Masquerade Ball" there was "conducted with the strictest propriety." Writing in the *Gazette* of May 30, "Aristippus" conceded that some people oppose masquerades, and he answered their objections: "In every city or town, of the size of Richmond, it is necessary that some public amusement be encouraged as a bar to gaming and vice; and none certainly are more innocent in their nature and more attractive to the youthful mind, and likely to promote the feelings of tenderness and sentiment, than the Theater, the Concert, and the Masquerade." In addition to cock fights and masquerades, Signior Manfreidi, "Artist of Agility and Rope Dancing" performed at the Hay Market during the first two weeks in June.[36]

The most interesting item in the *Gazette* of May 30 concerns progress on the new theatre:

Richmond, May 28th, 1804

At a meeting of the Committee appointed by the subscribers to a Theatre proposed to be erected in the city of Richmond.

Resolved, That the treasurer be directed to call for a second instalment of 50 dolls. upon each share, by the 1st day of June next.

> John Drew M'Caw
> J. W. Green
> J. Darmsdatt
> John Foster

In pursuance of the above resolution, the subscribers are desired to pay their second instalment to their treasurer, at the time above mentioned.

George Fisher, Treasurer

The plays.   *The Wedding Day* (May 7, 1804), a farce by Elizabeth Inchbald, was first acted at Drury Lane in 1794. It was acted in Philadelphia in 1795, New York in 1797, and Charleston in 1807. *Abaellino* was a five-act drama translated from Zschokke by William Dunlap. It was first acted at the Park Theatre in New York on February 11, 1801. It was acted in Charleston on February 8, 1802, and Philadelphia on February 22, 1811.

NINETEENTH SEASON

West and Bignall Company

June–September 1804

Chronicle.   The West and Bignall Company probably played in Petersburg or Norfolk during May and June. They returned to Richmond at the end of June and advertised the opening of a new season in the *Virginia Gazette* of Saturday, June 30, 1804: "The Theatre will open, for the season, this evening, with the celebrated comedy of *Speed the Plough*, succeeded by the musical entertainment of *The Farmer; or The World's Ups and Downs.* Mr. Downie, from the Philadelphia and Baltimore Theatres, will make his *debut* in the character of Bob Handy. Mr. Poe, from the Charleston Theatre, will likewise make his first appearance, on our boards, this evening." Although no characters were named in *The Farmer*, a full cast was given for *Speed the Plough:*

Sir Philip Blandford	Mr. Clark
Morrington	Mr. Clare
Sir Abel Handy	Mr. Hopkins
Bob Handy (from the Theatres	
Philadelphia and Baltimore)	Mr. Downie
Farmer Ashfield	Mr. Green
Henry (from the Charleston	
Theatre)	Mr. Poe

Evergreen	Mr. Martin
Bob Handy's Servant	Mr. Barrymore
Peter	Mr. Comer
Miss Blandford	Mrs. Green
Lady Handy (being her first appearance on this Stage)	Mrs. Downie
Susan Ashfield	Mrs. Hopkins
Dame Ashfield	Mrs. Clare

The advertisement was headed "Richmond Temporary Theatre." Doors opened at six, performance began at seven, and tickets were on sale at Mr. Pritchard's bookstore, at A. Davis's printing office, and at the theatre. Admittance, which was not specified, was probably one dollar.

On Wednesday, July 4, the *Gazette* announced for "This Evening a Comedy *The Dramatist; or Stop Him Who Can.* Also the Musical Entertainment *Sprigs of Laurel; or, The Rival Soldiers.*" No casts or other details were given. This seems thin fare for the Glorious Fourth; why not a patriotic splurge?

The note of nationalism was sounded belatedly on Saturday, July 7, when it was announced that "this Evening . . . will be presented (for the first time here) a new Comedy, written by a citizen of Charleston, and performed there, with considerable applause, called *Liberty in Louisiana.*" Afterpiece was "the Farce of *The Devil to Pay; or Wives Metamorphosed.*" No details were given.[37]

The *Gazette* of Wednesday, July 18, contains three items of interest: first, the announcement of *Secrets Worth Knowing* and *The Shipwreck, or the Sailor Boy* for Tuesday. Although one day late, the advertisement included full casts for both plays:

Secrets Worth Knowing

Greville	Mr. Bailey
Egerton	Mr. Rutherford
Rostrum	Mr. Downie
Undermine	Mr. Clare
April	Mr. Clark
Plethora	Mr. Comer
Nicholas	Mr. Hopkins
Valet	Mr. Poe
Butler	Mr. Martin
Coachman	Mr. Lynch

Mrs. Greville   Miss Melford
Rose Sydney   Mrs. Hopkins
Sally Downright   Mrs. Bailey

The Shipwreck

Selwyn   Mr. Poe
Michael Goto   Mr. Clark
Shark   Mr. Comer
Harry Hawser   Mr. Bailey
Dick   Mr. Martin
Stave (a Parish Clerk)   Mr. Hopkins
Plunderers and Sailors, by the rest of the company
Angelica   Mrs. Bailey
Fanny   Mrs. Hopkins
Sally Shamrock   Miss Melford

There was also an advertisement of *The Stranger* and *Rosina* for Thursday, July 19. Only the two titles were given; "for characters &c" we are told to "see hand-bills."

The most interesting item was this announcement:

To the public of Richmond, Manchester, and their vicinities. The Proprietress and Manager relinquishing their interest (for the present season) in the Richmond Temporary Theatre, after the 14th day of July, 1804, have given the use of the same to the *company in general*, together with the scenery, machinery, wardrobe, and every other apparatus thereunto appertaining— The ladies and gentlemen of Richmond, Manchester, &c, are therefore most respectfully acquainted that the management has been allotted to Messrs. Hopkins, Downie & Clare: who beg leave to assure their friends and the public that no exertion shall be wanting, on their part, to render the Theatre and its amusements worthy their attention. They further pledge themselves to produce such new Plays as can be procured, with other *nouvelle* entertainments as may appear congenial with the tastes and feelings of the auditors.

The "Proprietress" was Mrs. West, and the "Manager" was Green. Why they chose to make this arrangement is left unsaid. I suspect that both were heavily engaged in promoting the new theatre, which was at this time under construction and which seems to have been proceeding slowly.

The next advertisement appeared on Saturday, July 21. It announced for "This evening the historical Comedy of *Columbus; or, The First Discovery of America*." Afterpiece was "The Farce

of *The Mock Doctor; or, The Dumb Lady Cured.*" No casts were
given, but between pieces Mrs. Hopkins danced a *pas seul.*[38]

On Wednesday, July 25, was advertised for "This evening the
favorite Comedy, written by Coleman, called *The Heir at Law.*"
A complete cast was listed:

Daniel Dowlas (Baron Duberly)	Mr. Clare
Dick Dowlas	Mr. Bailey
Stedfast	Mr. Clark
Henry Moreland	Mr. Poe
Zekiel Homespun	Mr. Downie
Kentick	Mr. Rutherford
Waiter	Mr. Martin
Doctor Pangloss (L.L.D. & A.S.S.)	Mr. Hopkins
Lady Duberly	Mrs. Downie
Caroline Dormer	Mrs. Hopkins
Cicely Homespun	Mrs. Bailey

The performance also included "the original Epilogue" by Clare,
Bailey, Poe, Downie, Rutherford, Hopkins, Mrs. Downie, Mrs.
Hopkins, and Mrs. Bailey. Afterpiece was "the Farce of *Miss in
her Teens; or, a Medley of Lovers,*" for which no cast was given.[39]

On Saturday, July 28, was advertised for "This evening, the
Comedy *The Soldier's Daughter,*" with a complete cast. After-
piece was "the Farce of *The Virgin Unmask'd; or, An Old Man
Taught Wisdom,*" and between the two was "a Pantomimic
Interlude, *Harlequin Hurry Scurry; or the Rural Rumpus.*" Cast
was given for *The Soldier's Daughter* only:

Governor Heartall	Mr. Hopkins
Frank Heartall	Mr. Downie
Malfort, Sen.	Mr. Clark
Malfort, Jun.	Mr. Rutherford
Captain Woodley	Mr. Bailey
Mr. Ferrett	Mr. Clare
Timothy Quaint	Mr. Poe
Simon	Mr. Comer
Tom	Mr. Lynch
William	Mr. Martin
Widow Cheerly	Mrs. Bailey
Mrs. Malfort	Mrs. Hopkins
Julia	Master Downie
Mrs. Fidget	Miss Melford
Susan	Mrs. Clare[40]

The *Gazette* of Saturday, August 4, advertised "Nights of performance—Tuesdays, Thursdays, and Saturdays," and carried a long criticism of *Douglas*, which had been acted on Thursday:

The admired and truly affecting Tragedy of Douglas was performed on Thursday night last at the temporary Theatre in this city, in a style that surprised and delighted those that were present. Every thing that could be expected from a distinct conception of the character she represented from correctness of judgment and force of feeling, Miss Melford displayed. In spite of the disadvantages of a provincial accent and a size not perfectly adapted to the part she played, the feelings of Lady Randolph were exhibited with a degree of propriety and pathos, that sensibly affected the audience. Mr. Rutherford played young Norval in a very masterly manner. The grand and generous emotions of the youthful hero, seemed to transfuse themselves so readily into the bosom of the actor, and were so forcibly portrayed by his aspect, voice and gesture, as to occasion for several moments that delightful delusion and *complete reverie*, which constitute the proudest triumph of dramatic art. This gentleman in the performance of various parts, has exhibited decisive indications of talents and accomplishments that would enable him to succeed in a pursuit less embarrassed probably by obstructions to emolument, utility, and distinction, than the dramatic. The ferocity, dissimulation and sullen misanthropy of Glenalvon, were represented with great fidelity and force by Mr. Downie. His soliloquys in particular were delivered with marked propriety and energy. The capital defect probably in this gentleman's mode of acting, arises from an injudicious management of his voice. Mr. Clare deserved and received cordial applause in the character of Old Norval. He touched the "true chord" of sympathy, and more than once made the tear trickle "down beautiful blooming cheeks." The subordinate characters, altho' they did not call forth the exertion of the higher dramatic powers, were very properly sustained. The smallness of the audience was the more regretted by those who enjoyed the refined pleasures of the performance, because it appeared in no degree to damp the spirits or enfeeble the exertions of the performers.

An Admirer of the Drama

The writer of these remarks would be peculiarly pleased to read a moral analysis of the tragedy of Douglas. To him it appears radically vicious in its construction and tendency. True—It wakes the soul by tender strokes of art: but does it not—Rouse hateful passions and corrupt the heart?

Whatever its faults of "construction and tendency," *Douglas* remained a popular favorite well into the nineteenth century. It may be remembered as Dennis Ryan's choice for the opening night of June 21, 1784.

Play for "This evening" (Saturday, August 4) was "the Comedy, written by Thomas Holcroft, called the *Road to Ruin.*" Afterpiece was "the Musical Farce of *The Flitch of Bacon; or Dunmow Priory.*" Complete casts were listed for both pieces:

The Road to Ruin

Mr. Dornton	Mr. Clark
Harry Dornton	Mr. Downie
Mr. Sulky	Mr. Clare
Mr. Silky	Mr. West
Goldfinch	Mr. Hopkins
Jack Milford	Mr. Bailey
Mr. Smith	Mr. Comer
Hosier	Mr. Rutherford
Jacob	Mr. Poe
Tradesmen, clerks, Servants, &c by the rest of the Company	
Widow Warren	Miss Melford
Sophia	Mrs. Hopkins
Jenny	Mrs. Clare
Mrs. Ledger	Mrs. Downie

The Flitch of Bacon

Major Benbow	Mr. Hopkins
Justice Benbow	Mr. Clare
Captain Greville	Mr. Comer
Wilson	Mr. Bailey
Kilderkin	Mr. Rutherford
Nat Putty	Mr. Poe
Ned	Mr. Martin
Tipple	Mr. West
Country Lads and Lasses by the rest of the Company	
Eliza Greville	Mrs. Hopkins

I note with interest the appearance of Mr. and Mrs. Hopkins and of Mrs. Hopkins's future husband, Mr. Poe, in both pieces.

The same issue of the *Gazette* advertised "*A Pick Nick; or, A Cure for the Spleen*" at Mason's Hall by J. B. Baker, "(late from the Theatre, Boston)." Baker's program included "Gustavus Vasa's address to the Delecalions," "The American Tar," "Patriotic Address Written by J. D. Burke," and "Garrick's Bucks Have at Ye All."

On Wednesday, August 8, was announced for "This evening the Comic Opera *The Highland Reel* . . . to which will be added a Farce, never acted in the theatre, called *Modern Antiques, or, The Merry Mourners*." Complete casts were given for both plays:

The Highland Reel

Shelty, (the Piper)	Mr. Hopkins
Laird of Col	Mr. Saubere
Laird of Raisay	Mr. Martin
Captain Dash	Mr. Comer
Serjeant Jack	Mr. Clark
Sandy	Mr. Bailey
Charley	Mr. Downie
Crowdy	Mr. Rutherford
Benin	Mr. Lynch
McGilpin	Mr. Clare
Moggy McGilpin	Mrs. Hopkins
Jenny	Miss Melford

Modern Antiques

Cockletop	Mr. Comer
Frank	Mr. Downie
Joey	Mr. Hopkins
Napkin	Mr. Martin
Hearty	Mr. Clare
Thomas	Mr. Lynch
Mrs. Cockletop	Miss Melford
Mrs. Camomile	Mrs. Clare
Nan	Mrs. Downie
Belinda	Mrs. Hopkins

Between pieces Mr. Saubere recited "Snow Storm." This performance was advertised "for Benefit of Col. Quarrier, Intended as an Emolument for the use of the Theatre this season." The advertisement also stated that "tomorrow evening will be presented, the Tragedy of *Romeo & Juliet*," but no details were given.[41]

On Saturday, August 11, the *Virginia Gazette* advertised "a celebrated Comedy, in 3 acts (never performed here) called the *Maid of Bristol; or, The Lady of the Haystack*. As performed in

London, Philadelphia, and New York, with unbounded applause."
Afterpiece was "(by desire)" the farce, *The Lying Valet*. Cast was
given for the play, but not for the farce:

Lindorf	Mr. Poe
Giller	Mr. Clare
Shultzer	Mr. Rutherford
Captain Oakum	Mr. Clark
Shark	Mr. Comer
Ben Block	Mr. Downie
Dr. Cranium	Mr. Hopkins
Clod	Mr. West
Stella (Maid of Bristol)	Mrs. Hopkins
Mrs. Oakum	Miss Melford
Mrs. Shark	Mrs. Clare
Fanny	Mrs. Downie

The performance was "for the Benefit of Mr. & Mrs. Hopkins." I
note that Mrs. Hopkins was playing leading roles during this season.
Between pieces there was "an Olio to consist of Recitations, Songs,
and Dances," in which I assume Mr. and Mrs. Hopkins performed.

The *Gazette* of Wednesday, August 15, advertised for "Tomorrow
evening . . . the celebrated Tragedy of *George Barnwell; or the
London Merchant*. To which will be added the much admired
Farce, written by Geo. Colman, Jr . . . *The Wags of Windsor; or
The Man of All Trades*." No casts were given. Performance was
"for the Benefit of Miss Melford & Mr. Poe."

This issue of the *Gazette* carried another advertisement by
Baker, who now called himself "Brother J. B. Baker" and who
announced "a species of Entertainment, *Whims of the Moment;
or, A Brush to Rub Off the Rust of Care*" at the Mason's Hall,
Manchester, on Friday, August 17.

On Saturday, August 18, there was announced for "This Evening
the Comedy *The Soldier's Daughter*" and "the Musical Farce *The
Agreeable Surprise*." No casts were given. Performance was "for
the Benefit of Messrs. Wiedemeyer and Bogatch." Since neither
name appeared in the several casts of characters of this season, I
doubt that they were actors. They may have been scene painters
or musicians, the latter I suspect from the performance between
pieces of "Grand Military Music, on the Stage Assisted by

Amateurs—Consisting of Clarinets, Flutes, Bassoon, French-horn, Tambour de Bass and Drum."[42]

On Saturday, August 25, was advertised for "This evening the Tragedy of *Jane Shore.*" Afterpiece was "The Serious Pantomime of *Robinson Crusoe, and His Man Friday.*" Cast was given for *Jane Shore* only:

Lord Hastings	Mr. Downie
Duke of Gloucester	Mr. Clark
Catesby	Mr. Saubere
Sir Richard Ratcliffe	Mr. Comer
Bellmoure	Mr. Bailey
Duke of Buckingham	Mr. Poe
Bishop of Ely	Mr. Clare
Porter	Mr. Lynch
Servant	Mr. Martin
Dumont	Mr. Rutherford
Alicia	Miss Melford
Jane Shore	Mrs. Bailey

The performance was "for the Benefit of Mr. & Mrs. Clare." Between pieces was "an Allemande, by Mrs. Hopkins and Mr. Lynch."[43]

The *Virginia Gazette* of Wednesday, August 29, announced that, "on account of inclemency of the weather the entertainments intended for last evening were postponed until this evening." The entertainments were the "Admired Historical Drama never performed here *Deaf and Dumb; or The Orphan Protected*" and "An entire New Grand Heroic Spectacle, compiled by Mr. Saubere, called, *Albert and Rosalie, or the Midnight Bell.*" For characters we are told to "see bills." Performance was "for the Benefit of Messrs. Saubere & Comer," and we are assured that "no expense or pains has been spared in getting up [Saubere's] Spectacle in the best manner possible." We are further assured of an unusual precaution, which I have not found before: "Persons are employed to keep all noise from the outside of the theatre during the performance." Specialties between pieces were a "Comic Song (Caleb Quotem, or the Man of All Trades)—Mr. Hopkins," a "Recitation, (Eliza, a pathetic tale from Darwin)—Mrs. Rutherford," and a "Recitation in character, (Jacob Gawkey's Travels)—Mr.

Hopkins." Mrs. Hopkins gave the "original Epilogue to *Deaf and Dumb*."

The Richmond *Enquirer* carried theatre advertisements infrequently. On this date, however, it not only duplicated the *Gazette*, but added to it. We are told that "the Overture and Orchestra accompanyments [were] selected and composed by Mr. Decker." We are further told that Mrs. Hopkins (the only player named) played "Julio, (the Orphan under the name of Theodore,)" and that *Deaf and Dumb*, "never performed here [was] translated from the French of Monsieur Builley, and performed in London, New York, Philadelphia, and Boston with the most unbounded applause."

The last advertisement of the season appeared in the *Virginia Gazette* of Saturday, September 1. It announced for "This evening a Comedy *Heigho for a Husband, or the Female Fortune Hunters*, being a parody on Faquer's admired Comedy of *The Beaux Stratagem*." Afterpiece was "the Comic Opera *The Shipwreck; or the Sailor Boys*." Between the two was "a Pantomimical Ballet, called *The Scheming Milliners, or a Beau New Trimmed*," in the course of which was "an Allemande by Mrs. Hopkins, Mr. Poe, and Mr. Lynch. The whole to conclude with a Dance by the characters." No cast of characters was given for any of the three pieces. Performance was "for the Benefit of Messrs. Bailey and Martin."

This is the last record of performance this season. No closing date was specified in advertisements. I hypothecate a season of about eight weeks extending from June to September. If we estimate three performances per week, there should have been twenty-four; we have record of seventeen. The repertoire contained an unusual number of new plays, eighteen out of thirty-four, and included a variety of offerings: tragedy, comedy, farce, comic opera, pantomime. There were old favorites (*Romeo and Juliet, Douglas*) and contemporary successes of the London stage (*The Soldier's Daughter, The Maid of Bristol*). There was one probable American premiere: *Deaf and Dumb*, by Thomas Holcroft, on August 29. There was one play by an American author, *Liberty in Louisiana*.

At the close of the season the company probably went downriver to Petersburg or Norfolk (possibly both); three months later they were back in Richmond.

The plays. *Liberty in Louisiana* (July 7, 1804), a comedy in two acts by James Workman, was first acted in Charleston on April 4, 1804, and was published there during the year. It was acted in New York on May 12, 1804.

Secrets Worth Knowing (July 17, 1804), a comedy by Thomas Morton, had its premiere at Covent Garden on January 11, 1798, and its American premiere in New York on December 19, less than a year later. It was acted in Charleston on January 25 and in Philadelphia on February 5, 1799. *The Shipwreck*, a comic opera by the younger Colman, with music by Samuel Arnold, had its premiere at Drury Lane on December 19, 1796. It was acted in Philadelphia on March 2, 1798, and in New York on February 18, 1799. This is not the same play as *The Shipwreck* by Richard Cumberland, which had been acted in Charleston in 1774.

Columbus (July 21, 1804), a comedy by Thomas Morton, was first acted at Covent Garden on December 1, 1792. It was acted in Philadelphia on January 30, 1797, New York, September 15, 1797, and Charleston February 10, 1800. Odell describes the New York production as "scenic splendor unbounded." *The Mock Doctor* was a farce by Henry Fielding, first performed at Drury Lane in 1732. It was acted in New York in 1750, Charleston, 1754, and Philadelphia, 1759.

The Heir at Law (July 25, 1804), a comedy by George Colman, the younger, was brought out at the Haymarket on July 15, 1797. It was acted in Philadelphia on February 13, 1799, New York, April 24, 1799, and Charleston, January 8, 1800.

The Soldier's Daughter (July 28, 1804), a comedy by Andrew Cherry, was first acted at Drury Lane on February 7, 1804. Its American premiere was in New York on April 18, 1804. It was acted in Charleston on December 24, 1804, but did not reach Philadelphia until 1811. *The Virgin Unmask'd*, a farce by Henry Fielding, was first acted at Drury Lane in 1734. It was acted in New York in 1750, Philadelphia, 1759, and Charleston, 1800. *Harlequin Hurry Scurry* is recorded in Philadelphia in 1795 by Pollock, who attributes it to William Francis. I have found no record of performance elsewhere.

The Maid of Bristol (August 11, 1804), a melodrama by James Boaden, had its premiere at the Haymarket in August 1803 and its

American premiere in New York in December of the same year. It was acted in Charleston on April 12, 1804. *The Lying Valet* (August 11, 1804), a farce by David Garrick, was first acted at Goodman's Fields in 1741. It was acted in New York in 1750, Philadelphia, 1759, and Charleston, 1766.

The Review, or the Wags of Windsor (August 16, 1804), was a farce by George Colman, the younger, first acted at the Haymarket on September 2, 1800. It was acted in New York on May 13, 1803, and Charleston December 5, 1804, but did not reach Philadelphia until 1810.

Jane Shore (August 25, 1804), a tragedy by Nicholas Rowe, was brought out at Drury Lane in 1714. It was acted in New York, 1754, Charleston, 1763, and Philadelphia, 1766. *Robinson Crusoe,* a pantomime attributed to R. B. Sheridan, was performed at Drury Lane in 1781, New York, 1786, Philadelphia, 1787, and Charleston, 1794.

Deaf and Dumb, or the Orphan Protected (August 29, 1804) was probably Thomas Holcroft's adaptation of Jean Bouilly's *L'Abbé de l'Épée*, first acted at Drury Lane on February 24, 1801. Another adaptation by William Dunlap, titled *Abbé de l'Épée, or the Dumb Made Eloquent,* was first acted in New York on March 9, 1801. Hoole identifies the version which was acted in Charleston on January 23, 1802, as Dunlap's. The title advertised for the Richmond production, however, indicates Holcroft's version rather than Dunlap's; if so, this may have been its American premiere. I have found record of no other performance of Saubere's *Albert and Rosalie.*

Heigho for a Husband (September 1, 1804), a comedy by Francis Waldron, was brought out at the Haymarket on January 14, 1794. It was acted in New York on May 14, 1795, and in Philadelphia on April 24, 1797. *The Scheming Milliners* is attributed to William Francis by Pollock, who records a performance in Philadelphia in 1794. It was probably the same pantomime recorded by Odell in New York in 1811.

The players.   This was a company of able and experienced actors, most of whom had appeared in Richmond before. Newcomers included Mr. and Mrs. Downie and David Poe. Mrs. Hopkins, the former Miss Elizabeth Arnold, had married Charles Hopkins in 1802. He died in Washington on October 26, 1805, and she married David Poe on March 14, 1806. Names of twenty actors appear in advertisements of this season.

Between Seasons

September–December 1804

The last advertisement located was for September 1; I assume that the season closed then or soon after. Interest in the theatre continued, however, attested by a long article in the *Enquirer* of Wednesday, September 12, 1804. The writer, "Eugenius," is advocating an Academy for Richmond, where, he says,

there exists no permanent institution for the instruction of youth. In Richmond there are taverns and stores in abundance, but there is *no Academy.* A Theatre is now nearly compleated, a sum amply sufficient for this purpose, was readily collected by subscription; *but there is no Academy in Richmond. . . .* A lottery, the last resource of the desperate projector, was resorted to and granted [a $20,000 lottery had been approved by the State Legislature], but the tickets fell very slowly. The writer of these remarks, begs leave to invite the attention of young gentlemen in Richmond, to the following plans for accelerating and extending the sale of the tickets. No amusement is more rational and attractive than dramatic exhibitions. To act a play with propriety and spirit requires a combination of accomplishments brilliant and rare. A sound judgment, refined taste, exquisite sensibility and graceful elocution, are obvious and indispensible constituents of dramatic skill. These are qualities which every young man of liberal mind is anxious to cultivate and proud to display. Can any amusement be mentioned more improving and attractive, or more perfectly disconnected from whatever has a tendency to degrade and deprave the mind? Under these impressions I invite a sufficient number of young gentlemen of this place to unite for the purpose of acting some popular and instructive tragedy, Pizarro, Cato, Gustavus Vasa, The Force of Calumny, &c.–Let the monies collected, after deducting the incidental expenses of the exhibition, be appropriated to purchase tickets in the lottery, for building an Academy in Richmond.

"Eugenius" was, I think, Mr. Clare of the theatre company. Announcement of his performance with local amateurs was published in the *Virginia Gazette* on Saturday, September 29:

RICHMOND TEMPORARY THEATRE
Mr. Clare

With the greatest respect, begs leave to inform the Ladies and Gentlemen of Richmond, Manchester, and their vicinities, that in consequence of his having left the Theatre, and become a resident of this city, to follow his original profession, a number of young Gentlemen Amateurs have very generously offered their assistance, by performing a Play, Farce, and other Entertainments for his Benefit for the express purpose of enabling him to carry this, his determination, into proper effect—on which occasion he hopes for the kind indulgence and patronage of a generous and liberal public, which will be gratefully remembered.

This Evening, Saturday, Sept 29, will be presented, the celebrated Tragedy, written by Dr. Young, author of "Night Thoughts," &c. called *The Revenge.*

To which will be added, a Farce, called *Love-A-La-Mode*, with a variety of other Entertainments as expressed in the bills.

Tickets to be had at the Bell Tavern, at the Eagle Tavern, at Mr. Pritchard's Book Store, at A. Davis's Printing Office, and at the Theatre—price One Dollar. Doors to be opened at six, performance to begin at seven o'clock precisely.

Nothing was said about the lottery or the academy, but I assume that this production was the result of the proposal which had been made two weeks before. Confirmation of my assumption comes two weeks later, in the *Enquirer* of Saturday, October 13: "The Tragedy of the *Revenge* will be performed at the Temporary Theatre this evening, by a company of young gentlemen, for the benefit of the Richmond Academy. For particulars see bills."

Evidently there were two performances of *The Revenge*, the first for Mr. Clare, the second for the academy. Possibly there were others; I found record of just these two. No critic attests the success of the performances, but the lottery failed and the academy was not built. Mr. Clare did not act with the company during its next season, but he was with them when they opened the new theatre in January 1806.

TWENTIETH SEASON
West and Bignall Company
December 1804–February 1805

Chronicle. The company probably returned to Richmond early in December. The first advertisement appeared in the *Virginia Gazette* on Saturday, December 8, 1804. Headed "Richmond Temporary Theatre," it announced for "This evening the Comic Opera *Inkle and Yarico; or, The American Heroine.*" Afterpiece was "for the first time in this theatre, a Farce call'd *Raising the Wind.*" Casts were given for both plays:

Inkle and Yarico

Inkle	Mr. Poe
Sir Christopher Curry	Mr. Green
Camplay	Mr. Downie
Medium	Mr. Comer
Mate	Mr. West
Planters	Messrs. Martin & Briers
Trudge	Mr. Hopkins
Yarico	Mrs. Green
Narcissa	Mrs. Hopkins
Patty	Mrs. Downie
Wowski	Miss Melford

Raising the Wind

Plainway	Mr. Comer
Fainwould	Mr. Downie
Didler	Mr. Green
Richard	Mr. Poe
Sam	Mr. Hopkins
Waiter	Mr. Briers
Servant	Mr. Martin
Miss Durable	Mrs. Downie
Miss Peggy Plainway	Mrs. Hopkins

Again I note the appearance of Mr. and Mrs. Hopkins and Mr. Poe in both pieces. No specialties were advertised.

The next advertisement appeared in the *Enquirer* of Tuesday, December 11, and the *Virginia Gazette* of Wednesday, December 12. Headed "Richmond Theatre," it announced for Wednesday "(for the first time here) a Comedy, written by Cumberland, author of the *West Indian*, called *The Sailor's Daughter*. To which will be added the Farce of *The Wedding Day*." No casts were given, but the advertisement stated that doors opened "at half after 5 o'clock, and performance to begin at 6 precisely. Admittance — One Dollar. Nights of performance will be Monday, Wednesday, Friday, and Saturday."

The *Enquirer* of Thursday, December 13, announced that "Tomorrow evening, Dec. 14, will be presented (for the second time here) the new Comedy, called *Hearts of Oak*. To which will be added the farce of *All The World's A Stage*." No casts or other details were given. Identical advertisements appeared in the *Enquirer* and the *Virginia Gazette* on Saturday, December 15, announcing for "This Evening the Play of *The Stranger*" and "the Farce of *No Song No Supper*." No casts or other details were given. The same issue of the *Enquirer* also announced for "Monday Evening ... the Tragedy of *Abellino*, with the Farce of *Raising the Wind*." No casts were given.

On Wednesday, December 19, the *Gazette* announced for "This evening the celebrated play of *John Bull; or an Englishman's Fireside* ... to which will be added the Farce of *The Village Lawyer*." Casts were given for both plays:

John Bull

Peregrine	Mr. Green
Job Thornberry	Mr. Hopkins
Sir Simon Roachdale	Mr. Comer
Frank	Mr. Poe
The Hon. Tom Shuffleton	Mr. Downie
Lord Fitzbalaam	Mr. Briers
Dan	Mr. West
John Burr	Mr. Martin
Dennis Brulgruddery (with the original Epilogue)	Mr. Serson
(From the Theatre, Boston, being his first appearance here)	
Mary Thornberry	Mrs. Hopkins
Mrs. Brulgruddery	Mrs. Downie
Lady Caroline Braymore	Mrs. Green

The Village Lawyer

Scout	Mr. Green
Snarl	Mr. Downie

Charles	Mr. Poe
Justice Mittimus	Mr. Comer
Constable	Mr. Martin
Sheepface	Mr. Comer
Mrs. Scout	Mrs. Downie
Mary	Miss Melford

Under the heading "Richmond Theatre," the *Enquirer* of Thursday, December 20, respectfully informed the public "that the proceeds of this evening are the only rent the proprietor receives for the entire use of the buildings now occupied as the Temporary Theatre." The word "buildings" is clearly plural. Previous seasons since the fire of 1798 had advertised "Temporary Theatre, Market Hall." This "Temporary Theatre" was evidently at Major (or Colonel) Quarrier's, as advertised on December 21, 1803. Mordecai says that following the burning of the Academy Theatre, "Theatrical performances were afterwards held in the upper part of the old Market-house on Main and Seventeenth streets . . . and after that in Quarrier's Coach-shop on Cary and Seventh streets."[44] Possibly plays were acted in Quarrier's coach-shop, with an adjacent building used to store scenery. During the previous season the performance of August 8, 1804, had been advertised "for Benefit of Col. Quarrier, Intended as an Emolument for the use of the Theatre this season."

Plays advertised for Friday, December 21, were *The Busy Body* and *Raising the Wind*, with no casts given. This was the third performance of *Raising the Wind* this season.

On Saturday, December 22, the *Enquirer* advertised for "This evening . . . the play of *The Stranger*. To which will be added the Comic Opera of *No Song No Supper*." No casts were given. This was the second performance of this double bill this season.

On Tuesday, December 25, it was advertised that "Tomorrow Evening . . . will be presented the Tragedy of *George Barnwell; or The London Merchant*. To which will be added, the Farce of *The Lying Vallet*." No casts were given. Between the two was "a Comic Ballet Pantomime, called *Christmas Gambols; or Winter's Amusements*, with an exact representation of a Sleighing Match, over a Snowy Country. In the course of the Ballet, a Strathspey, by Mr.

Poe and Mrs. Hopkins; and a Mock Minuet, by Mr. Hopkins, Mr. West, Miss Melford & Mrs. Stuart."[45]

Folly gave "a Concert of Vocal & Instrumental Music" on Tuesday, January 1, 1805, "with the assistance of Mr. Hopkins and others." Since the theatre was dark on Tuesdays, the concert may have been given there; no place was mentioned in the announcement.[46] Hopkins was a member of the acting company, as, I suspect, were the "others" who assisted.

Of particular interest is the following advertisement, which appeared in the *Enquirer* of January 1, 1805:

SALES AT AUCTION

will be sold on Wednesday, the 2d January next, at 12 o'clock, on the premises, for approved negociable notes in the Bank of Virginia at 60 days,

Six Very Valuable Lots, known in Quesney's plan of the Academy or Theatre, Lot, No. 1, 4, 5, 6, 7, 9, the situation of which is inferior to very few, if any lots in the city of Richmond. The plan may be seen at the office of the subscribers.

December 25   Prosser & Moncure, V.M.'s

Another notice on page three of the same issue stated that the sale was postponed "until Tuesday next, the 8th instant."

From this notice I surmise that, despite John Marshall's chairmanship, raising money for the new theatre was slow and difficult, and now Mrs. West, probably advised by Marshall and Manager Green, was selling part of the land left her by her late husband in order to raise money for the completion of the theatre, which had been under construction for at least a year. I assume that sale of these lots produced enough money to finish the theatre, which was opened a year later.

At this time the *Virginia Argus* did not carry theatre advertisements. The issue of January 2, 1805, however, published a brief item on Cooper, then playing in New York. At the close of his New York engagement, he was to leave for Philadelphia and Charleston. He did not deign to play in Richmond's temporary theatre.

The next advertisement appeared January 3: "This evening . . . will be presented a celebrated Comedy, called *The Poor Gentle-*

man . . . to which will be added the Farce of *The Adopted Child*."
Between the two was a repetition of *Christmas Gambols*. Casts
were given for all three:

The Poor Gentleman

Lieutenant Worthington	Mr. Green
Doctor Ollapod	Mr. Hopkins
Sir Charles Cropland	Mr. Poe
Sir Robert Bramble	Mr. Comer
Frederick	Mr. Downie
Farmer Harrowby	Mr. Martin
Stephen Harrowby	Mr. Briers
Warner	Mr. Serson
Corporal Foss	Mr. West
Emily Worthington	Mrs. Hopkins
Miss Lucretia McTab	Miss Melford
Mary Harrowby	Mrs. Stuart
Dame Harrowby	Mrs. Downie

Christmas Gambols

Billy Puff	Mr. Hopkins
Tom Tough	Mr. Poe
John Bull	Mr. Briers
Lawyer Latitat	Mr. West
Double Chalk	Mr. Martin
Doctor Bolus	Mr. Downie
Sailor	Mr. Comer
Mrs. Latitat	Miss Melford
Sally Trueheart	Mrs. Hopkins
Betsy Crosstitch	Mrs. Stuart
Mrs. Bull	Mrs. Downie

The Adopted Child

Sir Bertram	Mr. Downie
LeSage	Mr. Poe
Spruce	Mr. West
Record	Mr. Hopkins
Michael	Mr. Green
Flint	Mr. Martin
Clara	Mrs. Hopkins
Lucy	Mrs. Green
Nell	Miss Melford
Jannette	Mrs. Stuart
The Adopted Child	Miss Green

This was Hopkins's benefit. In addition to three acting roles, he danced a "Mock Minuet" with West, Miss Melford, and Mrs. Stuart, and sang "a New Song called the Birth, Christening, Marriage, &c. of Dennis Brulgruddery." Mrs. Hopkins contributed her full share: she also played three acting roles and, in addition, joined Poe in a strathspey "in the course of the Ballet." Poe also played three roles in the course of the evening.[47]

On Saturday, January 5, the *Enquirer* advertised for "This Evening . . . the first time here, a Comedy called *Notoriety; or A Dash at the Day* . . . to which will be added, for the last time this season, the Farce of *Raising the Wind*." Casts were given for both plays:

Notoriety

Nominal	Mr. Green
Colonel Hubbub	Mr. Comer
Sir Andrew Acid	Mr. Hopkins
Lord Jargon	Mr. Downie
Clairville	Mr. Poe
Saunter	Mr. Martin
James	Mr. Briers
O'Whack	Mr. Serson
Lady Acid	Miss Melford
Miss Sophia Strangeways	Mrs. Green
Honoria	Mrs. Hopkins

Cast for *Raising the Wind* was the same as on December 8, 1804. This was Green's benefit; he played Nominal in *Notoriety*, Didler in *Raising the Wind*, and between the two recited Collins's "Ode on the Passions." Mrs. Green played Miss Sophia Strangeways in *Notoriety*. Despite the claim of "first time here," *Notoriety* had been acted in Richmond in 1796.

On Friday, January 11, the *Enquirer* announced for "This Evening . . . *The Point of Honor*, with the Comedy of *Robin Hood*." It was Miss Melford's benefit. No casts were given.

The next advertisement appeared on Friday, January 18. It announced for "This Evening . . . a celebrated Comedy, never performed here, called *Partnership Dissolv'd, or the Secret* . . . to which will be added (the first time these five years) the Musical Entertainment of *The Prize, or 2, 5, 3, 8*." Between the two was "a Pantomimical Ballet, entitled *The American Tar, or, Naval Gar-*

land." The only character named was Caroline in *The Prize*, played by Mrs. Green. This was Mrs. Hopkins's benefit. At the end of the play she sang "The Wounded Hussar," and "in the Course of the Ballet" danced a hornpipe and joined Poe and Briers in an allemande.[48]

The *Virginia Argus* of Saturday, January 26, advertised a concert at Free Mason's Hall on Wednesday, January 30, for the benefit of Master August Petticolas. Mr. and Mrs. Hopkins sang. Tickets were one dollar. Possibly because of the concert, performance in the theatre was on Tuesday instead of Wednesday. On Tuesday, January 29, the *Enquirer* advertised for "This Evening . . . a celebrated Tragedy, call'd *Venice Preserved, or a Plot Discovered* . . . to which will be added, the Comic opera of the *Agreeable Surprise.*" This was Mrs. Green's benefit, but no casts record her roles. There was, however, between pieces, a hornpipe by Miss Green.

Last advertisement of this season appeared Tuesday, February 12. It announced for "This Evening . . . the favourite Entertainment of *The Spoil'd Child.*" The only character named was Young Pickle in *The Spoiled Child*, played by Mrs. Hopkins. "In the course of the Evening" Mrs. Hopkins danced a hornpipe, and Mr. Hopkins sang "Old Woman of Eighty; with a comic dance in character." Performance began "at 1/2 past 6," and tickets were to be had "at Mr. Pritchard's Book-Store, at the office of *The Enquirer*, and at the Theatre."[49]

From this season there are records of fifteen performances, the first on December 8, 1804, the last on February 12, 1805. I assume a season of at least eight weeks. If there were (as advertised) four performances each week, there would have been at least thirty-two performances. There are records of twenty-six different plays, including tragedy, comedy, farce, ballet. There are no descriptions of elaborate stage effects, with the possible exception of the sleighing scene in *Christmas Gambols*. There were several musical productions, and frequent singing and dancing between pieces. There were six plays not previously recorded in Richmond: *The American Tar, Christmas Gambols, Hearts of Oak, Partnership Dissolved, Raising the Wind, The Sailor's Daughter*, of which one, *The Sailor's Daughter*, was an American premiere.

The season probably ended on February 12, or soon after. Quinn records "Green's Virginia Company" in Norfolk in April, Baltimore in June, and Washington from September 9 to December 21, 1805.[50] There was no legitimate theatre in Richmond until the opening of the new theatre in 1806.

The plays. *Raising the Wind* (December 8, 1804), a farce by James Kenney, was first acted at Covent Garden on November 5, 1803. It was acted in New York on May 14, 1804, and Charleston November 16, 1804.

The Sailor's Daughter (December 12, 1804), a comedy by Richard Cumberland, had its premiere at Drury Lane on April 7, 1804. It was acted in New York on March 15, 1805, and Charleston March 23, 1805, but did not reach Philadelphia until 1813. This Richmond performance is apparently its American premiere, eight months after its premiere at Drury Lane.

Hearts of Oak (December 14, 1804), a comedy by John Till Allingham, had its premiere at Drury Lane on November 19, 1803, and its American premiere in New York on May 14, 1804. It was acted in Charleston on May 6, 1805.

Christmas Gambols (December 26, 1804) was evidently a specialty prepared by the company for the occasion. It was not, I think, the same as *Christmas Gambols, or Harlequin in the Moon* presented in New York on December 26, 1801, or *Christmas Frolick, or Harlequin's Gambols* presented in Philadelphia on December 26, 1797. There was no Harlequin in the Richmond *Gambols.*

Partnership Dissolved (January 18, 1805) was a comedy by Edward Morris first acted at Drury Lane on March 2, 1799. Its American premiere was in Philadelphia on December 30, less than a year later. It is not recorded in New York or Charleston. Although Suzannah Rowson wrote a play titled *The American Tar*, said by Quinn to have been acted in Philadelphia on June 17, 1796, I think this Richmond "pantomimical ballet" was more likely the ballet by William Francis which Pollock records in the Chestnut Street Theatre on that date. Mrs. Rowson wrote plays (that is, acting with dialogue), while Francis composed pantomimes (acting without dialogue). The hornpipe and the allemande strongly suggest Francis rather than Rowson.

The players. This was essentially the same company that played the previous season; Briers, Serson, and Mrs. Stuart were new. Advertised casts list nine men, five women. There is no mention of scene painters or musicians. Mr. and Mrs. Hopkins sang frequently between pieces, and Mrs. Hopkins and Miss Green danced. Although descended directly from the old West and Bignall Company, this company was, I believe, managed by Green, advised and assisted by Mrs. West, and might properly be called the West and Green Company. I suspect that Green assumed managerial duties soon after West's death in 1799.

During this season the company lost its most valuable member, Mrs. J. West, the former Mrs. John Bignall, daughter of Thomas Wade West, who had played female leads for several years. Her obituary in the *Enquirer* of January 22 spoke of her as "the most distinguished ornament of the Virginia stage."

Hiatus

1805

The actors probably left Richmond in February to play in Petersburg and Norfolk. Sherman locates them in Norfolk in March and May. During the interval there was evidence of continuing interest in entertainment and drama, attested by several newspaper notices. On February 15 and again on February 22, 1805, the *Enquirer* published long articles on "The Young Roscius" on the English stage. On February 19 it carried an advertisement of Hay Market Gardens for rent or lease for one or more years. On March 9 the *Virginia Argus* advertised: "The Sixth and Last Volume of Warner & Hanna's *Select Plays* is just received at this office—where a few complete sets of the work in elegant binding are for sale." On April 10 it advertised: "Just published by Cook & Grantland and for sale at Minerva Printing office, the Farce of *Raising the Wind*." *Raising the Wind* had been presented at least four times during the previous season.

Hay Market Gardens was a popular amusement resort during these years. On Wednesday, August 28, the *Virginia Gazette* carried this announcement:

HAY MARKET GARDENS

The Ladies & Gentlemen of Richmond, and its vicinity are respectfully informed that Mr. Decker, Mrs. Hopkins, and Mr. and Mrs. Wilmot (late Mrs. *Marshall* of the Philadelphia and Charleston Theatres,) Having been induced by the solicitation of a few friends, to stay a night on their way to the Federal City, have taken the Hay-market Gardens. —And on Wednesday evening August 28th, propose giving an Entertainment, (in imitation of Vauxhall London,) of Vocal and Instrumental Music, (Assisted by the best Instrumental performers that can be procured).

The Room and Gardens will be brilliantly illuminated— Refreshments to be had at the Bar.

To begin precisely at 8 o'clock—Admittance one dollar—Tickets at Eagle Tavern.

Both Mr. and Mrs. Hopkins had played the previous season in Richmond. Evidently she either left the company, or the company was not performing at this time. I note the absence of her husband, who, had he been with her, would have assisted in the performance.

On September 25 the *Enquirer* regretted "the death of Mr. Hodgkinson, one of the most distinguished theatrical performers on the continent," and on November 5 noted the death "in the City of Washington, on Saturday the 26th inst [of] Mr. C. D. Hopkins, Comedian . . . one of the finest performers on the continent." Perhaps he was in Washington in August when Mrs. Hopkins performed in Richmond on her way to "the Federal City."

On December 19, 1804, Mr. Serson, "from the Theatre Boston," made his first appearance before a Richmond audience. On October 8, 1805, he announced in the *Enquirer*:

The Subscribers and the public in general, are most respectfully informed, that in consequence of the Broad Rock Races, and by desire of several subscribers, the Benefit intended for the *sick family of Mr. Serson*, and which was to have taken place This Evening, at the Washington Tavern, is postponed 'till Thursday Evening the 10th inst: when he solicits the patronage of a generous community; and he assures them, that he will use the utmost exertions to give satisfaction.

A number of Songs will be sung by a gentleman of Richmond.
Several detached Dialogues from different Comedy's, Farces,
&c. will be performed.
Appropriate scenery is painted, and a small stage erected.
The best music to be had in Richmond will be provided.
Several popular Recitations will be given.
The entertainment will close with a great variety of handsome
Deceptions.

This, I believe, was Richmond's nearest approach to theatre during
these interim months.

On December 4 the *Virginia Argus* advertised: "Just received
and for sale at this office A New Comedy, entitled the *School of
Reform or, How to Rule A Husband* in five acts By Thomas Morton, Esq." On December 10 the *Enquirer* advertised: "Just received
and for sale at the Enquirer Book-Store: 'Who Wants a Guinea?'
by Geo. Coleman, esq. Also, 'Honey Moon' by John Tobin, Es-
quire." Evidently drama was available in the closet if not on the
stage.

On December 12, the *Enquirer* advertised that "Schwicker, a
musician" had been engaged at Hay Market Garden, which "will
be kept open during the session of the General Assembly." On
the twenty-fourth the *Argus* advertised at the City Tavern: "Natural Curiosities," including "Adam & Eve in the Garden of Eden,"
a "Sheep with 5 legs," and a "wild black woman." Admission was
fifty cents. On the same date the *Enquirer* advertised: "A Live
Elephant, Just arrived, and will be exhibited at the Washington
Tavern . . . admittance 25 cents, children half price." On the
twenty-seventh the elephant was moved to "Mr. Brook's Tavern
in Manchester."

After a year of such meager fare, Richmond was ready for the
opening of the new theatre.

CHAPTER V

1806–1809

Chronicle.   The years from 1806 to 1812 may be considered a golden age of the Richmond theatre. There are records of ten seasons, a total of 171 performances by one of the strongest companies in America. We have evidence that the theatre was well attended, popular, and successful. A significant era in theatre history, and in the history of Richmond, ended in the disastrous fire of December 26, 1811.

The theatre that was opened in January 1806 was the one that burned six years later. It had been some years in building, and Richmond had had no permanent theatre for eight years. Under such circumstances, one would expect considerable publicity, even local pride, attending the opening of this theatre; but I have found no publicity, no boasting, no description of the new building. There is, of course, the famous picture of the fire; and accounts of the catastrophe by persons who survived it give some details: the audience (a full house) on the fatal evening consisted of about 650 persons; there were boxes, one staircase, a lobby, and one entrance to the pit and boxes, with a separate entrance to the gallery. There were windows through which persons escaped, and there was a "bull's eye" window in the west (front) gable. We know exactly where the building was located: for the next century the spot was occupied by an Episcopal church and marked by an ornamental memorial urn and a monument inscribed with the names of those who perished in the fire.

Newspaper files for 1806 are well preserved, but theatre advertisements are irregular. The first appeared in the *Virginia Gazette* on Saturday, January 25. Headed "Richmond New Thratee" (was the typographical error an ill omen?) it announced for "This evening . . . the Tragedy of *Douglas* . . . to which will be added, the Comic Opera of *The Romp*." Casts were given for both plays:

Douglas

Young Norval (being his first appearance here)	Mr. Sutton
Lord Randolph	Mr. Hughes
Old Norval	Mr. Clare
Glenalvon	Mr. Green
Officers, Servants, &c.	
Lady Randolph	Mrs. West
Anna	Mrs. Hopkins

The Romp

Old Cockney	Mr. Comer
Young Cockney	Mr. Wilmot
Old Barnacle	Mr. Bignall
Captain Lightly	Mr. Martin
Servant	Master Douglas
Priscilla Tomboy (the Romp)	Mrs. Wilmot
Penelope	Mrs. Bignall
Miss LeBlond	Mrs. Clare

Green, Comer, Martin, and Mrs. Hopkins were holdovers from the previous season; Sutton, Hughes, Mr. and Mrs. Wilmot were newcomers. The Mrs. West who played Lady Randolph was, I assume, the widow of former Manager Thomas Wade West; her daughter-in-law was always identified as "Mrs. West, junior." I hope that Mrs. West had the satisfaction of playing a leading role on the opening night of the new theatre which she had worked so long and hard to build. This may have been her last appearance; I located no later one, though records are, of course, incomplete. Her roles were taken over by Mrs. Green and Mrs. Placide. Entertainment between pieces consisted of a song by Mrs. Hopkins and a hornpipe by Master Douglas.

On Wednesday, January 29, was advertised for "This evening... the Tragedy of *The Gamester* ... to which will be added the Farce of *The Village Lawyer*." Casts were given:

The Gamester

Beverly	Mr. Green
Stokely (Being his first appearance here)	Mr. Sutton
Lewson	Mr. Bignall
Jarvis	Mr. Hughes

Bates	Mr. Clare
Dawson	Mr. Comer
Waiter	Master Douglas
Mrs. Beverly	Mrs. Wilmot
Charlotte	Mrs. Hopkins
Lucy	Mrs. Clare

The Village Lawyer

Sheepface	Mr. Wilmot
Scout	Mr. Green
Snarl	Mr. Comer
Justice Mittimus	Mr. Clare
Charles	Mr. Martin
Constables, &c.	
Mrs. Scout	Mrs. Clare
Kate	Mrs. Bignall

Despite his appearance as Young Norval on the previous Saturday, Sutton was again billed as "first appearance here." Between pieces there was "a Song" by Mrs. Green, and "the Song of the 'Old Commodore' in character by Mr. Comer."

This advertisement gave interesting details of house regulations:

No persons of color admitted to the pit or boxes.
No segars are permitted to be smoked in the box-lobby.
The music as well as the business of the stage being selected for the evening, it is presumed no particular tunes will be called for during the performance.
Doors to be opened at 5 o'clock and the performance commence at six precisely.
Admittance to boxes and pit 6 s. to the gallery 4s 6d.
Tickets to be had at Mr. Davis's Printing office and at the Office of the Theatre.[1]

I note that prices, which during the previous season had been one dollar, had reverted to shillings and pence, as in the 1790s. Also, I note the restriction on "persons of color." I found no mention of color in advertisements for the old Academy-theatre. In the temporary theatre, persons of color were not admitted. Now, with a new theatre, attendance was permitted on a segregated basis. Boxes and pit were lily-white; the gallery was Jim Crow. I recall no person of color in any audience of which I was a part in Richmond during the 1920s.

Under the heading "New Theatre," the *Enquirer* of Thursday, January 30, announced for "Tomorrow Evening . . . a favorite Comedy, called *Speed the Plough*. To which will be added, the farce of the *Irishman in London*." No casts or other details were given.

On Saturday, February 1, the *Gazette* advertised for "Monday evening . . . Cumberland's celebrated Comedy of *The Sailor's Daughter*." Cast was given:

Sir Matthew Morribund	Mr. Comer
Mandeville	Mr. Poe
Captain Sentamour	Mr. Green
Varnish	Mr. Martin
Vingleton	Mr. West
Hartshorn (the apothecary)	Mr. Hughes
Lindsay	Mr. Bignall
Raven	Mr. Wilmot
Shopman	Master Douglas
Servants &c.	
Louisa Davenant	Mrs. Wilmot
Julia Clareville	Mrs. Hopkins
Mrs. Hartshorn	Mrs. Bignall
Nurse	Mrs. Clare

Afterpiece was "the Farce of *The Devil to Pay; or Wives Metamorphosed*," for which no cast was given. Between pieces there was "a Song" by Mrs. Hopkins and a repetition of the "Old Commodore in character" by Comer.

The *Virginia Argus* of Tuesday, February 4, carried a short article on the theatre, which, it said, was liberally patronized. The prompter was advised to speak less loudly. On the same day, the *Enquirer* carried a long and interesting criticism of the performance of *The Gamester*, which had been presented the previous Wednesday. The play was praised for its moral qualities; Green and Mrs. Wilmot were lauded for their performance as Beverly and Mrs. Beverly, and Sutton was considered inadequate as Stukely:

THEATRICAL

There are few dramatical performances in the English language, which are entitled to higher commendation than the tragedy of the Gamester. It merits the eloquim of the critic, whether he considers the variety of its incidents, the intricacy yet just conduct of the plot, or the admirable lesson which it teaches to the greater portion of mankind. If we judge it by the strict dogmas we find it admirably correct; if by its influence on the audience truly interesting and pathetic. No situation in life can indeed be more admirably calculated to excite the tear of commiseration, than that which the author has selected. Surrounded by every object that can bestow happiness on earth; beloved, almost adored, by those who are nearest to his heart; the generous but deluded gamester falls a victim to a single vice. The story is not singular; it is too frequently exhibited in real life; and hence the excellence of the moral.

On Wednesday evening the lovers of the drama were gratified with the exhibition of this admirable tragedy. Beverly was supported with propriety and spirit by Mr. Green. The character was well adapted to his talents; and his voice, his gesture, and varied expression of countenance, deserve our highest approbation. In a word, Mr. Green is generally a *good* performer; in the Gamester he was *great*.

Of Mrs. Wilmot we dare not venture to say much, lest our unbounded admiration should lead us to expressions, which might be deemed hyperbolical by those, who were not witnesses to her performance. Let the tears and plaudits of a delighted audience speak her praise. So correctly, so feelingly did she perform, that our admiration of the actress was lost in our sympathy for Mrs. Beverly.

In Mr. Sutton we confess ourselves in some degree disappointed. A previous perusal of the play had led us to expect in Stukely, the elegance and artifice of Lovelace. We thought him the pliant, flexible, and smiling villain. Plausible in pretext, elegant in address we believed him, well calculated to lull the suspicions of a husband, and corrupt the virtue of a wife. But Mr. Sutton has apparently formed a different idea of the character, or else has not yet acquired sufficient skill to do it justice. To fill the part of Stukely with propriety, requires vigorous and various talents, improved by example, and mellowed by habit. We are not then to be surprised if a *young* performer fails in the attempt. Our strictures on Mr. Sutton are not however to be understood, as being given without qualification. He is indebted to nature for an excellent voice, and as the faults which he discovered are principally incident to beginners, we flatter ourselves with the expectation of seeing him, in a few months, no inconsiderable addition to our theatre.

We cannot leave this subject without remarking on the occasional, not to say, frequent inattention of the inferior performers, with regard to the commission of their parts to memory.

An enlightened audience cannot long indulgently overlook so gross and palpable a violation of propriety.

Richmond, Jan. 31   Philo-Dramatis

On Wednesday, February 5, was announced for "Tomorrow evening . . . for the first time in Virginia, a Comedy (written by George Coleman, jun. author of *John Bull, Poor Gentleman,* &c.&c.&c. and now performing in Boston and Charleston with distinguished applause) call'd *Who Wants a Guinea* (The Epilogue to be spoken by Mrs. Wilmot)." Afterpiece was "the Farce of *Miss in her Teens or, A Medley of Lovers.*" Casts were given for both plays:

Who Wants a Guinea?

Torrent	Mr. Comer
Heartly	Mr. Hughes
Hogmore	Mr. Bignall
Solomon Gundy	Mr. Green
Barford	Mr. Sutton
Jonathan Oldskirt	Mr. West
Sir Larry M'Murragh	Mr. Poe
Andrew Bang	Mr. Wilmot
Carrydot	Mr. Clare
Henry	Mr. Martin
Boy	Miss Green
Fanny	Mrs. Wilmot
Mrs. Glassonberry	Mrs. Clare
Amy	Mrs. Hopkins

Miss in Her Teens

Captain Loveit	Mr. Martin
Fribble	Mr. Wilmot
Flash	Mr. Green
Puff	Mr. Bignall
Jasper	Mr. Clare
Miss Biddy	Mrs. Hopkins
Tag	Mrs. Bignall[2]

During the previous season Miss Green had danced between pieces; her first acting role was apparently on March 26, 1804.

Who Wants a Guinea? was repeated on Saturday, February 8, with the same cast, except for Briers as Jonathan Oldskirt instead of West. Afterpiece was *Three Weeks after Marriage* with the following cast:

Sir Charles Racket	Mr. Green
Lovelace	Mr. Bignall
Woodville	Mr. Martin
Old Drugget	Mr. Comer
Servants &c.	
Lady Racket	Mrs. Wilmot
Dimity	Mrs. Bignall
Nancy	Mrs. Hopkins
Mrs. Drugget	Mrs. Clare

The advertisement added details about the boxes: "Places in the front boxes, securing four seats, and the whole side boxes, containing eight, may be had by applying at the theatre on the days of performance, between the hours of 10 and 2."[3] Evidently there were both front and side boxes, the latter twice as large, but the arrangement and the number of each remain unknown. There exists no diagram or sketch of the interior of the house.

The *Virginia Gazette* of Wednesday, February 12, advertised for "Tomorrow evening . . . a new Comedy, called *The Blind Bargain; or Hear it Out.* (As performed at the Theatre Royal Covent Garden, with unbounded applause.)" Afterpiece was *Three Weeks after Marriage.* Casts were given:

The Blind Bargain

Sir Andrew Analyse	Mr. Comer
Jack Analyse	Mr. Martin
Tourley	Mr. Green
Villars	Mr. Poe
Dr. Pliable	Mr. Clare
Giles Woodbine	Mr. Wilmot
Frank	Mr. Bignall
David	Master Douglas
James	[blank]
Mrs. Villars	Mrs. Wilmot
Miss Gurnet	Mrs. Clare
Sophia Woodbine	Mrs. Hopkins

The cast for *Three Weeks after Marriage* was the same, except that Woodville (now Woodly) was played by Poe instead of Martin. The *Gazette* of Saturday, February 15, advertised for "This evening . . . a Comedy written by Coleman the younger called *The Heir at Law*," with the following cast:

Doctor Pangloss	Mr. Green
Lord Duberly	Mr. Comer
Stedfast	Mr. Clare
Henry Moreland	Mr. Poe
Dick Dowlas	Mr. Martin
Zekiel Homespun	Mr. Wilmot
Kenrick	Mr. Bignall
Waiter	[*blank*]
John	Master Douglas
Lady Duberly	Mrs. Bignall
Caroline Dormer	Mrs. Hopkins
Cecily Homespun	Mrs. Wilmot

Afterpiece was *Miss in Her Teens*, for which no cast was given; presumably it was the same as on February 6.

On Wednesday, February 26, there was announced for "This Evening . . . for the first time in America, a Comedy, in three acts, written by Thomas Dibbins, esq. called *The Will For The Deed* with new Scenery and machinery, designed and executed by Mr. Stuart." Afterpiece was *The Midnight Hour*. Casts were given for both:

The Will for the Deed

Old Harebrain	Mr. Comer
Harry Harebrain	Mr. Poe
Antimony	Mr. Hughes
Capias	Mr. Briers
Motto	Mr. Green
Reference	Mr. Bignall
Acorn	Mr. Wilmot
Manly	Mr. Clare
First Bailiff	Mr. Martin
Second do.	Mr. Stowel
Waiter	Master Douglas
Mrs. Reference	Mrs. Bignall
Miss Manly	Mrs. Hopkins
Bar Maid	Mrs. Clare

The Midnight Hour

General	Mr. Hughes
Marquis	Mr. Martin

Sebastian	Mr. Bignall
Nicholas	Mr. Comer
Ambrose	Mr. Clare
Matthias	Mr. Wilmot
Julia	Mrs. Hopkins
Cicely	Mrs. Clare
Elora	Mrs. Wilmot[4]

Newspaper puffs are demonstrably unreliable, but this seems to have been the American premiere of *The Will for the Deed.* Curiously, the advertisement of Wednesday was repeated on Saturday.[5] Possibly the performance was postponed from Wednesday to Saturday; if so, "first time in America" would be March 1 instead of February 26.

Postponement was rare, but did occur, sometimes because of inclement weather, sometimes because of a leading actor's indisposition. The *Enquirer* of Tuesday, March 11, carried an elaborate apology by the manager for having, at the last moment, canceled the performance on Saturday, March 8, because of the sudden indisposition of Mrs. Bignall. The public were assured that "imperious necessity only" could have forced the cancellation. There is no record of the plays scheduled for performance on March 8.

The same advertisement announced for "This Evening . . . a celebrated play, in five acts, called *Abaellino, or, The Great Bandit.* To which will be added, the musical entertainment of *The Purse, or The Benevolent Tar.*" No casts were given. Between pieces there was a song by Mrs. Hopkins, and in the fifth act of *Abaellino* "a concert of vocal and instrumental music."

The *Virginia Gazette* of March 19 advertised for "Wednesday Evening . . . (never performed in Virginia) a celebrated Tragedy written by M. G. Lewis, esq. Author of the 'Castle Spector,' 'Adelmon,' &c.&c. and performed in London, New York, Philadelphia, and Charleston, with the most unbounded admiration, (with new Scenery, Dresses and Decorations) called *The True Patriot; or, Alphonso, King of Castile.* (for characters see bills)." The "new scenery" was described: "Act 2d, Orsino's Hermitage, with a rustic Tomb, raised to the memory of his wife, Victoria. Last scene, the outward Claudian Vault with the springing of a Mine, laid by the conspirators, and the rescue of Alfonso by Orsino."

Entertainment between pieces consisted of "Dr. Splash's Rambles; or A Cosmetic Excursion, For the benefit of the Ladies in First at Acton and Ealing, there faces is pealing; at Ilchester and Dorchester, Chickster, Porchester; at Woolwich & Highgate, and Dulwich and Rygate; at Beckington and Okington, Buckingham & Rockingham; at Birmingham, at Rockingham . . ." At this point the paper has been mutilated by clipping; I hazard that Dr. Splash's rambles ended in Richmond and whatever rhymes with it.

This was Mrs. Wilmot's benefit. She "respectfully informs the Inhabitants of Richmond and its vicinity, that having paid the utmost attention to the Entertainments selected for that evening, and particularly the regulation of the orchestra—She hopes to present them with a night's amuse [*sic*] worthy of their patronage." Tickets were to be had of "Mrs. Wilmot, at Mr. Goodwin's, near the Capitol; at Mr. Davis's printing-office; at Mr. Pumfrey's, and at the office of the Theatre, where places for the Boxes may be taken." Afterpiece was *The Padlock*. No casts were given. For characters we are told to "see bills."

On Saturday, March 22, the *Virginia Gazette* advertised for "Monday Evening . . . Shakespear's Tragedy of *Romeo and Juliet.* To which will be added the musical entertainment of *The Quaker; or, May Day Dower.*" No casts were given; we are again referred to bills of the day. This was the "Benefit of Mr. Stuart (Scene Painter)," and *Romeo and Juliet* was staged "with entire new Scenery and Decorations."

Another brief advertisement in the issue of Wednesday, March 26, announced for "Thursday Evening . . . (first time here) a much admired Comedy, written by Colley Cibber, esq. call'd *She Wou'd & She Wou'd Not; or The Kind Imposter.*" Afterpiece was *The Adopted Child*. No casts were given. This was Comer's benefit.

The issue of Saturday, March 29, advertised for "Saturday evening . . . a celebrated Tragedy, written by the Rev. Mr. Home, called *Douglas; or The Noble Shepherd.*" Cast was given:

Young Norval (for that night only)	Mrs. Wilmot
Lord Randolph	Mr. Comer
Old Norval	Mr. Clare
First Officer	Mr. Martin
Second Officer	Mr. Briers

Servant	Master Douglas
Glenalvon	Mr. Green
Matilda (Lady Randolph)	Mrs. Hopkins
(First time and for that night only)	
Anna	Mrs. Bignall

Young Norval was a featured role and a first-rate breeches part for Mrs. Wilmot. This was the benefit of Mrs. Hopkins. *Douglas* was followed by "a celebrated After-Piece (never presented in Virginia) called *The Follies of a Day; or, The Marriage of Figaro*," for which no cast was given.

The issue of Saturday, April 5, advertised for "Easter Monday ... the Grand Dramatic Romance, of *Blue Beard; or, The Fatal Effects of Curiosity* with new Scenery, Dresses and Decorations." The following cast was given:

Abomelique (Blue Beard)	Mr. Green
Selim (being his first appearance on this stage)	Mr. McDonald
Ibrahim	Mr. Comer
Schacabac	Mr. Wilmot
Hassan	Mr. Briers
1st Spahi	Mr. Bignall
2d do.	Mr. Martin
3d do.	Mr. Clare
Spectre	Mr. Santford
Spahis' slaves, Palaquin bearers, &c. &&&.	
Fatima	Mrs. Green
Irene	Mrs. Hopkins
Beda	Mrs. Bignall

Afterpiece was *The Midnight Hour* for the second time this season. No cast was given; presumably it was the same as on February 26.

The issue of Wednesday, April 9, advertised for "Thursday Evening . . . for the first time this season, the favority Comedy of the *Soldier's Daughter*." A complete cast was given:

Governor Heartall	Mr. Comer
Frank Heartall	Mr. Green
Malfort, Sen.	Mr. Clare
Malfort, Jun.	Mr. Poe
Captain Woodly	Mr. Martin
Mr. Ferret	Mr. Macdonald

Timothy Quaint	Mr. Bignall
Tom	Master Douglas
William	Mr. Santford
Widow Cheerly	Mrs. Green
Mrs. Malfort	Mrs. Poe
Mrs. Fidget	Mrs. Clare
Susan	Mrs. Bignall
Julia (Malfort's child)	Miss Green

This was Mrs. Green's benefit. Afterpiece was "the musical entertainment of *Tom Thumb*," and between pieces was "a Ballet called *Shelty's Frolic*." No casts were given for *Tom Thumb* and *Shelty's Frolic*.

During the previous season in the temporary theatre, Richmond newspapers had carried news of Thomas Abthorpe Cooper, the leading star of the American stage, in New York, Philadelphia, and Charleston. I found no advertisement of his appearance in Richmond then or now, but the *Enquirer* of Friday, April 11 (although carrying no theatre advertisement), published a long article by "Crito" on Cooper's appearance as Hamlet in Richmond on Saturday, April 5:

It is difficult to describe the vivid expectations of the audience, who attended the Richmond Theatre last Saturday Night to see, criticise and admire the celebrated Cooper. The notice was short, but the house was uncommonly crowded. Every heart throbb'd for the rising of the curtain and every eye gazed with anxiety for the scene that was to present them with the Prince of Denmark; next to Rolla, the favorite and perhaps the greatest character played by Cooper.

The scene at length was shifted and Hamlet appears at the footstool of the throne. Every thing about him was prepossessing. A mourning dress, rich and starred with brilliants; a figure of more than middling stature, firm without being athletic, and dignified, without affectation; a face, whose every feature seemed capable of expressing every emotion: such was the interesting object that stood forth before the audience. But it was not Cooper the player & the stranger, who appeared before you, with an eye expressive of curiosity & the blush of anxiety upon his cheek. It was Hamlet of Denmark, and at the very first glimpse, you saw the folded arm, the knitted brow, the indignant and discontented eye, which announced, that there was "something rotten in the state of Denmark."

In fact, you never saw Cooper once during the whole presentation. Most players are apt to drop the character they assume. They grow tired of it or they forget their dramatic existence. They turn and speak to the audience. They coquette with them, they try to find out the weak side of the house, and like an artful advocate, to that point they bend all their force. But Cooper commands the whole house by attempting to command Nobody; he forgets where he is, and recollects only the character which he personates. He never turns his audience into players, by speaking to them; when he should be speaking to the other dramatists on the stage.

To those who have not seen Cooper it would be difficult to describe the command which he has acquired over himself. How inimitable was his action, when he asked "What shall such a fellow as I do, *crawling between heaven and earth!*" His very motion which he mentioned, and as he gradually raised them into mid-air, his very fingers seemed to be convulsed, and to vibrate with the retching of his feelings.

The same attention to character is displayed in the pauses of his dialogue. Most players seem to think that the playing of a part consists in speaking it. Their dramatic character is as fugitive as the words which they pronounce. When they cease to talk they think their labor is at an end. Why? they may then oggle with the pit, or leer at each other; gnaw their nails, fish up their cravat or play as many "antic tricks" as their humor or conveniance may dictate. But Cooper is something more than a theatrical trumpet. When he ceases to speak, he still fills up the pauses of the dialogue with every emotion which the scene is calculated to inspire. It is the very look of Hamlet; the very gesture; the very spirit which seems to breathe in every limb and feature.

It would be tedious to speak of the differ [*Paper mutilated here*] would be drawing a full length portrait of the whole character of Hamlet. In the ghost scene he was uncommonly great; when he pronounced,

> —I'll call thee Hamlet,
> King, *father*, Royal Dane—

the house was melted by the mournful [tone] with which he spoke the epithet "father." And when in the same appeal he asks

> —why the sepulchre,
> wherein we saw thee *quietly inurn'd;*

it is difficult to give any idea of the complicated emotions which these two words expressed. It was grief for the death of a lost father, remonstrance for the disturbances which he caused to the living, and anxiety to avenge his wrongs, that seemed all to melt together into one voice.

In the picture scene with his mother, he exceeded even our warmest expectations. In the convent scene with Ophelia, he was impressive beyond description.

If Cooper has any prominent defects, they consist in the management of his voice. Now and then it has the hissing accent, & in the higher key of pronunciation, it seems sometimes to fail him.

In one word Cooper is scarcely inferior to Kemble, in his representation of Hamlet. In the "true sublime" of the Drama, he has no rival in this country.

Crito

"Crito," whoever he was, was a competent critic. Cooper's appearance, apparently for one evening only, was obviously the high point of a successful season in the new theatre. It marked for Richmond, the beginning of the star system which dominated the American stage during the nineteenth century. From Boston to New Orleans, local stock companies presented regular fare, with touring stars appearing for a few nights in featured roles, supported by the regular companies. Theatre critics and historians generally condemn the system, but it filled the theatres. Its pernicious effect is indicated in this article, which mentions no actor but Cooper.

The *Virginia Argus* of Tuesday, April 15, advertised for "This evening (the first time in Richmond) a Play in 5 acts, *The Wife of Two Husbands*," with the "Comic opera *Robin Hood, or Sherwood Forest*" as afterpiece. No casts were given. This was the benefit of Mr. and Mrs. Bignall, son and daughter-in-law of West's original partner. Entertainment between pieces consisted of "Bells Have at Ye All" by Mrs. Wilmot, a "New Song 'Tid Re I'" by Mr. Wilmot, and a hornpipe by Miss Green.

On Wednesday, April 30, was advertised for "Thursday Evening" a repetition of *The True Patriot; or Alfonso, King of Castile*. "To which will be added (never performed here) the admired Farce of *Honest Thieves*." No casts were given. Between pieces was "an entire new Pantomime Ballet, (never performed on any stage) selected from the most ludicrous incidents of various pieces (the music composed by Mr. Decker) called *The Victorious Tars; or, Avarice Overcome by Love*." This was Mr. Brier's benefit.[6]

The *Virginia Gazette* of Wednesday, May 7, announced for that evening a repetition of *She Would and She Would Not*, with *Miss in Her Teens* as afterpiece. No casts were given. The advertisement also respectfully informed the public that "there will be a performance every evening during the races. The entertainments will commence every evening at 7 o'clock precisely, without postponement, on any account." Notwithstanding the promise of future performances, this is the last advertisement of the season. I assume that handbills were distributed at the racetrack.

For the opening of the new theatre, this was a respectable, if not a spectacular, season, extending from January to May, 1806, perhaps four months. There are records of twenty performances, probably less than half of what was offered. There were thirty-three plays, including tragedy, comedy, farce, ballet. Of these, ten (*Who Wants A Guinea?*, *The Blind Bargain*, *The Purse*, *The Will for the Deed*, *The True Patriot*, *She Would and She Would Not*, *The Wife of Two Husbands*, *The Follies of a Day*, *The Honest Thieves*, and *The Victorious Tars*) were new to Richmond. There was one American premiere, *The Will for the Deed*, on February 26, and one pantomime ballet composed for the occasion and not presented elsewhere, *The Victorious Tars*, on March 1. There was one play of American authorship, *The Wife of Two Husbands* by William Dunlap. The feature of the season was Cooper's Hamlet on April 5, which occasioned the only piece of criticism.

It was a strong company of able and experienced actors. Names of fourteen men, six women, and two children are preserved. Thomas Abthorpe Cooper appeared as visiting star. Mr. Decker, who composed the music for *The Victorious Tars*, was probably leader of the orchestra. Mr. Stuart was scene painter. There were singing, dancing, and special stage effects. The season probably ended about the middle of May.

The plays.   *Who Wants a Guinea?* (February 6, 1806), a comedy by the younger Colman, was first acted at Covent Garden on April 18, 1805. It was acted in Charleston on November 27, 1805, and New York in January, 1806.

The Blind Bargain (February 13, 1806), a comedy by Frederick Reynolds, had its premiere at Covent Garden on October 24, 1804. It was acted in New York on May 13, 1805, and Charleston December 6, 1805.

The Will for the Deed (February 26, 1806), a comedy in three acts by Thomas Dibdin, was first acted at Covent Garden on March 24, 1804. It was acted in New York on March 26, 1806, advertised as "never acted in America." It was acted in Charleston on December 23, 1806. I found no record of performance elsewhere. This Richmond performance was apparently its American premiere.

The Purse (March 11, 1806), a musical farce by John C. Cross, was first acted at the Haymarket on February 8, 1794. It was acted in New York on February 23, 1795, and Charleston October 30, 1799.

Alphonso, King of Castile (March 19, 1806), a tragedy by M. G. Lewis, was first acted at Covent Garden on January 15, 1802. It was acted in New York on May 2, 1803, and Charleston December 1, 1804.

She Would and She Would Not (March 27, 1806) was an old comedy by Colley Cibber, first acted at Drury Lane in 1702. Its American premiere was in Philadelphia on May 26, 1794; it was acted in New York on May 9, 1803, and Charleston May 2, 1805.

The Follies of a Day (March 29, 1806), a comedy by Thomas Holcroft, had its premiere at Covent Garden on December 14, 1784; it was acted in Philadelphia in 1795, New York, 1799, and Charleston, 1801.

The Wife of Two Husbands (April 15, 1806) was a melodrama which William Dunlap adapted from *La Femme à deux Maris* by Pixérécourt. Its premiere was at the Park Theatre in New York on April 4, 1804, and it was acted in Charleston on November 20, 1805. There is no record of its performance in Philadelphia, and this is the only record of its performance in Richmond.

The Honest Thieves (May 1, 1806), a farce by Thomas Knight, was first acted at Covent Garden on May 9, 1797. It was acted in Philadelphia on March 30, 1798, Charleston, April 7, 1802, and New York, May 28, 1806. *The Victorious Tars* was evidently concocted by the company for the occasion. There is no record of performance elsewhere.

The players.   We know that Elizabeth Arnold married Charles Hopkins in 1802, and that he died on October 26, 1805. There has

been some uncertainty about the marriage of the widow Hopkins
to David Poe. In his biography of Edgar Allan Poe, Quinn repro-
duces the marriage bond from the original in the Henrico County
Courthouse in Richmond. It is dated March 14, 1806, but the
marriage was evidently postponed, or not announced. Quinn specu-
lates that it was performed between April 5 and April 9, with an
Easter honeymoon (April 6 was Easter Sunday). Mrs. Hopkins's
last advertised role was Irene in *Blue Beard* on Monday, April 7;
Mrs. Poe's first advertised role was Mrs. Malfort in *The Soldier's
Daughter* on Thursday, April 10.

Thomas Abthorpe Cooper was the outstanding star of the early
nineteenth-century American theatre. His picture is frontispiece to
Odell's second volume. Billed as "from Covent-Garden—first appearance here"—he made his American debut as Macbeth in
Philadelphia on December 9, 1796. He first appeared in New York
as Pierre in *Venice Preserved* on August 23, 1797. Nine days after
his Richmond appearance he appeared in Charleston, playing a
twelve-night engagement between April 14 and May 16, 1806. He
was almost without exception highly praised by critics, who generally considered him unexcelled in tragic roles. He is credited
with beginning the visiting-star system in the United States.

Between Seasons
May–August 1806

Probably about the middle of May, soon after the end of the
racing season, the company went downriver to Norfolk. The *Virginia Gazette* of Wednesday, June 4, 1806, carried an article on
Cooper as Beverly in *The Gamester* in the Norfolk theatre on
May 30. Green, Mrs. Wilmot, and other members of the Richmond
company were mentioned. Evidently Manager Green had arranged
during the previous season when Cooper played Hamlet in Richmond to meet in Norfolk. How long they played there I do not
know; they played in Petersburg also on their way back to
Richmond.[7]

During their absence there were fireworks at the Haymarket
Circus by M. Rosainville on Saturday, July 12; and on Wednes-

day, July 30, performances by Mr. Manfredi and Company at the Eagle Tavern. The company consisted of three ladies and two gentlemen; they did dancing, tumbling, and tightrope performing. Admission was one dollar, children half price. Days of performance were Mondays, Wednesdays, and Saturdays. "No segars to be smoked in the room during the performance."[8] The advertisement was repeated on August 2 and 9.

On Wednesday, August 13, the *Virginia Gazette* announced:

THEATRE

By a letter received at this office, from the manager of the Virginia Theatre, we are authorized to state to the public, that on Monday evening next, the Theatre of this town will certainly be opened, (for six nights only) when the celebrated Tragedy of the *Gamester* will be presented.

Beverly — By Mr. Cooper
Mrs. Beverly — By Mrs. Barret
From the New York Theatre

From the burst of applause, with which the present company of Tragedians have met with, both in Norfolk and Petersburg, promises to the visitors of the Richmond Theatre a degree of the utmost satisfaction. [*sic*]

Further advance press-agentry consisted of a long (one and a half columns) article in the *Enquirer* on Friday, August 15, entitled "Some Account of the Life of Mr. Cooper The Tragedian." Purportedly taken "from the Literary Magazine for 1804," the article consisted of a Cooper biography, concluding: "Such is the dignified Tragedian who is to represent the character of the Gamester next Monday night on the Richmond Stage."

TWENTY-SECOND SEASON
West and Bignall Company
August–September 1806

Chronicle.   Opening night was Monday, August 18, 1806: "The public are respectfully informed, that Mr. Cooper is engaged for six nights only; during which time no play will be repeated." The cast which supported Cooper in *The Gamester* was as follows:

Stukely	Mr. Green
Lawson (Being his first appearance on this stage)	Mr. Collins
Jarvis	[*blank*]
Dawson	Mr. Martin
Bates	Mr. M'Donald
Charlotte	Mrs. Green
Mrs. Beverly (From the Theatres, Boston, New York and Charleston, being her first appearance here)	Mrs. Barrett

Afterpiece was *The Prize*, no cast announced. Doors opened at six, with performance at seven-thirty; admittance was one dollar for boxes, seventy-five cents for gallery. Tickets were to be had at the newspaper office and at the theatre. Subscribers were requested to send to the newspaper office for their tickets.[9] The term *subscribers* meant, I think, persons who had subscribed to stock in the new theatre, and were entitled to tickets by virtue of stock ownership. A similar plan was used to finance Richmond's next theatre, which opened in 1819.

The *Enquirer* of Friday, August 22, carried a long critique of Monday's performance:

THEATRICAL

"The end of playing both at the first, and now, was, and is, to hold as 'twere the mirror up to nature; to shew virtue her own feature, scorn her own image, and the very age and body of the time, his form and pressure."

—Shakespeare

On Monday last, the anxiety of Richmond, was gratified by the exhibition of the "Gamester," in which Mrs. Barrett and Mr. Cooper, conducted the leading characters of Mr. and Mrs. Beverley. The performance of Mrs. B. was attended with frequent peals of applause, and was generally and highly admired. But I cannot acknowledge, that the moral beauties of the character, with which it so richly abounds, were so clearly displayed, or so fully impressed. The feelings were not seduced into that magic bondage, which causes the spectator to forget the illusive imagery before him, and which is the precious and desired moment of the dramatist, that he may steal upon the unguarded mind, and fix his moral purpose. There are few tragedies that teem with more interesting and distressing incidents than the "Gamester," but I could not discern one approving tear to bear evidence of the affecting scene, or the artist's skill. The dramatic talents of Mrs. B. may shine with more lustre in other characters, but in this there is a physical inaptitude that disqualifies her. Her gesture is not of a graceful and flexible style, but rather aukward and affected. Her voice is heavy and unhappy, which may arise from habit; but she expands her words with a solemn and lingering sound that tires the attention before the mind is acquainted with the thought. It is a just remark of Quintilian "that nothing can enter into the affections which stumbles at the threshold by offending the ear." But what I consider as the greatest *desideratum* is one of which she is altogether destitute; she professes no command over her countenance; not even in the most tragic moment, can she suppress an unskilful smile, which turns the pleading deception into mockery. Her eye which should discourse with the audience, and import its electric influence, is wandering and vacant; nor do I think that she has sufficiently studied the lesson of Hamlet "to suit the action to the word, and the word to the action." The author of the "Gamester" has acquired the most extravagant encomium, in painting *the living manners as they rise*. He has been styled the benefactor of mankind, for presenting this mirror to the world, in whose *polished convex*, vice beholds its haggard hue, and turns pale with reflected guilt. If then the author is entitled to such boundless applause, by what standard shall we fashion the eulogy, which is due to him whose dramatick genius can decay the vicious mind from its wily fold, can thaw and dissolve its cold ungenial form, and render it plastic to the stamp of virtue. Such is the skill of Godwin's pupil—the celebrated Cooper, that now treads upon the Richmond stage. His performance, in the character of Beverly, excited the most unwearied admiration. He is happily blessed by nature, and endowed by art, with all the qualifications that can form the tragedian, and ensure him the highest honors of the drama. His person is elegant and active, and his countenance beams with intelligence that informs you, he is perfectly acquainted with the theory of his play, and the moral it is intended to impress. His deportment is natural and unaffected, and his voice, though not the most happy, has sufficient compass to be heard distinctly. His articulation is clear and impressive, but his prosody sometimes rather turgid and imperfect. He appears anxious to acquire merited fame, but never stoops to employ those little arts and tricks which are too commonly used to excite the loud and fleeting plaudits of the pit. There is one impropriety which prevails upon the stage, the contageon of which not even Cooper has escaped, it is that of intrenching upon the language of the author. There are some of the performers guilty of this violation to a disgusting degree; they barely remember the thought, one half of which, they repeat in the polished style of the writer, and the other in their own sudden and imperfect language, which is a most unpardonable licence. It tends to create confusion on the mind of the auditor, & subtract from the merit of the writer, by conveying a fine sentiment in the alternate language of refinement and vulgarity. "O, reform it altogether, and speak no more than is set down for you, for there are of them, that will themselves laugh, to set on some quantity of barren spectators to laugh too."

The dramatick character of Cooper, although it may sometimes deserve the reproof of criticism, is surely of the most exalted order in this species of the drama. There are few who *have* been educated like him in the school of the tragic muse, he must therefore be frequently embarrassed by the want of confidence in his theatrical associates. In this disadvantage he may find an excuse for many imperfections, and it is one so just, that no candid mind can be so harshly disposed in its criticising, as not to admit its full measure of extenuation.

Spectator

Another Critique signed "A Looker-on," was received, but too late for this day's paper.

"Looker-on" was either unpublished or lost; but another discriminating and perceptive critique, this one by "Philo-Drama," appeared in the *Virginia Gazette* on Saturday, August 23:

On Monday night last the Richmond Theatre opened with the tragedy of the Gamester, when Mrs. Barret made her first appearance here as Mrs. Beverley. This is certainly one of the most finished patterns of female excellence in the whole compass of the English drama, and affords the finest opportunity to the actress for the exhibition of every passion and feeling in which tragedy delights. Her dignified resignation to the change of her fortune, her generous tenderness for the husband who had plunged her in ruin, her fear for the loss of his affections, her indignation at the infamous proposal of Stukely, her alarm for her husband's safety, her joy at the prospect of restoring him to liberty and happiness, and finally the horrid catrastrophe, which immediately succeeds, are occasions which call for all the varied powers which once distinguished a Pritchard, and more recently a Siddons. . . . But Mrs. Barret's dramatic qualifications are of a more circumscribed range. Her tall and stately figure as well as her impassioned voice and manner are better fitted for expressing the stronger workings of the soul than the tender touches of sentiment or the mild virtues of her sex. Indeed to exhibit that calm elevation of mind which rises above misfortune without degenerating into pompous rant on one side, or tameness on the other, is one of the highest efforts of the tragic art; and it must be confessed that where Mrs. Barret failed few are found to succeed. In a character better suited to her powers she will no doubt give more general satisfaction.

Stukely was performed by Mr. Green, who has rather too honest a face, and too much openess of manner, for the cool dissembling villain he represents. I have heard that when on one occasion at Drury Lane, this character was exhibited by Palmer, his performance was so animated and natural, that the audience, under a momentary illusion, gave a general hiss; thereby insensibly expressing their detestation of the character in the way they usually express their dislike to bad acting. Surely such a hiss as that was a more genuine compliment than the most clamorous applause. Tho' Mr. Green could not boast of this high compliment, his performance was generally spirited and correct, and very much to the satisfaction of the audience.

In one instance indeed, he was little entitled to the favor he received. After Stukely had lamely borne the insults of Lewson, he soliloquises on his cowardice, and, endeavoring to console himself under the mortifying reflection, adds, "yet fear brings caution, and caution security," &c. all of which the actor converted into a jest, and uttered with the same ironical air that would become Falstaff, where he says "the better part of valor is discretion, & that I have." And still farther to tickle the *refined* part of his audience, when Bates asks him "what is the matter," he attempts to foist in a miserable pun. Surely Mr. Green should be above paying a homage to his hearers which his own taste cannot but condemn.

Mr. Collins also now made his first appearance on this stage, in the character of Lewson. He possesses a good voice and may soon acquire a good delivery. If I mistake not he has only to conquer the diffidence which now represses him, and catch some of Mr. Cooper's fire to become a good actor.

Charlotte was represented by Mrs. Green, who received more than usual applause and I am decidedly of the opinion that her performance this evening did not shrink from a comparison with that of Mrs. Barret.

The character of Beverley was performed by the celebrated Cooper. The Richmond public, who had been once before gratified with an exhibition of his splendid dramatic powers, were now raised to the highest point of expectation, nor were they disappointed.

So perfect is Mr. Cooper in all the requisites of a good actor, that it is difficult to select any feature of his excellence by which he may be said to be characteristically distinguished. His figure is faultless, his gesture graceful and appropriate, his elocution smooth and clear, and his tones sweet and pathetic, or harsh or deep as the occasion justifies. His face, which is naturally handsome, most intensely expresses every varying emotion of his soul, though being of a grave cast, it is better suited to the vehement than the tender passions. But all these qualifications would go but little way in making him a first rate actor if he had not a sound judgment, a fine taste, and the most exquisite feelings. It is this combustion of excellences, so rarely united in one person, which enable him to enchain the attention, and melt the hearts of his hearers, and which have justly acquired him the appellation of the American Roscius.

But is this distinguished actor perfectly unexceptionable? No, Homer sometimes slumbers, and even Cooper has his faults. If a novice in stage criticism may presume to mingle a word of censure with his enthusiastic admiration, I would say that he does not always adapt the rapidity of his utterance to the occasion. There is an impressive solemnity in his pronunciation, which, in general, is that of a speaker whose mind feels the pressure of the subject, and whose tongue moves proportionally slow; and where there is doubt, or reasoning, or sentiment, this is proper enough, but I think I have witnessed too much of this deliberate elocution in sudden bursts of passion or in putting interrogatory. The mind of the hearer should not be suffered to out run the words of the speaker, and generally speaking this rule is a good test to inform us where the utterance should be rapid and where it may be slow.

The first appearance of Beverley was striking and impressive, and they who had never before seen Cooper, first felt, in the opening soliloquy the full power of tones over the human heart. When, soon afterwards, he says to Jarvis, "Recall past time then; or thro' this sea of storms and darkness, shew me a star to guide me. . . . But what canst thou?"

In pronouncing the last words, his tone, look, and accent most forcibly expressed a sudden recollection of his hopeless condition, and, yet a faint desire to hear a word of consolation from Jarvis. From the answer of the latter, I doubt whether all this was intended by the writer, but it is an instance of one of those superadded beauties which so masterly an actor can give the best productions, and of which indeed the best productions are most susceptible.

When Beverly comes from the gaming house, his bitter disappointment in the fond hopes he had cherished but a moment before, his recollection of his situation *then*, contrasted with what it lately was, his alternate suspicions of Stukely and his consequent self-reproach, rapidly as they are made to follow, were exhibited in the truest colors of nature. When in one of those moments of frantic suspicion he seized Stukely, who did not expect he would have pierced the trembling villain to the heart? And yet how suddenly and naturally in the tone of self-accusation, he exclaimed, "Pray thee forgive this language. I speak I know not what. Rage and despair are in my heart and hurry me to madness."

The soliloquy in the street was in Mr. Cooper's best manner yet shrouded as he was by the gloom of the night, and the far deeper gloom of mental anguish, there was a dignity and elegance in his appearance to which the spectator could not be insensible. It was perhaps so great as in some measure to weaken the effect that is properly dramatic.

But if he claimed our justest admiration in the previous scenes, what ought I to say to the awful spectacle he exhibited of Beverly's last moments. After taking the poison, and going through the interview with his wife and friends with the most touching expressions of a mind making its last struggle against the united agonies of grief, remorse, and dread of futurity, he slowly and solemnly sunk on his knees, and poured forth a prayer to the Almighty in tones so piteous and affecting . . . with a look so full of horror and the bitterest grief, that the whole house was petrified. A pin might have been heard to drop . . . each spectator, motionless, and breathless, fastened their eyes and ears on the expiring wretch and melted into tears.

Instead of weakening the effect by continuing the dialogue to the end, the curtain here judiciously dropped and waked the audience from their trance, to bestow those plaudits, which during the whole night they had almost forgotten to give.

Philo-Drama

On Wednesday, August 20, Cooper played Macbeth with Mrs. Barrett as Lady Macbeth, the only characters named. Afterpiece was *The Sultan*. On Friday, August 22, "he appeared in the character of Pierre in Otway's *Venice Preserved*." No other characters were named. On Monday, August 25, Cooper played Othello to Mrs. Green's Desdemona, with Green as Iago, the only characters named. Afterpiece was again *The Sultan*.[10]

Another long critique appeared in the *Enquirer* on Friday, August 29, written, I surmise, by the editor, Thomas Ritchie, since it is unsigned. Beginning with a quotation from Pope, the author devotes two-and-a-half columns to an analysis of Cooper's performance on Monday evening, with some general observations on the art of acting. Cooper "towers above his competitors. When Cooper speaks, it is impossible not to devour every sound which he utters: when Cooper listens, his eye, his lip, his forehead, his fingers are almost adequate to supply the cessation of his voice." Several scenes are singled out for special comment; I have deleted quotations of illustrative passages from the play:

In the Sword-scene with Brabantio, the calm, self-balanced intrepidity of the soldier broke forth, when he commanded all tumult to cease. . . . In the senate scene, his apologetic speeches were pronounced with the full force of conscious and triumphant innocence. . . . When he describes his first discovery of Desdemona's love, each feature of his face seemed again to glisten with the recollected joy. . . . In the Fracas-scene, where he cashiers Cassio, his powers of command were amply pourtrayed. . . . But it is in those scenes where the birth and progress of his jealousy is evolved, where still hesitating between the native unaffected honesty of Desdemona, and the artful evidences of her guilt that are accumulated by the villainous Iago, one while relapsing into the confidence of love, & at another reluctantly yielding beneath the plausible circumstances of suspicion, until his imagination completely rides ascendant and he determines that Desdemona should die; it is amidst this uproar of diversified and sublimated passions, that the mind of Cooper displays all its theatric treasures. . . . In the first scene of jealousy with Iago . . . Cooper soared above himself. Every limb, every feature seemed to be agonized on the rack! But it was his eye alone, haggard, wild, projected to the earth, and dimly bursting through his knitted eyebrow, that fixed almost every gaze. The Pit, who caught the full force of its expression, burst into the loudest plaudits. . . . In the 9th scene of the 4th act with Desdemona, Mr. Cooper delivered to admiration, that celebrated speech, wherein he places the horrors of un-requited and abused love, above all the other woes incident to man. . . . The dying scene of Mr. Cooper was worthy of the greatness in which he had lived. The *manner* of his death was an evident improvement upon Shakespeare's plan . . . [Cooper expires upon the line, "and smote him thus"] not like Shakespeare protracting his existence, until he had time to make another speech, abounding in a most miserable conceit
> I kissed thee ere I killed thee.—No way but this
> Killing myself, to die upon a kiss.

[There are, however, defects:] We place out of our criticism the form and texture of his limbs; though it must strike every eye that they are neither on the model of the Farnese Hercules nor of the Apollo Belvidere. We do not descend to a criticism upon *nature*, which Mr. Cooper can neither new-model nor improve: but it is to the *manner* in which he employs her powers, that we dedicate our strictures.

View Mr. Cooper as he *stands* attitudes will frequently strike you, that degrade the dignity of the character which he represents. Hogarth's "line of Grace" is not always the line of majesty. Mr. Cooper's shoulders are too often curved and shelving; his knees instead of being firm and solid in their articulation are flexible and bent; his feet instead of being projected apart into a suitable angle, are placed near and almost parallel to each other, somewhat resembling the attitude of Abel Drugger in Bell's Edition of the English plays. . . . The same want of energy accompanies his *motion*. In the technical language of the theatre, he does not properly *tread the stage*.

Mr. Cooper's voice is of a large compass of tones, and each tone is of exquisite music. Still that compass has its limits. Confined within a certain range of tones, it is sweet, loud and powerful. But raise it beyond a certain key, and it obviously falls short of the pitch which he attempts to produce, and the sound which is emitted is dissonant and harsh. . . .

No man on the stage so little "mouths" his speeches as Mr. Cooper. The tone of his voice is incomparably chaste, its volume almost mathematically suited to the pitch of his passion. But in a few instances perhaps "he overstepped the modesty" of their limits. Fearing to want dignity, his voice would assume a *rant* not supported by the weight of the sentiment; and sometimes fearing to lose its perspicuity, it would drawl and spin itself into a long hissing accent: "Like a wounded snake dragging his slow length along."

· · · · ·

Mr. Green supported the character of Iago with considerable skill. In his soliloquies, where the mask was completely taken off and the villain appeared in all his deformities, his representation was the greatest. But even in these solitary scenes, his deportment was not sufficiently marked by the savage joy of triumphant villainy. . . . Mr. Green's Iago had a sufficient appearance of *thought*, but it wanted the full expression of his feelings. This defect was still more obvious in his interesting interviews with Othello. While he is engaged in secret soliloquy his feelings flow from him as they arise in his bosom; no labour is necessary to restrain them, because no one is supposed to be present who might possibly notice and detect his deceptions. But in his scenes with Othello, the part which he plays is still more difficult. He has two characters to support; of the villain who secretly exults in the success of his own stratagems, and of him who is attempting to disguise his secret machinations, under the. appearance of disinterested friendship. The struggle between the secret enemy and the pretended friend are vehement, and give full scope to all the powers of the performer. The last should be represented to have the ascendency, when Othello's eye was turned upon Iago: the former, when not an eye was fixed upon him, and he was replaced as it were, in all the freedom of his soliloquies. These opportunities were frequent, because the mind of Othello was frequently absorbt by his own meditations. But the countenance of Mr. Green had almost a uniform expression, whether his companion's eye was upon him or not. He seemed actually afraid of indulging the exultation of his soul, lest Othello should turn too quickly upon him, and detect his imposture. —Throw however these defects aside, & the character of Iago was supported to admiration. Mr. Green has great skill in the various departments of the stage; he has still much greater capacities. . . .

Let the performers on the stage recollect, that Hamlet's advice to the profession is extremely imperfect. The duty of a player is of two different kinds; the *speaking* and the *underplaying* of the part. In all that Shakespeare has advised upon the subject, he has compleatly confined his lessons to the first of these duties; directing the players how to employ their *tongues*, how to "suit the action to the *word*," and to "*speak* no more than is set down" for them. He has unfortunately omitted all that constitutes the *under-play* of the character; the *looking* of the part, the sympethising attention, the gestures, the expressions of the face, which should go along with the scene *when* the performer has ceased his speech, or even retired into the background.

This is the part in which the performers of the Richmond stage are so inexcusably defective. . . . The great Cooper himself is a model, which they may not disdain to imitate.

Hamlet was advertised for Wednesday, August 27, with cast of characters:

Hamlet	Mr. Cooper
King	Mr. Martin
Polonius	Mr. Comer
Ghost	Mr. Barrett
Horatio	Mr. Collins
Laertes	Mr. Rutherford
Rosencrans	Mr. Bignall

Guildenstern	Mr. Macdonald
Player King	Mr. Briers
1st Grave Digger	Mr. Wilmot
Queen	Mrs. Barrett
Player Queen	Mrs. Bignall
Ophelia	Mrs. Wilmot

I found no critique of Cooper's Hamlet. Afterpiece was *Rosina*, with the following cast:

Belville	By a gentleman from New York, (being his first appearance here.)
Captain Bellville	Mr. Martin
Rustic	Mr. Bignall
William	Mr. Wilmot
First Irishman	Mr. Rutherford
Second Irishman	Mr. Macdonald
Reapers, &c.	
Rosina	Mrs. Wilmot
Phoebe	Mrs. Green
Dorcas	Mrs. Bignall

On Friday, August 29, the *Enquirer* announced for "This Evening" Cooper's benefit and "last appearance here," in "Shakespeare's celebrated Tragedy of *Richard the Third: or The Battle of Bosworth Field.*" No cast was given, nor is there any criticism of Cooper as Richard. This was undoubtedly Shakespeare as rewritten by Colley Cibber. Both Kean and Kemble played Cibber. Macready's experimental "restoration" was not played until 1821. Afterpiece was *Miss in Her Teens.*

Despite this advertised "last appearance," the *Virginia Gazette* of Wednesday, September 3, advertised "Mr. Cooper's last night but two" for "This evening." Evidently a successful engagement was extended. The play was *Jane Shore*, with the following cast:

Lord Hastings	Mr. Cooper
Dumont	Mr. Green
Duke of Gloster	Mr. Rutherford
Belmour	Mr. Collins
Catesby	Mr. Sears
Ratcliffe	Mr. Martin
Lord Darby	Mr. Bignall
Senator	Mr. MacDonald
Alicia	Mrs. Barrett
Jane Shore	Mrs. Wilmot

I found no criticism of Cooper's Hastings. Afterpiece was *Raising the Wind*, with the following cast:

Jeremy Didler	Mr. Green
Fainwou'd	Mr. Rutherford
Plainway	Mr. Comer
Richard	Mr. MacDonald
Waiter	Mr. Briers
Sam	Mr. Wilmot
Miss Plainway	Mrs. Green
Miss L. Durable	Mrs. Bignall

Saturday, September 6, was "Positively the last night but one of Mr. Cooper's performance," and the play was "(By Particular Desire)" a repetition of *Othello*. Afterpiece was *The Village Lawyer*. No casts were given.[12]

There is no record of Cooper's last night. He had been originally engaged for six nights and six different roles. I surmise that his success was such that he was held over for three additional performances, one of which was a repetition of *Othello*; perhaps the last was also a repetition of one of the original six plays. We have records of eight performances and seven roles. This Richmond season elicited the most detailed criticism extant of his performances in two of his greatest roles, Beverly and Othello.

The season continued after Cooper's departure. On Saturday, September 13, the *Virginia Gazette* respectfully informed the public that the theatre would reopen "for five nights only." Play for "This Evening" was "the admired commedy of *The Will; or School for Daughters*," with *The Padlock* as afterpiece. Between pieces Mr. Wilmot sang "Ted-re-i." No other names were advertised. There is no record of the other four performances.

The plays and the players. Of fifteen plays recorded this season (seven tragedies, seven farces, one comedy), all except *Macbeth* and *Othello* had been previously recorded in Richmond; these probably were performed earlier, and the record is lost. Both had been played in other American theatres during the eighteenth century: *Macbeth* in Philadelphia in 1759, New York, 1768, and Charleston, 1794; *Othello* in New York, 1751, Philadelphia, 1773, and Charleston, 1774. I assume that both were played in Richmond in the usual adaptations.

The company was essentially the same. Names of fifteen actors appear in the newspapers. Mrs. Barrett and Collins were advertised as first appearances. Assuming five performances (as advertised) after Cooper's departure, the season probably ended about the middle of September.

TWENTY-THIRD SEASON
West and Bignall Company
December 1806–February 1807

Chronicle. The only entertainment advertised between the actors' departure in September and their return in December was a "Grand Display of Fireworks at the Circus in the Hay-Market Gardens" on Wednesday evening, October 8, 1806: "The Garden and Ball Room are engaged for that night by Mr. St. Aubin, who will take care to have them elegantly illuminated for the occasion; and will also provide a good band of music for the accomodation of the Ladies and Gentlemen, who may honor him with their company at the Exhibition."[13]

On Wednesday, November 26, the *Virginia Gazette* carried this announcement: "The Richmond Theatre will open on Monday, Dec. 1st, 1806, with a play and farce, as will be expressed in the bills of the day. Days of performance during the winter, will be Monday, Wednesday, and Friday." There is no record of performances on Monday, Wednesday, and Friday, December 1, 3, and 5; "bills of the day" did not survive. The first newspaper advertisement appeared on Saturday, December 6. Perhaps this performance was advertised because it was in addition to the regular three-per-week schedule; the State Legislature was in session, and attendance was probably encouraging. Play for "This Evening" was *Who Wants a Guinea?* "(The Epilogue to be spoken by Mrs. Wilmot)." In the course of the play, Mr. Barrett sang "The Land of Potatoes." Afterpiece was *The Romp.* No casts were given.[14]

The next advertisement appeared on Wednesday, December 10, announcing for "This Evening" *The Castle Spectre* "with entire New Scenery, Dresses and Decorations." Again the epilogue was spoken by Mrs. Wilmot. A full cast was given:

Osmond	Mr. Barrett
Reginald	Mr. Green
Percy	Mr. Collins
Father Philip	Mr. Comer
Motley	Mr. Wilmot
Kenric	Mr. Huntingdon
Saib	Mr. Bignall
Hassan	Mr. Rutherford
Muley	Mr. Briers
Alaric	Mr. Martin
Angela	Mrs. Wilmot
Alice	Mrs. Bignall
Evelina (The Castle Spectre)	Mrs. Barrett

The play was enlivened by "the song and chorus of 'Megen Oh! Megen Ee!' with the glee of 'Listening Angels'—The principal vocal parts by Mrs. Green, Mr. Spear, Mr. Wilmot, Mr. Comer & a Gentleman of Richmond."

Scenic spectacles were described:

In Act 1st—A Gothic Hall in Conway Castle.

In Act 2nd—An Ancient Amoury with suits of Armour complete, arranged as in the Tower of London.

A Gothic Apartment with high arch'd windows, from which Percy escapes, by leaping into the arms of his followers.

In Act 3rd—The apartment of Angela with Sliding Pannel, Portraits of Reginald & Evelina—An Antique Bed and Doors, leading to the Oratory, which discovers the Castle Spectre.

In Act 5th—A gloomy Subterraneous Dungeon in Conway Castle, with excarvated [*sic*] roof & passages leading through the chasm of the Rock.

The whole of the Scenery entirely New—Designed and executed by Mr. Stuart.

Afterpiece was *The Padlock*, with the following cast:

Don Diego	Mr. Comer
Leander	Mr. Spear
First Scholar	Mr. Bignall
Second Scholar	Mr. Martin
Mungo	Mr. Wilmot
Ursula	Mrs. Bignall
Leonora	Mrs. Green

Doors opened at five o'clock, "the performance to commence at six precisely." Boxes and pit were six shillings, gallery, four and six.[15]

On Saturday, December 13, the *Virginia Gazette* advertised for "This Evening . . . Coleman's Celebrated Comedy, of *John Bull; or, an Englishman's Fireside* . . . to which will be added the Farce of *The Sultan; or A Peep into the Seraglio.*" Casts were given for both plays:

John Bull

Peregrine	Mr. Barrett
Job Thornberry	Mr. Rutherford
Sir Simon Rochdale	Mr. Comer
Frank Rochdale	Mr. Collins
Tom Shuffleton	Mr. Huntingdon
Dan	Mr. Wilmot
Williams	Mr. Spear
Steward	Mr. Bignall
John Burr	Mr. Martin
Dennis Brulgruddery	Mr. Green
(with the Epilogue Song)	
Lady Caroline Braymore	Mrs. Green
Mrs. Brulgruddery	Mrs. Bignall
Mary Thornberry	Mrs. Wilmot

The Sultan

Solyman, (The Grand Sultan)	Mr. Rutherford
Osmyn, (The Favorite Eunuch)	Mr. Comer
Grand Carver	Mr. Martin
Eunuchs, Guards, &c.	
Roxalana (The American Slave)	Mrs. Wilmot
Ismena (The Prussian Slave, with Songs)	Mrs. Green
Elmira (The Sultana)	Mrs. Bignall

The *Enquirer* of December 23 advertised the "Elegant Accomplishment" of fencing, "Taught by G. L. Barrett of the Theatre." There were also "Some beautiful Paintings to be had of Mr. Barrett," evidently a man of many talents.

"The celebrated tragedy of *Pizarro; or, The Spaniards in Peru* (with New Scenery, Dresses & Decorations)" was presented on Friday, December 26. Afterpiece was *The Prize*. No casts were given.[16]

On Saturday, December 27, the play was *The Castle Spectre*, "for the last time this season." The same description of scenery was advertised, and the principal roles were the same as on December 10, but there were some changes among the minor roles. For this performance Kenric was played by Martin (replacing Huntingdon), Hassan by Bignall (replacing Rutherford), Muley by Huntingdon (replacing Briers), and Alaric by Briers (replacing Martin). The role of Saib was omitted. Apparently Manager Green sought to strengthen the performance by these changes in the cast. Afterpiece was *Raising the Wind* with the following cast:

Jeremy Diddler	Mr. Green
Plainway	Mr. Comer
Plainwood	Mr. Collins
Richard	Mr. Huntingdon
Waiter	Mr. Briers
Sam	Mr. Wilmot
Miss L. Durable	Mrs. Bignall
Peggy	Mrs. Green[17]

The *Virginia Gazette* of Wednesday, December 31, announced for "This Evening . . . a celebrated Play in five acts, called *Abaellino; or The Great Bandit*." Complete cast was given:

Abaellino (the Great Bandit)	Mr. Green
Andreas Gritti, (Dodge of Venice)	Mr. Comer
Dandoli	Mr. Bignall
Canari	Mr. Huntingdon
Parozzi	Mr. Collins
Contarino	Mr. Spear
Memmo	Mr. Wilmot
Matheo	Mr. Martin
Cardinal Grimaldi	Mr. Briers
Flodoardo	Mr. Green
Iduella	Mrs. Bignall
Rosamonda	Mrs. Green

The production featured "a concert of Music" in act five. Afterpiece was "(for the first time in Virginia) the admired Farce, called *The Weathercock*," with the following cast:

Old Fickle	Mr. Comer
Tristram	Mr. Green
Briefwit	Mr. Spear
Sneer	Mr. Collins

Gardener	Mr. Bignall
Barber	Mr. Huntingdon
Servant	Mr. Martin
Variella	Mrs. Green
Ready	Mrs. Bignall

The Mountaineers was acted on Monday, January 5, 1807, but no advertisement records it; instead, there is a long criticism of the performance in the *Enquirer* of Thursday, January 8. This, evidently, is merely one of many performances which were unvertised, and hence are lost.

COMMUNICATION

Believing that the Stage, under proper Management, is one of the finest vehicles for the conveyance of morality, which human ingenuity has ever devised, I send you the following hasty sketches, attempted in a spirit of candour, as far as my feeble efforts will go, to point out its errors and to give Merit its due praise. It is no excuse for the badness of the performance, that I have written it in the midst of company and in great hurry. I present it to you, such as it is, "with all its imperfections on its head." I am aware that I have said some things calculated to offend the self love of some of the performers—but I will give my sentiments, such as they arise in my mind, or suppress them altogether. I conceive it a kind of moral cowardice to see a fault in any public institution and not dare to point it out. Under this impression I offer no apology for the freedom I have here used. If the persons of whom I have spoken, possess magnanimity, they will pardon me—if they do not, their pardon is not worth obtaining.

Mountaineers

On Monday night the lovers of the drama were gratified by the representation of this most interesting Comedy.

The *Dramatis Personae* were in one instance unfortunately arranged. Mrs. Barret would have made a much better Agnes than she did a Zorayda. Had the characters been reversed, the representation would have appeared far more natural. Unpleasant is the task of censure; but we shall never have good actors nor actresses, until their performances shall be severely criticized. The levity of Agnes was carried to excess; and as much as Mrs. Green deserves to be respected as an actress and a lady, she should yet be told that there is generally too much the appearance of affectation in her performances, and too great a desire manifested of exhibiting her charms. Mrs. Barret succeeds much better in a gay than a

serious character; poor Zorayda was made as solemn as a gentleman of the broad brim; this character was but illy sustained;
perhaps it is difficult to perform, filial affection, struggling with
religious zeal, and all powerful love, call for the tone, the gesture
the look of Mrs. Wilmot. Kilmallock, the Irish captive was tolerably well sustained by Mr. Barret, as also was Virolet by Mr. Collins.
The buffoonery of Mr. Wilmot, in the character of Sadi, calls for
the most marked disapprobation. The performance of Mr. Green,
in the character of Octavian, by far the most important in the
play, is literally above all praise. The attention is changed, the soul
is wrapt from the first moment of his appearance; iron tears were
shed on that night by eyes but little accustomed to weep; the
miser forgot his gold, and the buzy trifler his mighty nothings to
gaze upon Octavian; they were no longer in Richmond; they were
in the *Sieira de Ronda*; they burned with Octavian; they loved
with Floranthe: one fault, however is observable on the first
appearance of Octavian. . . .

This is very fine; but the Poet then proceeds with a most
unnatural thought; he suddenly withdraws Octavian from the con-
templation of his own miseries in order to score the days of his
affliction on the trunk of a willow; whoever has been for any time
"wedded to calamity," will *feel* that this *is* unnatural; it *was felt*
when the first soliloquy of Octavian was pronounced; it was a
most unlucky interruption to the train of feeling; we left Octavian
to chop the bark of a tree, until he returned again in character,
and resumed the broken chain of melancholy and maddening
reflections with—

Oh Octavian
Where are the times thy ardent nature painted
When fortune smiled upon thy lusty youth,
And all was sunshine?

When Said and Octavian are struggling and Agnes rushes from
the cave, nothing could surpass the beauty, propriety and interest
with which Mr. Green pronounced his part—surprise, interrogation,
reflection, indignation, deep agony were all in their turns exhibited
in a most masterly and pathetic style. . . .

Feeling as I did when I listened to this play, I am almost
tempted to say that never was there a more interesting character
drawn, than Octavian, and never could it have been more accurately represented. But were I to give specimens of Mr. Green's
excellence in this piece, I should have to copy the play; wherever
Octavian appears the character is sustained with rigid and critical
nicety and precision. In one scene the feelings are wound up to
a pitch that is positively painful;— the first interview between Oc-

tavian and old Roque, the servant of his mistress Floranthe, whom he supposes dead. . . .

That man's heart must be as rugged as "the forest oak or mountain pine" who would not melt at such a scene.

Similarly, *The School of Reform; or How to Rule a Husband* was acted on Monday, January 12, without advertisement. Record of its performance is a critical article published in the *Enquirer* on Saturday, January 17.

COMMUNICATION

On Monday evening, the *School of Reform or How to Rule a Husband*, was played at the Richmond Theatre.

This Comedy will not stand the test of a rigid scrutiny. In the first place, there is not a unity of action; and in the second, there is a confusion of incidents: but as I have as entire a disgust for the "cant of criticism" as ever Sterne had, I shall say no more in the way of censure of this play, but give it the merit, to which it is certainly entitled, of being, upon the whole, an agreeable and interesting comedy.

With respect to the *representation* of the piece, one general censure applies to every actor and actress on the stage—They transposed the collocation of the words, and mutilated the language of the author, uniformly to the injury of the force and meaning of the play.

Mr. Barret sustained the character of Lord Avondale with great judgment, force of expression and appropriate gesture. This is a very natural character—it is a compound of virtues and vices—it is not one of those "faultless monsters which the world never saw," that we too often see on the stage; but although it is one of those characters that we see every day, yet is it on that very account, the more difficult to perform; for it is much easier to draw a monster than a natural portrait—as it is much easier to write bombast, and fustian, than to write with the plain unadorned sweet simplicity of a Swift or a Goldsmith, so is it much easier to rant in tragedy, or be a buffoon in comedy, or by affection and levity, where the character does not require it, so excessivly to overact the part, that it not only ceases to be interesting or amusing, but gradually becomes odious and disgusting, than to perform a *natural* character. Mr. Barret did perform a natural character, but to my taste, with great excellence.

Mr. Comer represented General Tarragon with considerable success. The character was well suited to the actor, and the actor to the character, which I have observed to be the case oftener with

Mr. Comer than any other performer on the stage; for I do not think this gentleman possesses a flexibility of manner, or versatility of talent, calculated to please in different and opposite characters; Mr. Comer's tone of voice is monotonous, and his style of performance, to use the expression, too uniform and unvarying; but his gesture is generally suited to the meaning of the words he utters. Since Mr. Comer's first appearance on the Richmond stage, he has improved extremely; but after arriving at a certain point, whether from indolence, and want of study, or that nature has denied him farther excellence, it remains for him to shew—he stopt short and has continued pretty much the same for the several last past seasons.

Mr. Collins did not succeed in the character of Mr. Ferment. It is one of the commonest things in human life for persons to over-rate themselves; and this is Ferment's prominent weakness; and it brings him into ludicrous situations; but if I understand the author, he did not intend that he should overrate himself so very far, as Mr. Collins made him. He was represented as a very dolt—a creature in the unfortunate situation, of being unable to excite either admiration, pity or laughter. Ferment should have appeared much more respectable and dignified than he did, at the same time that his hobby-horses, his plans and his weak points, should have brought him into embarrassing and ludicrous situations, the mortification of which should have made his own self-love preceive and feel most poignantly—that to my apprehension, was the *point of character* to which Mr. Collins *was not up*. But Mr. Collins is a young & diffident man; good voice, genteel appearance; always has his part perfect; &, if, as I have heard, he continues to devote himself assiduously to theatrical studies, I think that he will one day arrive at considerable eminence in his profession—a profession, the influence of which upon the morals and manners of civilized society, and upon every species of excellence in forensic and senatorial elocution, has been so little understood, and so badly appreciated. It requires only that the lives of the actors and actresses should not be spent in the shameful dissipation that they too often are, and that they should perform none but good plays to render the stage more efficacious in "raising the genius and mending the heart" than the pulpit itself.

Mr. Spear in the character of Frederick was very unequal to his performance; sometimes he supported the part tolerably well; but in general, the manner of his acting, was tame and uninteresting; with a thick voice, mouthing very word; and his gesture altogether strained, aukward and unnatural.

Mr. Green did not support Tyke with his usual judgment. The serious parts of the character were done with considerable interest;

but the ludicrous *were not*: Mr. Green could not make Tyke a greater scoundrel than he was; but he certainly made him a much greater fool than the author intended. The word "yes" is constantly spelled as it should be; but Mr. Green uniformly pronounced it *ees* although from Tyke's acquaintance with "Jockey Lords," it might have been presumed that he would know how to pronounce a word so perpetually in use. Mr. Green is very far from being exempt from the general censure passed upon all the comedians, in the commencement of these remarks—if he did not "make free with the King's English," he certainly made very free with Mr. Morton's.

Mr. Huntington supported his character of the Old Man very well. This performer seems to stand upon a middle ground of eminence in his calling, from which he is never jostled, either by the laughter of comedy or the frenzy of tragedy; he is never very low in his style of performance; and he is certainly never very great.

Mrs. Barret in the part of Mrs. St. Clair, was much more correct in her performance, than she generally is in serious characters; patient melancholy and resigned grief were what Morton intended, and what Mrs. Barret exhibited.

Mrs. Green failed to excite any great degree of interest in the character of Julia; she has, to a great degree, that fault, from which I have seen few, very few performers exempt: They seem to suppose that they have done enough, and relapse into Mr. or Mrs. Such-a-one, until they have to speak again, and then they endeavor to resume the character they had thrown off. They represent scarcely half the character when they permit these vacant intervals, in their performances: they know not, or if they do, they avail not themselves of the knowledge, that the assuming a particular cast of countenance, and exhibiting appropriate gesture, often speak the language of the passions more forcibly than words themselves.

Mrs. Wilmot performed the character of Mrs. Ferment. This is the all important character in the under plot of *The way to rule a husband*, and was most properly assigned to Mrs. Wilmot. —Never for a moment, in look, gesture, or word, did Mrs. Wilmot, relapse, into Mrs. Wilmot. Mrs. Ferment alone was seen, heard, or understood; the hearty laugh of good-natured ridicule at the weaknesses of a husband, was so naturally *put on* by Mrs. Wilmot, that one cannot but believe that for the time, she actually felt as she appeared to feel. I presume that Horace's maxim will apply as well to mirth as to grief—*Si vis me flere &c.* "If you would have me weep, begin the strain." Mrs. Wilmot would have us laugh, and she began the strain; nor could the warmest wishes of her friends, nor her own self-love desire greater success than she obtained. Conscious that she is performing to admiration, she seems to thank the audience for that debt of applause which she knows they are *obliged* to pay her. Added to Mrs. Wilmot's natural and acquired talents for the stage, she is wise enough always to make herself mistress of her part; no improper pauses, no stammering, no tragic treading across the stage to get nearer the prompter, until he has benumbed and deafened the audience with his hollow sepulchral reminiscences.

The next advertisement appeared on Wednesday, January 14. Headed "Richmond Theatre," it announced for "This Evening, the historical Tragedy, written by John D. Burke, Esq. author of *The History of Virginia, Bethlem Gabor,* and *Oberon,* performed at the Theatres Boston, New York, Charleston, Philadelphia and Virginia, with distinguished applause . . . *Bunker Hill; or, The Death of General Warren.*" Cast was as follows:

General Warren	Mr. Barrett
Putnam	Mr. Huntingdon
Prescott	Mr. Bignall
Abercrombie	Mr. Collins
Governor Gage	Mr. Comer
Lord Percy	Mr. Spear
Sir William Howe	Mr. Briers
Serman	Mr. Wilmot
American Officer	Mr. Martin
Elvira	Mrs. Green
Anna	Mrs. Bignall

Afterpiece was *The Highland Reel* with Bignall as Shelty (the piper) and Mrs. Wilmot as Maggy M'Gilpin, the only characters named.[18] Shelty had been one of the most famous roles of Bignall's father.

The *Virginia Gazette* of Saturday, January 17, announced for

This Evening . . . a Play, interspersed with Songs and Patriotic Airs, (for the first time in Virginia) called *The Glory of Columbia; or, Patriotism and Independence* (written by Mr. Dunlap, of the N. York Theatre, and performed there and in Boston and Charleston, with most distinguished applause) being a play, representing the virtuous heroism of three Patriots, Williams, Van Vat and Paulding, who first secured Major Andre, and by a glorious contempt of pecuniary reward, as well as offered rank rescued their country from the impending evils, consequent upon Gen. Arnold's treachery; and exhibiting the capture of York town, by which the American Independence was secured.

Cast was as follows:

General Washington			Mr. Barrett
General Arnold			Mr. Huntingdon
Major Andre			Mr. Green
Capt. Bland			Mr. Collins
Mellville			Mr. Martin
Williams	the three		Mr. Wilmot
Van Pat	patriotic		Mr. Comer
Paulding	citizens		Mr. Spear
Dennis O'Bogg			Mr. Bignall
British Officer			Mr. Briers
Children			Miss Bignall and Miss West
Mrs. Bland			Mrs. Barrett
Honora			Mrs. Green
Sally Williams			Mrs. Wilmot

Afterpiece was a repetition of *The Sultan*. Cast was the same as on December 13, except that the featured role of Solyman "(the Grand Sultan)" was played by Huntingdon instead of Rutherford.

The Glory of Columbia was evidently a success, for it was repeated on Wednesday, January 21, with the same cast. Afterpiece was *The Waterman; or, the First of August*, with the following cast:

Tom Tug	Mr. Barrett
Bundle	Mr. Comer
Robin	Mr. Wilmot
Wilhelmina	Mrs. Green
Mrs. Bundle	Mrs. Bignall[19]

Theatrical activity usually coincided with Race Week and with sessions of the State Legislature. A prudent manager would naturally take his company to Petersburg or Norfolk during slack times, and play Richmond during the crowded and festive weeks. During this season the Legislature doubtless swelled the audiences; when the Legislature adjourned on January 22, the theatre continued.

On Saturday, January 24, the *Gazette* advertised for "Monday evening . . . (for the last time this season) the Tragedy of *Pizarro*; with other entertainments as will be expressed in the bills."

Neither cast nor afterpiece is named; there was, however, a comic song "The Yorshire Concert" by Wilmot. "Yorshire" I assume to be a misprint for "Yorkshire."

The *Virginia Argus* of Tuesday, January 27, carried a news story, reprinted from the *Petersburg Intelligencer*, on the performance of the Barretts and Master Barrett in *Douglas* "on Friday evening." Barrett and Mrs. Barrett had appeared regularly during this Richmond season, in addition to teaching fencing and producing "beautiful Paintings." Evidently they rehearsed Master Barrett in their spare time, then took him to Petersburg for his debut as young Norval. The parents played Old Norval and Lady Randolph. The performance elicited high praise from the Petersburg critic.

On Wednesday, January 28, the *Virginia Gazette* announced for "This evening (not played here these 12 years) an admired Comedy (written by Miss Lee) called *The Chapter of Accidents*. This elegant Comedy (the production of a justly celebrated female writer) has been selected by Mrs. Wilmot as one highly interesting to the ladies—at the same time that its originality of Character, and diversity of incident, render it eminently calculated to promote the entertainment of the lovers of Comic humour. (For Characters see Bills)." Afterpiece was "the Comic Opera *Tom Thumb The Great; or, The Lilliputian Hero*." This was Mrs. Wilmot's benefit, and tickets were to be had "as usual, and of Mrs. Wilmot at the Theatre." Between pieces there was "a Variety of New Songs."

The *Enquirer* of Thursday, January 29, reprinted from the *Charleston Courier* nearly a column of effusive praise of Master Barrett's performance of Young Norval. He probably toured Petersburg, Norfolk, and Charleston before returning to Richmond. The same issue advertised for "Friday, January 30, the tragedy of *Douglas, or The Noble Shepherd*" featuring Master Barrett "(only twelve years old)" as Young Norval. He was supported as follows:

Lord Randolph	Mr. Huntingdon
Glenalvon	Mr. Green
Old Norval	Mr. Barrett
Officers	Messrs. Bignall and Briers

Servant	Mr. Martin
Lady Randolph	Mrs. Barrett
Anna	Mrs. Bignall

All three Barretts appeared in the afterpiece, *The Adopted Child*, which was cast as follows:

The Adopted Child	Master Barrett (by particular desire and for that night only)
Sir Bertram	Mr. Huntingdon
Le Sage	Mr. Comer
Michael	Mr. Barrett
Record	Mr. Bignall
Spruce	Mr. Wilmot
Flint	Mr. Martin
Clara	Mrs. Wilmot
Lucy	Mrs. Green
Annetta	Mrs. Bignall
Nell	Mrs. Barrett

This was Mrs. Barrett's benefit and tickets were to be had "at A. Davis's Printing Office, Mr. Pumfrey's Book Store, & of Mrs. Barrett, at Captain Davidson's Tavern, near the Capitol."

Douglas included "a Scotch overture & Music, adapted to the piece; between the acts by Mr. Decker, leader of the band." There was also special entertainment between pieces:

End of the Tragedy, will be presented an Ollipodria, consisting of the following:
1. Comic Song—Mr. Wilmot
2. The Grecian Fabulist, or the Old Man, the Boy and the Ass, to exemplify the impossibility of pleasing everybody—Master Barrett
3. A favorite Song—Mrs. Wilmot
4. Recitation, Monsieur Ron Son, or the modern art of Quizzing—Mr. Barrett
5. Comic Song the Land of Pot-o-o-o-o-o
6. An address to the Volunteers of Richmond, written for the occasion—Mrs. Barrett
After which, Fencing in the following grades, will be exhibited, for that evening only, by Mr. and Mrs. Barrett.
1st Salute. 2d Carte & Tierce. Thrust by Master Barrett
3d Carte & Tierce Parade by Master Barrett
4th Counter, Carte & Tierce by Master Barrett
5th Counter Cartes & Tierce Pushed & Parade—by Father and Son. To conclude with the Salute.

Barrett had advertised to teach fencing the previous December. I trust that all his pupils attended the theatre for this demonstration. Fencing "by Mr. and Mrs. Barrett" I take to be a mistake for Mr. and Master Barrett.

Master Barrett's performance evoked two critical appraisals, both favorable. The first appeared in the *Virginia Gazette* on Wednesday, February 4:

Mr. Editor,

Always conceiving that Theatrical performances have a tendency of polishing the human understanding, and of introducing into civil society a fund of knowledge, which is capable of being universally diffused, and that such performances should undergo rigid scrutiny, or justly merited encomiums, indispensable necessary for the support of the institution, I send you the following communication, a lame attempt indeed to criticism, but impressed with the idea, that the discharge of this important duty should be otherwise neglected.

On Friday evening, was exhibited, to a numerous and respectable audience in this city, Home's excellent tragedy of *Douglas, or, The Noble Shepherd*, the part of young Norvel, by Master Barrett . . . the justly famed American Roscius. This being his first appearance in this city, it naturally excited the public curiosity; nor were the high and ardent expectations of the audience too dearly estimated—by his performance he meritoriously has affirmed the public sentiment of admiration that glowed with the liveliest anticipation previous to his appearance. It would be preposterous in me, so feeble is my capacity, to attempt, to delineate the several appropriate gestures, the elegance of expressive [*sic*] maintained by Master Barrett, during the performance, the sublimity of the spectacle when after the fatal conflict with Glenalvon, he hastened to perform the last filial duty, is to me expressive in no other terms but astonishment and admiration.

The dramatic talent of this youth if nurtured with due and proper attention, may perhaps at some future period eclipse even the famed Britannic Garrick—but if he possesses a genius which might be better devoted than to the stage, it would in my opinion be more commendable to give him an opportunity of displaying the talents, he doubtless possesses, on the civil or political stage, which may one day or other render him an useful ornament to society.

Certain it is however that his performance in the character of Norval has merited our warmest approbation. Not an exception can be drawn to the inimitable support which he gave it.

The manner in which Mrs. Barrett sustained the character of

Lady Randolph exceeded the highest expectations formed of her in the minds of the audience—she felt to perfection what she uttered—no intervals in which her attention was drawn by other objects (as some critics on the drama have observed) occurred—struggling with maternal affliction and at the same time maintaining a proper degree of fortitude, (as Home certainly intended)—the citizens of Richmond were at once transported into Caledonia, and beheld the real Lady Randolph.

Mr. Green supported Glenalvon with his usual ingenuity and address — It is so well known that this celebrated performer is incapable of erring in his dramatic exhibitions, that to pass a just encomium on his excellence that science, would require an eulogist, and not one so inadequate as I am to give it.

Mr. Barrett performed old Norval tolerably well.

Mr. Huntingdon was greater in Lord Randolph than I ever saw him. His gesture was rather aukward, but time and experience will efface that defect. He certainly possesses an articulation peculiarly adapted to the stage.

It is useless to comment on the performances of the rest in this tragedy, as they do not merit it.

I am sir, your obedient servant
A Patron

A more critical and perceptive piece, unsigned, appeared in the *Gazette* on Saturday, February 7. The writer considers that *Douglas*, "adheres as closely to the rules of the Drama, laid down by the critics, from Aristotle to Voltaire, as any in the English, or any other language." It is "entirely fictitious: plot, incidents, and characters; no light borrowed from history: the author, therefore, must alone be consulted as to the development of character." Had Home been present Friday, he would have approved entirely the performance of "that charming little fellow, the American Roscius, young Barrett." Other members of the cast come off less well. Huntingdon did not sustain Lord Randolph with propriety. The character is subtler than Huntingdon made him; he "missed the finer emotions in the nicer parts of the character." Green did not perform Glenalvon well: "It is useless to point out his defects; because he could perform it with critical propriety, and his omissions arose from neglect." Mrs. Barrett performed Lady Randolph "always well, most generally to admiration." Mr. Barrett as Old Norval "overacted his part. There was no necessity, that he should have manifested such extreme decrepitude, infirmity, old age and weakness as he did." Mrs. Bignall as Anna "did poorly with a part of great possibilities. It frequently requires an excellent performer to act a low part." Finally, Master Barrett "deserves great praise for so seldom committing a fault, from which I have never seen any actor exempt, Cooper excepted: that of talking to the audience, and looking at the Pitt and Boxes, instead of the person with whom the dramatist intended a dialogue to take place. Even in speaking a soliloquy, the audience should be forgotten; there ought to be as little communication between the performers and their auditors as possible."

Meanwhile, the *Virginia Gazette* of Saturday, January 31, advertised for Monday evening, February 2, *The School for Scandal,* with the following cast:

Sir Peter Teazle	Mr. Comer
Sir Oliver Surface	Mr. Spears
Joseph Surface	Mr. Huntingdon
Charles	Mr. Green
Crabtree	Mr. Wilmot
Sir Benjamin Backbite	Mr. Collins
Rowley	Mr. Briers
Moses	Mr. Bignall
Snake	Mr. Martin
Lady Teazle	Mrs. Wilmot
Maria	Mrs. Green
Lady Sneerwell	Mrs. Bignall
Mrs. Candour	Mrs. Barrett

Afterpiece was "the Comic Opera of *The Shipwreck*" with the following cast:

Selwyn	Mr. Collins
Harry Hawser	Mr. Green
Michael Goto	Mr. Huntingdon
Shark	Mr. Wilmot
Stake, (a Parish Clerk)	Mr. Comer
Dick	Mr. Spear
Plunderers	By the rest of the company
Angelica	Mrs. Green
Fanny	Mrs. Bignall
Sally Shamrock	Mrs. Wilmot

This was Comer's benefit. Entertainment between pieces consisted of a recitation, "The Seven Ages of Woman," by Mrs. Wilmot; "O Stay Sweet Fair," by Mrs. Wilmot, Mrs. Green, and Mr. Wilmot; a song in character, "The Old Commodore," by Comer; and a glee, "Oh! Lady Fair," by Mrs. Wilmot, Mrs. Green, and Mr. Wilmot.

On Wednesday, February 4, was announced for "This evening (for the first time in this Theatre) the Celebrated Play, being the introduction to the Tragedy of *Pizarro*, called *Cora; or, The Virgin of the Sun*." Afterpiece was *The Hotel; or, the Man with Two Masters*. For characters we are referred to the bills of the day. This was the benefit of Mr. Stuart, "Scene Painter and Machinist." Between pieces was a "Comic Song" by Wilmot, the favorite ballad of "Lillies & Roses" by Spear, and the favorite duet, "Of Plighted Faith" by Mrs. Wilmot and Mrs. Green.[20]

"Kotzebue's Celebrated Play of *Lover's Vows*" was acted on Saturday, February 7, with the following cast:

Baron Weldenham	Mr. Huntingdon
Count Caffel	Mr. Spears
Anhault	Mr. Green
Frederick	Mr. Collins
Verdon	Mr. Comer
Landlord	Mr. Martin
Cottager	Mr. Wilmot
Farmer	Mr. Bignall
Countryman	Mr. Briers
Agatha	Mrs. Barrett
Amelia	Mrs. Wilmot
Cottager's Wife	Mrs. Bignall
Girl	Miss Bignall

Afterpiece was "(for the last time this season) the admired Comic Opera of *The Weathercock*," for which no cast was given. This was Decker's benefit. Between pieces he performed with Weidemeyer, La Taste, and C. Southgate "a Favorite Quartett of Pleyels for Flute, Violin, Viola and Violincello." There was also "a new Scotch Song" by Mrs. Green, a comic song, "Murder in Irish," by Mr. Wilmot, and a new song, "The Violet Girl," by Mrs. Wilmot. "By Desire" the favorite glees of "Oh Lady Fair" and "Oh Stay Sweet Fair" were repeated by Mrs. Wilmot, Mrs. Green, and Mr. Southgate.[21]

Another item of interest appeared in the same newspaper:

NOTICE

By virtue of a Trust Deed executed to me by Mrs. Margaret West, I shall on Saturday the 28th Inst. expose to sale by Public Auction to the highest bidder for ready money, upon the premises, all the remaining part of that Tract Piece or parcel of ground heretofore undisposed, of situate, lying and being in the city of Richmond, and which is commonly called and known by the name of Quesnay's Academy ground; or so much thereof, as may be sufficient to pay and satisfy two installments of $1000 each, due to Mr. Yeamans Smith of the city of Richmond, and the cost and charges of executing this Trust.

Samuel M'Crow, Trustees
George Fisher

Margaret was the widow of Manager West, who died in 1799. She had previously sold some of her property, presumably to finance the building of the present theatre. Evidently she had borrowed on the remaining property. George Fisher was treasurer of the Committee which had raised money for the theatre. Does this indicate that the theatre was not making money? What was Mrs. West's investment in the theatre? I have no answers.

The *Virginia Gazette* of Wednesday, February 11, advertised: "Master Barrett, The Infant American Roscius's Last Appearance Here" for Thursday, February 12. *Douglas* was repeated, with the same cast. Afterpiece was "the Grand serious pantomime of *Don Juan; or, The Libertine Destroyed*," for which no cast was given. This was Mr. Barrett's benefit, and there was "a Pick Nick" between pieces: a recitation, "Alonzo the Brave and the Fair Imogene," by Master Barrett, a comic Irish song, "The Land of Potatoes," by Mr. Barrett, and "The Grecian Fabulist," by Master Barrett.

The same newspaper carried under the heading "Richmond Theatre," an enthusiastic puff for "a diamond to [*sic*] long buried in obscurity . . . a young gentleman of this city [who] is to make his appearance on our boards in the arduous part of Hamlet. . . . characters adequate to judge, declare him to be equal if not superior to the celebrated Cooper." The *Virginia Argus* of Friday, February 13, lent its columns to a similar piece by "a Friend," who told readers that the "young gentleman" was only seventeen years of age and had "never yet appeared on any stage." His talents are "great and splendid," and "his conception of this great character is very little if any inferior to the celebrated Cooper." The performance was on Saturday, February 14, Mr. Wilmot's benefit. Afterpiece was *The Prisoner at Large*. No casts were given, and the "young gentleman" remained unnamed. There was no criticism of the performance.

On Wednesday, February 18, the *Virginia Gazette* advertised "Last Night But one This Season. On Thursday evening . . . by the particular desire of several citizens, will be performed for the first time in any Theatre, a Play (written by a Young Gentleman of Richmond) called *The Road to Honor*." Cast was as follows:

Governor Wealthy	Mr. Huntingdon
Sir Andrew Acid	Mr. Comer
Old Manful	Mr. Barrett
Young Manful	Mr. Green
Young Acid (Captain of the Pirates)	By the Young Gentleman who performed Hamlet
Ranger	Mr. Martin
Spitfire	Mr. Stowell
Serjeant Scout	Mr. Briers
Blunt	Mr. Wilmot
Subtle	Mr. Spear
Trip	Mr. Collins
Bellona	Mrs. Wilmot
Pricilla	Mrs. Green

I suspect that *The Road to Honor* was written by the "Young Gentleman" who performed Hamlet. "Young Acid (Captain of the Pirates)" suggests a fat part, written by and for the "Young Gentleman." No critic appraised the merits of either the performance or the play, which, except for this record, is unknown.

Afterpiece was a repetition of *The Weathercock*, with the same cast as advertised for December 31, except that Barber, then played by Huntingdon, was now played by Stowell; and Ready, then played by Mrs. Bignall, was omitted. The evening was enlivened by three songs between pieces: "Tantivy," in character by Mrs. Green, "Dan the Head Waiter's journey to London," by Mr. Wilmot, and an untitled song by Mrs. Wilmot.

Last night of the season was Tuesday, February 24, when *Douglas* was repeated for the benefit of Master Barrett, "the Infant American Roscius." A puff in the *Enquirer* of this date informed the public that "the profits of this night's performance . . . will be exclusively appropriated to the education of this most promising child . . . at present, under the tuition of Dr. Haller, who is well known to be a professor of first-rate talents and learning." Afterpiece was "a Comedy in three acts, called *The Farm House; or, The Female Duellist.*" Between pieces the same specialties were performed as on January 30. The only character named was Young Norval Douglas, played by Master Barrett, "(only twelve years old)."

The season covered nearly three months, with performances recorded on every day of the week. If we assume an average of three performances per week, there should have been about thirty-five; we have records of twenty-one. Thirty-one different plays were performed: tragedy, comedy, comic opera, farce, spectacle, including seven not previously recorded in Richmond: *The Chapter of Accidents, The Glory of Columbia, The Hotel, The Road to Honor, The School of Reform, The Waterman, The Weathercock.* There was one American premiere of an English play, *The Hotel,* and one performance of a hitherto unknown play by a local author, *The Road to Honor.*

The company was essentially the same, though some new names were added. Its acting strength as compiled from advertisements was nineteen, with Green as manager. From available records, it was a long and successful season.

The plays. *The Weathercock* (December 31, 1806), a farce by John Till Allingham, was brought out at Drury Lane on December 18, 1805. Its American premiere was at the Park Theatre in New York on June 9, 1806, less than six months later. It was acted in Charleston on November 10, 1806, and Philadelphia December 21, 1810.

The School of Reform (January 12, 1807), a comedy by Thomas Morton, had its premiere at Covent Garden on January 15, 1805, and its American premiere in Charleston on February 3, 1806. It was acted in New York on April 16, 1806, and Philadelphia, February 28, 1812.

The Glory of Columbia (January 17, 1807), called by Odell "a very weak adaptation of the long-forgotten *Andre*," was written by William Dunlap to satisfy "the popular demand for patriotic spectacles . . . with a cheerful indifference to history," according to Quinn.[22] It was brought out at the Park Theatre, New York, on the Fourth of July, 1803, and was acted in Charleston on April 8, 1805.

The Waterman (January 21, 1807), a comic opera by Charles Dibdin, was first acted at the Haymarket in 1774. It was acted in Philadelphia in 1791, New York, 1793, and Charleston, 1794.

The Chapter of Accidents (January 28, 1807), a comedy by Sophia Lee, was brought out at the Haymarket on August 5, 1780. It was acted in both New York and Philadelphia in 1783 and in Charleston in 1794.

The Hotel (February 4, 1807), a farce by Thomas Vaughn, was first acted at Drury Lane on November 21, 1776. This Richmond performance was evidently its American premiere. I found no other record of its performance in America before 1822, when it was acted in New York.

The Road to Honor (February 19, 1807) "by a Young Gentleman of Richmond" was performed only once.

The players. This season included the appearance of Master George Barrett, aged twelve, "the Infant American Roscius," who played Young Norval in *Douglas* and title role in *The Adopted Child*. He had already appeared on stage as "Boy" in 1798 in a New York production of *The Stranger* with Cooper in the title role. His Young Norval was favorably received in Richmond, and future fame was predicted. Fulfilling the prediction, he became in later years the "Gentleman George" Barrett, favorite of the Park Theatre in New York and most famous light comedian of the American stage.

TWENTY-FOURTH SEASON

West and Bignall Company

May–June 1807

Chronicle. The *Virginia Gazette* of Saturday, May 23, 1807, respectfully informed the public that "the Richmond Theatre will be opened for a few nights beginning on Monday, May 25, [when] will be presented a Play (translated from the German of Kotzebue) *The Stranger; or, Misanthropy and Repentance* (for characters see bills)." Afterpiece was *The Prize*. Boxes and pit were six shillings, gallery, four and six. Tickets were to be had at A. Davis's printing office, Mr. Pumfrey's stationery store, and at the office of the theatre. "Subscribers are respectfully informed their tickets will be left at A. Davis's Printing office."

On Saturday, June 6, the *Enquirer* stated that "the celebrated Cowper is to be in Town this Evening, and it is to be hoped that the manager of our Theatre, will not fail to avail himself of this opportunity of gratifying the public by engaging Mr. Cowper for a few evenings at least." The advice was taken, but when Cooper appeared, or how many times, is unknown. Only one advertisement of his engagement is preserved. The *Virginia Gazette* of Saturday, June 13, advertised Cooper's "last night of performance." The play was *Othello*, with the following cast:

Othello	Mr. Cooper
Iago	Mr. Green
Roderigo	Mr. Huntingdon
Cassio	Mr. Hallam
Brabantio	Mr. Comer
Montano	Mr. Spears
Lodovico	Mr. Martin
Duke	Mr. Low
Gratiano	Mr. Bignall
Emilia	Mrs. Barrett
Desdemona	Mrs. Green

Afterpiece was *No Song, No Supper*, for which no cast was given. Between pieces Comer sang "Old Commodore" in character. Cooper possibly played seven roles on seven evenings between June 6 and June 13, but there was no other advertisement, and no criticism was published.

The next advertisement appeared in the *Virginia Gazette* on Wednesday, June 24, announcing for "This evening the *Historical Tragedy of Bunker Hill; or, The death of General Warren*." Afterpiece was "the serious Pantomime *The Death of Captain Cook, In the Island of O-Why-Hee*." No casts were given. Doors opened at six, performance began at seven, and tickets were to be had "as usual."

There are only these three advertisements this season. I do not know why there were no more. Newspaper files are in good condition. Certainly, the appearance of Cooper deserved newspaper notice in addition to the usual handbills. Only the *Othello* advertisement lists cast. From it, we glean names of ten actors, eight men and two women. Almost certainly there were others. And certainly there were other performances. Even if the season extended only from May 25 to June 24 ("for a few nights") there should have been a dozen performances. Records are incomplete and disappointing. We can document only six plays, all previously acted in Richmond, and there was no criticism. But Cooper did appear.

Hiatus
June 1807–September 1809

The company probably left Richmond in July 1807 to play in other Virginia theatres. It was never to be the same. When the theatre reopened, after a hiatus of more than two years, there were new management and a new company.

At least one of the company remained in Richmond to practice his profession: La Taste, of the orchestra. On August 10 he advertised a concert and ball at Hay Market Garden and later advertised a dancing school to be opened on Monday, September 21.[23]

Entertainment was scarce during the rest of the year. On December 4 the *Virginia Argus* advertised the "Famous African Horse," Spottee, on exhibition at the Washington Tavern. Spottee could "add, subtract, multiply and divide." Admittance was "50¢, children half price." There is no record of theatre during the winter of 1807-8.

On April 1, 1808, the *Virginian* advertised the opening of Hay Market Garden for the season. There was organ music, dancing, and fireworks. According to the *Enquirer* of April 29, the only living elephant in the United States was then on exhibit at the Washington Tavern, admittance twenty-five cents.

Somewhat closer to legitimate theatre was the performance of "Beauties of the Theatre" in the ballroom of the Eagle Tavern on

May 17. Scenes from *Douglas* and *School for Scandal* were acted by Mr. and Mrs. Ormsby. There was also "A Comic Piece in 2 acts *The Humerous Scotchman*," and "Songs & Recitations." Leader of the orchestra was Mr. H. Weidemeyer, who had been a member of the West and Bignall orchestra during the last season. The program was repeated on May 24 at Hay Market Garden.[24]

On July 8 the *Enquirer* respectfully informed the public that "Mr. & Mrs. Poe, Mr. Burk junr and Mrs. Shaw from the Boston theatre, intend to give an entertainment at the Hay-Market Garden on Monday evening next. Particulars in future advertisement." I assume that the entertainment was presented, although I found no other advertisement.

On August 9 Manfredi advertised rope dancing, tumbling, and dancing on the slack wire at Mason's Hall on August 10. Admittance was fifty cents. On August 12 he advertised that "Miss Catherine and Miss Miniguina" would perform with him. Then on August 23 he advertised "a new Pantomime, called *The Old Man seeking his own Fancy, or Harlequin, Dead and Alive.*" Cast consisted of Manfredi as Clown, Miss Catherine as Columbine, Mr. Copene as Old Man, Mr. John as Magician, and Master Glorious as Harlequin. The pantomime was repeated on August 26, with the addition of Mr. Entwine as Doctor. On August 27, "Miss Catherine's benefit," the pantomime was called *"Harlequin's Skeleton and Ghost"*; and on August 31, "the Benefit of Miss Miniguina & the Little American," it was *"Harlequin Transformed into a Bull Dog."* Most ambitious program was on September 3: "the new Double Dance, called the *Triumph of the King of Mogul*, being the second time it has been exhibited in the United States." The evening concluded with "a Pantomime called *Harlequin Pastry Cook*," with the following cast: Clown, Manfredi; Columbine, Miss Catherine; Old Man, Mr. Copene; Magician, Mr. John; Harlequin, the Little American.[25]

Competition to Manfredi's troupe came from Webster, who on August 12 offered in the Bell Tavern assembly room "an entertainment consisting of Dialogue and Songs, written by Dibdin, called *Song Smith; or Rigmarole Repository.*" Admittance was one dollar.[26]

On Friday, November 11, appeared this notice: "Mr. Simon

Respectfully informs the ladies and gentlemen of Richmond and Manchester that he has arrived in town with his company, and will open the theatre on Saturday the 12th of November to perform Rope Dancing, Tumbling, Pantomimes & & which will be explained in the bills. His exertion and zeal will be exerted to merit public patronage." Another performance was advertised for Thursday, November 17, "if weather permits."[27]

"Rope Dancing, Tumbling, Pantomimes, Italian Shades, & &" were advertised in the theatre for Tuesday, December 6, 8, and 10 by Alarcon. Performance began at seven, admittance "half a dollar."[28]

On December 27 Martin advertised performances at the theatre "During the sitting of the Legislature." Performances were given on December 27 and 31, 1808, and on January 5, 14, 21, and 31, 1809. January 21, was "the Benefit of Mrs. Martin, who will perform the most surprising and wonderful Feats of Activity and Dexterity, aided by Mr. Martin as Clown." Martin's last performance on January 31 consisted of "New and frolicksome tricks of dexterity, The Celebrated Phantasmogoria, never exhibited before, with several curious paritions, viz: the apotheosis of Washington, the Boat of Charon, Dives' Tomb destroyed by a shower of fire, the Giant of Goliah, natural as life &.&.&."[29] This may have been the same Martin who had previously acted with the West and Bignall company.

The dancing school of John La Taste was advertised again on March 10, and on July 11 there was "Grand Fire Works by Mr. Lewis." The second night of "the Young American Orator, The Infant Roscius, only Seven years old" was advertised for Hay Market Garden on Wednesday, July 19. He gave recitations from the English classics and sang a number of serious and comic songs. Leader of the band was Weidemeyer.[30]

On August 22 the *Enquirer* carried this brief notice: "We are authorized to state, that the Richmond Theatre, under the management of Messrs. Green & Placide, will be opened early next month." Possibly in anticipation of the coming season, G. Greenhow advertised on August 25 "For Sale—One Share in the Richmond Theatre Company."[31]

CHAPTER VI

1809–1811

TWENTY-FIFTH SEASON
Placide and Green Company
September–October 1809

Chronicle. The Charleston season closed on April 11, 1809. Sherman locates the company in Norfolk in May. They may also have played in Petersburg on their way to Richmond, where they arrived probably about the middle of August. The season opened on Saturday, September 2, with *Venice Preserved* and *The Weathercock*. A brief announcement respectfully informed the public that "the Richmond Theatre will be opened on Saturday Evening," and named the plays, but gave no cast or other details.[1]

The next advertisement included casts for the two plays which were performed on Wednesday, September 6. They were "(for the first time here) a Grand Melo Drama *The Fortress*" and "a Musical Drama called *The Hunter of the Alps* (written by Mr. Dimond, jun. author of *The Hero of the North* &c.)":

The Fortress

Count Everard	Mr. Caulfield
Valbron	Mr. Clark
Oliver	Mr. Fox
Count Adolphus	Mr. Byrne
Vincent	Mr. Sully
Philip	Mr. Ringwood
Thomas	Mr. Spear
Petras	Mr. Utt
Soldier	Mr. Jones
Celestine	Mrs. Clark
Alice	Mrs. Placide
Palina	Mrs. Bray

The Hunter of the Alps

Felix	Mr. Fox
Rosalvi	Mr. Clark
Jeronymo	Mr. Bray
Juan	Mr. Spear
Baptista	Mr. Ringwood
Marco	Mr. Byrne

Pietro	Mr. Jones
Julio Di Rosalvi	Master H. Placide
Florio Di Rosalvi	Miss S. Sully
Helene Di Rosalvi	Mrs. Placide
Genevieve	Mrs. Clark
Claudine	Mrs. Bray
Ninette	Mrs. Utt
Rosetta	Mrs. Simpson

Between play and afterpiece was "a Ballet Dance . . . performed by children only called *The Bird Catcher; or, The Merry Girl.*" The children were Miss Sully as Lubin "(the bird catcher)," C. Placide as Lucette "(the merry girl)," with Masters H. Placide, T. Placide, and M. Sully as "Hunters, &c." The ballet concluded with "an allemand by Miss S. Sully and Miss C. Placide." Doors opened at six with "curtain to rise at seven precisely." Tickets at one dollar, children half price, were to be had at the newspaper office and the theatre. Subscribers were requested to send to the newspaper office for their tickets.[2]

The *Virginia Gazette* of Friday, September 8, advertised for that date "(never performed here) a Celebrated Comedy, written by Moreton, called *Town and Country; or, Which Do You Like Best?*" Afterpiece was *Fortune's Frolic; or, the True Use of Riches.* Casts were given for both plays:

Town and Country

Reuben Glenroy	Mr. Caulfield
Trot	Mr. Clark
Cosey	Mr. Sully
Plastic	Mr. Fox
Rev. Owen Glenroy	Mr. Ringwood
Captain Glenroy	Mr. Spear
Hawbuck	Mr. Bray
Armstrong } Ross }	Mr. Utt
Williams	Mr. Byrne
Robert	Mr. Jones
Hon. Mrs. Glenroy	Mrs. Placide
Rosalie Somers	Mrs. Green
Mrs. Trot	Mrs. Clark
Mrs. Moreen	Mrs. Simpson
Goody Hawbuck	Mrs. Utt
Taffline	Mrs. Bray

Fortune's Frolic

Robin Roughhead	Mr. Sully
Old Snacks	Mr. Ringwood
Mr. Frank	Mr. Clark
Rattle	Mr. Fox
Clown	Mr. Byrne
John	Mr. Jones
Margery	Mrs. Simpson
Dolly	Mrs. Clark
Miss Nancy	Mrs. Bray

Between pieces Miss Sully danced a hornpipe. The advertisement stated that "during the Season, no Play will be repeated, nor will there be any Postponement on account of weather."

Most of the advertisements of this season appeared in the *Virginia Gazette*, and tickets were on sale at that office; but the only piece of criticism appeared in the *Enquirer* on September 12. Unsigned and headed "For *The Enquirer*," the piece first quoted Pope's Prologue to Addison's *Cato* ("To wake the Soul, by tender strokes of art . . ."), which was cited as "the office of the Tragic Muse." The office of the comic muse "may be expressed in the other words of the same poet, 'To shoot the Follies living as they rise.' " Exclusive of Dr. Johnson's consideration of plays as "of the public stock of harmless pleasure," plays have two principal offices: "to show us what man *is*, and exhibit *models of what he ought to be*." The essay continued:

In the exhibition of these offices, the Drama has made rapid advances, since those primeval days, when Thespis used to wander about in his cart and stain his face with the leys of wine. But there is still great scope of improvement, but in the species and manner of scenes to be exhibited. There is besides great scope, in what may be called the *machinery of the plot*. Every thing should be omitted which detracts from the *probability* of the representation, and destroys its resemblance to real life; such as *Asides*; many Soliloquies; & songs, where they are struck up on a sudden, without being called for by any person on the stage.

There is nothing, which so much determines the taste of the Manager, or the success of his labours, as the choice of his dramas. What an immense scope is left to his selections, both in the varities of scenes which are exhibited, and in the different lights in which these are hit off by different authors. Some display the

effects of *Love*—others the torture of *jealously*—some the maddening energy of *Ambition*—and others, the ridiculous or fatal
effects of fashionable vices. These are infinitely diversified by their
exhibition. The age of Charles 2d has a *mannerism* of its own,
peculiarly distinct from that of 1800. Beaumont and Fletcher mistake lewdness for love, and scurrility for wit. —The genius of
Sheridan and Holcroft is chaste, attic, descriptive of the feelings
of the heart, or the ruling follies of the day.

The Manager should select the finest productions of Sheridan,
Cumberland, Holcroft, Colman, Moreton—every drama that is
recommended by the lustre of its sentiments, the elegance of its
dialogue, the keenness of its wit, the beauty of its plot and the
ridicule of fashionable follies.

Every thing should be exploded, which partakes of the indecent,
the gross, the scurrilous or the buffoon. Where the Manager persists
in foisting these upon the stage, they should be hissed and hooted
off by the audience. Thus, what shall we think of the Entertainment exhibited on Friday night of "Fortune's Frolic;" where the
audience was entertained with such low-lived expressions, as
"feasting bellies, and filling guts?"

Let them repeat the affecting, though not always the appropriate
lines of Johnson's Prologue delivered at the opening of Drury Lane
in 1747,

> Ah! let not Censure term our fate our choice,
> The Stage but echoes back the public voice;
> The Drama's laws, the drama's patrons give,
> For we that live to please must please to live.

The company, who now grace the boards of the Richmond
Theatre are worthy of public encouragement. The Manager deserves our thanks for his exertions and his care. The Scenery is
uncommonly elegant. The Music is extremely fine. The Players
generally speaking *good*!

In the whole range of the *Dramatis Personae* Mrs. Placide is our
favorite—her voice sweet, pathetic and so expressive, that you can
scarcely mark the *emphasis* of her words—her eye brilliant and
penetrating—her countenance, robed in all the varieties of passion—
her gestures, so happily attempered to the part, which she represents—her full understanding of her character—her never ceasing
attention to the scene in which she is engaged—*her* never forget-
ting, that she is on the stage, and yet her always playing her part
so naturally, as to make *us* forget it—stamp her with the reputation
of being one of the best actresses, which has ever adorned the
Theatre of Virginia. She is in my respects similar to our old favorite, Mrs. J. West. As the celebrated Mrs. Merry was, she is deficient

in the portability and grace of *person*—but who can control the operations of nature?

Has she then no *fault*? She has a few—which may be easily illustrated by the fable of Momus. . . . We may pass the same encomium on Mrs. Placide; only her tongue does not *creak* enough. Her voice is sometimes so low, that its sweetest accents do not reach the listening ear. Her manner too, is sometimes extravagant and unnatural.

Mrs. Green has touched this horizon but once this season; but she was soft, interesting & picturesque—more artless, and far more unaffected than we have ever seen here.

Mr. Caulfield has strong tragic powers; a noble and commanding person; a fine voice—his greatest danger lies in "tearing the passion all to rags;" in travestying the serious into the deeply tragic. He overcharges the picture with too much colouring; he overacts his part beyond the modesty of nature; as the Representation of Reuben Glenroy too strongly demonstrated. Let these exuberances be corrected.

Mr. Clark deserves every credit for the zeal, with which he labours to serve the public. No man's part is better committed to memory—no man better feels his character. His representation of Rosalin in the Hunter of the Alps was to the life; but his voice, though strong, is often harsh, untunable and grumbling. He can certainly *modulate* it better than he does; as well as soften down the *angular* movements of his arms. His improvement, since he last visited the Richmond boards, is at least an earnest of the amelioration which future perseverance and energy may infuse into his acting.

Mr. Fox is good in many parts. His representation of Robert in the Curfew, was to the life modest, chaste, and empressive. A little more simplicity would greatly improve him. It is obvious that nature has given him fine teeth and good eyes—and no less obvious by the use he makes of them, that he knows it too.

In all the characters, which breathe fun and mirth and revelry, Mr. Sully stands one of the greatest heroes of the Buskin. His part of the gate-keeper in "The Fortress," was performed to admiration. His greatest sin, is not so much in the want of powers, as of a *constant desire to exert them.*

Mr. Ringwood is fraught with a large share of the *comica vis*— His Irishisms, his humour, his representations of low life, are faithful copyists of nature. As the Lieutenant, in the Fortress, he was truly great—But in the serious character of Parson Glenroy, he appeared to be out of his element. " 'Tis not the *inky cloak*, nor customary suits of solemn black, that can denote" *him* truly.

Mr. Bray, *as far as we are acquainted*, is one of our favorites.

He represented the Simple quaker, to the life, and in the character of Hawbuck in the Comedy of "Town and Country," he was *true Yorkshire*. The comic character is *forte*; in which as a Gentleman justly observed to us, no man ever better understood the Art of divesting himself of all appearance of Intelligence. —We hope soon to have the satisfaction of hearing him sing the favorite song of the "Potatoe Merchant," which a learned judge of the United States declares, he would at any time walk five miles to hear him sing.

For the present, we shall dismiss "our friends, the players" with a few simple rules, which, if they please, they may put alongside those of Hamlet's advice to them:

1. When on the stage, never to forget that they are there; never to coquette with the audience—to address themselves only to the scene in which they are engaged.

2. Not to think their representative character is over, when they have done *speaking*—but to fill up their intervals of the dialogue with proper *action*—and to remember, that when off the stage, we do not cease to *feel*, though we cease to *speak*.

3. Never to speak to each other, except to forward the business of the drama—and above all, never to point to the audience; lest the audience should take it to be a pointed insult to themselves.

This is the only record of *The Curfew*, which was evidently produced some time between opening night, September 2, and the appearance of this criticism on September 12.

The *Virginia Gazette* of September 12 advertised for Wednesday, September 13, "(for the first time here) a celebrated Drama called *The Wanderer; or The Rights of Hospitality*." Afterpiece was *The Review*, and between the two was a "Ballad, called *The Wood Cutters*. To be performed by Miss Sully, & Master H. Placide." An advertisement in the *Virginia Argus* of this date adds Miss Placide to the cast. No cast was given for *The Review*, but there was a full cast for *The Wanderer*:

Gustavus Adolphus (Heir-apparent to the Throne of Sweden	Mr. Spear
Sigismond (Son to John late King)	Mr. Caulfield
Count Valdestein	Mr. Fox
Count Sparre	Mr. Sully
Banor (Col. in the Swedish Army)	Mr. Clark
Serjeant'	Mr. Utt

Olaus	Mr. Jones
James	Mr. Byrne
Ramsay (A Scotchman in	
Valdestein's service)	Mr. Ringwood
Countess Valdestein	Mrs. Placide
Christina	Mrs. Green
Officers and Soldiers	Gentlemen of
	the Company

On Friday, September 15, was advertised for that date "a celebrated Tragedy in five acts, call'd *George Barnwell, or The School for Profligates.*" Cast was given:

Thorowgood	Mr. Clark
Uncle	Mr. Ringwood
George Barnwell	Mr. Fox
Trueman	Mr. Spear
Blunt	Mr. Sully
John	Mr. Byrne
Keeper	Mr. Utt
Officer	Mr. Jones
Millwood	Mrs. Placide
Lucy	Mrs. Clark
Maria	Mrs. Green

The feature of the evening was "(for the first time here) a Grand Allegorical Pantomime, Spectacle; interspersed with Song, Recitation, &c. called *Cinderella; or, The Little Glass Slipper*, Invented by Mr. Byrne, and performed at the Theatre Royal Drury Lane, upwards of one hundred nights: and at Philadelphia and Charleston, with unbounded applause." Full cast was listed:

Prince	Mr. Placide
	Mr. Bray
	Mr. Fox
Lords	Mr. Clark
	Mr. Byrne
	Mr. Spear
	Mr. Jones
Attendants	Mr. Utt
	Mr. Ringwood
Pedro	Mr. Sully
Cinderilla	Mrs. Placide
Sisters	Mrs. Clark and Mrs. Utt

Deities

Venus	Mrs. Green
Graces	{ Mrs. Bray { Miss Placide (Miss Green
Cupid (with a Dance)	Miss Sully
Hymen and Cupids	Little Masters

Scenery, which was "Entirely New," was elaborate:

Scene I.—Represents the Bower of Venus, with a view of the sea, Mount Ida, &c.—a richly ornamented Sailing Boat, Ropes, Garlands of Roses, &c.,—Dance of Graces.—The Roses and Flowers disappear; and in their place a Bright Cloud descends, which ascends again with Venus, the Nymphs, &c.
Scene II.—The Prince's Palace—Statue of Diana, &c.
Scene III.—Cinderella's Kitchen, in which a Pumpkin changes into a rich Carriage, and four white Rats into four Horses richly caparisoned.
Act II.—Scene I.—A Grand Banquet prepared in a splendid Ball Room with a beautiful Arch, ornamented with a Time-Piece, the hand of which Cupid (at the approach of twelve) characteristically puts back an hour, to please Cinderella, when, instantaneously, the figure of Time indignantly removes it to its proper place. Dance, &c.
Scene III.—The Garden of Venus.—The planet Venus descends, strikes a Rose-Bush, which changes to a splendid Car, which Cupid ascends with.
Scene V.—An elegant Hall, in which all the Ladies of the Court, come to have the slipper tried on.
Scene VI.—The prince's Hall changes to the Palace of Venus: Nymphs and Cupids are discovered—The Altar of Hymen, &c.—To conclude with the Marriage of Cinderella and the Prince.

The advertisement concluded with the notice that "Pamphlets descriptive of the Pantomime, to be had at the Printing-office of Messrs. Davis's, Mr. Ritchie, and at the Bar of the Theatre."[3] Regrettably, no copy of the pamphlet survives.

We return to more conventional fare on Wednesday, September 20, when *Hamlet* was acted with the following cast:

Hamlet	Mr. Green
King	Mr. Clark
Horatio	Mr. Spear
Polonius	Mr. Fox

Laertes	Mr. Sully
Rosencrans	Mr. Byrne
Guildenstern	Mr. Jones
Player King	Mr. Utt
Osrick	Mr. Byrne
Ghost	Mr. Caulfield
Grave Diggers	Messrs. Bray and Jones
Ophelia	Mrs. Green
Queen	Mrs. Placide
Player Queen	Mrs. Clark

Eleven men are listed, which was probably the entire strength of the company, since Byrne doubled as Rosencrans and Osric. No special effects were advertised. Afterpiece was "(for the first time here) the Musical Entertainment *My Grandmother; or The Living Picture*," for which no cast was listed.[4]

On Friday, September 22, the *Virginia Gazette* announced for that date "a Grand Musical Romance (for the first time here) interspersed with Dance, Song, Chorusses, &c., called *The Forty Thieves* as performed at the Theatre Drury Lane, with unbounded applause, for two seasons." The elaborate production evidently strained the company's acting strength, since there was considerable doubling in the advertised cast:

Casim Baba, (the rich Brother)	Mr. Jones
Ali Baba, (the poor Brother, a woodcutter)	Mr. Green
Ganem, (his son)	Mr. Spear
Mustapha, (the Cobler of Bagdad)	Mr. Sully
Selim, (Chief of the Caravan)	Mr. Byrne
Abdalla, (Capt. of the Thieves)	Mr. Caulfield
Hassarac, (Second Captain)	Mr. Fox
Their Followers	Messrs. Utt, Bray, &c.
Zaide, (wife of Casim Baba)	Mrs. Utt
Cogia, (wife of Ali Baba)	Mrs. Clark
Zelia, (Daughter of a Bashaw)	Mrs. Bray
Morgiana, (Slave to Casim Baba and Zelie's Sister)	Mrs. Green
Orcobrand, (Genius of forest and protector of the Thieves)	Mr. Clark
War ⎫	Mr. Utt ⎫
Famine ⎪ His	Mr. Byrne ⎪
Fraud ⎬ Attendants	Mr. Spear ⎬
Rapine ⎭	Mr. Jones ⎭

Ardenella, (Fairy of the Lake and protectress
    of Ali Baba's family)   Mrs. Placide
Principal Sylph   Miss Placide
Gossamer   Miss S. Sully

The play was staged "with entire new Scenery, Decoration, &c"
which was described:

ACT 1st

Scene 1st—opens with a view of the Fairy's Grotto; at the
extremity of a Lake by Moonlight—The Sylphs and Fairies form a
dance. After which the Fairies enter in a Chariot, drawn by two
white Swans—The back of the scene opens and discovers a wood,
with Ali Baba and his son, on the road to the Forest.

Scene 2d—The Forest—The Robber's Cave. A distant view of
the Mountains; where are seen passing among the Rocks, Forty
Thieves on Horseback. The Banditts enter, pronounce the Charm
and the enchanted cave opens with a tremendous sound. The cara-
van with the Bashaw's Daughter is seen to pass over the mountains,
who are attacked by Banditts, and the prisoners confined in a
cavern.

Scene 4th—Inside of the Wood-Cutter's Cottage.

ACT 2d

A Grand view of the inside of the Magic Cavern.

Scene 5th—A Garden by Moonlight. The Oil Jars are discovered,
where the Robbers are concealed, in which Forty Thieves are
destroyed by a Woman.

Scene 6th—Inside of the Robbers; Cave opens, and discovers
Abdalia and Zelie, guarded by Furies—At the moment the cruel
Enchanter is going to execute his threatened vengeance, the power
of the Fairy interposes, Ardenella enters. Orcobrand is siezed by
Demons, and sinks into a flaming Gulph.—The scene changes to
a Grand Subterranean and Perspective View of the Fairy's Palace
with a moving Cascade.

Music was "by Mr. Kelly," and novelty was piled on spectacle.
Sully introduced "a new Song, written by Mr. Emery of Covent
Garden Theatre, called 'Cuddy Clump's Visit to London—or, a
Peep at the Forty Thieves.'" Afterpiece was *High Life below
Stairs*, with a "Mock Minuet by Sir Harry, and Mrs. Kitty." Cast
was given:

Lovel	Mr. Sully
Freeman	Mr. Clark
Philip	Mr. Caulfield
Sir Harry	Mr. Fox
Lord Duke	Mr. Spear
Coachman	Mr. Utt
Kingston	Mr. Jones
Fiddler	Mr. Placide
Kitty	Mrs. Placide
Cook	Mrs. Utt
Lady Charlotte	Mrs. Clark
Lady Bab	Mrs. Bray

The *Gazette* of Tuesday, September 26, advertised "The last night, but one, of Performance, until the Company returns from Fredericksburg" for "Wednesday evening." Feature of the evening was "(for the first time here) A Grand Melo Drama called, *Tekeli, or, The Siege of Montgatz*," with the following cast:

Hungarians

Count Tekeli	Mr. Caulfield
Wolf (his friend)	Mr. Sully
Conrad (the miller)	Mr. Green
Isidore	Mr. Spear
Hussar	Mr. Jones
Frank	Mr. Valentine
Citizens, &c. &c.	

Austrians

Count Carraffa (the General)		Mr. Utt
Edmund (his Lieutenant)		Mr. Clark
Bras de Fer }	Soldiers {	Mr. Bray
Maurice }		Mr. Fox
Dancers {		Miss Placide
		Miss J. Placide
		Miss S. Sully

The play was staged "with New Scenery and Decorations":

In Act I.—A Forest, in which the disguised Tekeli and Wolf escape from the Austrian Soldiers.

In Act II.—The inside of the Mill of Zeben, with a Bridge across the Torza in the Back ground.

In Act III.—A view inside of the Fortress of Montgatz, changes to the Ramparts, with a grand Battle between the Hungarians &

Austrians, in which Tekeli, assisted by Alexina, who in a single combat vanquishes an Austrian officer, is victorious, and Montgatz saved.

Afterpiece, also "(for the first time here)," was the farce "written by Coleman" of *We Fly by Night; or, the Long Stories*, with the following cast:

General Bastion	Mr. Clark
Winlove	Mr. Spear
Skipton	Mr. Jones
Ferret	Mr. Sully
Gaby Grim	Mr. Bray
Count Grenoville	Mr. Placide
Humphrey	Mr. Caulfield
Stubby	Mr. Fox
Lady Lynx	Mrs. Utt
Emmy Bastion	Mrs. Bray
Countess	Mrs. Clark
Mrs. Stubby	Mrs. Placide

On Friday, September 29, was announced for "This evening a Comedy (never performed here) *Time's A Tell Tale*." Afterpiece was *My Grandmother*. Casts were given for both:

Time's a Tell Tale

Sir Arthur Tessel	Mr. Spear
Sir David Delmar	Mr. Clark
Blandford (his first appearance here)	Mr. Rutherford
Query	Mr. Sully
Record	Mr. Jones
Hardacre	Mr. Green
Young Hardacre	Mr. Caulfield
M'Gregor	Mr. Utt
Toby	Mr. Valentine
Lady Delmar	Mrs. Bray
Zelida	Mrs. Green
Miss Laurel	Mrs. Clark
Olivia Windham	Mrs. Placide

Act II included "An Illuminated Naval Fete Champetre with a Ballet Dance by Miss Placide, Miss S. Sully, and Miss J. Placide."

My Grandmother

Sir Matthew Medley	Mr. Clark
Vapour	Mr. Fox
Dicky Gossip	Mr. Sully
Souffrance	Mr. Placide
Woodley	Mr. Spear
Waiter	Mr. Jones
Charlotte	Mrs. Clark
Florella	Mrs. Placide[5]

This, I assume, was the same cast as on September 20, when no cast was advertised.

Last performance of the season was Tuesday, October 3, when *The Poor Gentleman* was acted with the pantomime of *Care and Mirth, or Harlequin Skeleton* as afterpiece. Casts were given for both:

The Poor Gentleman

Lieut Worthington	Mr. Caulfield
Corporal Foss	Mr. Clark
Sir Charles Cropland	Mr. Spears
Sir Robert Bramble	Mr. Rutherford
Humphrey Dobbins	Mr. Jones
Farmer Harrowby	Mr. Utt
Stephen Harrowby	Mr. Bray
Ollipod	Mr. Sully
Frederick	Mr. Fox
Servant to Charles Cropland	Mr. Valentine
Emily Worthington	Mrs. Green
Miss Lucretia Mactab	Mrs. Clark
Dame Harrowby	Mrs. Utt
Mary	Mrs. Bray

Care and Mirth

Harlequin	Mr. Sully
Clown	Mr. Placide
Pantaloon	Mr. Ringwood
Lover	Mr. Spear
Swiss Valet	Mr. Bray
Neptune	Mr. Utt
Waiter	Mr. Jones
Care (the Magician)	Mr. Clarke
Mirth	Mrs. Clarke

| Pantalina | Mrs. Utt |
| Columbine | Mrs. Bray |

The production included a variety of changes and leaps by Harlequin as well as special stage effects: "The pantomime will commence with the Magic Tree, which is changed to a Pedestal, and Harlequin discovered on it. The celebrated Gladiator Scene.— The escape of Harlequin, with the Clown, on the prongs of a Pitch-Fork. The death of Harlequin with the laughable Scene between the Clown and the Animated Skeleton. The piece to conclude with a view of the Grotto of Neptune."[6] I assume (no disrespect to Manager Placide) that "the Grotto of Neptune" was adapted either from *Cinderella* or *The Forty Thieves*.

There are records of eleven performances between September 2 and October 3, 1809. If these were opening and closing nights, and if there were three performances each week, there should have been more, but this season, though brief, is unusually well recorded. During eleven evenings, twenty-one different plays were presented, a variety ranging from old reliable tragedy (*Venice Preserved, Hamlet*) to the latest popular successes of the London stage (*The Curfew, The Wanderer, Tekeli*). Twelve were new (or previously unrecorded) in Richmond: *Care and Mirth, Cinderella, The Curfew, The Fortress, The Forty Thieves, The Hunter of the Alps, My Grandmother, Tekeli, Time's A Tell Tale, Town and Country, The Wanderer,* and *We Fly by Night*. Most notable aspect of this season's program was romantic spectacle such as *Cinderella* and *The Forty Thieves*; this I attribute to Placide, the new manager, whose special talent was ballet and pantomime.

The company consisted of at least fourteen men and six women, with (I think) three boys and five girls. Of these, Mr. and Mrs. Placide, Mr. and Mrs. Green, Mr. and Mrs. Clark (sometimes Clarke), and Mrs. Simpson had been with the company in Charleston during the 1808-9 season. Spear (or Spears) and Rutherford had played in Richmond during recent seasons with Green. The company evidently left for Fredericksburg immediately after closing night.

The plays. The *Curfew* was performed some time between opening night, September 2, 1809, and the publication of a critical review on September 12. A drama by John Tobin, it was first acted at Drury Lane on February 19, 1807. Its American premiere was in Charleston on January 8, 1808, and it was acted in New York on March 4, 1808.

The Fortress (September 6, 1809), a melodrama by Theodore Hook, had its premiere at the Haymarket on July 16, 1807, and its American premiere in New York on April 22, 1808. It was acted by this company in Charleston on January 14, 1809. *The Hunter of the Alps*, a musical farce in two acts by William Dimond, was first acted at the Haymarket on July 3, 1804, and first acted in America in New York on May 2, 1805. It was staged several times during 1807 and 1808 in Charleston by this company.

Town and Country (September 8, 1809), a comedy in five acts by Thomas Morton, was brought out at Covent Garden on March 10, 1807. It was first acted in America in New York on November 2, 1807, and was acted in Charleston on December 30 of the same year.

The Wanderer (September 13, 1809) was an adaptation of Kotzebue's *Edward in Schottland* by Charles Kemble. It was first acted at Covent Garden on January 12, 1808, and first acted in America in Charleston on December 16, 1808. It was acted in Washington in 1810 and Philadelphia, 1832.

Cinderella (September 15, 1809), the "grand allegorical pantomime . . . invented by Mr. Byrne," was first recorded in Charleston on February 13, 1807, and was performed nine times during that season. It was performed in New York on August 17, 1807, Philadelphia, February 26, 1812, and Baltimore, June 9, 1814.

My Grandmother (September 20, 1809), a musical farce by Prince Hoare, was first acted at the Haymarket on December 16, 1793. It was first acted in America in Philadelphia on April 27, 1795. It was acted in New York in 1796 and Charleston in 1800.

The Forty Thieves (September 22, 1809) is ascribed by Nicoll to George Colman, the younger; but Odell says that Sheridan, Ward, and Kelly all contributed.[7] It was first staged at Drury Lane on April 8, 1806, and its American premiere was in Charleston on December 18, 1807. It was produced in New York on March 20, 1809, and Philadelphia, December 26, 1810.

Tekeli (September 26, 1809), a melodrama which Theodore Hook adapted from Pixérécourt, was brought out at Drury Lane on November 24, 1806. It was first acted in America in New York on December 21, 1807. It was acted in Charleston in 1808, Alexandria, 1810, and Philadelphia, 1812. *We Fly by Night*, a farce by George Colman, the younger, was first acted at Covent Garden on January 28, 1806, and first acted in America in New York on February 27, 1807. It was acted in Charleston on June 1, 1807, and in both Baltimore and Philadelphia in 1818.

Time's a Tell Tale (September 29, 1809), a comedy by Henry Siddons, was brought out at Drury Lane on October 27, 1807, and had its American premiere in New York on April 18, 1808. It was acted in Charleston on November 25, 1808.

The pantomime *Care and Mirth, or Harlequin Skeleton* (October 3, 1809) appears to be much like one called *Care and Mirth; or Harlequin Restored*, which was performed in New York in 1801; *Harlequin's Skeleton* (no subtitle) was performed in Philadelphia in 1790. Since the New York pantomime included Placide as Clown and Mrs. Placide as Columbine, I assume that this one was similar.

The players.   Alexander Placide was once "first rope dancer to the King of France"; later, he and his troupe were "received with singular applause in the Theatres Royal of Dublin, Bath, Bristol, and Norwich; also at Sadler Wells."[8] Placide landed at Charleston in 1791, and went from there to New York, where he made his American debut on January 25, 1792. He performed in Boston and Philadelphia during 1792, and in 1794 became manager of the French Theatre in Charleston. Later he joined the West and Bignall Company which played in Charleston during the 1790s. Both Placide and Mrs. Placide played with West and Bignall in Richmond between October 1795 and January 1796, taking leading roles in several pantomimes and ballets. "In 1796 he had married Charlotte Sophia Wrighten, member of the Boston Theatre Company then playing in Charleston, had opened Vaux-Hall Gardens, a fashionable summer resort, and had in general established himself as a worthy citizen of the community."[9] He acted as co-manager with John B. Williamson and Edward Jones, and upon Jones's death in 1799 became manager, with Williamson as acting manager. He was manager from 1799 until his death in 1812.

The Sully family was enumerated in Chapter 2. The Placides are comparable in both number and fame. There was, first, Alexander, the head of the family, who came to America in 1791 accompanied by "Madame Placide," who performed with him. Willis hints that their relationship may have been less than marriage and that she returned to France when he married (legally) Miss Wrighten in Charleston in 1796.[10] I would rattle no skeletons in Placide genealogy. There were numerous progeny, several of whom made careers on stage. The Master H. Placide who appeared this season grew up to become the noted Henry Placide of New York and London renown. Odell considered him "perhaps the best all-round actor in America."[11] There were two girls, Misses Caroline and Jane Placide, of whom Jane continued to perform with her father's company until his death. Caroline, first as Miss Placide, later as Mrs. Waring and Mrs. Blake, became famous in comedy roles. Miss Eliza Placide, later Mrs. Asbury, was not mentioned in the advertisements of this season, nor was her brother, Thomas. On July 14, 1812, the New York *Columbian* advertised the opening of the Olympic Theatre, Anthony Street, under the management of Twaits, Placide, and Breschard; on August 3, the same paper advertised a benefit for "the widow Placide and her Six Children."[12] Evidently Alexander Placide died in New York between July 14 and August 3, 1812. The Placide family dominated the Richmond stage between 1809 and 1812.

J. W. Green made his debut in Richmond in the leading role of Bellamy in *The School for Soldiers* on November 24, 1796. He had played in Philadelphia with the Wignell and Reinagle Company in 1794, '95 and '96. On June 24, 1796, he married Miss Williams, who had played with the same company during the same years. He played leading roles with the West and Bignall Company until West's death in 1799. Between 1799 and 1807 he seems to have assisted Mrs. West in managing her theatrical affairs, gradually taking over the management of the company. Mrs. West was apparently in financial difficulties in 1807, and I suspect that the company, which her husband had organized in 1790, deteriorated at that time. During the 1807-9 hiatus, Green went to Charleston, where he joined Placide as acting manager for the seasons of 1808-9 and 1809-10.

The "Master M. Sully" of this season cannot be the Matthew Sully, Jr., who played adult roles in 1793. I suspect that he was the grandson of the senior Matthew Sully. Similarly, "Miss Sully" and "Miss S. Sully" cannot be among the five daughters of Matthew, Sr. They were probably his granddaughters. The original five girls were all married in Charleston before 1800, and their father announced his retirement from the stage in 1800. I assume that after 1800 "Sully" is Matthew Sully, Jr.

TWENTY-SIXTH SEASON

Placide and Green Company

October 1809–January 1810

Chronicle.   The Fredericksburg season was brief. On Friday, October 20, 1809, the managers of the Richmond Theatre respectfully informed the public that "on Monday evening next, the Theatre will be re-opened, with the famous comedy, called the *Soldier's Daughter.*" Afterpiece was "for the first time here, a farce called *Plot and Counterplot.*" Between play and farce was "a Ballet Dance, to be performed by children, called *Jack in Distress.*" No casts were listed. The advertisement specified details of tickets and house regulations, which were the same as the preceding season except that doors now opened at "quarter past five o'clock—Curtain to rise at quarter past six precisely." [13]

The *Virginia Argus* of Tuesday, October 24, advertised for Wednesday "(for the second time here)" *Tekeli*, which had been presented on September 27. *Jack in Distress* and *Plot and Counterplot* were repeated. No casts were given.

The first advertisement to list casts appeared in the *Virginia Gazette* on Friday, October 27, when *The Wheel of Fortune* was acted with the following cast:

Penruddock	Mr. Green
Sir David Daw	Mr. Bray
Tempest	Mr. Rutherford
Woodville	Mr. Clark

Sydenham	Mr. Spear
Henry Woodville	Mr. Fox
Weazel	Mr. Clough
Jenkins	Mr. Jones
Woodville's Servant	Mr. Utt
Mrs. Woodville	Mrs. Placide
Emily Tempest	Mrs. Green
Dame Dunkley	Mrs. Clark
Maid	Mrs. Utt

No specialties were advertised between pieces. Afterpiece was *The Children in the Wood*, with the following cast:

Lord Alford	Mr. Spear
Sir Rowland	Mr. Clark
Walter	Mr. Sully
Apathy	Mr. Bray
Gabriel	Mr. Fox
Oliver	Mr. Placide
Ruffians	Messrs. Jones & Utt
Boy	Master H. Placide
Lady Alford	Mrs. Placide
Josephine	Mrs. Green
Winnifred	Mrs. Utt
Girl	Miss S. Sully

This advertisement announced Mrs. Green's benefit for Monday, October 30. The *Gazette* of that date contains no mention of the performance.

There was, however, a big advertisement in the issue of Tuesday, October 31, which introduced *The Robbers* with this puff, written, I suspect, by Green:

. . . of this most extraordinary production, it is probable that different opinions may be formed by the critics, according to those various standards by which they are in use to examine and to rate the merit of dramatical compositions: but all will acknowledge it to abound with passages of the most superior excellence, and to exhibit situations the most powerfully interesting that can be figured by the imagination. This Tragedy touches equally those great master springs of *Terror* and *Pity*. It exhibits a conflict of passions, so strong, so varied, and so affecting, that the mind is never allowed to repose itself; but is hurried on thro' alternate emotions of *compassion* and *abhorrence,* of *anxiety* and *terror,* of *admiration* and *regret,* to the catastrophe. The language too, is

bold and energetic, highly impassioned and perfectly adapted to
the expression of that sublimity of sentiment which it is intended
to convey. It has been translated into every *European* language,
and performed at the various *Theatres* with a success correspondent to its merit.

Cast was as follows:

Count De Moor	Mr. Caulfield
Charles De Moor	Mr. Clark
Francis De Moor	Mr. Rutherford
Speigelberg	Mr. Sully
Switzer	Mr. Fox
Roller	Mr. Green
Schufterg	Mr. Bray
Grimm	Mr. Utt
Kozinki	Mr. Spear
Herman	Mr. Clough
Razman	Mr. Bray
Commissary	Mr. Jones
Amelia	Mrs. Placide

Eleven men was probably the entire strength of the company,
since Bray doubled.

Following the tragedy was a ballet, *The Hunters and the Milk
Maid* "(by children only)." Miss Sully played Jerome, Master H.
Placide, Collas, and Miss C. Placide, Collet, "the Milk Maid." There
were "Hunters, Dancers, &c." In the course of the ballet was intro-
duced "the celebrated Gavotte De Vestris, by Miss C. Placide and
Miss Sully." The evening concluded with "the much admired
Musical Farce of *The Quaker; or, The May Day Dower*," with the
following cast:

Lubin, with the original songs	Mr. Fox
Steady	Mr. Caulfield
Solomon	Mr. Sully
Farmer Easy	Mr. Clough
First Countryman	Mr. Utt
Second Countryman	Mr. Jones
Gillian	Mrs. Green
Florella	Mrs. Clark
Cicily	Mrs. Utt

This was the benefit of Mr. and Mrs. Clark.

On Friday, November 3, the *Virginia Gazette* announced for "This evening for the first time here a celebrated Tragedy, in five acts, written by M. G. Lewis, called *Adelgitha; or, The Fruits of a Single Error*." Cast was as follows:

Michael Ducas	Mr. Green
Guiscard	Mr. Fox
Lothair	Mr. Rutherford
Tancred	Mr. Jones
Alciphron	Mr. Clough
Dercetus	Mr. Clark
Rainulf	Mr. Ringwood
Julian	Mr. Spear
Adelgitha	Mrs. Placide
Imma	Mrs. Green
Claudia	Mrs. Clark
Abbess of St. Hilda	Mrs. Utt

Afterpiece was "the Grand Historical Pantomime of *La Perouse; or The Desolate Island*," with the following cast:

Europeans

Perouse, (the Navigator)	Mr. Placide
Captain of the Frigate	Mr. Fox
Officer	Mr. Rutherford
Child of Perouse	Master M. Sully
Chimpanzee (Ourang outang, or large ape)	Mr. Sully
Madame Perouse	Mrs. Green
Conge (Servant to Madame Perouse)	Mrs. Bray

Natives of a Neighboring Island

Kanko (Umba's Lover)	Mr. Caulfield
Nagaski (Umba's Father)	Mr. Ringwood
Ostepalaw	Mr. Jones
Tetasimar	Mr. Spear
Potoomora	Mr. Utt
Umba	Mrs. Placide

The advertisement included a long description of spectacular scenic effects in *La Perouse*, with a shipwreck and Perouse struggling in the waves, a grotto of the island, seashore with a boat crossing in perspective, wild dances by savages, a snow scene, and a frozen

lake. There are also details of Perouse's friendship with a chimpan-
zee (played by Sully), the arrival of Mme. Perouse with marines in
a rescue vessel, and the climactic rescue of Perouse and spouse just
as they are about to be burned at the stake. This was Mrs. Placide's
benefit, and she took leading roles in both tragedy and pantomime.
Entertainment between pieces consisted of "Tid-Re-I" by Sully,
"Shakesperian Address" by Rutherford, and "Feyther and I" by
Bray. Fox's benefit was advertised for Monday, but there is no
record of the performance.

The next advertisement appeared on Tuesday, November 7,
announcing for Wednesday *Wild Oats* and *The Honest Thieves*. No
casts were given. This was the benefit of Mr. and Mrs. Bray. Entertainment between pieces consisted of a comic song, "The Grinders"
by Sully, a song, "The Rose," "(written and composed by Mr.
Bray)" by Fox, a hornpipe by Mrs. Bray, and a comic song, "The
Potatoe Merchant, or, The Yorkshire Irishman" by Bray. Tickets
were to be had "as usual, and at Mr. Lewis Adam's Book Store." [14]

The *Virginia Gazette* of Friday, November 10, advertised for
"This evening Shakespeare's Tragedy of *Macbeth* (with the original
music by Locke.)" Cast was as follows:

Macbeth	Mr. Green
Macduff	Mr. Caulfield
Duncan	Mr. Clough
Malcolm	Mr. Rutherford
Banquo	Mr. Clark
Fleance	Miss Sully
Lenox	Mr. Spear
Seyton	Mr. Ringwood
Hecate	Mr. Fox
First Witch	Mr. Bray
Second Witch	Mr. Sully
Third Witch	Mr. Utt
Lady Macbeth	Mrs. Placide
Gentlewoman	Mrs. Clark

This was Davenant's version of *Macbeth*, for which music was
composed by Lock, and the advertisement specified: "The Vocal
Parts, by Mrs. Green, Mrs. Clark, Mrs. Bray, and Messrs. Fox,
Caulfield, Bray, Spear, Ringwood, Utt, Sully, &.&." The tragedy
was followed by the ballet *The Hunters and the Milk Maid*, first

performed on October 31, in which the same children took the same roles. The evening concluded with "the Musical Entertainment of *The Spoiled Child*," for which no cast was given.

The custom was to distribute playbills, even when elaborate advertisements such as this one were placed in newspapers. One playbill distributed on this date survives in the Harvard Theatre collection. It repeats the advertisement, then adds the complete cast of *The Spoiled Child*:

Little Pickle (with Songs)	Miss Sully
Old Pickle	Mr. Ringwood
John	Mr. Bray
Thomas	Mr. Clough
Cudden	Mr. Jones
Tag (the Rhyming Lover)	Mr. Sully
Maria	Miss Placide
Miss Pickle	Mrs. Clark
Susan	Mrs. Bray
Margery	Mrs. Utt

This performance was Caulfield's benefit, and the public were informed that Mr. and Miss Sully's benefit would take place "on Monday Evening next." Monday evening was November 13, but no record of the performance exists.

The *Virginia Gazette* of Tuesday, November 14, advertised for Wednesday "the Comedy *The Honey-Moon*" and "a Comic Interlude (never performed here) called *The Invisible Girl*." Both casts were given:

The Honey-Moon

Duke of Aranza	Mr. Green
Count Montalban	Mr. Spear
Balthazar	Mr. Clark
Rolando	Mr. Rutherford
Lampedo	Mr. Sully
Campillo	Mr. Clough
Lopez	Mr. Jones
Iliana	Mrs. Placide
Volante	Mrs. Green
Zamora	Mrs. Clark
Hostess	Mrs. Utt

The Invisible Girl

Captain Allclack	Mr. Fox
Lord Transit	Mr. Jones
Sir Christopher Chatter	Mr. Clough
Melchisedeck	Mr. Ringwood
Tom	Master H. Placide
Harriot	Mrs. Clark

At the end of the fourth act of _The Honey-Moon_ there was an "original Dance by the Characters." _The Invisible Girl_ was followed by a "Hornpipe (with Skipping Rope)" by Miss Sully, and a "Song (Chapter of Fashions)" by Mr. Sully. Afterpiece was "for the second time here) the Musical Entertainment of _Love Laughs at Locksmiths_" with the following cast:

Totterton	Mr. Fox
Captain Beldare	Mr. Spear
Vigil	Mr. Ringwood
Risk	Mr. Sully
Solomon Lob	Mr. Bray
Grenadier	Mr. Jones
Lydia	Mrs. Green

This was Rutherford's benefit, "Tickets to be had of Mr. Rutherford at the Virginia Inn, and at the usual places."

On Friday, November 17, there was announced for "This evening _The History of King Lear and His Three Daughters_." Cast was as follows:

Lear	Mr. Green
Burgundy	Mr. Jones
Cornwall	Mr. Spear
Albany	Mr. Clough
Kent	Mr. Rutherford
Glos'ter	Mr. Clark
Edgar	Mr. Caulfield
Edmund	Mr. Fox
Oswald	Mr. Sully
Pages	Masters Green and Sully
First Knight	Mr. Ringwood
Goneril	Mrs. Clark
Regan	Mrs. Placide
Cordelia	Mrs. Green

Lear was followed by "a Pantomime Interlude called *Harlequin Hurry-Scurry, or The Devil Among the Trades-folk*" with the following cast:

Harlequin, (with a leap)	Mr. Sully
Taylor, (with the Comic song of Mrs. Bond)	Mr. Bray
Carpenter	Mr. Clough
Cooper	Mr. Jones
Cobler	Mr. Ringwood
Bricklayer	Mr. Utt
Master	Mr. Clark
Columbine	Mrs. Placide
Miliner	Mrs. Green
Mantua Maker	Mrs. Clark
Washerwoman	Mrs. Utt
House Maid	Mrs. Bray
Country People, Lasses, &c. &c.	

The performance concluded with "a Double Allemand, by Mrs. Placide, Mrs. Sully and Mrs. Green."

Afterpiece was "the favorite Farce of *The Jew and The Doctor; or a Prescription for Happiness*," in which Green played Abednego "(the benevolent Jew)." No other characters were named. This was Green's benefit, and he played two leading roles. In addition, Mrs. Green played Cordelia, and the milliner in the pantomime, with an allemande. Master Green appeared as a page in the pantomime, but Miss Green was not mentioned; perhaps she was among the "Country People, Lasses, &c. &c." Tickets were to be had "as usual—and of Mr. Green near the Theatre."[15]

We come now to a run of fourteen performances for which no casts were advertised. Notices are brief. Of hundreds of handbills which were undoubtedly distributed, none survives. The *Virginia Gazette* of Tuesday, November 21, advertised for "This evening the Comedy *The School of Reform, or How to Rule a Husband*. To which will be added (for the first time in Virginia) A Grand Heroic Pantomime, in two acts, called *Jupiter & Europa or The Jealousy of Juno*." Between pieces Sully sang "Knowing Joe, or the Show Folks," and Bray sang "The Potatoe Merchant." *Jupiter and Europa* was spectacularly staged, "with new Scenery, Dresses,

& Decorations." The advertisement included an elaborate "Story of the Pantomime":

Jupiter having heard of the beauty of Europa, descends in his Eagle in search of her—is followed by Juno in her Car drawn by Peacocks . . . transforms himself into a white Bull—Europa and nymphs are at first afraid of him under his metamorphis, but perceiving his gentleness they approach, admire and adorn him with Garlands, and Europa at length seats herself on his back, instantly he proceeds to the sea, and swims to the opposite shore. . . . Juno enraged, ascends her Car, and crosses the Sea in pursuit of them.

Act II opens with "a Temple to which nymphs enter to tell of Europa's fate." This is followed by a "Scene among the Rocks," in which Jupiter and Europa are pursued by Juno and soldiers. "A Fiery Dragon enters, & destroys all the soldiers, but is attacked and slain by Cadmus." Further scenes exhibit pavillions, forts, and palaces. There is a combat between Jupiter and the Prince. In the final scene Europa, disenchanted by Jupiter, is "married in great splendor to Prince Nicanor, her original intended." As might be expected, this extravaganza was for Manager Placide's benefit.

On Friday, November 24, the *Gazette* announced for "This evening the Comedy *The Heir at Law*" and the "Musical Farce of *Lock & Key*." The play was followed by "The original Epilogue By the Company." House regulations were given:

Doors to be opened at half past five o'clock—Curtain to rise at half past six precisely.
Tickets to be had at the office of *The Virginia Gazette* and at the office of the Theatre.
Admittance to Box and Pit, One Dollar—Gallery 75 cents—Children half price.
Subscribers are requested to send to the office of *The Virginia Gazette* for their Tickets.
The public are respectfully informed, that *Smoking Segars* in the Theatre, *is prohibited*.

On Tuesday, November 28, the *Gazette* advertised for Wednesday, *John Bull, Jack in Distress,* and *The Hunter of the Alps. Jack in Distress* had been performed by the children of the company twice during this season, and *The Hunter of the Alps* during the previous season.

The bill for Friday, December 1, was *Adelgitha* and *Plot and Counterplot*, both previously performed this season. The advertisement stated that "in future the days of performance will be on Monday, Wednesday, Friday & Saturday."[16] It also announced for Saturday, December 2, *The Mountaineers* and *Cinderella.* Octavian in *The Mountaineers* was one of Green's favorite roles; *Cinderella* had been presented during the previous season.

The Forty Thieves and *The Irishman in London* were performed on Wednesday, December 6. Between them, Sully sang "Four and Twenty Fidlers," and Bray sang "The Potatoe Merchant."[17]

Plays for Friday, December 8, were "*The History of King Lear, and His Three Daughters.* Also the Farce of *The Honest Thieves, or The Faithful Irishman*"; for Saturday, December 9, "*Pizarro; or the Death of Rolla.* Also the Comic Pantomime of *Harlequin Pastry Cook*"; and for Wednesday, December 13, *The Point of Honor; or, the School for Soldiers* and the "magnificent Heroic Pantomime *Don Juan, or The Libertine Destroyed.*"[18] None of the advertisements gave further details.

On Friday, December 15, the *Gazette* informed the public that "there will be no performance until tomorrow (Dec. 16th) on account of preparations for the performance of the Historical Melo-Drama (for the first time here) called *The Indian Princess or The First Settlement of Virginia.*" Afterpiece was *The Village Lawyer.* Between pieces Fox sang "Tom Starboard," and Sully sang "The Spring of Shelala." *The Indian Princess* was staged "with new decorations and scenery, painted for the Drama by Mr. Holmes."[19]

On Wednesday, December 20, was performed "(for the first time here) A new Comedy *Man and Wife; or More Secrets Than One.*" Afterpiece was "the musical Entertainment *Sprigs of Laurel; or, The Rival Soldiers.*" On Friday, December 22, was performed "(for the first time here) a Grand Romantic Cabalistic Melo-Drama being the production of M. G. Lewis, esq. author of *The Monk,* called *The Wood Demon, or The Clock has Struck.*" Afterpiece was *The Critic.* On Tuesday, December 26, was performed "the Comedy *Wives as They Were, and Maids as They Are.* Also (for the first time here) a new Comic Pantomime called *The Devil on Two Sticks, or The Magic Chamber* with new Scenery and Decorations."

On Friday, December 29, was performed *The Soldier's Daughter* followed by "for the first time here, the Grand Burletta of *Midas, or the Assembly of Dieties*."[20] None of the advertisements gave further details.

The long run of brief announcements was broken on Saturday, December 30, when the *Virginia Patriot* announced for "This evening the Tragedy of *The Gamester*" and *The Highland Reel* with casts for both:

The Gamester

Beverly	Mr. Green
Stukely	Mr. Rutherford
Lewson	Mr. Fox
Jarvis	Mr. Clark
Dawson	Mr. Spear
Bates	Mr. Clough
Servant	Mr. Jones
Mrs. Beverly	Mrs. Placide
Charlotte	Mrs. Green
Lucy	Mrs. Utt

The Highland Reel

Sandy	Mr. Fox
Charley	Mr. Spear
M'Gilpin	Mr. Ringwood
Crowdy	Mr. Rutherford
Captain Dash	Mr. Caulfield
Sergeant Jack	Mr. Clark
Laird of Coll	Mr. Clough
Laird of Raisey	Mr. Jones
Shelty (the piper)	Mr. Sully
Moggy M'Gilpin	Mrs. Clark
Jenny	Mrs. Green

This was Rutherford's benefit. He played two roles, and between pieces gave a comic recitation, "Giles Jollup, the Grave, and the Brown Sally Green." There was also a comic song, "Murder in Irish," by Sully, a recitation, "Alonzo the Brave and the Fair Imogene," by Fox, and a "Comic Song" by Bray. From similarity in titles, I suspect that Rutherford's "comic recitation" was a parody of Fox's "recitation," a popular poem by M. G. Lewis.

On Tuesday, January 2, 1810, the *Argus* advertised for "Tomorrow" *Town and Country* and *The Fortress*, both of which had been acted during the previous season. No casts were given.

When *The Indian Princess* was presented for the first time, on December 16, 1809, no cast was advertised. For a second performance on Thursday, January 4, 1810, the *Virginia Patriot* advertised the complete cast; presumably it was the same:

Europeans

Captain Smith	Mr. Green
Delavar	Mr. Clough
Lieutenant Rolf	Mr. Rutherford
Percy	Mr. Spear
Walter	Mr. Sully
Larry	Mr. Ringwood
Robin	Mr. Bray
Talman	Mr. Utt
Alice	Mrs. Clark

Soldiers and Adventurers, &c.
Virginians

Powhatan, (the King)	Mr. Clark
Nataquas, (his Son)	Mr. Jones
Niami, (a Prince)	Mr. Fox
Grimosco, (a Priest)	Mr. Caulfield
Pocahontas, (a Princess)	Mrs. Placide
Nima	Mrs. Bray

The play was to be followed by the ballet *Jack in Distress* and the pantomime *The Devil on Two Sticks*, both of which had been performed this season.

This entire performance was evidently canceled. The *Virginia Patriot* of Saturday, January 6, carried this interesting item:

THEATRE

The lovers of the drama were on Thursday evening gratified by the appearance of Master Payne in the character of Douglas. It is doing but sheer justice to this young gentleman, to state, that this character was supported with great ability. The style of his performance was evincive of fine feelings and correct taste. It was a subject of regret to many that the entire play was not performed, instead of omitting some highly interesting parts. From the performance of Octavian this evening much pleasure may be expected.

The same issue informed the public that "an arrangement has been made with Master Payne (who has lately performed in Philadelphia,

Baltimore, New York, and Boston, with such distinguished success) for Seven Nights in this Theatre." Nights of Master Payne's performances were specified as Saturday of this week, Monday, Tuesday, Wednesday, Thursday, and Friday of next week, "after which the Theatre will close this season."

As I reconstruct events, Thursday's issue of the *Patriot* had gone to press when Master Payne put in an unexpected appearance and was immediately engaged by managers Placide and Green, who canceled the advertised performance of *The Indian Princess*, plastered the city with handbills announcing Master Payne as Young Norval in *Douglas*, and filled the theatre. I have no handbill to support my surmise, but the attenuated version of *Douglas* indicates haste and inadequate rehearsal.

Following Payne's debut on Thursday, the theatre was dark on Friday while the company prepared *The Mountaineers* for Saturday, January 6. It was announced in the *Patriot* of that date, with Master Payne in the leading role of Octavian, followed by the pantomime *Harlequin Hurry Scurry*, and the farce *High Life below Stairs*. On Monday Payne played Hamlet, on Tuesday, Rolla in *Pizarro*, on Wednesday, Frederick in *Lovers' Vows*, on Thursday, Selim in *Barbarossa*, on Friday, Romeo, and on Saturday, Lothair in *Adelgitha*, six major roles on six consecutive evenings.[21]

Newspaper advertisements are brief and incomplete. Afterpiece to *Pizarro* was *The Prize; Barbarossa* was followed by the children's ballet, *The Hunters and the Milk Maid* and *The Spoil'd Child*, with the comic songs of "The Cosmetic Doctor" by Sully and "The Potatoe Merchant" by Bray between. *Romeo and Juliet* included "In Act 1st, a Grand Masquerade. End of Act 4th, a Funeral Procession to the Tomb of Juliet, with a solemn Dirge, &c&c." It was followed by "A New Pantomime, interspersed with Song and Dance, called *Moiza & Lindor, or The Traitor Punished*," which included a concert and ball in act one and a combat with small swords between Lindor and Smith in Act II. Afterpiece was *The Honest Thieves*.[22] Although Friday was advertised as Master Payne's benefit, last night of his performance, and last night of the season, there was an encore on Saturday when Payne made his final appearance and the season closed. He appeared again with this company during their Charleston season in March.

Of Master Payne's eight plays, only one, *Barbarossa; or, the Downfall of the Tyrant of Algiers*, was new to Richmond. Of three pantomime interludes and four farce afterpieces recorded during Master Payne's eight nights, only one, the pantomime *Moiza and Lindor*, was new. I have found no record of it elsewhere.

Surprisingly, Master Payne's eight performances produced no critical response. There is evidence that the engagement was a financial success, at least. Three days after his final appearance, a "Communication" to the *Enquirer* publicized his take:

Young Payne played in this Theatre for eight nights [eight roles are listed] . . . . He was entitled to half the profits and a clear benefit besides—$1710 was the amount of his receipts during this short period—10 days—what a blind Goddess is Fortune! —There is no disparagement intended to this youth—he has a fine genius, fine powers of conception, and in many scenes is a most astonishing actor. —But here is a lad, just springing into life, without the laboured accomplishment of years, reaping $1700 in ten days— while our judges of Courts of Appeals, whose heads are almost grey in the service of their country, who have exhausted the midnight oil in study, and devoted entire days to their accomplishment in their profession, & now unsealing the foundations of sacred justice to their countrymen, are about to receive, *perhaps*, only $2000 for a tedious *year* of public service. —Is it because men care more for their amusements than for solid substantial services?[45]

The Communication is unsigned. As far as I know, it was unanswered. I leave unresolved the relative merits of the bench versus the boards. There was a similar protest in 1786 when Hallam and Henry left Richmond with a clear profit of £1,500 after a season of six weeks.

This season was successful in many ways. It extended for nine weeks, with records of thirty-three performances. Certainly there were others, but the records are comparatively good, if incomplete. A total of fifty-six plays is recorded, including tragedy, comedy, farce, melodrama, comic opera, pantomime. There were some spectacular stage effects, and much singing and dancing. There was a good balance between old favorites and current successes. Eighteen plays were new to Richmond: *Adelgitha, Barbarossa, Harlequin Pastry Cook, The Honey-Moon, The Hunters and the Milk Maid, The Indian Princess, The Invisible Girl, The Jew and the Doctor, Jupiter and Europa, King Lear, Lock and Key, Love Laughs at Locksmiths, Man and Wife, Moiza and Lindor, La Perouse, Plot and Counterplot, The Wheel of Fortune,* and *The Wood Daemon.* There was one play by an American author, *The Indian Princess.*

The company was the same. This season there are records of thirteen men and five women. There were four girls (Miss Sully and Miss S. Sully, Miss Caroline Placide and Miss Jane Placide) and four boys (Master Sully, Master M. Sully, Master Green, and Master Henry Placide). It was a strong company, ably managed by Placide and Green. The feature of the season was the engagement of Master Payne as star. The season closed on January 13; the company opened in Charleston on February 6, and played there until May 16.

An epilogue of dramatic composition belongs to this season. In 1798 a political satire written by B. H. Latrobe in Richmond was acted on the Richmond stage, and on February 19, 1807, *The Road to Honor,* by a "Young Gentleman,'" was performed. We come now upon another play of local authorship.

The *Visitor* was a biweekly literary magazine established in Richmond in February 1809 by John Lynch and Charles Southgate. In February 1810 it became a weekly, and began to carry news, but for a year it was more magazine than newspaper, publishing fiction, poetry, and essays. The issue of December 16, 1809, published "Theatrical anecdotes," signed "Z," mostly about Garrick and Macklin. The feature of the issue was the beginning of a history of the English stage, published in four installments (January 13, March 10 and 24, 1810) beginning with the liturgical drama and ending with Mrs. Siddons, whom "the writer of this article has had the pleasure of witnessing." All four articles were signed "A. B."

Of particular interest is the publication in two installments (December 30, 1809, and January 13, 1810) of *Steali, or, the Lady of the Gaol,* "A Melodrama in one act." It is introduced by the following "Theatrical Communication":

Mr. Visitor,

I congratulate you and other admirers of rational refinement on the improving taste of the public, evinced by the encouragement which has been given to the representation of Pantomimes and Melodramas in our Theatre this season, and having a penchant to contribute my mite to the progress of that improvement, I take the liberty, through the medium of your paper, of recommending to the all-accommodating attention of *Messieurs Placide & Green* the following chef d'oeuvre of its kind.

The interest, you will observe, as is usual in such pieces, is of a German tinge; and the characters and the circumstances are all of them foreign, not only to our country, but to the ordinary rules of dramatic writing: indeed, some persons to whom I have shown the manuscript, which was bequeathed to me by a ingenious young man, now no more, have suspected that it is nothing more than a translation; but this, you know, in these enlightened days, can be no impediment to its success.

My constant attendance at the Theatre has given me some knowledge of the scenic art, and therefore, to alleviate the task of the managers as much as I can, I have cast the piece myself; and such a scrupulous regard to figure and talents, as, when added to the superlative merit of the composition, will doubtless render it eminently productive: in which opinion, I remain,

Yours, &c.
David Dangle

Steali
Or, The Lady of the Gaol
A Melodrama, in one act

Bluffenberg, Lieutenant of Police, a sleeping and consequently a silent character	Mr. Placide
Count Von Snarl, Governor of a District	Mr. Clark
Count Steali, an unfortunate Nobleman	Mr. Rutherford
Smacko, formerly a taylor, but now coachman to Bluffenberg	Mr. Bray
Snappenfield, a Police officer	Mr. Sully
Miss Bluffenberg, the Lieutenant's daughter	Mrs. Utt
Liskina, a waiting maid	Mrs. Clark
Officers, Citizens, Dancers &c.	

The place of action, is Strasbourg and the environs.
Scene—a Street in Strasbourg
Enter Von Snarl . . .

The author's satire is already apparent: his target the European melodrama and scenic pantomime of Placide's repertoire. Placide, a Frenchman whose command of English was probably less than perfect, cast himself (wisely, I submit) in pantomime roles. He was originally "Rope dancer to the King of France." The play is a burlesque melodrama, not without wit, heavy satire, and broad humor. It is sometimes clever, outrageous in characterization, preposterous in plot, redolent with puns. I doubt that its author expected to see it on the Richmond stage. It appeared in print, however, while the company was playing; I assume they read the concluding installment, published (coincidentally, I am sure) on January 13, closing night of the season, before they left Richmond. Perhaps they carried copies to Charleston. There is no record of stage production of *Steali*.

The plays.   *Plot and Counterplot* (October 23, 1809), a farce by Charles Kemble, was first acted at the Haymarket on June 30, 1808. Its American premiere was in New York on November 18, 1808. It was acted in Charleston by this company on February 14, 1810.

The Wheel of Fortune (October 27, 1809), a comedy by Richard Cumberland, was brought out at Drury Lane in 1795 and acted in Philadelphia and New York in 1796.

The Hunters and the Milkmaid (November 1, 1809) was evidently composed by members of this company. The only record of its performance elsewhere was in Charleston, where it was performed on February 21, 1810. It was perhaps similar to *The Two Hunters and the Milkmaid* which was performed in 1795.

Adelgitha (November 3, 1809), a tragedy by M. G. Lewis, had its premiere at Drury Lane on April 30, 1807, and its American premiere in New York on November 14, 1808. It was acted in Charleston by this company during both preceding and succeeding seasons, on February 13, 1809, and February 21, 1810. *La Perouse* was the subject of a pantomime by John Fawcett presented at Covent Garden on February 28, 1801, but this Richmond production was probably the one by Charles Smith which was performed by Placide's company in Charleston eight times between 1803 and 1809. A Perouse pantomime (no author named) was brought out "for the first time," according to Odell, in New York on January 1, 1811. William Dunlap wrote a play on the subject, which is not known to have been acted.

The Honey-Moon (November 15, 1809), a comedy by John

Tobin, had its premiere at Drury Lane on January 31, 1805, and its American premiere in New York on May 29, only four months later. It was acted in Charleston on May 31, 1805, and Philadelphia, January 25, 1811. *The Invisible Girl* may have been the same as *The Invisible Mistress*, listed by Nicoll among plays of unknown authorship. The Richmond production was probably the same play acted by this company in Charleston on April 11, 1809. A play by the same title was acted in New York on January 26, 1807, and in Baltimore and Philadelphia in 1810. In Richmond it was called a comic interlude, in Philadelphia a musical farce, essentially the same. *Love Laughs at Locksmiths*, a musical farce in two acts by George Colman, the younger, was first acted at the Haymarket on July 25, 1803. It was acted in New York on May 23, 1804, Charleston, May 31, 1805, and Philadelphia, January 25, 1811.

The version of *Lear* which was acted in Richmond (November 17, 1809) was almost certainly Nahum Tate's adaptation with the infamous happy ending. The fool (omitted by Tate) does not appear in a full cast of characters. Garrick played Tate's version; Shakespeare's ending was restored by Edmund Kean in 1823. *The Jew and the Doctor*, a farce by T. J. Dibdin, was first acted at Covent Garden on November 23, 1798. Its American premiere was in Charleston on February 11, 1800. It was acted in New York in 1808 and Philadelphia in 1814.

Jupiter and Europa (November 21, 1809) was almost certainly the same pantomime staged in Charleston on March 2, 1803, and New York July 4, 1806. Mr. and Mrs. Placide were in all three productions. I assume that it was composed by Placide or some member of this company.

Lock and Key (November 24, 1809), a musical farce by Prince Hoare with music by William Shield, was first acted at Covent Garden on February 2, 1796, and first acted in America in New York on March 17, 1797. It was acted in Charleston in 1802, Washington, 1803, Baltimore, 1815, and Philadelphia, 1816.

Harlequin Pastry Cook (December 9, 1809) was probably the same pantomime recorded in Philadelphia on November 21, 1794, and in New York on July 15, 1805. There is no record of its performance in Charleston by this company.

The Indian Princess, or La Belle Sauvage (December 16, 1809) was written by James Barker of Philadelphia, and first performed there at the Chestnut Street Theatre on April 6, 1808. It was acted in New York on June 14, 1809. Although the Richmond subtitle (*"The First Settlement of Virginia"*) suggests G. W. P. Custis's *Pocahontas, or the Settlers of Virginia*, this play was definitely Barker's. Custis's treatment of the same subject was not produced until 1830.[23] Barker's play was produced in Charleston by this company during both the preceding and following season; Custis's play was not produced there until 1858. Barker used John Smith's *General History of Virginia* as his source, taking liberties with history (as did Smith) and producing "an entertaining play, with a romantic atmosphere." This was "the first Indian play by an American to be performed." It was produced at Drury Lane on December 15, 1820, "the first well authenticated instance of an original American play being produced in London after an initial performance in America."[24]

Man and Wife (December 20, 1809), a comedy by Samuel Arnold, had its premiere at Drury Lane on January 5, 1809, and its American premiere in New York on May 5, just four months later. It was acted in Charleston on March 12, 1810, and Philadelphia, February 22, 1812.

The Wood Daemon (December 12, 1809), a melodrama by M. G. Lewis, had its premiere at Drury Lane on April 1, 1807, and its American premiere in New York on May 9, 1808. It was acted in Charleston in 1809 and Philadelphia in 1823.

Barbarossa (January 11, 1810), a tragedy by Dr. John Brown, had its premiere at Drury Lane in 1754 and was acted in New York, Charleston, and Philadelphia before 1800. Its performance in Charleston in 1794 by the West and Bignall Company leads me to suspect earlier performance in Richmond.

The pantomime *Moiza and Lindor* (January 12, 1810) is not recorded elsewhere. I assume that it was concocted by the company for the occasion.

The players.   John Howard Payne is famous as the author of "Home, Sweet Home"; students of American history know that he served as consul at Tunis; students of American drama remem-

ber him as the author of *Brutus, Thérèse, Clari, Charles the Second*
and *Richelieu*, all popular successes; his acting career is less well
known, though notable. He was once famous as a child prodigy.
Born in New York in 1791, he was publisher of the *Thespian
Mirror* at the age of fourteen. Odell publishes a full page illustration of him as Young Norval, the role in which he made his
New York debut on February 24, 1809: "Not quite eighteen years
of age, and looking younger, handsome and debonair, he at once
awakened interest and achieved astonishing success. At standing
water between man and boy, he aimed at the highest tragic parts,
and so long as he graced the American boards, he was acclaimed
and followed." His engagement is assessed as "a sea-mark for the
season, and indeed for the history of the American theatre as a
whole."[25]

The four Sully children who appeared this season were probably
grandchildren of Matthew, Sr. I hope the "Sully" who was with
the company was their father. "Master Green" was, I assume, the
son of Mr. and Mrs. J. W. Green; I do not know his name.

TWENTY-SEVENTH SEASON
Placide and Green Company
August–October 1810

Chronicle. The company played in Charleston from February 6
to May 16, 1810, with both Cooper and Master Payne appearing
during the season. On June 26 the *Virginia Patriot* reported that
"Master Payne is performing at the Norfolk Theatre with the most
distinguished applause." Presumably he was supported there by
the Placide and Green Company.

In Richmond an exhibition of waxworks at the City Tavern
included Washington, Bonaparte, John Wesley, Blackbeard the
pirate, and "Othello Moor of Venice, Fair Desdemona his wife;
she is represented lying asleep, Othello being in the act of stabbing
her with a dagger."[26]

In May the equestrian company of Pepin and Breschard
performed at the "(new erected) Circus in Hay Market Garden."
The company included Seigne, Codet, Menial, Gayetano, Master

Felix, and Master Diego. Prices were: "Boxes $1. Pitt 75 cents. Coloured People 50 cents." Evidently "Coloured People" were accommodated in a segregated section, less desirable than either boxes or pit.[27]

The *Enquirer* of June 12 carried the advertisement of Darraq, a French dancing master "lately arrived," who opened a dancing academy. The *Virginia Argus* of July 10 advertised a "Travelling Theatre" in the large chamber next the post office. There were wax figures, as well as "Balancing, Tumbling, Leaping," and Don Carlos performed feats of agility and skill on the slack wire. All for 50 cents, Children 25. The *Enquirer* of July 31 announced that Martial Metyer, fencing master of St. Mary's College, Baltimore, would open a fencing school as soon as sufficient scholars enrolled. He resided at the Virginia Inn.

At this time Richmond was supporting a variety of entertainment: concerts, dancing, equestrian performances, fireworks, cockfights, horse racing, not to mention occasional traveling ventriloquists, acrobats, and exotic beasts. Population had almost doubled in the past decade: from 5,737 in 1800 to 9,735 in 1810. As capital of Virginia, Richmond housed the Offices of state government and the State Legislature, which attracted lawyers and politicians from throughout the state. The trial of Aaron Burr in 1807 had created national publicity, and throughout the nation Richmond was thought of as the home of Marshall, Jefferson, Madison, Monroe, and the Virginia aristocracy. The docks were busy, commerce was thriving, and the theatre on Shockoe Hill near the Capitol was flourishing.

The first announcement of real theatre appeared in the *Virginia Patriot* on August 3:

TO THE LOVERS OF THE DRAMA

We announce with considerable pleasure, that the company of Comedians, which has lately given so much satisfaction at Norfolk and Petersburg, are about to return to this city. We are assured that this agreeable event will take place about the 20th of the present month.

Some performers of great merit having joined the company, since their last visit to this place, the Managers and the audience will enjoy the mutual and reciprocal pleasure—the one of imparting, and the other of partaking of the most rationaly, agreeable, and instructive amusements which are known to exist in any part of the civilized world.

While therefore we are blest with peace, and with plenty; while industry every where meets a most ample reward; we can not doubt that the approaching exhibitions, will be not less acceptable to the citizens, than the remuneration will be to the performers.

To the talents and exertions, as well as correct and gentlemanly deportment of Messrs. Green and Placide, every one can bear witness. It is to that unceasing ability and disposition to please that much has been and much may be yet ascribed. It is from liberal encouragement only that the best talents can be obtained and excited to exertion. We believe that the managers have done all that can be expected from them. They will only ask to be received and treated according to their merits.

The theatre opened on Saturday, August 18, "with the celebrated play of the *Castle Spectre*." Afterpiece was "for the first time here" the "Musical Entertainment" *Of Age Tomorrow.* Casts were given for both:

The Castle Spectre

Osmond	Mr. Green
Reginald	Mr. Clark
Percy	Mr. Rutherford
Henric (from the New York Theatre)	Mr. Collins
Father Philip	Mr. Caulfield
Motley	Mr. Jones
Hassan	Mr. Clark
Saib	Mr. Utt
Muley	Mr. Foster
Alaric	Mr. Austin
Angela (from the N. York Theatre)	Mrs. Poe
Alice	Mrs. Clark
Evilina (the Castle Spectre)	Mrs. Placide

Of Age Tomorrow

Baron Willinghurst (Being his first appearance in this Theatre)	Mr. Twaites
Baron Piffleberg	Mr. Collins
Molkus	Mr. Caulfield
French Hair-Dresser	Mr. Placide

Servant	Mr. Austin
Lady Brumback	Mrs. Clark
Sophia	Mrs. Green
Maria	Mrs. Poe

Doors opened at six, with performance at seven. Tickets were to be had at Mr. Davis's Printing Office and the Theatre. "Subscribers Tickets will be left at the Printing Office."[28] Clark's doubling in *The Castle Spectre* leads me to suspect that the company's acting strength for male speaking-roles was nine. Manager Placide cast himself as "French Hair-Dresser" in the farce, but evidently preferred not to undertake an English-speaking role. I suspect that his fractured English and French mannerisms created tremendous comic effects in *Of Age Tomorrow.* I note also that Mrs. Poe, who had played in Richmond frequently during the past decade, as Miss Arnold, Mrs. Hopkins, and Mrs. Poe, was now billed as "from the N. York Theatre."

The *Virginia Patriot* of Tuesday, August 21, advertised for Wednesday "M. G. Lewis's Celebrated Tragedy of *Adelgitha, or The Fruits of a Single Error*," with the following cast:

Michael Ducas	Mr. Green
Guiscard (From the N. York Theatre for that night only)	Mr. Robertson
Lothair	Mr. Rutherford
Dercetus	Mr. Austin
Alciphron	Mr. Foster
Rainulf	Mr. M'Donald
Julian	Mr. Jones
Tancred	Mr. Barton
Adelgitha	Mrs. Placide
Imma	Mrs. Green
Claudia	Mrs. Clark

Afterpiece was "the much admired farce of *The Jew & Doctor*" with the following cast:

Abednego (the Jew)	Mr. Twaites
Doctor Specific	Mr. Clark
Old Bromley	Mr. Rutherford
Mr. Changeable	Mr. Collins
William	Mr. Jones
Charles	Mr. Austin

Mrs. Changeable	Mrs. Placide
Emily	Mrs. Green
Betty	Mrs. Clark

On Friday, August 24, the *Patriot* announced for "This evening the Play *The Curfew*," with the following cast:

Danes

Fitzharding (his first appearance here)	Mr. Young
Conrad	Mr. Caulfield
Armstrong	Mr. Jones
Herman	Mr. Collins
Robbers (disguised as Minstrels)	Messrs. Utt, Foster, &c.

Normans

Hugh de Tracy	Mr. Clark
Robert	Mr. Twaits
Bertrand	Mr. Rutherford
Walter	Mr. Collins
Philip	Mr. M'Donald
Vassal	Mr. Austin
Friar	Mr. Utt
Matilda	Mrs. Placide
Florence	Mrs. Poe

I note Collins's doubling as a Dane and as a Norman; twelve men were listed in thirteen parts, the entire strength of the company, I presume, excepting, of course, Manager Placide. *The Curfew* was followed by "a Ballet performed by Children, *The Wood Cutters; or, The Merry Girl*" in which the wood cutters were "Master Henry and Miss Jane Placide." The Merry Girl was "E. Placide (not six years of age)" who danced a *pas de deux* and a *pas seul*. The evening concluded with "the Musical Entertainment of *We Fly By Night, or, Long Stories*," cast as follows:

General Bastion	Mr. Clark
Winlove	Mr. Foster
Skiptown	Mr. Jones
Ferret	Mr. Twaits
Gabby Grim	Mr. Collins
Count Grenoville	Mr. Placide
Humphrey	Mr. Robertson
Stubby	Mr. Rutherford
Lady Lynx	Mrs. Utt

Emma Bastion	Mrs. Poe
Countess Grenoville	Mrs. Clark
Mrs. Stubby	Mrs. Placide

Manager Placide's good judgment is evident in his casting himself in a role where his French accent would be no handicap.

The play for Wednesday was the comedy *Town and Country* with the farce *The Irishman in London*. Complete casts were given:

Town and Country

Reuben Glenroy	Mr. Robertson
Frost	Mr. Clark
Cosey	Mr. Twaites
Plastic	Mr. Jones
Rev'd Owen Glenroy	Mr. Rutherford
Capt. Glenroy	Mr. Rutherford
Hawbuck	Mr. Collins
Armstrong	Mr. Utt
Robin	Mr. Austin
Dwindle	Mr. M'Donald
William	Mr. Foster
Hon. Mrs. Glenroy	Mrs. Placide
Rosalie Somers	Mrs. Green
Mrs. Trot	Mrs. Clark
Mrs. Moreen	Mrs. Clark
Goody Hawbuck	Mrs. Utt

I do not know whether to explain the doubling of Rutherford and Mrs. Clark as necessary for a full cast or as a printer's error. This was, I suspect, the full strength of the company.

The Irishman in London

Capt. Seymour	Mr. Foster
Mr. Calloony	Mr. Rutherford
Mr. Frost	Mr. Clark
Murtoch Delany (with the song of Paddy's wedding)	Mr. Twaites
Edward	Mr. Jones
Cymon	Mr. Collins
Louisa	Mrs. Placide
Caroline	Mrs. Green
Cubba	Mrs. Clark[29]

The program for Friday was "a Melo Drama, *The Wood Daemon, or, The Clock Has Struck,* to which will be added a Melo Drama called *The Tale of Mystery."* Two melodramas on one program was unusual. *The Wood Daemon* had "Scenery, Dresses and Decorations . . . entirely new." No casts or other details were given, but the Advertisement stated: "There will be a performance on Saturday night."[30] I have found no record of Saturday's performance.

The *Enquirer* of Tuesday, September 4, advertised for Wednesday "the Grand Drama interspersed with Dance, Song, Choruses, &c." of *The Forty Thieves,* with Twaits as Mustapha "(the Cobbler)," the only actor named. Afterpiece was *High Life below Stairs.*

"The grand Dramatic Romance, written by Colman, interspersed with Song, Dance, Processions, &c. called *Blue Beard or Female Curiosity"* was performed on Friday. No casts were given, but a description of scenery was included: "Act 1st—View of a Turkish Village. The Train of Abomelique appears crossing the mountains to claim his intended bride—Grand march and chorus. Act 2d—The Magic Chamber—Grand view of an illuminated Turkish Palace— This Scene entirely new. Act 3d—The exterior of Blue Beard's Castle.—The Cavern of death where Fatima is rescued from the power of Blue Beard by Selim, who destroys the Tyrant." Afterpiece was "the comedy in three acts called *Animal Magnetism."*[31]

On Friday, September 14, the *Enquirer* carried a long criticism of *The Road to Ruin,* presented "on Monday evening last," September 10. It was written "For the Enquirer," headed "Richmond Theatre," and unsigned. Although lavish in praise, it is not a puff but a genuine piece of theatrical criticism written by a knowledgeable and perceptive critic. Green, Twaits, and the Youngs are particularly commended:

On Monday evening last was presented Holcroft's elegant Comedy of *The Road to Ruin.* The city of Richmond has scarcely ever before witnessed a theatrical exhibition so elegantly furnished. The parts were well cast, and sustained with the highest spirit. Almost every character was, in itself, a feast.

Mr. Green, in the character of old Dornton gave us a picture of a father, which the streaming eyes of the audience, attested to be drawn from nature. The variety and excellence of this gentleman's theatrical powers, entitle him to laurels more rich and luxuriant than he has ever yet worn. He has, indeed, been always highly esteemed as an actor; yet we have scarcely been just to him.

Mr. Young exhibited the character of young Dornton with a vivacity and intelligence which gives us the promise of a banquet throughout the season. We hope that the example of spirit and nature which he has set in genteel comedy, will be followed. The tragic strut and deeptoned declamation are too frequent on our stage. Some of our actors seem to think that it requires a hollow voice, and a dragging, solemn enunciation, to give emphasis and effect to a striking sentiment. There cannot be a greater mistake; and it is wonderful that they do not themselves observe the superior effect which is produced upon the audience, when one such sentiment escapes in the manner of real life and conversation. Is not the stage intended to represent real life, and can the illusion ever be so strong and so fine as when the dialogue is carried on exactly after that manner which we see constantly around us?— For Heaven's sake, let us have no more vault toned awful ranting— no more dragging and drawling over the best passages of a poet, until all their fire dies, and all their spirit evaporates. Our actors have certainly read the criticism which Fielding puts into the mouth of Partridge, in his novel of Tom Jones—yet they seem to have mistaken the compliments real, when they are only ironical, and the censures sincere when they form the finest panegyrick. Thus when Garrick, in Hamlet, sees the ghost, the workings of nature which he exhibits, impart the contagious tremor to the frame & voice of Partridge, & he declared it is no acting; for he should have done so exactly himself, if he had seen a ghost—But when the King, according to the manner which prevailed upon the London stage, before the aera of Garrick, begins to square himself and strut and rant, Partridge is entirely relieved of all his sympathy, and exclaims, with great delight, "Ah, that's it—any body may see, *that is acting*;" as if it were not the chief business of an actor to make us forget that he is acting.* (**Ars est celare artem*.) We will not make a personal application of these hints; a good natured man has no pleasure in censuring; but he begs that the performers will, themselves, compare their voice & manner with that of nature around them & of themselves, when off the stage, & they will find it easy to make the application.

Let them only ask themselves for one moment, what is it that gives Mr. Twaits the just success which he enjoys?—It is the unaffected ease and nature with which he enters into his character. In Goldfinch, on Monday night, he deserved and received the highest applause; the character was not caricatured, it was nature's self; it was neither degraded by buffoonery, nor distorted by affectation, but exhibited with a just and beautiful precision. This gentleman certainly stands unrivalled in the line of characters in which he has shewn himself here: we have had others that have attempted them, but in the hands of Mr. Twaits, they have a new air & interest—It is easy to discern through the lowest character which [he] impersonates, the superior intelligence which directs his action.

But what shall we say of Mrs. Young, when in the character of Sophia, she came bounding on the stage in all the effulgence of beauty & with all the graces sporting around her? Could she have seen the electric stroke of delight which darted through the house, she would in her turn, have had a feast. Never was the character better supported either on this, or the other side of the Atlantic. She gave us a picture of rustic wildness, simplicity and innocence, which every hearer felt to be true to the life and which rendered her one of the most interesting beings on earth. When she came leaping over the chord, when she twirled her handkerchief into the form of a babe and dandled it on her knee, when sitting on the floor, she opened her plumb cake and drew forth the valentine, when afterwards in a fit of jealousy she tore the valentine to pieces, threw it on the floor & burst into tears, in short, in every incident which belonged to her part, she seemed to us to hit it with inexpressible felicity. We congratulate the city on such an acquisition to the Theatre.

The "Grand Dramatic Romance of *Blue Beard*" was repeated "(by particular desire)" on Wednesday, September 12. Cast was given:

Abomelique (Blue Beard)	Mr. Clark
Ibrahim	Mr. Caulfield
Selim	Mr. Foster
Schacabac	Mr. Twaits
Hassan	Mr. Utt
Skeleton	Mr. Austin
Spahis	Messrs. M'Donald, & Barton &c.
Fatima	Mrs. Green
Irene	Mrs. Clark
Beda	Mrs. Placide

Presumably this was the same cast as September 7, when no cast was advertised. *Blue Beard* was followed by "the much admired interlude" of *Blue Devils* "for the first time here." Cast was given:

Meagrim	Mr. Twaits
Demison	Mr. Clark
James	Mr. Rutherford

| Bailiff | Mr. Utt |
| Annette | Mrs. Young |

This is the second record of the appearance of Mrs. Young, who had been praised for her performance of Sophia in *The Road to Ruin* on Monday, September 10. The evening concluded with *The Spoiled Child*, with the following cast:

Old Pickle	Mr. Clark
Tag	Mr. Twaites
John	Mr. Rutherford
Thomas	Mr. Austin
Richard	Mr. M'Donald
Little Pickle (with songs)	Mrs. Poe
Miss Pickle	Mrs. Clark
Maria	Mrs. Green
Margery	Mrs. Utt[32]

On Friday, September 14, the *Virginia Patriot* announced for "This evening, a celebrated Drama, in 3 acts, performed with more applause than any other modern production, called *The Foundling of the Forest*." An elaborate cast was advertised:

Count de Valmont	Mr. Young
Baron Longueville	Mr. Clark
Florian (the Foundling adopted by Valmont)	Mr. Rutherford
Bertrand (Valet to Longueville)	Mr. Green
Le Clair (Valet to Florian)	Mr. Twaits
Sanguine } Bravos in the pay	{ Mr. Utt
La Noire } of Longueville	{ Mr. M'Donald
Gaspard (an old domestic)	Mr. Collins
Geraldine (niece to de Valmont)	Mrs. Young
Rasabella (her woman)	Mrs. Green
Monica (an old Peasant)	Mrs. Clark
Unknown Female	Mrs. Placide
Domestics, Peasants, Dancers, &c.	

Afterpiece was "the Musical Entertainment of *My Grand Mother, or The Living Picture*," for which no cast was given.

On the same date the *Virginia Argus* carried a summary of the plot, a typical romantic story of virtue (Valmont) versus villainy (Longueville), separation and reunion, and mistaken identity (Florian, the foundling, turns out to be Valmont's son). It was a lavish production, attested by this "Description of Scenery":

Act 1st Scene 3d—a Forest and Storm.—Scene 4th, Another part of the Forest, more entangled and intricate, the Tempest becomes violent, & the stage appears alternately illuminated by lightning and enveloped in darkness.

Scene 5, The outside of a Cottage in the Wood, a light beaming in the casement.

Act 2d, The castle garden decorated for a Fete—a sham combat with the Broad Sword and Shield between Master and Miss J. Placide—A Pas Seul by Miss E. Placide, not 6 years of age.

Act 3d, The river bank, the Rhine flows across the stage at a distance, on one side a pavilion, through the lower windows of which a light appears, the moon has just risen above the German bank, and sheds its radiance upon the water.

Such efforts did not go unrewarded. In the *Enquirer* an unnamed critic singled out Green and Mrs. Placide for special praise, with a more restrained evaluation of Mrs. Young:

On Friday Evening last, we were presented with Mr. Dimond's beautiful drama of the Foundling in the Forest. The characters were well cast, and the representation went off with much eclat.

Mr. Green played the part of the repentant Bertrand—in a style of execution which did him considerable credit. His struggles, his halting between the fear of his master & the remorses of conscience, the final triumph of virtue, and his resolution to serve and save Eugenia, were hit off in his very best manner. He felt what he said, and he made us feel it too. Mr. G. has powers, which should be oftener exerted. They are the spark of the flint, whose corruscations always delight us.

Mrs. Placide was the soft, the noble Eugenia—sometimes wild, and always interesting—whether she was chaunting the piercing notes of the maniac, or pouring her pathetic prayers at the feet of the inhuman Longueville, she always irresistibly commanded the attention of the audience. —The sweet voice of Mrs. Placide, her noble air, the sweet and elevated cast of her countenance, the precision and discernment with which she acts, the deep interest which she takes in the scene, all stamp her as the favorite child of the drama:

How often did we *forget* to applaud her because we were wrapped up in the reverie created by her enchantment! How often did the hands refuse to meet, lest the ears should lose any of her accents! A silence, still as that of the grave, was the only praise which we could give her.

In fine, where shall we discover her equal? She is the Merry of the Virginia Theatre—all her blemishes are those of Nature, all her

virtues are her own. This eulogium comes like a day after the
fare—but it is of itself of sufficient proof that it is not a puff for
a Benefit night—it is the pure tribute due to merit—it is just,
because it comes from the heart.

The noble Geraldine did not suit Mrs. Young as well as the
artless Sophia. She should pour more soul into her acting. She was
most interesting, when she spoke the least. "Her tongue too oft
destroyed the magic of her eyes." A statue may please us—but
wonder and extacy are the fruits of higher powers—"words that
breathe," and looks and attitudes "that burn." —Motive and exertion, however, may crown Mrs. Y. with the finest wreathes of the
Tragic Muse.[33]

The *Virginia Patriot* of Friday, September 14, announced that
"Mrs. Placide's Benefit will take place on Monday Evening," but I
found no record of performance on that date. Next record of performance was on Wednesday, September 19, when "Mrs. Cowley's
justly admired comedy, in five acts, called *Which Is The Man, or
The Soldier of Honor"* was presented. It was followed by "a Ballet
to be performed by Children only: *The Bird Catchers*. To which
will be added (for the first time in Virginia) a National Drama in
three acts, written by Doct. Joor of South Carolina, called *The
Battle of Eutaw Springs and Evacuation of Charleston*." The performance was "for the Benefit of Mr. & Mrs. Clark," but no casts
were advertised. There was, however, a description of scenery:

Act 1st—A view of the American Encampment.
Act 2d—Battle at the Eutaw House, between the American and
British forces.
Act 3d—A Grand Transparent view of Charleston on Fire. —The
Evacuation of Charleston by the British—a view of Charleston
Harbor, Fort Johnston and Sullivan's Island, with the British Fleet
at Anchor—Entrance of the American Army—the Genius of Ameri-
ca descends and recites The Standard of Liberty; the Eagle of
Columbia appears crowning Green with Laurels, and bearing the
following inscription,
The Southern States are Free.[34]

The *Enquirer* of Friday, September 21, published "The Standard
of Liberty," which it says was "written by Mrs. Rowson and recited by Mrs. Placide, on Wednesday night, in the character of the
Genius of Columbia." It consists of about a hundred lines of
heroic couplet, recounting the fall of Troy, whence the warlike

Eagle flew to Rome, then because of avarice and vice she sought another home: Columbia. It is snide of me to mention anent this rousing patriotic production that Manager Placide was French and most of the actors English.

The *Virginia Patriot* of Friday, September 21, carried a typical puff for the evening's bill of *The Belle's Stratagem* and *Matrimony; or, the Test of Love*:

The Company which now graces the Richmond Boards, shines in genteel Comedy. A Proof of this appears in the entertainment afforded by the representation of the "Road to Ruin" & "Town and Country." The bill of fare which is this night offered to the Audience will put forth the strength of the Company in its best lights. The Belle's Stratagem is one of the best comedies in the whole range of the Drama, and indeed it is not surprising, for as an artist is best acquainted with his own tools, the fair Authoress, may be supposed to know all the arts and stratagems of the Belle's. "Matrimony" appropriately follows on the heels of the "Stratagems." It is a farce peculiarly humorous and chaste; it needs no other eulogium than that it is from the pen of Mr. Kenney, the author of the exquisit piece of humour, "Raising the Wind." This night offers then a rich banquet to the lovers of genteel Comedy, Critics, and all the laughter-loving sons of Momus. The feast is spread by the fair hand of Mrs. Poe whose dramatic excellence as well as long exertions in the cause of the public will certainly ensure her that liberal compensation, which she so justly deserves.

A brief advertisement in the same issue named the plays but gave no casts. It was Mrs. Poe's benefit. During *The Belle's Stratagem* she sang "While Strephon Thus You Teaze Me," and in the masquerade in the third act danced a double allemande with Placide. This was her last recorded performance of the season. Quinn conjectures that Rosalie was born in December.[35] Edgar was now almost two years old. David was not with his family at this time; as far as we know, he never rejoined them.

The *Patriot's* brief and conventional puffing was far exceeded by a long unsigned article in the *Enquirer* of the same date. The author apologized for "another Theatrical critique. . . . Indeed, I should not perhaps have troubled you at all, had I not been a confirmed enemy of every species of Monopoly, and really deemed it a moral duty to admonish justice that her scales are not held

even." Mrs. Placide, Mr. Green, and Mr. Twait, he says, have mo-
nopolized praise. "Much better were it instead of lavishing praise
where praise can add no fame, to take aspiring genius by the hand
and help it from obscurity." Rutherford, Collins, and Young get
brief and favorable mention:

But the object of these remarks, Mr. Editor, is yet behind the
curtain. It is true, a man who has ever been accustomed to esteem
modesty and *woman* synonymous terms, and who has always been
more ready to kneel at the shrine of beauty than before the image
of a saint, feels some diffidence in introducing a lady in the
columns of a news paper. Yet he gathers strength from the resolution, that no observation of his shall tinge the cheek of modesty
with a blush nor cast one stain on the vestal robe of virtue. Thus
self justified, he enters on the task, confidently believing that the
public will be prepared to welcome with the same approbation
which marks her entrance on the stage, the introduction of Mrs.
Poe. From an actress who possesses so eminently the faculty of
pleasing, whose powers are so general and whose exertions are so
ready, it would be unjust to withhold the tribute of applause. Were
I to say simply that she is a valuable acquisition to the Theatre, I
should dishonor her merit and do injustice to the feelings of the
public. It is true she has never yet been called to the higher characters in tragedy, and it is proper that she never should be for she
who is so well calculated to fill the heart with pleasure, should
never be required to shroud it in gloom. On the first moment of
her entrance on the Richmond boards, she was saluted with the
plaudits of admiration, and at no one moment since has her reputation sunk. Her "exits and her entrances," equally operate their
electric effects, for if we expect to be pleased when Mrs. Poe
appears, when her part is ended, our admiration ever proclaims
that our anticipations have been more than realized. It is needless
to review the various characters in which her excellence has been
displayed. I think I may be pardoned for asserting, that taking her
performances from the commencement to the end, no one has
acquitted himself with more distinguished honor. If it be excellent
to satisfy the judgment and delight the heart, then Mrs. Poe is
excellent. If it be the perfection of acting to conceal the actor,
Mrs. Poe's name is a brilliant gem in the Theatrick crown. In a
word, as no one has received more than she of the public applause,
no one is better entitled to the public liberality.

Were I to say more, Mr. Editor, perhaps I should forget the
character I have assumed. In regard to Mrs. Poe, for a reason which
the glass will tell her, it is a difficult thing to separate the *actress*

from the *woman*; no wonder then, if it should be also difficult to separate the *critic* from the *man*. Even were Aristarchus himself to rise from the dead to sit in judgment on her acting, he would find it necessary to put a strong curb upon his feelings. For if he did not, instead of criticising the *player*, he might find himself perhaps, in the situation of Shakspear's Slender, dolefully heaving the lover's sign and pathetically exclaiming, "Oh! Sweet Anna Page."

And now after thanking you for your complaisance, I will bid you good night—first however, assuring you that this is no *benefit puff* for the writer is a stranger to both Richmond and Mrs. Poe. Yet he sincerely hopes that on this night, the full horn of plenty may be emptied into her lap, and that she may moreover, reap in its fullest extent, the still richer reward of merited approbation.

Another puff in the same issue of the *Patriot* tells us that Saturday, September 22, is Caulfield's benefit, the plays *King Lear* and *The Devil to Pay*. Caulfield's merits "are too well known to need as an additional recommendation the feeble aid of the writer's pen." Caulfield's roles for the evening are not mentioned; and Twaits, not Caulfield, played Lear:

To enlarge upon the merits of a tragedy so well known and so universally admired as King Lear, would be both superfluous and impertinent. There is not in the whole compass of the drama a play more strongly calculated to display the powers of the actor and to interest the feelings of the audience.

It ought not also to pass unobserved, that the theatrical entertainments of this season have hitherto been almost entirely in the comic line, and that the introduction of a tragedy, and especially of one so excellent, will have all the zest of novelty and variety to recommend it.

If, after what has been already said, any additional inducement to witness the performance can possibly be wanting, it may be found in the pleasure of beholding the astonishing versatility of talents in the inimitable Twaits. This favorite actor, on that evening, plays Lear in the tragedy, and those who have already admired the various and unrivalled excellence of his comic powers will be delighted to find that he is equally qualified for the impassioned scenes of tragedy; equally at home in the sock and buskin.

On Tuesday, September 25, the *Patriot* advertised for Wednesday "a celebrated Comedy in five acts, by Moreton, author of *Speed the Plough, Columbus,* &c. called *A Cure for the Heart Ache.* To which will be added (for the first time here) a Grand Romantic Melo-Drama, in two acts, called *Valentine & Orson.*" No casts were given. Between pieces Mrs. Young performed "a Hornpipe with a Skipping Rope." The *Virginia Argus* of September 26 announced "the Part of the Green Knight, by Mr. Metyer, who has kindly offered his services as an Amateur, for that night only, and will during the Drama, Fight three different Combats." Metyer was the fencing master who had advertised in July. Perhaps some of the actors were among his pupils. Combats were frequent on the Richmond stage. Although no cast was named, the advertisement gave nearly a column to a "Prospectus" of the action of *Valentine and Orson,* a good illustration of the spectacular stage effects of the Placide and Green repertoire:

Act I Scene I A new Scene representing the town and city gates of Orleans. A grand procession with colours, standards and trophies
Scene II Garden of the Convent
Scene III Palace. The King on his Throne with attendants &c.
Scene IV An Apartment in the Palace
Scene V A new Scene—The Forest of Orleans—In the centre, a large Tree; at the back, a Cavern. Combat between Valentine & Orson
Act II Scene I A new Scene—The exterior of a Palace
Scene II An Apartment in the Palace
Scene III Palace Garden with a superb Banquet
Scene IV An Encampment of the Green Knight—Knights hung on a Tree; being vanquished. Magic Shield hung up, guarded by a Saracen Priest. Combat between the Green Knight and Eglantine. Orson & Green Knight fight; Green Knight vanquished. Valentine's soldiers rush on and conquer the Saracens. Thunder. The Genius Pacolet descends on a Cloud; addresses the characters.
Scene V Castle of the Giant Ferragus. Two Fiends rush out on Valentine & Orson; but are overthrown and sink. A Lion enters. Valentine presents the magic Ring and the Lion disappears. Pacolet is seen in place of the monster; and conducts Valentine and Orson to his Castle.
Scene VI Magic Chamber in the Castle
Pacolet touches the golden Oracle, which speaks . . . Pacolet addresses the Oracle, which falls; and sinks. Valentine's hand joined to Eglantine & Orson's with Florimonda's. The Genius

signifies his approbation; addresses them; and mounts in the air.
Scene VII   A Brilliant Hall illuminating a Grand Procession.

Both the *Enquirer* and the *Virginia Patriot* on Friday,
September 28, carried this advertisement:

The Subscribers to the Richmond Theatre, are respectfully
informed one year's interest upon the shares, commencing July 1st
1810, will be paid upon application at the Theatre every morning,
this, and the next week, by

J. W. Green

September 27, 1810

Evidently the melodramatic spectacles were popular; I take Green's
announcement as evidence that the theatre was well attended and
financially successful.

The same issue of the *Patriot* announced Rutherford's benefit
for "This evening." Plays were *The Suspicious Husband* and *Robin
Hood*, but no casts or other details were given.

Collins's benefit was announced for Saturday, but no record
exists of the performance. *The Foundling of the Forest* was advertised for Tuesday "(for the second time here)" with *The Purse* as
afterpiece, but no casts were given.[36]

There was competition at Hay Market Garden where Martin
advertised an "Ascension in a Balloon" and a brilliant display of
fireworks at 5:30, admission one dollar, children half price. De-
ferring to superior spectacle, the theatre advertisement respectfully
informed the public that "the performance on this evening, will
not commence until half past seven o'clock, on account of Mr.
Martin's exhibition at the Gardens." The advertisement stated
further that "there will be a performance on Wednesday, Thursday, and Friday this week (being the last until after the Petersburg
Races) beginning each night at a quarter before seven."[37]

The last recorded performance of this season was on Friday,
October 5, when *Town and Country* and *The Children in the
Wood* were presented. The advertisement gave no casts or other
details.[38] There is no record of the performances on Wednesday
and Thursday.

The *Virginia Argus* of Friday, October 5, advertised a
performance for "Tomorrow evening, being the last until the

twenty-second of this month." I think it likely that the company closed in Richmond on Saturday and opened in Petersburg the following week, but there is no record of performance on Saturday.

While the company played in Petersburg, Martin moved his "exhibition" into the theatre for a week. He was evidently a man of many talents. The performance consisted of two parts: first, "Philomathematical Experiments, Magic Art and Deceptions"; second, "the True and Celebrated Phantasmagoria in its highest degree of perfection." Admittance was seventy-five cents to box and pit, children fifty cents, and gallery fifty cents.[39]

The *Enquirer* of Tuesday, October 9, printed an amusing anecdote about Twaits, who is "the Foote of our Stage":

His comic humor not only raises the ready laugh in the fictitious scenes of the Drama, but he can *play a part* for himself. He studies in the school of Momus, as well as of Melphomene. He not only embodies the ideas of others, but he can draw upon the stores of his own wit. —He is in character as a Punster or a Player.

Some time during the last week, T. came forward, on a Benefit night, to receive the *rich* reward of public favor. Pit, Boxes, and Galleries were crowded on the occasion—it was no Irish Benefit, as some gentleman of the sock have found it to their cost—the catastrophe must have been a pleasant one for the hero of the night—for he pocketed not less than $670.

The story tells that Twait was robbed by a Negro servant in his hotel, but recovered his money, and the thief was taken before a local magistrate:

This *Denouement* took place, on Friday night—but a very few moments before the curtain was to rise on the stage. The temple of Melpomene was opened—the fires were lighted on her altar, and we cannot say a *crowd*, but a certain number of spectators had attended to witness the mystic rites of the goddess—The play was to be "Town and Country"—in which Mr. Twaits was to play the part of the London Cit, the "comfortable" Mr. Cosey—but instead of a fictitious part on the stage, he was hurried before the civil magistrate, to act his own cause before the public. In the mean time, the audience grew impatient—sticks and palms began to testify their dissatisfaction—and Mr. Young thought proper to come forward with an apology, and an assurance that Mr. Rutherford should read the part, until the real Mr. Cosey could appear.

Two acts passed over, with book in hand—when the curtain arose upon the 3d, Mr. T. advanced to the front of the stage, agitated and tremulous, to make his apologetic bow, to the company: "Ladies and Gentlemen, I have to apologize to you for not appearing sooner; but you have been informed of the motives of my absence. I have been before a magistrate; and I am happy to say, that the thief is secured and the money which I had received from your generous hands, is recovered from the villainous ones which had taken it from me. (*applause.*) Everything has been settled to my satisfaction; and, *this is what, I call, being comfortable"* (a thunder of applause.) The reader will most relish the expression, who knows how favorite a one it is with Mr. Cosey.

Twait's benefit is not mentioned in extant advertisements, but it is interesting to know that receipts were $670 on that night. At one dollar each it would have been a full house. The performance of *Town and Country* for which he arrived late must have been on Friday, October 5.

Between August 18 and October 5 there are records of seventeen performances, a season of approximately seven weeks. Thirty-four different plays were presented, a varied repertoire, in which romantic spectacle was featured. Nine plays were new to Richmond: *Animal Magnetism, The Battle of Eutaw Springs, The Blue Devils, The Foundling of the Forest, Matrimony, Of Age Tomorrow, The Suspicious Husband, Valentine and Orson,* and *Which Is the Man.* There was one play by an American author: *The Battle of Eutaw Springs.*

Newspaper advertisements name twenty-four performers: fifteen men, six women, two girls, one boy. One local amateur (the fencing master, Metyer) appeared. No visiting stars appeared, but it was a strong company and a successful season.

The previous season ended with a parody of the popular European romantic melodrama being then presented on the Richmond stage. This season ends on a melancholy and moralistic note. On October 5 the *Enquirer* published an "Epilogue to the Tragedy of *Douglas,*" said to be "the production of a very young man." Romantic in tone, neoclassic in form, it consists of about a hundred lines of heroic couplet beginning "The woods and wilds with melancholy gloom/Now silent mourn around Matilda's tomb" and ending "Alike prepar'd for instant death, or life,/May every soul swell 'midst the jarring strife." I doubt that it was ever spoken from the stage.

The plays.   *Of Age Tomorrow* (August 18, 1810), a musical farce in two acts by T. J. Dibdin, with music by Michael Kelly, was first acted at Drury Lane on February 1, 1800. Its first American performance was in New York on November 6, 1806. It was acted in Philadelphia on December 22, 1810, and Charleston, February 1, 1811.

Animal Magnetism (September 7, 1810), a comedy by Elizabeth Inchbald, was first acted at Covent Garden in 1788, and first acted in America in New York in 1793. It was acted in Charleston on March 16, 1810, and Philadelphia, December 3, 1831.

The Blue Devils (September 12, 1810), a one-act farce by George Colman, the younger, was first acted at Covent Garden on April 24, 1798, and first acted in America in Charleston on April 19, 1802. It was acted in New York in 1806 and Philadelphia in 1818.

The Foundling of the Forest (September 14, 1810), a romantic drama by William Dimond, had its premiere at the Haymarket on July 10, 1809. Its American premiere came just four months later, in New York on November 27. It was acted in Charleston on April 11, and Philadelphia, December 3, 1810.

Which Is the Man? (September 19, 1810), a comedy in five acts by Hannah Cowley, was brought out at Covent Garden in 1782. It was acted in Philadelphia in 1792, New York, 1795, and Charleston, 1804. *The Battle of Eutaw Springs* was written by William Ioor of South Carolina and first staged in Charleston on January 10, 1807. Quinn says that it was acted in Philadelphia in 1813. "It is a chronicle play of patriotic text rather than dramatic effectiveness. The central historical character is General Green, who is visited at times by the Genius of Liberty, which in Charleston was embodied in the attractive person of Mrs. Young. Captain Laurence Manning is the youthful hero, and the humor is furnished largely by a British soldier, appropriately named Queerfish."[40]

Matrimony (September 21, 1810), a comic opera in two acts by James Kenney, was first acted at Drury Lane on November 20, 1804, and first acted in America in New York on May 17, 1805.

It was acted in Charleston in 1807 and Philadelphia in 1811.

Valentine and Orson (September 26, 1810), a romantic melodrama in two acts by T. J. Dibdin, was brought out at Covent Garden on April 3, 1804, and was first acted in America in New York on April 15, 1805. It was acted in Charleston in 1806 and Philadelphia in 1811.

The Suspicious Husband (September 28, 1810), a comedy in five acts by Dr. Benjamin Hoadly, was first acted at Covent Garden in 1746. It was acted in New York in 1754, Philadelphia, 1759, and Charleston, 1763. I suspect an eighteenth-century performance in Richmond of which record is lost.

The players.   Mrs. Poe's last recorded appearance had been on April 10, 1806, just after her marriage to David Poe. Since then they had played in Philadelphia, New York, and Boston. They appeared in "an entertainment" at Hay Market Garden on July 11, 1808, billed as "from the Boston theatre."

The most notable newcomer to the company was William Twaits, who before coming to America had played with Macready's company in Birmingham. He was brought to this country by William Wood, co-manager of the Old Drury of Philadelphia, and played there before moving to New York, where he made his debut as Caleb Quotem in *The Review* on June 21, 1805. Odell says that his success was "immediate and overwhelming."[41] Between 1805 and 1810, he played leading roles on the New York stage. Although naturally endowed for comic roles, in which he made his greatest successes, he also played Richard III, Prince Hal, and King Lear. In Richmond as in New York, he played leading roles in both comedy and tragedy, ranging from Lear to Cosey.

TWENTY-EIGHTH SEASON
Placide and Green Company
October–November 1810

Chronicle.   Before the last season closed for the Petersburg races, the company advertised that the theatre would reopen on October 22, 1810. The first advertisement appeared in the *Virginia Patriot* of Tuesday, October 23, announcing *The Poor Gentleman* and *Don Juan* for Wednesday. No casts were given, but house regulations stated that doors opened at 5:30 with performance at 6:30: "Tickets to be had at this office, and at the office of the Theatre. Days of performance, Mondays, Wednesdays and Fridays." A brief notice in the issue of Friday, October 26, announced for "This evening" *John Bull* and *No Song, No Supper*. "Mr. and Mrs. Clark's Benefit" was also advertised for "Saturday evening," but there is no record of performance on Saturday. On Tuesday, October 30, the *Enquirer* advertised for Wednesday the "Grand Historical Melo Drama, written by James Barker of Philadelphia, & performed at the various Theatres on the Continent with unbounded applause— called the *Indian Princess or the First Settlement of Virginia*." Afterpiece was *Love Laughs at Locksmiths*. No casts were given. The *Virginia Patriot* of Friday, November 2, announced "For the Benefit of the Poor of the City of Richmond" performances of *The Heir at Law* and *The Children in the Wood* on "this evening," with *Pizarro* and *Love Laughs at Locksmiths* on Saturday. No casts were given. Another brief notice on Tuesday, November 6, advertised for Wednesday the "celebrated Drama, in four acts, written by Mrs. Inchbald, *The Child of Nature*," which was followed by the "grand Melo Drama, *Tekeli, or The Siege of Montgatz*." No casts or other details were given.

Speed the Plough was advertised for Friday, followed by "for the first time here, a Grand Historical Pantomime, in two acts, called *Telamachus in the Island of Calypso*." For characters and description of scenery we are told to "see Bills." This was Manager Placide's benefit. Between pieces he danced a hornpipe on the tightrope and displayed the flag in a variety of attitudes. "Afterwards he will dance with two boys fastened to his feet; likewise with two men attached to his feet in the same manner." After the dancing "a grand collection of historical paintings" was exhibited, described as "Brook Watson, Lord Mayor of London, fighting a shark," "The Burning of the Philadelphia Frigate by Stephen Decatur," "The Bombardment of Tripoli," and "The Battle of Bunker's Hill." Pamphlets descriptive of the paintings were to be had at the door of the theatre and at Adams's Book Store for

12½ cents. The artist was not named.[42]

The Manager in Distress was advertised for Wednesday, November 14, with Green playing the Manager. It was his benefit and "Positively the last night this season." Other parts were taken by Collins, Foster, Twaits, Caulfield, Utt, M'Donald, and Mrs. Clark, but their roles were not specified. "In the course of the prelude" Caulfield gave "(by particular desire) Imitations of the following London Performers:"

> Mr. Bensley in *Mountaineers*
> Mr. Parson in *Heiress*
> Mr. Palmer in *Henry 8th*
> Mr. King in *Heiress*
> Mr. Kemble in *Hamlet*
> Mr. Johnson in *London Hermit*
> Mr. Aichin in *Henry 8th*
> Mr. Suet in *My Grandmother.*

The Manager in Distress was followed by *The Provoked Husband, or a Journey to London*, and the evening concluded with a repetition of *Love Laughs at Locksmiths.*[43]

This was not the last night of the season. The *Virginia Patriot* of Friday, November 16, carried this notice: "The Managers of the Theatre respectfully inform the public that they have made arrangements with Mr. Dwyer, from the late Theatre Drury Lane, to perform six nights—His first performance will be this evening … when will be presented the Comedy of *The Dramatist*." The *Virginia Argus* of this date announced for "This evening" *The Dramatist* with Dwyer as Vapid, and *The Devil to Pay, or, Wives Metamorphosed* with Twaits as Johnson.

On Tuesday, November 20, the *Virginia Patriot* respectfully informed the public that "the Play advertised for yesterday evening, is postponed until this evening." The *Enquirer* of the same date advertised for "This evening" *The West Indian* with Dwyer as Belcour and another repetition of *Love Laughs at Locksmiths*. It also carried a brief puff on Dwyer, "who has considerable stage effect—his person genteel, his manners easy, and his acting stampt with vivacity and fire. —He shines most in *genteel comedy*. His representation of the ardent and lively Belcour in Cumberland's West Indian is pronounced to be his forte, and one of the

chastest personations of that character, which has ever appeared."
There is no further record of Dwyer's performance. I assume he
played six roles on six evenings; we have record of two.

Although only eight actors are named during this season, which
is characterized by brief advertisements, this was the same company which had played the previous season, with, of course, the
addition of Dwyer as visiting star. During a season of four weeks,
there are records of ten performances and fifteen different plays,
three of which were new: *The Manager in Distress, The Provoked
Husband*, and *Telemachus*. The company probably left Richmond
soon after November 20; they opened in Charleston on January 9,
1811.

The plays.   The "historical pantomime" *Telemachus* (November 9,
1810) may have been adapted from the play by the Reverend
George Graham published in Dublin in 1763. I suspect that it was
mostly the work of Alexander Placide, who presented it first in
Charleston on March 31, 1798, and in New York on July 29, 1801.

The Manager in Distress (November 14, 1810) was a prelude
written by George Colman, the elder, and first acted at the Haymarket on May 30, 1780. It was acted in New York on May 10,
1802, and Charleston, January 19, 1809. *The Provoked Husband*
was a comedy which Colley Cibber completed from John Van-
brugh's manuscript of *The Journey to London*. It was first acted
at Drury Lane in 1728, and was acted in New York, 1752,
Philadelphia, 1754, and Charleston, 1763.

The players.   John Dwyer, from Drury Lane, made his American
debut as Belcour in New York on March 14, 1810. Odell charac-
terizes him as "the elegant Dwyer . . . representative of the airy,
debonair gentleman of English comedy." Between March 14 and
April 18 he played an "immense sweep of comedy roles . . . representing the very best in the comedy of the last twenty-five years
of the eighteenth century."[44] He played with the Placide-Green
Company in Charleston in January 1811 and was in Philadelphia
during the same year.

TWENTY-NINTH SEASON
Placide and Green Company
August–October 1811

Chronicle.   The Charleston season opened on January 7 and closed on May 20, 1811. Hoole lists Alexander Placide, manager, and William Twaits, acting manager. The Greens were not with the company in Charleston. The company may have visited Savannah during the summer, and they may have played Norfolk and Petersburg on their way back to Richmond, where they arrived early in August.

The first advertisement appeared in the *Enquirer* of August 13, announcing that the "Richmond Theatre will open on Wednesday evening, August 14th, with the play of *The Wonder* and the musical entertainment of *The Purse or Benevolent Tar.* In the course of which Mr. Smalley from the Theatre Royal Covent Garden and late from New York, will introduce the popular Ballads of 'The Bay of Biscay O,' 'The Galley Slave,' and 'The Thorn.' " No other actors were named, and no further details were given.

On Friday, August 16, was presented "the much admired Play in 5 acts, call'd *The Suspicious Husband.* To which will be added the much admired musical Entertainment, call'd *The Padlock.*" Leonora was played by Miss Thomas "(her first appearance)," and Leander by Mr. Smalley, who introduced the favorite songs of "Just like Love" and "The Streamlet." No other actors were named. Doors opened at six, with performance at seven. Tickets were to be had at Mr. Davis's Printing Office, and at the Theatre. "Subscribers Tickets will be left as usual."[45]

On Monday, August 19, was presented "the celebrated Commedy in 5 acts, call'd *She Stoops to Conquer, or The Mistakes of a Night.* To which will be added, the much admired musical Entertainment, call'd *Rosina, or Love in a Cottage.*"[46] No casts were given.

The *Virginia Argus* of Thursday, August 22, advertised for that date, "Never Performed Here . . . a new Play in 5 Acts call'd *The Doubtful Son; or Secrets of a Palace.* To which will be added the Musical Entertainment of *Sprigs of Laurel; or, Rival Soldiers.*"

The same advertisement appeared in the *Enquirer*, but the *Virginia Patriot* added: "The public are respectfully informed some alterations in the characters of the Farce has taken place different from the advertisement in the bills."

Rosina	Miss Thomas
Phoebe	Mrs. Clark
William	Mr. Twaits
First Irishman	Mr. Green

Evidently the complete casts were advertised in the handbills, but not in the newspapers.

The *Virginia Argus* of Monday, August 26, announced for "This Evening . . . a Play in three acts, call'd *The Point of Honor, or School for Soldiers*." The only character named was Durimel, played by "Mr. Anderson (From the New York Theatre, his first appearance here.)" Afterpiece was "the Grand Historical Pantomime call'd *Don Juan, or The Libertine Destroyed*.

The *Enquirer* of August 27 advertised *Macbeth* and *Care and Mirth, or Harlequin Skeleton* for Thursday, August 29. However, the *Virginia Argus* of August 29 announced for "This Evening . . . a Comedy in 5 acts, call'd *The Road to Ruin*. To which will be added the much admired comic Farce of *The Irishman in London*." I suppose we should accept the *Argus* advertisement, since it appeared on the day of the performance. There is no reason given for the change. It is possible that the *Enquirer* advertisement erred as to date and that *Macbeth* and the Harlequin pantomime were presented on Tuesday, August 27, the date the advertisement appeared, followed by *The Road to Ruin* and *The Irishman in London* two days later. No casts were advertised.

The bill for Monday, September 2, was "the celebrated comedy in three acts, called *The BirthDay; or The Reconciliation*" and "the Grand Historical Pantomime called *La Perouse; or The Desolate Island*," but no advertisement gave further details.[47]

On Tuesday, September 3, the *Virginia Patriot* advertised for "Wednesday Evening . . . the celebrated Tragedy of *Adelgitha; or The Fruits of a Single Error*. To which will be added for the first time in this Theatre the celebrated opera of *Paul and Virginia*." The only additional detail is that "Nights of performance" will be

"Mondays, Wednesdays & Fridays."

The *Virginia Argus* of September 5 respectfully informed the public that "in consequence of the sudden indisposition of Mrs. Placide, the Play for tomorrow, Friday Evening the 6th Sept. is unavoidable changed to the much admired Comedy of *The Grandfather's Will, or The Old Batchelor in the Straw*. After the Play the much admired favorite Pantomimic Ballet, to be performed by children only, call'd *The Hunters and the Milk Maid*. To which will be added the much admired musical entertainment of *The Agreeable Surprise*, the part of Lingo by Mr. Twaits." The bill is confirmed by advertisements in the *Enquirer* and the *Patriot* of September 6, the latter adding that *The Grandfather's Will* is a comedy in five acts, but no advertisement listed casts.

"The Grand Drama of the *Forty Thieves*" was acted on Monday, September 9, with "the Comedy of *Ways & Means*" as afterpiece. No details were given.[48]

The *Enquirer* of September 10 respectfully informed the public that "Mr. Robertson from the N.Y. Theatre is engaged and will make his first appearance on Wednesday evening . . . in the much admired Comedy of *Town and Country*." Afterpiece was *The Spoiled Child*. No casts or other details were given.

The Mountaineers was advertised for Friday with Robertson as Octavian and Twaits as Sadi. Afterpiece was the pantomime of *Care and Mirth, or Harlequin Skeleton*, with Smalley as Harlequin, Placide as Clown, and Mrs. Young as Columbine, the only characters named. The *Virginia Patriot* of Friday added that *The Mountaineers* would include in act two "the favorite Glee, of 'Ye High Born Spanish Noblemen,'" and that "in the course of the Pantomime, will be introduced the Magic Tree, and the Laughable Scene of the Gladiator, the Magic Chair, and a Leap by Harlequin six feet high, with other Leaps and Changes, &c."[49]

Everyone Has His Fault and *Of Age Tomorrow* were acted on Monday. Between pieces Smalley sang "The Life and Death of Tom Moody (the Huntsman)." No further details were given.[50]

The first advertisement of this season to give casts of characters appeared in the *Virginia Patriot* of Friday, September 20. It announced for that date *Abaellino, the Great Bandit* with the following cast:

Abaellino	Mr. Robertson
Andrias Gritto	Mr. Clark
Canari	Mr. Burke
Dandoli	Mr. Utt
Parozzi	Mr. Anderson
Contarino	Mr. Young
Falieri	Mr. Laurent
Memmo	Mr. Smalley
Matheo	Mr. Caulfield
Flodoardo	Mr. Robertson
Rosamunda	Mrs. Green
Iduella	Mrs. Clark

Abaellino was followed by "the Grand Allegorical Pantomime Spectacle, interspersed with Songs, Dance and Recitation, called *Cinderella; or The Little Glass Slipper*," with the following cast:

Prince	Mr. Placide
Lords	Messrs. Caulfield, Clark, Young & Burke
Attendants	Messrs. Laurent, Potter & Utt
Pedro	Mr. Smalley
Cinderella	Mrs. Green
Sisters	Mrs. Clark & Utt
Venus	Mrs. Young
Graces	Mrs. Poe, Miss Thomas & Miss Placide
Cupids	By Little Masters

The *Virginia Argus* of Monday, September 23, announced for that date *The Foundling of the Forest*, "After which will be performed, the interlude of *The Songster's Jubilee*; To conclude with the musical entertainment of *The Review, or Wags of Windsor*." The only character named was Caleb Quotem in *The Review*, played by Twaits. "Nights of Performance" were Monday, Wednesday, and Friday. At this time the *Virginia Patriot* was evidently distributed locally on the evening before the printed date. The issue dated September 24 carried an advertisement of the performance of the previous evening, giving program details not carried by the *Argus*, and a polite puff for Smalley on the occasion of his benefit. *The Songster's Jubilee* was described as "an entire new interlude consisting of Songs, Duetts, &c":

Duet — "How Sweet in the Woodlands" By Miss Thomas
& Mr. Smalley
Song — "How Happy when Edward was kind" By Miss
Thomas
Song — "Old Vulcan, or Columbia and Liberty" By Mr.
Smalley
Duet — "The Bird that sings in Yon Cage" By Mrs. Green
& Mr. Smalley
And for this night only, the celebrated Song of "Black
Eyed Susan"
And G. A. Stevens celebrated description of A Storm,
In character By Mr. Smalley

The puff, which was "Communicated" (written perhaps by
Manager Green), stated that Smalley was

a gentleman of great comic talents. . . . Some minds are suited for
tragedy; but it generally leaves upon the minds of those lovers,
dark and gloomy reflections; whereas, genteel comedy enlivens the
ideas, and leaves behind the most pleasing and delighted aspects.
Mr. Smalley, tho' in a declining state of health has always exerted
himself, and put in action his mental and corporeal powers, to
please, and has seldom failed to put the audience in a roar. In the
characters of Baron Piffleberg, Pedro, and O-rang-o-tang, he has
seldom been equalled, but never surpassed.

Another lavish advertisement with casts of characters and details
of program appeared in the *Patriot* on Tuesday, September 24,
announcing for "Wednesday evening . . . a celebrated Comedy in
Five Acts written by Holcroft, author of *The Road to Ruin* &c
called *The Deserted Daughter*." Cast was as follows:

Dr. Mordent	Mr. Clark
Cheveril	Mr. Green
Lenox	Mr. Young
Item	Mr. Twaits
Grime	Mr. Burke
Clement	Mr. Foster
Donald (a Scotchman)	Mr. Robertson
Lady Ann	Mrs. Green
Joanna (the deserted daughter)	Mrs. Young
Mrs. Sarsnet	Mrs. Clark
Mrs. Endfield	Mrs. Utt

The play was followed by a "Musical Divertisement" consisting of:

An Antique Song (in character of an old woman) call'd "Hard
    times, or Always Grumbling" by Mr. West
Song — "The Tuneful Lark" Miss Thomas
Song — "The Thorn" Mr. Smalley
Comic Song — "The Yorkshireman's Concert and Voyage to
    America" Mr. West
Song — "Crazy Jane" (without accompaniments) Miss Thomas
Song — "The Love Letter" Mr. Smalley

Afterpiece was "(for the first time here) a new and favorite Farce
performed in the various Theatres on the continent with unbounded applause, called *A Budget of Blunders*." Cast was as
follows:

Mr. Growley	Mr. Caulfield
Le Doctor Dablancour	Mr. Twaits
Doctor Smugface	Mr. Burke
Captain Belgrave	Mr. Foster
Tom	Mr. Anderson
Waiter	Mr. Laurent
Post Boy	Master H. Placide
Sophia	Mrs. Young
Bridget	Mrs. Poe
Deborah	Mrs. Clark

This was the Clark's benefit. A small advertisement in the *Enquirer*
of September 24 added only that Mr. West was "from the Philadelphia Theatre."

On Friday, September 27, was advertised for "This evening"
The Road to Ruin with a complete cast:

Goldfinch	Mr. Twaits
Old Dornton	Mr. Green
Harry Dornton	Mr. Young
Jack Milford	Mr. Caulfield
Sulky	Mr. Clark
Silky	Mr. Burke
Hosier	Mr. Anderson
Jacob	Mast. Henry Placide
Waiter	Mr. Laurent
Servant	Mr. Cain
Widow Warren	Mrs. Clark
Sophia	Mrs. Young
Jenny	Mrs. Utt

Entertainment between pieces consisted of "by particular desire and positively for this night only 'The Old Commodore' (In character—By Mr. Smalley)." Afterpiece was "a National Drama, in three acts, written by Dr. Joor, of South Carolina, called the *Battle of the Eutaw Springs, and Evacuation of Charleston.*" Complete cast was given.

AMERICANS

Maj. Gen. Green	Mr. Young
General Marion	Mr. Caulfield
General Moultrie	Mr. Anderson
Colonel Henderson	Mr. Clark
Capt. Laurence Manning	Mr. Green
Old Sly Boots	Mr. Utt
Young Sly Boots	Mr. Burke
M'Girt	Mr. Clark
Plunderers	Mr. Laurent & Mr. Cain
Emily Bloomfield	Mrs. Poe

BRITISH

Colonel Stuart	Mr. Foster
Major Barry	Mr. Laurent
Lieutenant	Mr. Cain
Mathew Queerfish	Mr. West
Officers, Soldiers, &c.	

The advertisement included a description of scenery similar to the one given for the previous performance (September 19, 1810) with the added attraction of martial music: "In the course of the Afterpiece the gentleman of a Military Band of Richmond, in full uniform, have volunteered their services to perform several National Airs." This was Caulfield's benefit; he played General Marion and Jack Milford, presumably to a full house.[57]

Although dated Tuesday, October 1, the *Virginia Patriot* advertised that "This Evening, (Monday) Sept. 30, will be presented Shakespeare's celebrated Tragedy of *Othello; or, The Moor of Venice.*" Cast was given:

Othello	By a gentleman, being his first appearance on any stage
Iago	Mr. Green
Roderigo	Mr. Twaits

Cassio	Mr. Robertson
Brabantio	Mr. Clark
Duke of Venice	Mr. Anderson
Lodovico	Mr. Burke
Montano	Mr. Young
Gratiano	Mr. Caulfield
Messenger	Mr. Cain
Desdemona	Mrs. Young
Amelia	Mrs. Placide

Afterpiece was "the Grand Dramatic Romance of *Blue Beard; or Female Curiosity.*" No cast was given for *Blue Beard*, which was staged "with additional Scenery, Machinery, and Decorations," identical with but less elaborately described than in the previous performance on September 7, 1810. Entertainment between pieces consisted of songs by Smalley and Miss Thomas, with "a Comic Song" by West. This was the benefit of the Youngs. The advertisement stated that there would be a performance "every night this week." The same issue announced that "on Tuesday evening, October 1, will be presented a Play in Five Acts, called *The Doubtful Son; or, Secrets of a Palace.*" Afterpiece was *The Poor Soldier*. No casts or other details were given. There is no record of performances on Wednesday or Thursday. The next advertisement appeared in the *Virginia Patriot* of Friday, October 4, announcing for that date *Pizarro* and *The Jew and the Doctor*. The only character named was Rolla, played "by the gentleman who performed Othello." Between pieces there were again songs by Smalley and Miss Thomas, with another "Comic Song" by West.

The *Virginia Argus* of Monday, October 7, announced for that date *Laugh When You Can*, with the following cast:

Gossamer	Mr. Twaits
Bonus	Mr. Green
Mortimer	Mr. Robertson
Sambo	Mr. Young
Delville	Mr. Clark
Costly	Mr. Burke
Charles Mortimer (a child)	Miss Clark
Farmer Blackbrook	Mr. Caulfield
Gregory	Mr. Laurent
Waiter	Mr. Foster
Mrs. Mortimer	Mrs. Placide

Emily	Mrs. Young
Dorothy	Mrs. Utt
Miss Gloomly	Mrs. Clark

Entertainment between pieces consisted of "a Comic Song" by West and "a Bravura Song" by Miss Thomas. Feature of the evening was

(for the first time here) a Grand Nautical Spectacle, in three acts, interspersed with Songs, Duetts, and Chorusses, called *Black Beard, the Pirate* written by T. Cross, Esq. and performed at the Theatre London one hundred and fourteen nights successively. The public are respectfully informed, that this interesting spectacle has been in preparation for a considerable time, and is now brought forward with new Scenery, Machinery, and Dresses.

Blackbeard, (the Pirate)	Mr. Placide
Gunner	Mr. Caulfield
Carpenter	Mr. Utt
Caesar	Mr. Smalley
William	Mr. Foster
Drunken Negro	Mr. Laurent
Pirates	Messrs. Clark, Burk, &c.
Lieut. Maynard, (a Naval Officer)	Mr. Anderson
Abdallah, (a Moorish Prince)	Mr. Young
Nancy, (disguised as a Midshipman)	Mrs. Clark
Orra, (Black Beard's wife)	Mrs. Placide
Almeida, (a Moorish Princess)	Mrs. Young
Slaves	Mrs. Utt, Miss Placide, &c.
Sailors, Moors, Slaves, &c.	by Supernumeraries
Slave Girl, (with a Song)	Miss Thomas

Mrs. Poe did not appear in either cast. This was Mrs. Placide's benefit, and Manager Placide was obviously making every effort. The advertisement included a long summary of the action of *Black Beard*, with special attention to elaborate stage effects:

Act I. Scene I—The Stage represents the Cabin of Black Beard's Ship; Black Beard and his Pirates are discovered carousing and singing. Caesar holds a candle and Black Beard snuffs out the light with a Pistol. A ship is seen through the cabin windows under full sail. Orders are given to clear the ship for action, and the scene changes to main Deck and Forecastle. An engagement between the pirates and a Turkish ship, the latter attempts to board, are repulsed, taken, and the Moorish Prince and Princess made prisoners.

Act II. A picturesque view of the sea coast, with Black Beard's Pavillion & Bower. The ship arrives, Black Beard, &c. land from the boat. A dance by the "Slaves." Scene II. The interior of Black Beard's house. Scene III.—Court Yard of the Castle. Scene IV.—A picturesque view of the country. A natural bridge. Sea at a distance. The Pearl sloop of war is seen to arrive: Lieutenant Maynard and part of his crew land in search of Black Beard.

Act. III—Cabin of the ship. The Moon seen rising through the cabin windows—Black Beard having in vain endeavored to gain the affection of the Princess Almeida; he becomes enraged, and as he attempts to seize her, the Ghost of Orra, his murdered wife, appears. Scene II—A view between decks. Scene III. Powder Magazine. Scene the last, the Pearl sloop and the Revenge grapple—after a dreadful conflict, Black Beard is killed and thrown into the sea. The Revenge is seen on fire and sinks. The crew of the Pearl gives three cheers, and the curtain falls.

Mrs. Poe's benefit on Wednesday, October 9, was advertised in three newspapers, but no casts for the evening were listed. Plays were *Alexander the Great* and *Love Laughs at Locksmiths*, with a "Comic Song" by West, and the children's ballet *The Hunters and the Milk Maid* between.[52] We can assume that Mrs. Poe appeared; we know that she was ill at this time. We can also surmise that little Eddie, now almost three years old, may have appeared in the ballet, which, as usual, was performed "by children only."

The *Virginia Patriot* of Friday, October 11, advertised for that date *The Stranger* and *Inkle and Yarico*. Casts of both were given:

The Stranger

The Stranger	By the gentleman who performed Othello and Rolla
Count Wintersen	Mr. Foster
Baron Steinfort	Mr. Young
Solomon	Mr. West
Tobias	Mr. Clark
Peter	Mr. Smalley
Francis	Mr. Caulfield
Children	Miss Clark and Miss Placide
Mrs. Haller	Mrs. Green
Countess Wintersen	Mrs. Poe
Charlotte	Mrs. Clark
Savoyard (with a song)	Miss Thomas

Inkle and Yarico

Inkle	Mr. Young
Sir Christopher Curry	Mr. Green
Captain Camply	Mr. Foster
Medium	Mr. Clark
First Planter	Mr. Anderson
Second Planter	Mr. Rose
Trudge	Mr. Twaits
Yarico	Mrs. Placide
Narcissa	Miss Thomas
Wouski	Mrs. Clark
Patty	Mrs. Utt

This was Miss Thomas's benefit; in *The Stranger* she played Sovoyard "(with a song)"; in *Inkle and Yarico*, Narcissa; and between pieces sang again, followed by "a Vocal and Rhetorical Description of London Ballad Singers" by West, and "The Commodore" in character by Smalley. Mrs. Poe did not appear in *Inkle and Yarico*; Countess Wintersen was her last recorded role. This was "the last night of performance until after the Fredericksburg and Petersburg Races." I assume that the company played in Fredericksburg and Petersburg during the races; they were gone less than two weeks, reopening in Richmond on October 22. As usual, however, I consider that the season ended when the company left town.

Omitting the questionable performance of *Macbeth* and *Care and Mirth* on August 27, we have records of twenty-three performances between August 14 and October 11. Forty-six different plays were presented, including the children's ballet *The Hunters and the Milkmaid*. Repertoire included tragedy, comedy, farce, opera, pantomime, ballet, with a good balance between old favorites (*Alexander the Great, The Poor Soldier*) and novelties. Eight plays were new to Richmond: *The Birthday, Black Beard, A Budget of Blunders, The Deserted Daughter, The Doubtful Son, The Grandfather's Will, Laugh When You Can,* and *Paul and Virginia*. There is no record that *Othello* caused either comment or controversy. As far as we know, it was witnessed by whites in pit and boxes, and by nonwhites in the gallery. The degree of pigmentation of the makeup worn by the gentleman amateur who played Othello is unknown.

The company was perhaps stronger than ever before. Some of the ablest actors in America appeared regularly. Seventeen men, seven women, two girls, and one boy were named in advertisements. I include among women, Miss Thomas, who took adult roles and sang; Miss Placide and Miss Clark, I classify as girls. The one named boy was Master Henry Placide. I have no clue as to the identity of the gentleman amateur who played Othello, Rolla, and The Stranger.

Mrs. Poe was a regular member of the company this season. In his meticulous biography of her son, Quinn records details of her residence in Richmond at this time. There is no record of Edgar's appearance on stage. I consider his appearance likely, and cite three probable times: in *The Hunters and the Milkmaid*, the ballet performed twice "by children only," and particularly on the occasion of his mother's benefit, October 9; also, in *Cinderella* on September 20, when "Cupids" were played "By Little Masters." The only boy named in advertisements was Master Henry Placide. Both "Hunters" and "Cupids" are clearly plural. At least one more boy was needed. Little Eddie was almost three, beautiful, talented, precocious. Obviously he would have made a darling Cupid. His mother was ill. Not to have brought her little son on stage, particularly on her benefit night, would have been an egregious neglect of golden opportunity which Managers Placide and Green should not have committed.

The plays.   *The Doubtful Son* (August 22, 1811), a drama in five acts by William Dimond, had its premiere at the Haymarket on July 3, 1810, and its American premiere in New York on October 12, just three months later. It was acted in Philadelphia on February 6, and Charleston, February 20, 1811.

The Birthday (September 2, 1811), which T. J. Dibdin adapted from Kotzebue's *Der Bruderzwist*, was first acted at Covent Garden on April 8, 1799. Its American premiere was in Charleston on January 24, 1801. It was acted in Philadelphia in 1814 and New York, 1820.

Paul and Virginia (September 4, 1811), a musical drama by James Cobb with music by Joseph Mazzinghi and William Reeve, was first performed at Covent Garden on May 1, 1800. Its American premiere was in New York on May 7, 1802. It was acted in Charleston in 1805 and Philadelphia, 1813.

The only record I have found of the five-act comedy *The Grandfather's Will* (September 6, 1811) is in Hoole, who records performances in Charleston in 1805, 1806, 1807, and 1811, but identifies no author. I suspect that it was the work of some member of this company.

The Deserted Daughter (September 25, 1811), a comedy in five acts by Thomas Holcroft, had its premiere at Covent Garden on May 2, 1795, and its American premiere in New York on February 24, 1796. It was acted in Philadelphia on April 29, 1796, and Charleston, February 29, 1812. *A Budget of Blunders*, a farce by Greffulhe, was first acted at Covent Garden on February 16, 1810. It was acted in Philadelphia on January 30, 1811, New York, February 15, 1811, and Charleston, February 29, 1812.

Laugh When You Can (October 7, 1811), a comedy by Frederick Reynolds, was brought out at Covent Garden on December 8, 1798. It was acted in Charleston on February 3, 1800, New York, February 12, 1800, and Baltimore, November 2, 1810. *Black Beard, the pirate* was presented in Charleston on May 14 and 20, 1811. Hoole lists the author as Sawyer. There was a Blackbeard play by Lemuel Sawyer of North Carolina, described by Quinn as "an amusing farce," published in Washington in 1824, and containing "satire on political conditions of the time." It "seems not to have been produced."[53] The play acted in Charleston and Richmond was, I think, not Sawyer's farce, but a pantomime (called a "Ballet" in the advertisements, Nicoll says) by James C. Cross (not T. Cross, as advertised in Richmond) first presented at Covent Garden on October 15, 1798, as *The Genoese Pirate; or, Black Beard*, and included in Cross's *Circusiana*, published in 1809, as *Blackbeard; or, the Captive Princess*.[54] This was not, I think, the same Blackbeard play recorded by Odell in New York; casts of characters are quite different. James C. Cross of Nicoll, Volume III (*Late Eighteenth Century Drama*), is, I assume, John C. Cross of Nicoll, Volume IV (*Early Nineteenth Century Drama*). They are cross-referenced between volumes. I suspect that Manager Green's "J. Cross" in longhand may have become "T. Cross" in print.

THIRTIETH SEASON

Placide and Green Company

October–December 1811

Chronicle. Advertisements in all three Richmond newspapers announced the company's return from Fredericksburg and Petersburg and the performance "on Tuesday Evening, October 22d, 1811," of *The Poor Gentleman* and *Rosina*, but none gave casts or further details. The next performance was also advertised in all three newspapers. The *Enquirer* and the *Virginia Argus* announced for "Friday Evening . . . the much admired Comedy in 5 acts, called the *Rivals*, to which will be added the Grand Pantomime of *La Perouse; or the Desolate Island.*" The *Virginia Patriot* of Friday, October 25, added a long description of scenery and action almost identical to the one which accompanied the performance of *La Perouse* on November 3, 1809.

"Shakespeare's celebrated tragedy in 5 acts, called *Macbeth*" was performed on Monday. Afterpiece was *The Farmer*, with Twaits as Jeremy Jumps, the only player named.[55]

The *Virginia Patriot* of Tuesday, October 29, respectfully informed the public that "in consequence of the extensive preparations making for the New Play, there will be no performance until Thursday evening, when will be presented a Melo-Dramatic Romance called *The Lady of the Lake* (Taken from the poem of Walter Scott) The scenery painted by Mr. West, The Banners and Trophies by Mr. Graime. To which will be added the celebrated Comedy in three acts called *The Midnight Hour.*" No casts or other details were given.

There was competition at the City Tavern: a "Museum of Wax-Figures, as Large as Life, Living Animals & Mechanism" including "A Living African Leopard" and an "African Ape" which would perform "the Manuel Exercise at the Word of Command." The program concluded with "the Yankee setting fire to his big gun." The exhibition lasted one week, with "good music during the Exhibition." Admittance was "25 cents—Children half price." In addition, profiles were taken "and elegantly framed."[56]

On Monday, November 4, was performed "the celebrated

Dramatic Romance, in 3 acts, called *The Lady of the Lake*."
Afterpiece was "Sheakspeare's celebrated Comedy in 3 acts called
Catharine and Petruchio." No casts were given, but doors opened
at 5:30 and performance began at 6:30. Tickets were to be had
"at Mr. Davis' Printing Office and at the Theatre" and "Subscribers' Tickets will be left as usual." [57]

The first advertisement to list casts appeared in the *Virginia
Patriot* of Tuesday, November 5, announcing for "Wednesday
evening . . . the favorite Comedy of the *Busy Body*" with the
following cast:

Marplot (Busy-Body)	Mr. Twaits
Sir George Airy	Mr. Green
Sir Francis Gripe	Mr. Burke
Sir Zealous Traffic	Mr. Clark
Charles	Mr. Young
Whisper	Mr. Anderson
Butler	Mr. West
Servant	Mr. Hanner
Miranda	Mrs. Green
Isabinda	Mrs. Young
Patch	Mrs. Placide
Scentwell	Mrs. Utt

Afterpiece was "a Melo-Drama called *The Wood Daemon, or The
Clock has Struck*" with the following cast:

Hardyknute (Count Holstein)	Mr. Robertson
Culpho (the Count's steward)	Mr. West
Wilikind	Mr. Burke
Oswy	Mr. Foster
Rolf	Mr. Hanner
Ghost of Count R——ic	Mr. Anderson
Guardian Spirit of Holstein	Mrs. Clark
Sangrida (the Wood Daemon)	Mr. Clark
Hacho (a Giant)	Mr. Utt
Una	Mrs. Green
Clotilda	Mrs. Placide
Paulina	Miss Thomas
Ghost of the Countess Alexina	Mrs. Utt
Leolyn	Master Placide
Knights, Peasants, Officers, &c	By Gentlemen of the Company

Entertainment between pieces consisted of a "Comic Song" by

West, and "Sigh Not for Love" by Smalley. This was Mrs. Green's benefit.

The program announced for Friday, November 8, was "a Comedy, in five acts, written by M. G. Lewis, author of the *Castle Spectre, Alfonso, Adelgitha*, &c as performed with the most unbounded applause in London, New York, and Charleston, called *Rivers; or, The East-Indian*." Afterpiece was *The Highland Reel*. No casts were given. Entertainment between acts consisted of a "Comic Song, descriptive of English Courts of Law, called 'the Assizes'" by West, "Trumpet Song—'He was famed for Deeds of Arms'" by Smalley, "Song—'Heigho'" by Miss Thomas, and "Song—'The Beggar Boy's Petition'" by Smalley. Also, "in the course of the Evening, the Gentlemen of the orchestra will (by particular desire) play several favorite American National Airs, also A Variety of Scotish Tunes."[58] From the operas, musical farces, pantomime ballets, and frequent songs between pieces, we may assume an adequate orchestra, though it seems to be taken for granted. Names of musicians never appear in advertisements; we can only conjecture as to the size and composition of the orchestra.

This performance was Mrs. Clark's benefit. In a later announcement of another benefit, Mrs. Clark "respectfully informs the Public" that her previous benefit had, on account of the weather, been postponed to "the following Evening," which was Saturday, November 9, and even then the weather "prevented several families from attending the Theatre." Her second benefit was on Wednesday, November 27.[59]

We have noted that the *Virginia Patriot* was distributed on the day before the dateline. The issue dated November 12 announced that "This evening, Monday, Nov. 11th, will be presented a Favorite Tragedy, in 5 acts (not performed here for many years) written by Henry Brooke, called *Gustavus Vassa: or, The Deliverer of His Country*." A complete cast was advertised:

Gustavus Vassa	Mr. Robertson
Christiern	Mr. Green
Arvida	Mr. Young
Peterson	Mr. Clark
Laertes	Mr. Rose

Anderson	Mr. Caulfield
Siward	Mr. Anderson
Arnoldus	Mr. Burke
Messenger	Mr. Hannar
Officer	Mr. Utt
Christina	Mrs. Young
Augusta	Mrs. Placide
Mariana	Mrs. Clark
Gustava	Miss Clark

Afterpiece was "Shakespeare's much admired farce of *Catharine and Petruchio*." No cast was given. Entertainment between pieces consisted of "A comic Song 'The Life and Death of George Barnwell'" by West, a "Song" by Miss Thomas, and a "Dance, 'The Shantreuse,'" by Miss Placide. This was Robertson's benefit.

The same issue advertised for Wednesday, November 13, "the Grand opera" *Lodoiska*, "a whimsical interlude, called *Mother Goose's Rambles To Richmond* in which will be presented a view of the Capitol," and "the Farce of *The Prisoner at Large*." No casts were given. This was West's benefit. Between pieces he sang "Hard Times or Always Grumbling (in character of an old woman)." The advertisement stated that *Lodoiska* had been "in preparation a great part of the season and will be brought forward with entire new scenery":

Scene I Evening. A Moated Castle on the border of an extensive forest—distant mountains terminate the view—the setting sun reflecting on the surrounding objects. The draw bridge of the castle is let down over which passes the Baron and his army.
Scene II Morning. The internal part of the castle, presenting the court yard terrace and tower where Lodoiska is imprisoned which terminates with the moat and the battlements.
Scene III A Gothick Hall. The Tartars break into the castle, which they set fire to in several places, flames break forth—the Armoury falls to pieces and discovers an extensive view of the court yard explosions, towers, and battlements fall, the princess Lodoiska is rescued from the Smoaky ruins—The Baron and his army are defeated and the piece concludes with a Grand Chorus.

The next advertisement announced that, "for the Benefit of Mr. Twaits on Friday Evening will be presented Shakespeare's Celebrated Play in 5 acts, Called *The Merchant of Venice*. The part of Shylock by Mr. Twaits. After the play a Mock Italian Song by Mr. Twaits. To which will be added by particular desire, the much admired musical entertainment, called *The Agreeable Surprise*." A later advertisement added "a Comic Song 'The Assizes' " by West, and a "Song" by Miss Thomas; neither notice gave casts.[60]

Complete cast was given for *The Beaux Stratagem* on Monday, November 18, when Manager Green took his benefit:

Archer	Mr. Green
Aimwell	Mr. Young
Sullen	Mr. Clark
Freeman	Mr. Anderson
Foirgard	Mr. Caulfield
Gibbet	Mr. Utt
Hounslow	Mr. Rose
Bagshot	Mr. Hanner
Boniface	Mr. Burke
Scrub	Mr. Twaits
Lady Bountiful	Mrs. Utt
Dorinda	Mrs. Young
Mrs. Sullen	Mrs. Placide
Cherry	Mrs. Clark

Afterpiece was *Raising the Wind*. Between pieces Mrs. Green sang "a New Song, 'The Slumbring Soldier,' " West sang "a Comic Song, 'Meg of Wapping,' " Miss Thomas sang "a Song," and Twaits sang "a Song, 'Cosmetic Doctor, or a Man for the Ladies.' "[61]

Evidence of a successful season is the following notice, which appeared in the *Virginia Patriot* on Tuesday, November 19: "A meeting of the subscribers to the Richmond Theatre is requested on Thursday evening, at 5 o'clock, at the Washington Tavern; at which time, and place, the manager will be prepared to pay the interest upon the subscriptions for the present year. Monday, 18th, Nov. 1811."

The same issue advertised that "on Wednesday Evening, Nov. 20, will be presented (not performed here these five years) Shakespeare's celebrated historical play, in 5 acts of *King Henry IVth; or The Humors of Sir John Falstaff*." Only five of the cast of characters were named:

Sir John Falstaff	Mr. Twaits
Hotspur	Mr. Robertson

Henry, prince of Wales	Mr. Burke
Sir Richard Vernon	Mr. Anderson
Lady Percy	Mrs. Young

Afterpiece was *The Turnpike Gate* with the following cast:

Crack	Mr. Burke
Robert Maythorn	Mr. Rose
Joe Standfast	Mr. Green
Peggy	Mrs. Placide

Between pieces Mrs. Green sang "a Song," West sang a "Comic Song, 'Geo. Barnwell,'" and Miss Thomas sang a "Bravura Song, 'Too Happy when Edward was kind.'" The performance was for the benefit of Anderson, Burke, and Rose.

On Friday, November 22, was performed "a Comedy in Five Acts, written by Mrs. Inchbald, called *I'll Tell you What or An Undescribable Something.*" Afterpiece was *The Poor Soldier.* Between pieces was "a Ballet by Children, called *The Bird Catchers: or, The Merry Girl.* The parts by Miss Jane Placide, Miss E. Placide, Master Placide, Oliver, &c."[62] I do not know whose child Oliver was, and I am unable to read the name as a misprint for "Edgar," but I cannot resist the speculation that little Eddie Poe was on stage while his mother was dying at home. This performance, "For the Benefit of the Poor of this City," may well have included her.

On Tuesday, November 26, was advertised for "This Evening (Monday) . . . for the 3rd time here, the celebrated Melo-Dramatic Romance—called *The Lady of The Lake* . . . to which will be added the Grand Opera of *Lodoiski.*" No casts were given; but *The Lady of the Lake* was staged "with new Scenery, Dresses, and Decoration. The Scenery painted by Mr. West—Banners and Trophies by Mr. Graim." The public was respectfully informed that "the pieces advertised for this Evening will be performed for the last time this season, as the Scenery must positively be removed on the following day." The advertisement was headed "Last week But one."[63]

Plays were regularly presented on Mondays and Wednesdays. Between performances on Monday the twenty-fifth and the twenty-seventh, Lefolle and Taylor "of the Richmond Theatre" advertised for Tuesday a "Grand Vocal and Instrumental Concert" at the Eagle Tavern. A complete program was given in the *Virginia Patriot* of Friday, November 22. The first number was Haydn's Grand Overture by the "full orchestra," evidently the theatre orchestra, which included: Lefolle, violin; Taylor, flute; Gallaher, clarinet; Ribes, violin. There were others, I assume, but only these names and instruments are given. There were songs by Miss Thomas, Mrs. Green, Twaits, and Southgate. Tickets were on sale at the Eagle and Washington taverns, and at Fitzwhylsonn and Potter's bookstore.

On Wednesday, November 27, for Mrs. Clark's benefit, the plays were Morton's comedy *The Way to Get Married* and O'Keeffe's farce *Modern Antiques*. Between them, Miss Thomas sang "a Song," West sang a "Comic Song, 'Ben Buckstay's Ghost,' " and Mrs. Young danced "a Hornpipe with the Skipping Rope." No casts or other details were given.[64]

The *Virginia Patriot* of Friday, November 29, advertised for that date a repetition of *Henry IV* with Twaits as Falstaff and Robertson as Hotspur, the only characters named. Afterpiece was the "historical pantomime" of *Telemachus in the Island of Calypso*. Between pieces was a "Song by Mrs. Green and a "Comic Song" by West. The advertisement included this description of scenic effects in *Telemachus*:

> In act Ist—Beautiful representation of Calypso's Grotto.
> Act I—A Storm. Telemachus and Minerva (under the form of Mentor) are saved from the wreck, and introduced to Calypso who entertains them and shows Telemachus the portrait of his father Ulysses.
> Act II—Wisdom triumphant over love—Mentor discovered constructing a ship, to carry Telemachus out of the Island: Cupid enraged orders the nymphs to follow him and set fire to the ship, to prevent his going; but Mentor first throws Telemachus from a high rock into the sea, and himself afterwards, in order to swim to another ship which he sees near the coast."

This was Mrs. Poe's benefit. She had not appeared since October 11. I think she did not appear on stage at her benefit. Advertisement of the performance was accompanied by this announcement in the *Patriot*:

MRS. POE'S BENEFIT

In consequence of the serious and long continued indisposition of Mrs. Poe, and in compliance with the advice and solicitation of many of the most respectable families, the managers have been induced to appropriate another night for her benefit—Taking into consideration the state of her health, and the probability of this being the last time she will ever receive the patronage of the public, the appropriation of another night for her assistance, will certainly be grateful to their feelings, as it will give them an opportunity to display their benevolent remembrance.

An even more pathetic note appeared in the *Enquirer* of the same date: "To the Humane Heart: On this night, Mrs. Poe, lingering on the bed of disease and surrounded by her children, asks your assistance and *asks it perhaps for the last time.* The Generosity of a Richmond Audience can need no other appeal. For particulars see the Bills of the day."

"Cumberland's Celebrated Comedy, of *The Wheel of Fortune: or The Misanthrope*" was acted on Tuesday. Afterpiece was the "Grand Nautical Spectacle in three acts, interspersed with Songs, Duets, and Choruses, called *Black Beard, the Pirate.*" No casts were given, but the advertisement included a long description of scenic effects in *Black Beard* identical with that advertised on October 7. "The celebrated Comedy of *The Road to Ruin*," "a Pantomime Ballet, called *Vauxhall Garden*," and "the much admired Farce of *The Lying Valet*" were acted on Friday. No casts or other details were given. "The celebrated Play, of *Rivers: or The East Indian*" and "the much admired Farce *Of Age Tomorrow*" were acted on Saturday, but no details were given.[65]

The *Virginia Patriot* of Tuesday, December 10, carried this announcement:

DEATHS

Mr. Casper Flisher, an old inhabitant of this city.

Mrs. Poe, of the Richmond Theatre. Her friends are requested to attend her funeral to day at ten o'clock.

The *Enquirer* of the same date carried this:

Died on last Sunday morning, Mrs. Poe, one of the Actresses of the Company at present playing on the Richmond *Boards*. —By the death of this Lady the Stage has been deprived of one of its chief ornaments —And, to say the least of her, she was an interesting Actress; and never failed to catch the applause and hold the admiration of the beholder.

The two issues carrying Mrs. Poe's death notices also carried advertisements of performance on Wednesday of "the celebrated Comedy in 3 acts called *The Birth-Day: or, The Reconciliation.* After which will be performed for the 2nd time here, an Interlude (translated from the French) called *The Blue Devils.* The whole to conclude with the much admired Pantomime, called *Whim Upon Whim, or, Harlequin Vagaries.*"

"Shakespeare's very Celebrated Tragedy of *Hamlet, Prince of Denmark*" was acted on Friday with Green as Hamlet, the only character named. Afterpiece was *The Weathercock. The Rivals, Vauxhall Garden,* and *Fortune's Frolic* were acted on the following Wednesday, but no details were given.[66]

The program advertised for Saturday, December 21, was "the much admired Comedy of *Town & Country; or Which do You Like Best,*" with Robertson as Reuben Glenroy, the only character named. Afterpiece was "the Musical Entertainment, of *Ella Rosenberg.*" Between pieces was "a Song" by Miss Thomas, "a Hornpipe" by Durang, and "a Comic Song called 'The Yorkshire Concert'" by West.[67] This was Robertson's benefit, and the *Enquirer* of December 21 carried a handsome puff:

MR. ROBERTSON'S BENEFIT
"Good wine needs no bush"

Merit, *in any line*, is worthy of its reward. The discerning people of this City will not, surely then, let Mr. Robertson behold the unpleasant spectacle of a thin Audience at his benefit on this evening. He had selected an excellent play and afterpiece for our amusement; and his Reuben Glenroy is confessed to be among the most finished performances on the stage. As a general player, Mr. R. has particular merit. The way in which he has risen, if it could be laid open to the public eye, would entitle him to greater applause. In some characters, he is great—I have never seen the generous throb of sympathy circulate more freely and forcibly in our Theatre, than when he played Gustavus Vasa. —May I not add that Mr. R. is a native of America, and that a large and amiable family is dependent on his exertions? and that independently of these, his hand is "open as day to melting charity," as in the case of Mrs. Poe. —Surely these are claims which a Richmond audience will not suffer to be overlooked.

The *Virginia Patriot* of Tuesday, December 24, advertised for "This Evening, Monday . . . an entire New Play, translated from the French of Diderot, by a Gentleman of this City, called *The Father; or Family Feuds*." Afterpiece was "(for the first time here) the Favorite New Pantomime, of *Raymond & Agnes: or, The Bleeding Nun*." No casts were given. Entertainment between pieces consisted of a "Song" by Miss Thomas, a "Comic Song" by West, a "Dance" by Miss E. Placide, and a "Hornpipe" by Miss Placide. This was the benefit of Manager Placide. The performance, however, was postponed: "The New Play, entitled the *Father, or Family Feuds*, intended to have been performed for the Benefit of Mr. Placide on last evening, owing to his indisposition, added to the badness of the weather, has been deferred until Thursday Evening next, at which time the performance will positively take place. —For Characters in the Play, and a description of the afterpiece, see Bills."[68] Performances were regularly on Mondays and Wednesdays, but since Wednesday was Christmas, the performance was postponed from Monday the twenty-third to Thursday the twenty-sixth.

In addition to the advertisement, the *Patriot* carried a long article, unsigned but obviously written by a competent and well-informed person, on the stage in general and *The Father* in particular:

THE DRAMA

It is ever with the liveliest pleasure that we view the laudable efforts of the votaries of literature to reform the abuses which exist in it, and to effect the restoration of true taste. In the various departments of literature none more imperatively calls for reform than the Drama; for none has suffered more from the influence of a corrupt and vitiated taste. The British Drama has, indeed, woefully degenerated since the era of Cumberland and Coleman. For the genuine and legitimate comedy of the last century, a spurious and unnatural species of Dramatic representation has been introduced, equally absurd and preposterous, and at once destitute of the sober charms of truth and of those imposing attractions which fancy when united to taste can give to fiction. In the Pantomimical and Melo Dramas which now triumphantly reign on the English stage sound has been substituted for sense and scenery for sentiment; and the Car of Thespsis, which in the ages of Menander and Terrence, as well as in the better days of the British Drama, was surrounded by Wit, Humour and Mirth—by the Graces and the Passions, is now too often disgraced by low buffoonery and insipid mimickry. The cause of this degeneracy may, doubtless, be traced to the extent of the London Theatres, which renders it nearly impossible for the voice to be heard without resorting to that false kind of declamation too far out of nature to be tolerated—Hence, in England, modern dramatists have been compelled to address the eyes and ears rather than the understanding; and to degrade man from the loftly dignity of an intellectual, into a merely sensual being. But, as the same cause of degeneracy does not exist here, where our Theatres are upon a smaller scale, we should no longer perpetuate, by our encouragement, or by a disgraceful and servile imitation, the abuses we have complained of, but should give our warmest support to the true and legitimate Drama.

The preceding observations have been produced, by our hearing that a Comedy in five acts, called "The Father" or "Family Feuds" translated from the French of the celebrated Diderot, by a Citizen of Richmond is shortly to be presented on our Theatre. We have perused this interesting Drama. It breathes throughout the whole the purest morality and the most affecting pathos; in short, it is a family picture of masterly design, and exquisite colouring. The anxieties, the struggles of the parental heart on the most trying occurrences—the wild, yet noble enthusiasm of youthful and impassioned sensibility—the shrinking reserve of spotless delicacy—the calm and steady attitude of undeviating honor—the perils the alarms of indigent and unprotected innocence and beauty—the torments of ambition, egotism and avarice—the wretchedness of selfish and morose celibacy—are all strongly exhibited in the various scenes of the interesting Drama under consideration. It would be sufficient evidence of the merit of "*The pere de famille*" that it has been noticed with approbation even by the fastidious La Harpe in his *Cours de literature*, "a monument" says a writer of celebrity, "raised to the glory of the French nation" & that it has been praised by Voltaire and other eminent critics; but, a still higher evidence is, that it has enjoyed, and still continues to enjoy, in the country of its birth, the most flattering applause. We therefore congratulate the public on the refined banquet thus prepared for them. The Theatre may, and ought to be a school of morals as well as a place of elegant recreation. The translator of this celebrated Comedy needs no eulogium from our pen. He has already acquired such marked distinction by the purity and classical elegance of his English style, that any farther praise from us would be superfluous. The public however will be gratified to learn that the peculiar adoptation of the characters of the play to the talents of the performers, is such, as to enable each to display his best stile of acting. Mr. Green we understand is to fill the part of the Father—a virtuous & humane man and an affectionate parent, whose tranquility is disturbed by the solicitude resulting from the impetuous passions of a favorite son. The character of the Commodore is extremely well adapted to the comic powers of Mr. Twaits. Mr. Young, the hero of the piece, has an arduous and laborious task to perform in the character of St. Albin; but from his usual attention to his parts, the public have unquestionably a right to anticipate his success. Mrs. Placide's talents are so admirably adapted to every species of dramatic representation, that it is needless to say that the character of Cecilia is suited to them. It is with pleasure we understand that Sophia, the heroine of the piece, is to be undertaken by Mrs. Young, as the artlessness and simplicity of this character will derive a superadded recommendation from the unaffected grace, and fanciful elegance which peculiarly distinguish that deservedly admired actress; and, which, in all those characters, wherein we discover a perfect union of nature—of spotless purity, youthful sensibility and unsophisticated innocence, have acquired her such universal homage. It is one of the excellencies of this play, that the action is vivid, continued & rising to a climax, & that the interest it inspires is kept alive throughout the whole piece. We are perfectly sure that the public will be highly gratified with this admirable comedy, and that they will be inspired with an additional motive to afford it their fostering patronage when they understand that Mr. Placide has selected it for his benefit.

Despite this effusion, *The Father, or Family Feuds* is not known to have been acted again. Casts for December 26 are taken from the playbill for that date:

Monsieur Dorbeson	Mr. Green
St. Albin	Mr. Young
Commodore	Mr. Twaits
Germuil	Mr. Anderson
Le Bon	Mr. Burke
Philip	Mr. Rose
Le Brie	Mr. Durang
Police Officer	Mr. Utt
Duchemp	Mr. Hanna

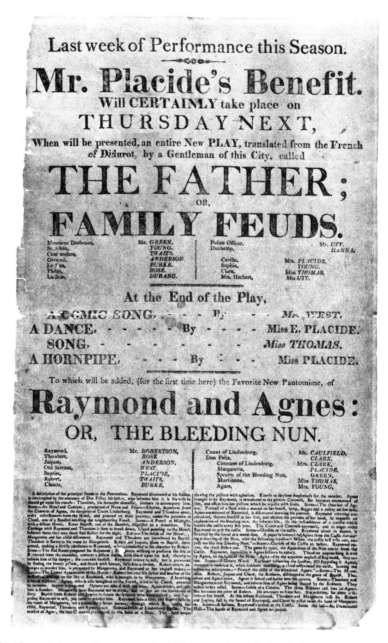

Placide and Green Company playbill, December 26, 1811. (Courtesy Virginia State Library.)

Cecilia	Mrs. Placide
Sophia	Mrs. Young
Clara	Miss Thomas
Mrs. Herbert	Mrs. Utt

This was Manager Placide's benefit, and there were specialties between pieces: a comic song by West, a dance by Miss E. Placide, a song by Miss Thomas, and a hornpipe by Miss Placide. Afterpiece was "(for the first time here) the Favorite New Pantomime, of *Raymond and Agnes: or, The Bleeding Nun*" with the following cast:

Raymond	Mr. Robertson
Theodore	Mr. Rose
Jaques	Mr. Anderson
Old Servant	Mr. West
Baptist	Mr. Placide
Robert	Mr. Twaits
Claude	Mr. Burke
Count of Lindenburg	Mr. Caulfield
Don Felix	Mr. Clark
Countess of Lindenburg	Mrs. Clark
Margaretta	Mrs. Placide
Spectre of the Bleeding Nun	Mrs. Green
Marvianna	Miss Thomas
Agnes	Mrs. Young

The playbill included

a description of the principal scenes in the Pantomime. Raymond discovered at his studies, is interrupted by the entrance of Don Felix; his father, who informs him it is his wish he should go upon his travels: Theodore, his favourite domestic, intreats to accompany him. Scene—An Hotel and Convent; procession of Nuns and Friars—Chorus, departure from the Convent of Agnes, the daughter of Count Lindenburg. Raymond and Theodore enter, order refreshments from the Hotel, and proceed on their journey, under the guidance of Claud, one of a Banditti infesting the neighbouring Forest. Scene—A Forest at Midnight, with a distant Hovel. Enter Baptist, one of the Banditti, disguised as a woodman. The Carriage with Raymond and Theodore is seen to break down. Claud pointing to the Hovel, informs them they may there find shelter for the night. Scene—The inside of the Hovel . . . Margaretta and her child discovered. Raymond and Theodore are introduced by Baptist. Theodore is shewn to his room by Margaretta. Robert and Jaques, sons to Baptist, enter armed, making a servile obedience to Raymond, who is conducted to his chamber by Robert. Scene— The Bed Room prepared for Raymond; Margaretta wishing to preserve the life of Raymond from the assassins, conveys a pillow stained with blood upon his bed, thereby to inform him of his danger; she conceals herself. Raymond retires to rest, but is prevented by finding the bloody pillow, and struck with horror, falls into a swoun. Robert enters, attempts to murder him, is prevented by Margaretta, and Raymond at her request retires. —Scene—The Lower Apartments of the Hovel. Robert informs his father and brother of the ineffectual attempt on the life of Raymond, who is brought in by Margaretta. A knocking is heard without. Agnes, who is also benighted in the Forest, is led in by Claud, attended by a servant. Supper is prepared. Opiates are mix'd with the wine. Agnes drinks, and falls into a slumber. Margaretta begs Raymond not to drink but to pretend the semblance of sleep. Baptist sends Robert and Jaques to secure the servants who have retired; and supposing Raymond at rest prepares to murder him. Raymond siezes him; and Baptist falls by the hands of Margaretta, who points to a secret avenue through which she, taking her child, Raymond, Theodore and Agnes escape. Scene—Inside of Lindenburg Castle. The mother of Agnes, the late Countess portrayed in the habit of a Nun. The Count enters viewing the picture with agitation. Kneels to implore forgiveness for the murder. Agnes brought in by Raymond, is introduced to the present Countess, she becomes enamoured of him, and offers him her picture which he rejects with scorn. Scene—The chamber of Agnes. Portrait of a Nun with a wound on her breast, lamp, dagger and a rosary on her arm. Agnes enamoured of Raymond, is discovered drawing his portrait. Raymond entering unperceived, throws himself at her feet, and obtains the promise of her hand, he requests an explanation of the bleeding nun, she informs him, it is the resemblance of a spectre which haunts the castle every fifth year. The Count and Countess approach, and in anger order Raymond to quit the castle. Scene—Outside of the castle. Raymond about to depart, is diverted by the sound of a mandoline. A paper is lowered by Agnes from the Castle containing a drawing of the Nun, with the following scroll—"When the castle bell tolls one, expect me like this Bleeding Nun." —Scene—Outside of the Castle as before. Raymond enters, the clock strikes one. The gates fly open, the Apparition of the Nun comes from the Castle. Raymond, supposing it Agnes follows [in] extacy. Theodore approaching is met by Agnes, in the habit of the Nun. Agitated by the apparent neglect of Raymond, they retire. Scene—A Dreary Wood. Raymond following the spectre, still supposing it Agnes, attempts to embrace it, when suddenly vanishing, a cloud arises from the earth, bearing the following inscription—"Protect the child of the murdered Agnes." —Scene—The Mountains. Robert, Jaques and Claud, the Robbers, discovered at the grave of Baptist. Theodore and Agnes enter, Agnes is seized and borne into the cavern. Scene—Theodore and Margaretta meet Raymond, and inform him of Agnes being seized by the Robbers. They hasten to her relief. Scene—Inside of a Cavern. The three Robbers cast lots for Agnes. She becomes the prize of Robert. He attempts to seize her. She resisting, he aims a stiletto at her breast. At this instant Raymond, Theodore and Margaretta rush in. Robert and Jaques, fall by the sword of Raymond, and Claud by pistol from the hand of Margaretta. Scene—A Salloon. Raymond's arrival at the Castle. Scene the last—An Illuminated Hall—The hands of Raymond and Agnes are joined.[69]

From later accounts we know that only the first act of the pantomime was presented.

One final advertisement announced for "Friday evening . . . a celebrated Tragedy, written by M. G. Lewis, called *Adelgitha, or Fruits of a Single Error*. To which will be added the Comic Opera of *The Adopted Child*."[70] There was no performance on Friday, December 27, for the theatre burned Thursday night.

This season, opening on October 22 and ending on December 26, was evidently one of Richmond's most successful. There are records of twenty-four performances and of forty-five different plays, including tragedy, comedy, farce, opera, pantomime, ballet. Thirteen plays were new to Richmond: *Catharine and Petruchio, Ella Rosenberg, The Father, Gustavus Vasa, I'll Tell You What, The Lady of the Lake, Lodoiska, Mother Goose's Rambles to Richmond, Raymond and Agnes, The Rivals, Rivers, Vauxhall Garden,* and *Whim upon Whim.* The season included the American premiere of *The Lady of the Lake.*

This was a particularly strong company, with Twaits outstanding in comedy, and Green and Robertson in tragedy. There was an abundance of musical talent, and four members of the orchestra were named: Gallaher, clarinet; Lefolle, violin; Ribes, violin; Taylor, flute. West and Graim painted scenery. Fifteen men and six women were named, plus three girls and two boys. This season was the climax of the Placide-Green Company; it deteriorated rapidly after December 26, 1811. Although it opened in Charleston on

January 31, 1812, it would never again be one of the strongest companies in America. Richmond, too, would never be the same again.

The plays.   R. B. Sheridan's *The Rivals* (October 25, 1811) had its premiere at Covent Garden on January 17, 1775. It was acted in New York on April 21, 1778, Philadelphia, November 10, 1778, and Charleston, March 10, 1800.

The Lady of the Lake (October 31, 1811) was evidently the American premiere. Sir Walter Scott's poem was published in 1810, an immediate and sensational success. The first dramatic adaptation was by T. J. Dibdin, first acted at the Surrey on September 24, 1810, and published in 1810. Another version by E. J. Eyre was acted in Edinburgh on January 15, 1811, and published in 1811. Either might possibly have reached Richmond by October 1811, but I suspect that this was Dibdin's version. *The Lady of the Lake* (probably Dibdin's) was acted in Philadelphia on January 1, 1812, Charleston on February 28, 1812, and New York on May 8, 1812.

Catharine and Petruchio (November 4, 1811) was almost certainly David Garrick's adaption of *The Taming of the Shrew*, first acted at Drury Lane on January 21, 1756. It was acted in Philadelphia in 1766, New York, 1768, and Charleston, 1774. I suspect earlier performance in Richmond of which record is lost.

Rivers, or the East Indian (November 9, 1811), a comedy by M. G. Lewis, had its premiere at Drury Lane on April 22, 1799. It was acted in New York on November 17, 1800, and Charleston, March 15, 1804.

Gustavus Vasa (November 11, 1811), by Henry Brooke, is famous in theatre history as the first play banned under the Licensing Act of 1737. Originally scheduled for production at Drury Lane, it was first acted in Dublin on March 12, 1744. An account of the censorship was published by Herbert Wright in 1919. Nicoll considers it "a well-constructed and well-written dramatic work." It was acted in New York in 1789, Philadelphia in 1790, and Charleston in 1794, where it was advertised as an "elegant Tragedy [which] breathes throughout the strongest spirit of Liberty and Patriotic Zeal; and is truly worthy of representation on the American stage."[71] I note that it was not performed in America until after the Revolution. Since the Charleston production was by the West and Bignall Company, I suspect a performance in Richmond by the same company during the 1790s, of which record is lost.

Lodoiska (November 13, 1811), by J. P. Kemble, had its premiere at Drury Lane on June 9, 1794. It was acted in Charleston in 1807 and New York, 1808. *Mother Goose's Rambles to Richmond* was evidently a comic pantomime, probably with dancing, gotten up by the company. Manager Placide loved pantomimes and dancing.

I'll Tell You What (November 22, 1811), a five-act comedy by Elizabeth Inchbald, was first acted at the Haymarket on April 18, 1785. It was acted in both New York and Philadelphia in 1793. There is no record of a performance in Charleston.

Vauxhall Garden (December 6, 1811) was evidently a pantomime ballet gotten up by the company. I found no record of its performance elsewhere. I suspect it was the same as the ballet *French Vauxhall Gardens,* which was performed on December 30, 1796.

Whim upon Whim (December 11, 1811) was another Harlequin pantomime, probably by Manager Placide, in which he took a leading role.

Ella Rosenberg (December 21, 1811), a comic opera by James Kenney with music by M. P. King, had its premiere at Drury Lane on November 19, 1807. It was acted in New York on June 15, 1808, Charleston, March 22, 1809, and Philadelphia, December 12, 1810.

The Father (December 26, 1811) was "translated from the French of Diderot by a gentleman of this city." I am unable to identify the gentleman-translator. His work was not published. It was acted just this once, on the night of the fire. The pantomime of *Raymond and Agnes* was based upon M. G. Lewis's famous novel *The Monk*, published in 1796. The pantomime, which Odell calls "a showy and unpleasant thing," was performed in New York several times in January 1804. It was "received by a crowded house with deepest attention, and honored at its conclusion with loud applause."[72]

CHAPTER VII

December 26, 1811

THE FIRE

The Richmond theatre burned on Thursday, December 26, 1811. Accounts of the fire are given by Little, Mordecai, and Stanard.[1] But the best account is by Thomas Ritchie, editor and publisher of the *Enquirer*, who was in the audience:

OVERWHELMING CALAMITY

In the whole course of our existence, we have never taken our pen under a deeper gloom than we feel at this moment. It falls to our lot to record one of the most distressing scenes which can happen in the whole circle of human affairs. —The reader must excuse the incoherence of the narrative; there is scarce a dry eye in this distracted city. Weep, my fellow-citizens; for we have seen a night of woe, which scarce any eye had seen, or ear hath heard, and no tongue can adequately tell.

How can we describe the scene? No pen can paint it; no imagination can conceive it. A whole theatre wrapt in flames—a gay and animated assembly suddenly thrown on the very verge of the grave—many of them, oh! how many, precipitated in a moment into eternity—youth; and beauty, and old age and genius overwhelmed in one promiscuous ruin—Shrieks, groans and human agony in every shape—this is the heart-rending scene that we are called upon to describe. We sink under the effort. Reader! excuse our feelings, for they are the feelings of a whole city.

Let us collect our ideas as well as we can. On Thursday night a new play & a new after piece were played for the benefit of Mr. Placide. Crowds swarmed to the theatre—it was the fullest house this season—there were not less than 600 present. The play went off—the pantomime began—the first Act was over. The whole scene was before us—and all around us was mirth and festivity. Oh God! what a horrible revolution did one minute produce! The curtain rose on the 2d Act of the Pantomime—the orchestra was in full chorus; and Mr. West came on to open the scene—when sparks of fire began to fall on the back part of the stage, and Mr. Robertson came out in unutterable distress, waved his hand to the ceiling, and uttered those appalling words—"The house is on fire." His hand was immediately stretched forth to the persons in the stage-box to help them on the stage—and aid their retreat in that direction. This is all that we caught of the stage—the cry of *fire, fire,* passed with electric velocity through the house—every one flew from their seats to gain the lobbies and stairs.

The scene baffles all description. The most heart-piercing cries pervaded the house. "Save me, save me." Wives asking for their husbands, females and children shrieking while the gathering element came rolling on its curling flames and columns of smoke—threatening to devour every human being in the building. Many were trod under foot—several were thrown back from the windows from which they were struggling to leap. The stair-ways were immediately blocked up—the throng was so great that many were raised several feet over the heads of the rest—the smoke threatened an instant suffocation. We cannot dwell on this picture. We saw—we felt it—like others, we gave up ourselves for lost—we cannot depict it. Many leaped from the windows of the first story, & were saved—children and females and men of all descriptions were seen to precipitate themselves on the ground below—most of these escaped; though several of them with broken legs, & thighs, and hideous contusions. Most if not all who were in the pit escaped. Mr. Taylor, the last of the musicians who quitted the orchestra finding his retreat by the back way cut off leapt into the pit whence he entered the semicircular avenue which leads to the door of the Theatre, & found it nearly empty. He was the last that escaped from the pit! how melancholy, that many who were in the boxes did not also jump into the pit and fly in the same direction. But those who were in the boxes, above and below, pushed for the lobbies—many, as has been said, escaped through the windows—but the most of them had no other resource than to descend the stairs, many escaped in that way—but so great was the pressure that they retarded each other; until the devouring element approached to sweep them into eternity. Several who even emerged from the building were so much scorched that they have since perished—some even jumped from the second window—some others have been dreadfully burnt.

The fire flew with a rapidity, almost beyond example. Within 10 minutes after it caught the whole house was wrapt in flames.— The colored people in the gallery most of them escaped through the stairs cut off from the rest of the house—some have no doubt fallen victims. The pit and boxes had but one common avenue— through which the whole crowd escaped, save those only who leaped through the windows.

But the scene which ensued—it is impossible to paint. Women with disshevelled hair; fathers & mothers shrieking out for their children, husbands for their wives, brothers for their sisters, filled the whole area on the outside of the building. A few, who had escaped, plunged again into the flames to save some dear object of their regard—and they perished. The Governor perhaps shared this melancholy fate. Others were frantic, and would have rushed to destruction, but for the hand of a friend. The bells tolled. Almost the whole town rushed to the fatal spot.

The flame *must* have been caught to the scenery from some light behind—Robertson saw it, when it was no longer than his arm—Young saw it on the roof, when it first burst through. Every article of the theatre was consumed; as well as the dwelling house next to it. But what is wealth in comparison of the valuable lives which have gone forever?—The whole town is shrouded in woe. Heads of families extinguished forever—many and many is the house, in which a chasm has been made that can never be filled up.—We cannot dwell on this picture—but look at the following catalogue of the victims, and then conceive the calamity which has fallen upon us. —We must drop the pen—when we have time to collect a more particular account, we shall give it everafter. Oh miserable night of unutterable woe!

The same issue of the *Enquirer* carried an account of official actions taken on the morning after. There was an Ordinance, a Resolution, and a Report:

AN ORDINANCE, Concerning The Conflagration Of The Theatre
In The City Of Richmond
(Passed at 11 o'clock, Dec. 27th, 1811.)

Whereas, the fire which took place in the Theatre, on the 26th inst. has brought upon our City a calamity unknown in the annals of our Country, from a similar cause, depriving society of many of its most esteemed & valuable members, & inflicting upon the survivors, pangs the most poignant & afflicting; & the Common Hall, participating of those feelings, & being desirous of manifesting their respect for the remains which have been preserved from the conflagration, & to soothe & allay as much as in them lies, the grief of the friends & relatives of the deceased:

Be it therefore ordained by the president & Common Council of the City of Richmond, in Common Hall assembled: And it is hereby ordained by the authority of the same; that Doct. Adams, Mr. W. Hay, Mr. Ralston & Mr. Gamble, be and they are hereby authorised & empowered to cause to be collected & deposited in such urns, coffins or other suitable inclosures, as they may approve, all the remains of persons, who have suffered, which shall not be claimed by the relatives, & cause the same to be removed to the public burying ground, with all proper respect and solemnity, giving to the citizens of Richmond and Town of Manchester, notice of the time of such interment and providing the necessary refreshments; and they shall have further authority to cause to be erected over such remains, such tomb or tombs, as they may approve with such inscriptions as to them may appear best calculated to record the melancholy & afflicting event.

And be it further ordained by the authority of the same, that the Constable of this City, be authorized to communicate to the Citizens, that it is earnestly recommended that they will abstain from all business, keeping their shops, stores, compting houses and offices shut for forty eight hours, from the passing of this ordinance.

And be it further ordained that no person or persons shall be permitted for and during the term of four months from the passage hereof to exhibit any public show or spectacle, or open any public dancing Assembly within this City under the penalty of six dollars & sixty six cents for every hour the same shall be exhibited.

The Commissioners appointed by this ordinance, shall have authority to draw upon the Chamberlain for the amount of any expence by them incurred in executing the same.

Copy   N. Sheppard, C.C.H.

The Resolution follows:

At a very numerous Meeting of the citizens of Richmond, Manchester and others convened at the Capitol on Friday, the 27th instant. —The Mayor of this City in the Chair—The following Preamble and Resolution were moved and unanimously adopted:

This City having been visited by a calamity the most distressing with which society can be afflicted, which has deprived us of many of our most valuable citizens, pervaded every family and rendered our whole town one deep and gloomy scene of woe; the extent of which at this time cannot be accurately ascertained.

Resolved therefore, that three proper persons in each ward be appointed to go round and procure the most accurate information of the names and numbers of such of our citizens and others who have fallen a sacrifice by the burning of the Theatre last evening and that some persons in Manchester be requested to perform the same service in that town; and that they make Report thereof to the Mayor.

. . . . .

Resolved, That it be recommended to the citizens of Richmond to observe Wednesday next, as a day of humiliation and prayer, in consequence of the late melancholy event, and to suspend on that day their usual occupations.

Resolved, That the committee appointed by the Common Hall, to collect the remains of the deceased, be also requested to regulate the time and order of the funeral procession.

Resolved, That the members of the Legislature, the Executive and the Judiciary branches be respectfully requested to attend on this melancholy occasion.

Resolved, That the Reverend Mr. John Buchanan and Mr. John Blair, be requested to prepare a funeral sermon for the occasion to be delivered by one of them on Wednesday next in the Church on Richmond Hill.

Resolved, That the citizens of Richmond be requested to wear crape for one month in token of the deep sense universally entertained of this severe visitation.

Resolved, That the inhabitants of this city and town of Manchester, be respectfully requested, and such strangers as may wish to join in this melancholy occasion, be most cheerfully permitted to contribute towards the monument to be erected over the deceased, in aid of the public funds to be contributed by this corporation.

Resolved, That a committee consisting of the following Gentlemen, viz. Gen. John Marshall, Thomas Taylor, Joseph Marx, William Fenwick and Benjamin Hatcher be appointed to receive contributions and to make such arrangements in concert with a committee from the Common Hall as may be necessary for erecting the monument designated by an Ordinance passed this day.

Resolved, that although this meeting have no reasons whatever to believe that this melancholy catastrophe has been produced by design, a Committee consisting of Thomas Ritchie, William Marshall and Samuel G. Adams, be appointed to enquire into its causes, for the purpose of submitting this statement for the information of the world.

And then the Meeting adjourned.

                                                                    Benjamin Tate, Mayor

The committee appointed to prepare a list of the dead reported promptly, and the funeral was scheduled for Saturday, the twenty-eighth.

The *Enquirer* of Tuesday, December 31, contained additions and corrections. Changes were made in funeral arrangements, and the funeral was postponed to Sunday. Ritchie's account of the funeral follows:

INTERMENT OF THE DEAD

The arrangements for this melancholy occasion could not be completed before Sunday—and as the place of interment had been changed from the Church to the area where the Theatre stood, to that fatal and devoted spot, the funeral procession did not move, as was originally contemplated by the Committee, from the Baptist-Meeting-House, near the Theatre, there the relics lay, to the Church where the interment was intended to be made.

The mournful procession began at Mr. Edward Trent's on the main street where the remains of the unfortunate Mrs. Patterson lay. —In front, the Corpse—then the Clergy—Ladies in carriages—the Executive Council—Directors of the Bank—Members of the Legislature—the Court of Hustings—Common Hall—Citizens on foot & on horse back. —Why paint the length and solemnity of the line? They moved up the main street untill they struck the cross street leading to the Bank—here they were joined by the Corpse of poor Juliana Harvie, who expired at her brother-in-law's, the Cashier of the Bank—they moved up the Capitol Hill, and at the Capitol were joined by the bearers of two large Mahogany boxes, in which were enclosed the ashes and relics of the deceased. —The mournful procession then moved to "the devoted spot;" and in the centre of the area where once stood the pit, these precious relics were buried in one common grave. The service for the dead was read by the Rev. Mr. Buchanan. —The whole scene defied description. A whole city bathed in tears!—How awful the transition on this devoted spot!—A few days since, it was the theatre of joy and merriment—animated by the sound of music and the hum of a delighted multitude. It is now a funeral pyre! the receptacle of the relics of our friends—and in a short time a monument will stand upon it to point out where their ashes lay!

Editor Ritchie, who had rushed into print his distraught first account of the "overwhelming calamity," now added a longer and more detailed account:

NARRATIVE

We cannot paint the details of the scene Thursday night—No description can do justice to its horrors—and there were so few persons so cool and self-collected as to accurately paint any part of the mass of woes which fell in a moment upon us. Some scenes are so fraught with horror, that a delicate pencil would have to skip them—Besides, time enough has not been had to bring together an accurate group of woes.

It is painful to touch upon the catastrophe of those who have gone forever. Their ashes are in the grave—but their memories are entombed in our hearts.

The Generous and worthy [Governor George W.] Smith, who but a few days since was crowned with one of the highest honors which Virginia can bestow, is snatched from his country, his distracted family, his children and his friends!! It is not certainly known whether he had effected his escape from the building and rushed again into the flames to save his child—There is a confusion in the story, and perhaps it is as well if it never were cleared up!

Abraham B. Venable, the President of the Bank of Virginia; a man who has filled out public stations with very high repute; who has been in the H. of R. and in the Senate of the U.S. during the most interesting periods—he too is gone! He has left no wife or children; but a long train of relatives and friends to weep his loss. —He was in the box with ladies; he begged them not to be precipitate or impatient; but was at length driven towards a window in the lobby, with a crowd of others. The suffocating smoke came rolling on. Mr. V. and some who were with him were thrown down. Mr. Noland fell towards the window and was saved; Mr. V. fell the other way and perished in the smoke!

Many doubtless perished in the same way. The volume of smoke, which could not at first escape through the roof, was bent downwards; black, dense, almost saturated with oily vapours. Many were suffocated by it, who might have had strength enough to leap the windows. —Several were saved by the fresh air which they inhaled at the windows—or even at a cranny.

Poor Botts! a man of astonished assiduity and attainments at the bar, has perished with his wife & her niece—he fell perhaps a victim to his hopes. He thought it more prudent to sit still with his wife, while the crowd passed by; but her sister-in-law Mrs. Page, yielding to the sympathetic impulse of her fears, rushed foward and is saved. —What a seal has death set upon his family! At one fell swoop, five helpless children are converted into Orphans.

How heavily has the hand of death fallen upon the family of the Harvies! Poor mourners, deeply indeed have ye drunk of the cup of affliction. Within 5 short years we had numbered among the dead, the venerable John Harvie, the distinguished Lewis Harvie, the amiable Mrs. McCraw the interesting little boy of Dr. Brokenbrough. But by one blow, the distressed mother, Mrs. Harvie, has lost her noble and high-souled daughter, Juliana, her excellent son E. J. Harvie, and that sweet little girl, Mary Whitlock, her beloved Grand-daughter!!! Reader, conceive if you can, what you never can have felt.

Lieut. James Gibbon, of the U.S. Navy, has gone with the rest! Young as he was he had tasted of the cup of affliction. He was taken captive in the Philadelphia, and immured in the prisons of Tripole.—On this fatal night, he and Mr. Jno. Lynch were in the same box with Mrs. Ballego, Miss Conyers, Mr. Venable & others—when the alarm was first given, they endeavored to quiet the apprehensions of the ladies, but when the front scene was in flames, they reached over for Miss Conyers who had sunk motionless below—they took her over; they held her between them, in a state of insensibility, her head falling over Mr. Lynch's left arm. In this manner they proceeded towards the head of the stairs, when Gibbon said "Lynch, leave Sally to me. I am strong enough to carry her: she is light and you can save somebody else." Mr. L. replied, "God bless you, Gibbon, there is the stair," and then turned round to seek some of the other ladies. Poor Gibbon and his lovely & interesting companion, sunk together.

We must drop this recital. —We have already stated the deaths of Mrs. Gerardin and her sweet boy—of Mrs. Gibson, whose husband is perhaps now on his way from Europe; what a blow upon his heart!—of the venerable Mrs. Page; of Mrs. Lesslie; of the lovely Nancy Green, the daughter of Mr. Green, the Manager; of the amiable Mrs. Greenhow. The particulars of most of their fates are wrapt in oblivion. Their ashes are in the grave.

Let us change the scene. —It is a far more grateful task to describe the fate of those who have, as it were, miraculously escaped. It is some relief to our feelings, to contemplate those who seem again to have "re-visited the realms of light." It is almost as if the grave had given them again from its jaws. —We are sorry, indeed, that our limits do not permit us to give any but hasty snatches and sketches of events.

Mr. John G. Jackson was overcome by the suffocating smoke and fell senseless. His last recollection was that his feet were descending; but whether the floor or stairway were broken or he had reached the descent, he was not conscious—but insensibly he descended to the level of the pit where a strong current of fresh air revived him, as he lay amongst a heap of prostrate persons. He struggled to rise and found himself on his feet with a lady clinging to him and beseeching him to save her. With difficulty he found the door, not being acquainted with the house, but at last he emerged with the lady, when the fire was pouring through the front windows, and ere they had advanced far, the roof tumbled in.

Mr. M. W. Hancock carried with him to the play, his niece, the two Miss Herons and 3 boys. When the alarm was given, he did all in his power to save his proteges—but was at last separated from them all. The flames were approaching with a degree of fury perhaps never exceeded. Hitherto the scene had been all bustle, confusion and consternation; it now changed to one of a awful horror and desperation that beggars all description. He attempted to reach the centre window in the lobby of the lower boxes. He at last succeeded in mounting on the heads of the crowd betwixt him and the window, and finally reached it, surrounded by the un- availing and afflicting cries of those suffocating around him. He stepped within the window and with difficulty raised the lower sash—he thrust his feet out when the sash was suddenly pressed down and caught his feet betwixt it and the sill. He extricated the foot but could not the other, until those behind him who had sufficient strength left to mount over him and the lower sash which kept him down, did so. He found himself so far gone from suffocation that he gave himself up as lost—the flames however rushed over his head and the introduction of fresh air at the bot- tom of the window gave him new life. Those behind him being no longer able to keep him down, he with a last effort raised the sash, extricated his foot and jumped out. —It gives us sincere pleasure to add that the 3 boys and girls whom he carried with him have all escaped with their lives.

Mr. John Lynch was the only person who passed the window after Mr. Hancock. After he had left poor Gibbon, he met with a variety of horrid adventures. All was utter darkness in the Lobby, and suffocation threatened. It was an awful crisis—and but that one of the windows was burst open and let in fresh air, he thinks all in the lobby must have perished, at length he reached the win- dow, where he found a gentle man fixed fast, whom he since believes to have been Mr. Hancock. After an awful lapse, the flames were rushing on in all directions, his hair caught fire, hope deserted him; he was struck with horror at the idea of being burnt alive. He rushed towards the window, waving his hands as quick as possible over his head & clothes. This was a dreadful moment; he saw many drop down on each side of him suffocated—the window was not free, & he was scarcely on the bottom of it when he heard an awful crash behind him. He threw himself out and providence preserved him.

Mr. Robert Greenhow precipitated himself down the stairs over firebrands and bodies, with his fine son in his arms—and was saved.

Mr. Head Lynch made a wonderful escape with his child. His lady was saved by a strong man's pulling her by the hair of the head over the bodies in the stair-way.

Mr. Stetson fell in the lobby with his head to the wall—but for a crack which his mouth accidentally caught, he would have died for want of air—the fresh air that streamed through it revived him enough to lift his head to the window—a fresh draught of air re- vived him, and he jumped out.

Mr. Gordon was saved in a state of insensibility. His Lady was saved by jumping through a window & clinging to a man, and her little daughter by hanging to her mantle. They had 3 children there, and not one of them was lost.

Several individuals were active in risquing the lives of their fellow-creatures. Dr. McCaw let down several from the window— Mr. Doyle, Mr. Grant and others, who were out, received many as they were let or jumped down.

In addition to Ritchie's account, this issue printed the report of the committee appointed to investigate the disaster. It is the most detailed and judicious of all accounts, and should, I believe, be accepted as reliable and authoritative.[3]

REPORT

OF THE COMMITTEE OF INVESTIGATION

We the Committee, appointed by our Fellow-Citizens "to enquire into the causes of the melancholy catastrophe" which took place in this city on Thursday night last; a catastrophe, which has spread a gloom over a whole city, and filled every eye with tears; have given to this melancholy duty all the attention in our power. —We feel it due to ourselves; it was due to our weeping fellow-citizens; it was due to the world to collect all the lights which might serve to elucidate an event whose effects are so deeply written on our hearts. —We have seen every person who was behind the scenes, that was best able to assist our enquiries— we have heard their statements, and after sifting them as accurately as possible, beg leave to submit the following report to our afflicted citizens:

On the night of Thursday last, the Pantomime of "The Bleeding Nun, or, Agnes and Raymond" came on for representation after the Play was over. In the first Act, amongst other scenes, was the scene of the Cottage of Baptist the Robber, which was illuminated by a chandelier apparently hanging from the ceiling. When the curtain fell on the first Act and before it rose on the end, this chandelier was lifted from its position among the scenery above. It was fixed with 2 wicks to it; one only of them had been lit; yet when it was lifted above, *this fatal lamp was not extinguished*. Here is the first link in the chain of our disasters! The man who raised it, does not pretend to deny it—but pleads that he did so in consequence of an order from some person, whom he supposed authorised to direct him. That person was behind him; the voice had reached him, without his seeing the person, and he does not pretend positively to recognise him. We have not the most distant idea that there was the slightest mischievous intention in the order or in the act—it was inattention—it was the grossest negligence. The lifter of the lamp says that he was aware of the danger, and remonstrated against the act; yet yielded with too fatal a facility to the re-iterated orders of a person whom he saw not, but supposed authorized to direct him. We cast not the slightest imputations upon the Managers or any of the regular Comedians of the state— their positions at the moment as well as other circumstances, forbid the idea that the order ever passed from their lips; yet the act was done. The lighted lamp was lifted—the torch of destruction gleamed at the top of the stage.

Mr. Rice (the Property-man of the Theatre) says, that he saw the scene was aware of the danger of its remaining in that position; and spoke to one of the carpenters, three times repeatedly, "Lower that lamp and blow it out." He did not see it put out; for he was drawn by his business to another part of the stage.

Mr. West declares that he was passing by to commence the 2nd Act of the Pantomime, and saw the lamp up and heard Rice giving directions to the Carpenter to extinguish it.

Mr. Cook (the regular carpenter of the Theatre) declares that he saw the carpenter, alluded to above, attempting to let down the lamp immediately after the order to let it down had been given; that he has no doubt this attempt was made in consequence of the order, that he saw the cords tangle and the lamp to oscillate several inches from its perpendicular position. The chandelier above was moved by two cords which worked over two pulleys inserted in a collar-beam of the roof; and the straight line from the beam to the lamp was, Mr. Cook thinks, about 14 or 15 feet. Thus some idea may be had of the *degree* of oscillation.

Mr. Anderson (one of the Performers of the Theatre) says, that he had remarked, even before the representation, how unskillfully the chandelier had played; and that an attempt to move it had caused it to ride circularly round.

Mr. Yore (another of the workmen of the machinery,) most conclusively confirms this statement. He saw, that in the attempt to lower the lamp, as it was perched among the scenery, the carpenter had failed in his effort; that he then jirked it and jostled it; that it was thus swerved from its perpendicular attitude, and brought into contact with the lower part of one of the front scenes. The scene took fire; the flame rose, and tapering above it to a point, must have reached the roof, which was elevated 6 or 7 feet on above the top of the scene.

We were assured, that there was not one *transparent* scene hanging; that is, a scene coated with varnish and extremely combustible—that there was only one *paper* scene hanging, which Mr. Utt the Prompter declares, was removed 6 or 8 feet behind the lamp. Thirty-five scenes were at that moment hanging, exclusive of the flies or narrow borders which represent the skies, roofs, &c.—and of these, 34 were canvass paintings; which though not extremely combustible on the painted side, are on the other so well covered with the fibres of the hemp as to catch the flame.

Efforts were made to extinguish the flame. Mr. Cook, the carpenter, ascended into the carpenter's gallery, but in vain. He *did* succeed in letting down some of the scenes upon the floor, under an idea that this was the surest means of extinguishing the flame; but he could not distinguish the cords of the scene, that was then on fire. The roof soon caught, and the sense of danger compelled him to fly for his life.

The committee must now be under the necessity of drawing the attention of our fellow-citizens, to the events which took place in front of the curtain. Mr. West states, that immediately on his entering the stage to go on with his part, he heard some bustle behind the scenes which he conceived to be a mere fracas—the cry of "fire" then saluted his ears, which gave him no serious apprehensions, as he knew that little accidents of this description had often taken place; that he heard some voices exclaim "don't be alarmed," which exclamation he repeated through a solicitude to prevent hurry and confusion; that he had not at that moment seen any flakes of fire fall behind the scene; but seeing them at length falling from the roof, he retired behind the scene and found the whole stage enveloped in flames; that he attempted to pull down some of the hanging pieces; when finding it unavailing, he attempted to make good his own retreat.

Mr. Robertson, who was the only performer besides, that came before the audience, assured the Committee, that at the moment when he first discovered the flame, it was no longer than his handkerchief; that he repaired immediately to the stage, as near the orchestra as he could come: "there he conveyed to the audience, not wishing to alarm them, by gesticulation to leave the house; that in the act of doing that, he discovered the flames moving rapidly, and then he exclaimed "The house (or the Theatre) is on fire;" that he went directly to the stage-box where some 3 or 4 ladies were sitting, intreating them to jump into his arms; that he could save them by conveying them through the private stagedoor; & that he still intreated, until he found it necessary to make his own escape; that his own retreat by the private door was intercepted by the flames: that he found it necessary to leap into the stage-box, & join the general crowd in the lobby; that he gained one of the front windows; assisted in passing out some 10 or 12 females, but at last found it necessary to throw himself from the window."

This narrative is due to the exertions of a gentleman, who first sounded the alarm; & to whom there are a few who have not done that justice which he deserves—Let us now return to the transmission of the fire—where the point of flame reached the roof. The roof was unfortunately not plaistered & sealed—there was a sheathing of plank, pine plank we are told, nailed over the rafters; & over these, the shingles. The rosin of the pine had perhaps oozed out of the plank, though the heat of our summer's sun, stood in drops upon it. Yet however this may have been, no sooner did the spire of the flame reach the roof than it caught. The fire spread with a rapidity through this combustible material, unparallelled, certainly never equalled by any of the too numerous fires which have desolated our city—In 4 or 5 minutes at least, the whole roof was one sheet of flame—it burst through the bulls-eye in front—it sought the windows where the rarefied vapour sought its passage; fed by the vast column of air in the hollows of a Theatre, fed by the inflammable pannels & pillars of the boxes, by the dome of the pit, by the canvass ceiling of the lower boxes, until its suffocated victims in the front were wrapt in its devouring flame or pressed to death under the smoulding ruins of the building.

Here might we pause in our melancholy task. We have traced the conflagration to the fatal lamp, lifted as it was lit, then jirked & jostled, out of its perpendicular position, to the scenery—to the roof; until every thing was enveloped in its fury. —But there is one part of the subject which though it does not fall strictly within the letter of the *Resolution*, or perhaps the line of our duty, is yet too interesting to be passed over. Why, *this fatality*? Why have *so many* victims perished on this melancholy occasion? It cannot be said, that it was the combustibility of the building and the rapidity of the fire, great as they undoubtedly were, which altogether produced this mortality of the species—for we cannot believe, if large vomitories had been erected for the passage of the crowd, if there had been doors enough to admit them, that more than *one-tenth* of an audience should have perished on the occasion.

It was in the opinion of the Committee that this ill construction, of the theatre itself, was principally its cause. How numerous were the occasions on which it had long before been said, as the crowd was slowly retiring at the end of a play. "Suppose the house were on fire, what should we do?" —Yet we slept with too fatal a security over the evil—we trusted and we are ruined.—New doors were not opened; the winding staircase was not straitened, the access to the avenues of the theatre was not enlarged.

Even the relics of our fellow citizens as they lay, pointed out the causes of this fatality. They were found strewed in heaps at the foot of the narrow stair case which lead from the boxes—and though with less profusion, on the ground immediately *under* the lobby of the boxes above, from which lobby their retreat down the stairs had been intercepted by the crowd which choaked them up. On that fatal night, there were in the Pitt & Boxes 518 dollar tickets and 80 children—exclusive of 50 persons who were in the galleries. Of these, 598 had to pass through one common avenue, and although all the spectators in the Pitt may have escaped, except a few who may have jumped into the Boxes, yet the crowd in the Lower and Upper boxes had no other resource than to press through a narrow angular stair-case, or to leap the windows. —The Committee, not being particularly conversant with the construction of theatres, have requested Mr. Twaits, one of the Managers of this Theatre, to furnish us with his ideas on the subject. He has favoured us with a statement which we beg leave to incorporate with our report, in the words following, to wit:

"By the request of the Committee of Enquiry into the cause of the late dreadful calamity at the Theatre on the night of the 26th instant, I assert, that the loss of so many valuable lives, and the distress which is felt by all on the occasion, is wholly attributable to the construction of the late Theatre and its materials.

"In all Theatres, that I have seen, except the late one, there have been three distinct and separate doors of entrance—one to the Boxes, one to the Pit and one to the Gallery. The late Drury-Lane Theatre had in the centre of each side a spacious hall, with broad and straight stair-cases, which terminated in the Lobbies of the Boxes; three entrances to the Pit, one in the front and one on each side; and four entrances to two Galleries, two on each side. These avenues were firm and commodious, and in their construction presented every facility for escape, when any danger assailed the audience. Miserable reverse! In the late Richmond Theatre, but one entrance to the Boxes and Pit, and that so narrow, that two persons could scarcely pass at the same time—the way then lying through a gloomy passage to a narrow winding stair-case, which terminated in as narrow a Lobby. —It is, therefore, evident, that this ever to be lamented loss, which has at once deprived your city of some of its brightest ornaments, and desolated many families, is wholly attributable to the malconstruction of the late Theatre, which certainly offered no means of speedy escape. The rapidity of the conflagration must have been caused by the unfinished state of the building, there being no plastered ceiling or wall to prevent the communication of flame."

The Committee cannot close their melancholy labours without expressing one hope, that irreparable as our own calamities have been we may not have suffered altogether in vain; that our own misfortunes may serve as beacons to the rest of our countrymen, and that no theatres should be permitted to be opened in the other cities of the U.S. until every facility has been procured for the escape of the audience.

All who have written about the fire state that seventy-two persons perished. This, I think, is the number who perished in the fire or soon enough thereafter to be included in the mass funeral. There were, however, five victims who died later, making a total of seventy-seven.[4]

As news of the disaster spread, resolutions of condolence poured in. Congress unanimously passed a resolution that members "wear crape on the left arm for one month, in testimony of the national respect and sorrow for the unfortunate persons who perished in the fire at Richmond." In Richmond the officers of the Nineteenth Regiment resolved to wear black armbands for two months, in memory of the loss of their commanding officer, Col. George William Smith, recently elected governor.[5]

In Petersburg, Falmouth, and Norfolk, citizens wore badges of mourning and abstained from public exhibitions and dancing assemblies.[6] So too Alexandria, Fredericksburg, Smithfield, and Winchester. Several communities collected funds for the relief of the sufferers.[7] Similar resolutions were received from Raleigh, Savannah, Charleston, Philadelphia, Zanesville, Boston, and the Commonwealth of Massachusetts.

In addition to these public and official resolutions and memorials were numerous private obituaries and eulogies. Grief expressed itself in both prose and verse.[8] Of particular interest among eulogies and elegies are those inspired by Nancy Green, daughter of Manager J. W. Green, who had frequently performed in the theatre in which she died. The *Enquirer* of January 18, 1812, carried these "Lines on the Death of Miss Green (By J. W. C.)":

> No more, sweet Green—alas! no more!
> Thy smile shall bless our weeping eyes—
> Now on a far, an unknown shore,
> Thou breath'st the air of other skies.
>
> Ah! in what terrors, what alarms
> Thy soft, thy tender spirit fled!
> When struggling for a father's arms,
> The flames enroll'd thee with the dead.

How friendship, while she lisps their names,
Still shudders at the dreadful doom
That wrapt in undistinguished flames,
The hoary head! and beauty's bloom!

Still shall the tear of pity flow,
While memory haunts that dreadful scene,
And every heart that bleeds for woe,
Shall draw its deepest sigh for Green!

Miss Green was commemorated in both prose and verse in the *Virginia Patriot* of February 4.[9]

At the time of the fire, West and Robertson were on stage; they and the others, both actors and stage crew, escaped through the stage door. Apparently there was no ill-feeling toward them, no attempt to blame them for the disaster; indeed the official report explicitly exonerated them. Nevertheless, they were in desperate straits. Alongside horror, grief, and official exoneration, the *Enquirer* of December 31 published this brief piece of pathos:

TO THE CITIZENS OF RICHMOND

In the sincerity of afflicted minds, & deeply wounded hearts, permit us to express the anguish which we feel for the late dreadful calamity, of which we cannot but consider ourselves the innocent cause. From a liberal and enlightened community we fear no reproaches, but we are conscious that many have too much cause to wish they had never known us. To their mercy we appeal for forgiveness, not for a crime committed, but for one which could not be prevented. Our own loss cannot be estimated but by ourselves—'tis true (with one exception) we have not to lament the loss of life—but we have lost our friends, our patrons, our property, and in part, our homes.—Nor is this all our loss—In this miserable calamity we find a sentence of banishment from your hospitable city. No more do we expect to feel that glow of pleasure which pervades a grateful heart, while it receives favours liberally bestowed. Never again shall we behold that feminine humanity which so eagerly displayed itself to soothe the victim of disease, nor view with exultation the benevolent who fostered the fatherless, and shed a ray of comfort on the departed soul of a dying mother. Here then we cease—the eloquence of Grief, is Silence.

James Rose   William Anderson
Hopkins Robertson   Thomas Burke
Chas. Young   A. Placide

Charles Durang	J. W. Green
William Twaits	Wm. Clark

Allusions to Miss Green as the "one exception," to Mrs. Poe as the "dying mother," and to Edgar and Rosalie as "the fatherless" are clear.

The company probably took the first ship downriver. They were to meet further misfortune; they met it gallantly, as this item in the *Virginia Patriot* of January 24 attests:

Norfolk, January 20

The undersigned, passengers in the sloop Experiment, Captain Hall, from this port to Charleston, beg that he will accept their tribute of grateful acknowledgment for the skill, attention and humanity, which he in every instance, so eminently displayed during their late calamitous and perilous situation.

Confident, that no possible blame can in any way attach to Captain Hall, for the loss of the vessel, they sincerely feel for his misfortune, and must ever remember with sentiments of gratitude that skill to which (next to an all-wise Providence) they are so eminently indebted for the preservation of their lives—that attention and humanity, so liberally exerted to soften the horrors, and alleviate the distresses of their situation.

With sincerest wishes for his future welfare and prosperity, they beg leave to subscribe themselves his much obliged friends,

Thomas Caulfield	Mr. Thomas
Thomas Burke	Miss Thomas
Thomas West	Mr. Dunlap
Mrs. West	Wm. Anderson
Charles Durang	P. Ribes
A. Colburn	P. Gallagher
P. Grain	A. Placide, jr.
Mrs. Grain	Mr. Pendleton
Archibald Lord	Mr. Hanna
John Utt	James Rouse
Mrs. Utt	

This was the main body of the company. The absence of Placide, Green, Twaits, Robertson, Young, and Clark is notable. As managers, and perhaps shareholders, they may have stayed in Richmond to settle accounts; they did not expect to return. Despite shipwreck, the actors reached Charleston, where they opened on January 31. They did not open, however, without taking precautions to allay the fears of a community which was well aware of what had happened in Richmond. Hoole writes:

Upon the disastrous burning of the Richmond Theatre, December 26, 1811, Placide wrote a letter to the *Courier* (January 4, 1812), explaining that "more than *one hundred* bodies were taken from the flames. . . . I saved nothing . . . my music, scenery, wardrobes, everything fell a prey to the flames." He hurried home, added more exits, changed the seating arrangement of the Charleston, and had the City Council to inspect and announce that the building was safe—"in case of fire, *thirteen doors* open into the street, by which the *House* can be emptied, almost in an instant."[10]

Other managers were concerned, and they took pains to assure the public that their theatres were safe. On January 14, the *Enquirer* reprinted from the Philadelphia *American Daily Advertiser* a letter signed "Warren & Wood" which began: "Since the late most afflicting occurence in Richmond, the public attention has been naturally called towards the state of the New Theatre, and the means of safety in a moment of alarm. In reply to numerous enquiries on this subject, please to insert the following statement." The letter gives details of the construction of the house, arrangement of lobbies, corridors, and doors, and assures the public that it can be emptied "in perfect safety in less than five minutes from the occurrence of any serious alarm."

On January 18 the *Enquirer* reprinted nearly a column on the New York theatre: "The Managers of the New York Theatre deploring in common with their fellow citizens of the United States, the dreadful calamity occasioned by the burning of the Theatre at Richmond, and anxious, as far as human precaution can, to guard against the possibility of a similar accident, have solicited many of the most competent judges to an examination of the Theatre in this city." Details of construction are specified, with the conclusion that "if the said building was to take fire, there could be no possible danger to the audience." The report was signed by John E. West, Thomas Taylor, William Bridges, and John J. Holland. Appended was a concurring statement signed by nine firemen, and a final statement signed by six prominent citizens attesting the foregoing. I note that there were now six doors, two of which were recently added.

Among all the memorial resolutions and services there seems to have been a sense of condolence; I detect no imputation or insinuation of blame or bigotry. Recalling the long tradition of Puritanical opposition to the stage, we recognize this disaster as an opportunity to exploit. We should bear in mind also that wherever bigotry surfaces it is but the tip of the iceberg. That tip was not long in surfacing.

Among the many poems occasioned by the fire was one reprinted from the Philadelphia *Freeman's Journal* with a note on "the folly of ascribing to divine vengeance the accidents which result from human indiscretion."[11] On January 16 the *Enquirer* printed "A Card" from a friend "who sincerely laments the late mournful event that has taken place in Richmond; begs permission to recommend to the serious attention of its inhabitants, Doctor Witherspoon's Essay on the nature and effects of the Stage."

That there was, if not open gloating, at least a smug and righteous sense of satisfaction that Providence had given godless playgoers their just dessert is evidenced in the *Enquirer* of January 23:

A WORD TO THE WISE!

Extract of a letter from a respectable Friend of the City of N.Y. to his Correspondent in this City.

Although I do not approve of theatrical entertainments, yet I am far from the erroneous opinions of traditionary fanatics and bigots; who are too apt to attribute such accidental catastrophes to the angry judgments of their great and merciful creator, of whose divine attributes they must certainly be ignorant. —If such accidents only happened to Theatres and Dancing Assemblies, I will allow they would then have some room to plead in support of such a horrid opinion; but as such dreadful conflagrations have happened to the assemblies in Churches (so called,) and Meeting Houses, where the object of meetings was to perform solemn Worship to, and adoration of the Almighty God, surely they would not say, that these cases were also judgments from on high! I think that people of all sects ought rather to tremble and shudder in contemplating on the subject of such uncharitable and monstrous doctrines.

Just two days later the *Enquirer* carried a news story on "Another Earthquake" which was distinctly felt Thursday morning about nine o'clock:

These are indeed times of wonder. Comets—eclipses—tornadoes—earthquakes—in the age of superstition these were held to be portentous signs. Powers of the physical world are yet not satisfied? Are not your omens already out? Does not the conflagration of the theatre verify your superstitious auguries? Are not the ashes of our citizens enough? But this is the language of superstition. To the eye of the bigot, there seems to be a mysterious sympathy between the revolutions of the moral and physical world. But truth abjures such absurdities. . . . Away then with these chimeras! They are only worthy of those ingenious days of witchcraft. . . . Whether it be a dream or a vision of a bigot, just let loose from prison, they are equally at war with the lessons of philosophy.

Perhaps it was Editor Ritchie's eloquence anent the earthquake which provoked "a word in Season" from "A Subscriber" who in the *Virginia Patriot* of January 31 accused Ritchie of being an infidel:

Let him study the Bible and pray to God for grace to understand it, and he will find in it everything calculated to make man useful and happy here and hereafter; he will then learn also that all calamities with which God in his providence suffers the children of men to be afflicted, are so many rebukes as signal tokens of God's displeasure against us as sinners, and he will cease to revile such as are disposed to join in supplications to the throne of grace that God may overrule the late and never-to-be-forgotten calamity of the night of the 26th of last month, for the promotion of the best interests of the sufferers.

On February 13 the *Virginia Argus* published a letter from Oliver Whipple of Georgetown to the mayor of Richmond. Whipple sent sympathy and over two columns of "Crumbs of Comfort For the Mourners of Richmond." He interspersed frequent Biblical quotations among references to the Greek and Roman theatres. He commented on the "hard-hearted uncharitableness of many who class themselves among *professing Christians*" yet who say "This is God's work! he has come to inflict deserved justice and avenge himself of this wicked people." Whipple asserted that "a Play may be . . . perfectly moral and instructing, may open and enlarge our ideas, expand the mind, and lead the thoughts to comprehend sublime themes."

He was soon contradicted. The *Virginia Patriot* of February 25 carried a "Communication" signed "a Friend to Sound Doctrine," which accused "Oliver Whippel" of misquoting and perverting scripture. There were unmistakable references to those who were "devoured by the flaming element in the midst of gaiety. . . . It certainly is a dangerous and unevangelical doctrine to say that sinful mortals, hurled away, by an act of Providence, in the midst of gaiety and mirth, are like the prophet Elijah,—on a chariot of fire, translated to the heavenly domains."

The *Patriot* of March 3 published a "Counter Communication" signed "A Friend to Common Sense and Feeling" in which "A Friend to Sound Doctrine" is said to be "destitute . . . of delicacy, sensibility, and sentiment" in presuming to question "the truly humane & christian doctrine contained in the benevolent and good hearted address of Oliver Whipple Esq." Not only is "A Friend to Sound Doctrine" "A *Caviller*," he is a "Slave-holding Caviller," who daily commits "sins and abominations" by his slave-holding.

We should conclude, I fear, that the theatre fire was exploited by some purveyors of piety, who saw in it not only God's avenging sword but justification of their own bigotry. On the other hand, there was a genuine and widespread outpouring of sympathy and sorrow.

Among the local committees appointed at the time of the fire was one charged with the erection of an appropriate memorial. Among the many poems published in local newspapers was an elegy of nine four-line stanzas in which the poet, "Virginiensis," imagined himself "inscribing a memorial on the monument about to be erected on the fatal spot where the Theatre stood."[12] Poetic imagination foreshowed the event.

The committee consisted of John Marshall, Joseph Marx, Ben Hatcher, William Fenwick, and Thomas Taylor. They designated William Dandridge, cashier of the Bank of Virginia, to receive subscriptions for the monument. On February 6 the *Enquirer* published a long description of a proposed monument designed by Mr. Hiort, "an Amateur of the Fine Arts." Hiort proposed an elaborate obelisk, exhibiting such scenes as "the figure of Humanity . . . weeping o'er the ashes of her children; a distant view of the Capitol, and an angel flying with a scroll of the calamity to

Heaven." Benjamin Henry Latrobe, who had established himself in Richmond upon his arrival from England and who designed for Richmond the theatre that was not built in 1798, was also interested in the memorial. He proposed a monument to "consist of a block 32 feet square, on which a pyramid 48 feet high would rise, and within there should be a chamber 20 or 24 feet square. On the inner walls should be carved the names of the victims and the appropirate inscriptions; in the center there would be a memorial statue, 'a kneeling figure, representing the city . . . mourning over an urn.' A sketch embodying the idea still exists."[13]

Meanwhile an "association for building a church on Shockoe Hill," of which E. J. MacMurdo was treasurer, was raising money and making plans.[14] This association, the monument committee, and the Common Hall agreed that the monument and the church should be one, the Monumental Church. Possibly the Common Hall's appropriation of $5,000 helped to bring the church association and the monument committee together. The decision was doubtless approved by Chairman John Marshall, an Episcopalian.

Robert Mills, a protégé of Latrobe, was named architect, and the church was designed and constructed by him. It is considered one of his "most original and successful achievements." The cornerstone was laid on August 4, 1812, and the church was consecrated on May 4, 1814, when "the Reverend Mr. Buchanan performed Divine Service, and the Rev. Mr. Wilmer preached an appropriate sermon." Immediately afterward Treasurer MacMurdo informed pew-holders of an annual assessment of fifteen percent of the cost of the pews. Payments were to be made quarterly, with the first installment due on June 1.[15]

As chairman of the committee which had built the theatre that burned, Marshall was an obvious choice for chairman of the committee which erected the memorial. Three members of that committee were members of the Monumental Episcopal Church: William Fenwick held pew number thirty-six; Thomas Taylor held pew number eighty-six; John Marshall held pew number twenty-three. Joseph Marx was a prominent Jewish businessman of European birth. Benjamin Hatcher was probably a Presbyterian.[16] I suspect that Marshall, a prominent Episcopalian and delegate to the diocesan convention, may have influenced the decision to turn the monument into an Episcopal church.

The choice of Mills rather than Latrobe as architect may also have been influenced by him. Latrobe had satirized the Federalists in *The Apology*, which had been acted in Richmond in 1798, and Marshall was Richmond's greatest Federalist. When Marshall presided at the trial of Aaron Burr in Richmond in 1807, Latrobe, as a friend, if not an accomplice, of Burr, was in Richmond under subpoena. Although both Mills and Latrobe were friends of Jefferson, I suspect that Marshall may have favored Mills.

The church itself is historic, and its history has been written.[17] The building still stands. An urn outside enclosed the ashes of the dead, and their names were inscribed on a monument between the two pillars of the portico.

One final grace note may be added: the *Richmond News Leader* of October 17, 1975, carried a picture of the church above the headline "Monumental Church Restoration Due." Restoration was "expected to begin within three weeks," to cost half a million dollars, and to extend over seven years. "Monumental Church is important architecturally because it is the only one of Mills' five domed churches to survive."

Meanwhile, plans for building in Richmond the first theatre designed by the father of American architecture lie fallow.

Appendixes

The Theatre That Was Not Built

With minor exceptions, such as concerts in the Eagle Tavern and Curtis's £140 theatre that was sold by the vendue master in 1793, the Richmond theatre during the 1790s was the academy built by Alexander Quesnay in 1786 and first occupied by the Hallam and Henry Company in the autumn of that year. Descriptions of spectacular scenic effects and lavish productions of such plays as *The Tempest* and *Romeo and Juliet* attest its adequacy. Although Seilhamer says that it was designed to hold sixteen hundred people, there is no description of it. As far as I know there exists neither a drawing of its exterior nor a diagram of its interior. We know that it had boxes, gallery (upper boxes), and pit; but there are no details either of lavish furnishings or of stage design and equipment. It housed the Virginia Constitutional Convention of 1788. John Marshall, who frequented the theatre, left records of his expenditures for tickets, but left no comment on the house, the audiences, or the plays. We might expect the architect Latrobe, who attended the theatre, made friends with the players, and wrote a play which was produced there, to have left some record of his opinion of the edifice, but evidently he did not. If he had, I suspect it would have been a highly competent and highly critical professional analysis, invaluable as a record.

What Latrobe left, however, is even more valuable: a proposal for a new theatre. Following Latrobe's journal, his biographer, Talbot Hamlin, writes:

The only theatre in Richmond was an old and rather tumble-down building in the outskirts of the town, uncomfortable and architecturally uncouth, and above all ill-fitted for the elaborate scenery and the spectacles West liked to present. . . . a new building was necessary, and Latrobe—who knew the theaters of England and the Continent—was manifestly well qualified to be its architect. In his journal he says that he had begun the designs for the theater, hotel, and assembly rooms (in one building) on December 1, 1797, and completed them on January 6, 1798.[1]

The completed plans were soon made public. The proposal was dated January 22, just sixteen days after Latrobe completed his plans, and just eight days before the old theatre burned. It was signed by Maj. Alexander Quarrier and B. Henry Latrobe. Alexander Quarrier was a coach-maker who had come to Richmond from Philadelphia in 1786. At this time Latrobe had both his residence and his office at Quarrier's Court, on the canal at the foot of Seventh Street. He had executed some minor commissions, but this was his first major architectural design in America. The project was to be financed by subscription, details of which were published. The announcement appeared in the *Observatory* on June 28, 1798, but it is dated January 22 and almost certainly had been published previously. Identification of the site as "the ground upon which the Theatre now stands" is evidence that it was written before the theatre burned on January 30.

It is proposed to erect in the City of Richmond, a Building to contain an Hotel, Assembly-rooms, & a commodious Theatre.

To comprize the particulars of the scheme in an advertisement, would be impossible, but the following are its principle features.

A subscription shall be opened, consisting of 270 Shares of 100 Dollars each, payable by instalments of 10 Dollars per month, during the course of the present year.

A specific contract for the completion of the building in conformity to the design, and in a given time will be entered into with the most ample security for its performance, whereby the usual disappointments in Building by subscription will be avoided.

The whole proceeds, or rents of the building shall be divided half yearly, among the subscribers.—at the rate of rent now established in Richmond, the shares are calculated to produce 9¼ per cent.

The site of the Building, is the ground upon which the Theatre now stands. Conditional agreements highly advantageous to the subscribers, have been entered into with Mr. West, who has undertaken to build the interior parts of the Theatre at his own expence, and according to the design. All the Building except the internal part of the Theatre will be vested in the Subscribers, or their representatives in perpetuity.

All the Designs are finished, and Mr. Latrobe, the Architect, will attend every morning from 10 to 12 at Major Quarrier's to exhibit, and explain them.

                                                   Alexander Quarrier
Richmond, January 22, 1798   B. Henry Latrobe, B.

The subscription of "270 Shares of 100 Dollars each" would have produced $27,000, which was to finance the construction of the building, including the hotel and the assembly rooms. I note with interest the statement that "conditional agreements highly advantageous to the subscribers, have been entered into with Mr. West, who has undertaken to build the interior parts of the Theatre at his own expense, and according to the design." Evidently West and Latrobe worked together in designing the theatre. The extent of West's financial contribution is unknown, though it must have been substantial. The completed building would certainly have cost well over $30,000.

West had already built theatres in Charleston (1793), Norfolk (1795), Petersburg (1796), and Fredericksburg (1797); at the time of his death in 1799 he had almost completed one in Alexandria. He was obviously qualified. The collaboration of West and Latrobe brought together the two men in America best equipped by experience and talent for the building of a theatre.

During his residence in Richmond, Latrobe drew up plans for three major buildings: a church, a penitentiary, and this hotel-assembly-theatre. Of these, only the penitentiary was built. Plans for the other two, however, are preserved. Hamlin (a professor of architecture) discusses each of the three in considerable detail. Our concern is primarily with the theatre, which, however, must be seen in relation to the whole edifice: the hotel, the ballroom, and the theatre.

Hamlin considers Latrobe's design "remarkable for its time." The hotel, he says, was "far in advance of the usual taverns and hotels of its time"; and the ballroom, or assembly room, had it been erected, "would have been the outstanding American interior of its day." The theatre, however, was "the climax of the design":

The brilliant use of intersecting circular curves to give greater depth to the boxes and the gallery opposite the stage—and incidentally longer and roomier lobbies—would appear to be unique at the time. Equally remarkable is the interior, which like the plan is apparently without precedent. The ceiling over the auditorium proper is a shallow half dome. On either side, the fronts of the stage boxes are brought out toward the center sufficiently to create a narrow vertical plane, and this is carried across from side to side as a low, paneled, segmental arch, with a slightly conical coffered ceiling behind over the forestage and running back to the proscenium opening. This ceiling and the fronts of the side boxes form the only "proscenium arch," for the opening of the stage runs clear from one side to the other and the lunette beneath the segmental ceiling is filled with drapery—probably intended to be a permanent valance—gathered up to a great American eagle in the center. An examination of plates of late-eighteenth-century theatres in England, France, Germany, and Italy reveals not a single scheme of this type; only a decade or more later do the nearest approaches to such a simplicity of ceiling design, so visually satisfactory, so definitely focussed on the stage, appear in European examples. . . . In form and elegant simplicity of treatment the entire composition is extraordinary and in advance of its time. Had it been built it would have given Richmond not only a ballroom the equal (except in size) of any in England but also a theater interior simpler, finer, and more distinguished as a unit than almost any standing anywhere in Europe in 1797.[2]

Professor Brooks McNamara is equally impressed by the Richmond theatre that was not built. After analyzing and evaluating theatres throughout the United States, McNamara concludes that Latrobe's proposed Richmond theatre was "perhaps the most important architectural effort of the late eighteenth century." He compares it to James Watt's Theater Royal in Birmingham, built in 1795, and to William Strickland's Chestnut Street Theater of 1822. "But it is clear that Latrobe's building, had it been completed, would have been far more handsome than either of these structures, and indeed a better house than anything ever seen in England aside from the great theaters of London."[3]

The most important feature of Latrobe's theatre McNamara considers to be the entrance to the pit, which was from the rear center of the auditorium:

As in many modern theaters, a flight of stairs led directly up into the pit from the lobby. . . . The central aisle that Latrobe's auditorium anticipates, uncommon in the eighteenth century, became the common entrance system in many English and American theaters in the early years of the nineteenth century. . . . Latrobe's playhouse designed for Richmond marked the first steps toward a new era in auditorium design.[4]

He also considers the design of the stage "as much in advance of its time as the auditorium":

> The absence of proscenium doors and the raking of the stage wings . . . are extraordinarily unconventional for so early a building, and the proscenium opening (more than fifty feet) is far wider than that seen at most eighteenth century playhouses. . . . It is probable that Latrobe intended the scenery in his theater to be shifted by the English groove system. . . . The comparatively generous use of space behind the proscenium arch . . . demonstrates that the backstage facilities at the Richmond building would have been far superior to those at the Chestnut Street Theater as it was remodeled and enlarged in the early nineteenth century. Indeed, although it was a smaller house, the Richmond theater would have contained backstage space almost as good as that to be found at London's Covent Garden.[5]

These analyses are supported by eight diagrams and sketches reproduced from Latrobe's sketchbooks, which are preserved in the Maryland Historical Society. McNamara concludes: "Thus, in the design of the stage as well as the auditorium, the proposed Richmond playhouse illustrates both a transition to the theater of the nineteenth century and the highest point of American theater architecture in its day."[6]

In the 1960s there were efforts to build Latrobe's theatre in Richmond. In his concluding paragraph, Professor McNamara writes: "As these chapters are being written, it seems likely that the playhouse will finally be erected on a site not far from the original location chosen by Latrobe himself." It was not to be. "City Council employed a Baltimore firm to determine whether or not the City of Richmond should support with public funds the construction costs. . . . It was recommended that public funds for such construction should not be used. . . . The Latrobe Theatre project is now defunct."[7] A model of the twice-proposed theatre now sits in the Valentine Museum.

In 1798 Richmond did not build what would have been beyond compare the finest theatre in America because Richmond could not raise $27,000; and the father of architecture in the United States moved to Philadelphia. In 1800, not just New York, Philadelphia, and Charleston had fine theatres; so did Petersburg,

Norfolk, and Alexandria. In Richmond, what had been for a decade one of the best acting companies in the nation continued to play in the "Temporary Theatre, Market Hall."

NOTES

1. Hamlin, pp. 86-87.
2. Ibid., pp. 119-20.
3. *The American Playhouse in the Eighteenth Century* (Cambridge, Mass., 1969), p. 143.
4. Ibid., p. 151.
5. Ibid., pp. 151-54.
6. Ibid., p. 154.
7. Mrs. Stuart Gibson to Martin Shockley, Apr. 21, 1971.

Acting Companies by Seasons

This appendix lists by companies and seasons all players known to have appeared on the Richmond stage between 1784 and 1812. Companies are identified by managers, as the Hallam and Henry Company and the West and Bignall Company, although the former referred to itself as the American Company and the latter as the Virginia Company. Most names of players are taken from newspaper advertisements; a few come from playbills; a few from notices of benefits, critical articles, and such sources.

Newspaper and playbill casts of characters gave surnames only except in rare instances when two actors with the same surname appeared in the same cast, as "Bignall" and "J. Bignall." Surname only was used for the head of a family; for example, "Sully" meant Matthew Sully, Sr., while "M. Sully" meant Matthew Sully, Jr. With unmarried daughters, advertisements followed contemporary Anglo-American custom. The eldest daughter was "Miss Sully"; younger sisters were identified with initials; thus, "Miss Sully" for Charlotte, "Miss E. Sully" for her younger sister Elizabeth. In the case of large and intermarried families, such as the Sullys, Wests, and Bignalls, confusion is inevitable.

In text I have followed the usage of my sources, with explanation where necessary. Here, however, where I attempt to identify all known players as fully and clearly as possible, a different procedure is called for. First names and initials have been added whenever I am sure or reasonably sure of identifications; question marks are used for probable identifications. Surname only is used when I am unable to identify an individual. For instance, before 1800 "Sully" meant Matthew Sully, Sr.; after 1800 "Sully" meant his son Matthew Sully, Jr.; in these lists the younger Sully is always Matthew Sully, Jr. Similarly, before 1800 "West" meant Thomas Wade West, manager and head of the family; after his death in 1799, "West" probably meant his son, previously identified by initial or name. "Tom West," "T. West," and "West, Jun."

are most likely he, the son of Thomas Wade West, and he is designated Thomas(?) West throughout.

Comments on actors are made in text in a Players section at the end of each season. Many of these actors can be traced in New York, Philadelphia, Charleston, and other theatres; some were, or became, famous; others remain obscure. Spelling has been regularized and variations indicated: "Clark" and "Clarke" were almost certainly the same man; he signed his name "William Clark"; Lewis Hallam's son is referred to as "Mirvin," "Mirvan," and "Marvin" by different writers; I use "Mirvin."

With a few exceptions, this appendix is a catalogue of players, actors whose names appeared on playbills and in advertised casts of characters. Of course, there were others in every company—musicians, scene painters, stage hands, costume mistresses, prompter, box office keeper, etc., whose names usually went unknown.

Acknowledging the inevitability of error and the fallibility of probable ascriptions, I hope that this attempt to identify players from this period of the American theatre will prove useful to other scholars.

FIRST SEASON
Dennis Ryan Company
June–December 1784

Five men	*Three women*
William Godwin	Mrs. Hyde
Lewis	Mrs. Lewis
Dennis Ryan	Mrs. Smith
Smith	
Thomas Wall	
	One girl
	Miss Wall

SECOND SEASON

Dennis Ryan Company (?)

November 1785

No names are recorded of this hypothetical company playing a hypothetical season. We know only that "the Managers of the playhouse" were negotiating with the Common Hall for permission to perform. We have reason to believe that permission was granted.

THIRD SEASON

Hallam and Henry Company

October 1786

Only Hallam and Henry are named in Richmond, but we know that the Hallam and Henry Company played in Richmond at the opening of the new Academy-Theatre of A. M. Quesnay. Actors named for this hypothetical company are those who acted with Hallam and Henry in New York. Miss Storer later married Henry; Miss Tuke married Hallam.

Eleven men

Charles Biddle
Lewis Hallam, Jr.
Joseph Harper
Heard
John Henry
Kenna
I. Kenna
Owen Morris
Dennis Ryan
Thomas Wignell

Stephen Woolls

Six women

Mrs. Joseph Harper
Mrs. Kenna
Mrs. Owen Morris
Mrs. Remington
Miss Maria Storer
Miss Tuke

FOURTH SEASON
William Verling Company (?)
November–December 1787

Mrs. Rankin was the former Mrs. Remington.

Seven men   *Five women*

Bisset   Mrs. Gifford (Giffard)
Kidd   Miss Gordon
Lake   Mrs. Parsons
Lewis   Mrs. Rankin
Parsons   Mrs. Smallwood
Rankin
Welles

FIFTH SEASON
West and Bignall Company
August 1790–January 1791

Eleven men   *Six women*

Charles Biddle   Mrs. John Bignall
John Bignall   Mrs. Walter Davids
Diddep   Mrs. Hyde (Hide)
Mirvin Hallam   Mrs. Lewis
Lewis   Miss Wade
Richards (Richard Crosby)   Mrs. Thomas Wade West
Solomon
Tobine
Walpole   *One boy*
Thomas Wade West
Whipple   Master Davids

SIXTH SEASON
Godwin and Company
July 1791

Three men

Charles Busselot
William Godwin
Hodgson

One woman

Mrs. Charles Busselot

SEVENTH SEASON
West and Bignall Company
October–December 1791

Eleven men

Andrews
John Bignall
John Bignall, Jr.
Cleland (Cleveland?)
Courtenay (Courtney)
Mirvin Hallam
J. Kenna
Riffetts (Riffet)
Riley (Reilly)
Sheldon
Thomas Wade West

Seven women

Mrs. John Bignall
Mrs. Walter Davids
Mrs. Decker
Mrs. John Johnson
Mrs. Kenna
Mrs. J. Kenna
Mrs. Thomas Wade West

Two boys

Master Davids
Master West

EIGHTH SEASON
West and Bignall Company
August–December 1792

This season marks the American debut of the famous Sully family.

Thirteen men

Andrews
John Bignall
John Bignall, Jr.
Courtenay (Courtney)
Mirvin Hallam
Hamilton
Kenna
J. Kenna
Riffetts (Riffits)
Lawrence Sully
Matthew Sully
Matthew Sully, Jr.
Thomas Wade West

Nine women

Mrs. John Bignall

Mrs. Walter Davids
Mrs. Decker
Mrs. Kenna
Mrs. J. Kenna
Miss Charlotte Sully
Miss Elizabeth Sully
Mrs. Matthew Sully
Mrs. Thomas Wade West

One boy

Master Thomas Sully

Two girls

Miss Harriet Sully
Miss Harriet West

NINTH SEASON
Curtis and Company
August 1793

Only Curtis is named in contemporary Richmond newspapers.

TENTH SEASON
West and Bignall Company
September–December 1793

Mrs. Chambers was the former Miss Charlotte Sully.

Eighteen men

Isaac Bignall
John Bignall
John Bignall, Jr.
Chambers
Clifford
Edgar
Greenwood
Mirvin Hallam
Hamilton
Henderson
Kedey
Marriott
Murray
Riffetts (Riffet)
Lawrence Sully
Matthew Sully
Matthew Sully, Jr.
Thomas Wade West

Eleven women

Mrs. John Bignall

Mrs. Chambers
Mrs. Decker
Mrs. Edgar
Mrs. Gray
Mrs. Henderson
Mrs. Kedey
Mrs. J. Kenna
Mrs. Marriott
Mrs. Murray
Mrs. Thomas Wade West

Two boys

Master Chester Sully
Master Thomas Sully

Two girls

Miss Elizabeth Sully
Miss Julia Sully

ELEVENTH SEASON

West and Bignall Company

October 1795–January 1796

Ann (West) Bignall, daughter of Thomas Wade and Margaret (Sully) West and widow of John Bignall, Sr., married James(?) West before the season began. Thomas (or Tom) West was probably Thomas Wade West, Jr., though he never styled himself that way. Miss Harriet West later married Isaac Bignall.

Eighteen men

John Bignall, Jr.
Dubois
Duport

Ten women

Mrs. Decker
Mrs. Edgar
Mrs. Gray

Edgar
Francisquy
Gray
Jones
Latte
Marriott
Munto
Samuel Nelson
Alexander Placide
Matthew Sully
Val
James (?) West
Thomas (?) West
Thomas Wade West
W. West

Mrs. Kenna
Mrs. Moore
Mrs. Samuel Nelson
Mrs. Alexander Placide
Mrs. Val
Mrs. James(?) West
Mrs. Thomas Wade West

Three boys

Master Duport
Master Gray
Master West

One girl

Miss Harriet West

TWELFTH SEASON
West and Bignall Company
November 1796–January 1797

Twelve men

Bartlet
Copeland
Douvillier
Fitzgerald
J. W. Green
Heely
Morton (Moreton)
W. H. Prigmore
Matthew Sully
Gavin Turnbull
Thomas (?) West
Thomas Wade West

Seven women

Mrs. Douvillier

Mrs. Fitzgerald
Mrs. Graupner
Mrs. J. W. Green
Mrs. Shaw
Mrs. Gavin Turnbull
Mrs. Thomas Wade West

One boy

Master Shaw

One girl

Miss Harriet West

THIRTEENTH SEASON

West and Bignall Company

Autumn 1797–January 1798

Eight men   Thomas Wade West

John Bignall, Jr.
J. W. Green   *Three women*
Lathy
Matthew Sully   Mrs. **J. W. Green**
Gavin Turnbull   **Mrs. Gavin Turnbull**
James (?) West   **Mrs.** James (?) West
Thomas (?) West

FOURTEENTH SEASON

West and Bignall Company

December 1798–April 1799

Thirteen men   *Six women*

John Bignall, Jr.   Mrs. John Bignall, Jr.
J. W. Green   Mrs. Decker
Daniel M'Kinzie (M'Kenzie)   Mrs. J. W. Green
Charles Lace Radcliffe   Mrs. Watts
Matthew Sully   Mrs. James (?) West
Matthew Sully, Jr.   Mrs. Thomas Wade West
Taylor
Tubbs
Watts   *Two girls*
James (?) West
Thomas (?) West   Miss Elizabeth Arnold
Thomas Wade West   Miss Gillespie
Williams

FIFTEENTH SEASON

West and Bignall Company

October 1799

The one newspaper advertisement announced the opening of the
season and named the company as the "Virginia Company of
Comedians," but named no members of it.

SIXTEENTH SEASON
West and Bignall Company
August–October 1802

Only two players are named: James(?) West and M'Kenzie, who was, I assume, the Daniel M'Kinzie of season fourteen.

SEVENTEENTH SEASON
West and Bignall Company
January 1803

Only two players are named: Sully and Mrs. West, Jr. The former, I assume, was Matthew Sully, Jr.; his father had announced his retirement from the stage in 1800. The latter was probably Mrs. Thomas(?) West. The scenery was by Mr. Jones.

EIGHTEENTH SEASON
West and Bignall Company
December 1803–April 1804

Fifteen men	*Six women*
Bailey	Mrs. J. W. Green
Barrymore	Mrs. Lynch
Cane (Alexander Cain?)	Miss Melford
Clare	Mrs. Story
William Clark (Clarke)	Mrs. Thomas(?) West
Comer	Mrs. Thomas Wade West
J. W. Green	
Charles Hopkins	
Daniel M'Kenzie	*Two girls*
John(?) Martin	
Rutherford	Miss Decker
Santford (Sanfort)	Miss Nancy Green
Story	
Matthew Sully, Jr.	
Thomas(?) West	

NINETEENTH SEASON
West and Bignall Company
June–September 1804

Mrs. Charles Hopkins was the former Miss Elizabeth Arnold.

Fourteen men	Rutherford
	Saubere
Bailey	Thomas (?) West
Barrymore	
Clare	
William Clark (Clarke)	*Six women*
Comer	
Downie	Mrs. Bailey
J. W. Green	Mrs. Clare
Charles Hopkins	Mrs. Downie
Lynch	Mrs. J. W. Green
John (?) Martin	Mrs. Charles Hopkins
David Poe	Miss Melford

TWENTIETH SEASON
West and Bignall Company
December 1804–February 1805

Miss Nancy Green appeared as a dancer.

Nine men	Thomas (?) West
Briers	
Comer	*Five women*
Downie	
J. W. Green	Mrs. Downie
Charles Hopkins	Mrs. J. W. Green
John (?) Martin	Mrs. Charles Hopkins
David Poe	Miss Melford
Serson	Mrs. Stuart

TWENTY-FIRST SEASON

West and Bignall Company

January–May 1806

Mr. Decker composed music, and Mr. Stuart painted scenes. Elizabeth (Arnold) Hopkins married David Poe between April 7 and April 10. Thomas Abthorpe Cooper appeared as visiting star.

Fourteen men

John Bignall, Jr.
Briers
Clare
Comer
J. W. Green
Hughes
M'Donald (MacDonald)
John (?) Martin
David Poe
Santford
Stowell
Sutton
Thomas (?) West
Wilmot

Six women

Mrs. John Bignall, Jr.
Mrs. Clare
Mrs. J. W. Green
Mrs. Charles Hopkins (Mrs. David Poe)
Mrs. Thomas Wade West
Mrs. Wilmot

One boy

Master Douglas

One girl

Miss Nancy Green

TWENTY-SECOND SEASON

West and Bignall Company

August–September 1806

Thomas Abthorpe Cooper again appeared as visiting star.

Eleven men

George L. Barrett
John Bignall, Jr.
Briers
Collins
Comer

Sears
Wilmot

Four women

Mrs. George L. Barrett

J. W. Green
M'Donald (Macdonald)
John (?) Martin
Rutherford

Mrs. John Bignall, Jr.
Mrs. J. W. Green
Mrs. Wilmot

TWENTY-THIRD SEASON
West and Bignall Company
December 1806–February 1807

One local amateur appeared as Hamlet. Green was manager; Decker was leader of the orchestra; Stuart was scene painter and machinist; La Taste, C. Southgate, and Weidemeyer were musicians.

Twelve men

George L. Barrett
John Bignall, Jr.
Briers
Collins
Comer
J. W. Green
Huntingdon
John (?) Martin
Rutherford
Spears
Stowell
Wilmot

Four women

Mrs. George L. Barrett
Mrs. John Bignall, Jr.
Mrs. J. W. Green
Mrs. Wilmot

One boy

Master George H. Barrett

Two girls

Miss Bignall
Miss Harriet West

TWENTY-FOURTH SEASON
West and Bignall Company
May–June 1807

Thomas Abthorpe Cooper appeared as star.

Eight men

John Bignall, Jr.

John (?) Martin
Spears

Comer
J. W. Green   *Two women*
Mirvin Hallam
Huntingdon   Mrs. George L. Barrett
Low   Mrs. J. W. Green

TWENTY-FIFTH SEASON

Placide and Green Company

September–October 1809

This was a new company, with Alexander Placide as manager and J. W. Green as assistant manager.

Fourteen men

John Bray
James (?) Byrne
Thomas Caulfield
William Clark (Clarke)
Gilbert Fox
J. W. Green
J. (?) Jones
Alexander Placide
Ringwood
Rutherford
Spear (Spears)
Matthew Sully, Jr.
John Utt
Valentine

Six women

Mrs. John Bray

Mrs. William Clark (Clarke)
Mrs. J. W. Green
Mrs. Alexander Placide
Mrs. Simpson
Mrs. John Utt

Three boys

Master Henry Placide
Master John Placide
Master M. Sully

Five girls

Miss Nancy Green
Miss Caroline Placide
Miss Jane Placide
Miss Sully
Miss S. Sully

TWENTY-SIXTH SEASON
Placide and Green Company
October 1809–January 1810

This was essentially the same company from the previous season.
Master John Howard Payne appeared as star at the season's close.

Thirteen men

John Bray
Thomas Caulfield
William Clark (Clarke)
Clough
Gilbert Fox
J. W. Green
J. (?) Jones
Alexander Placide
Ringwood
Rutherford
Spear (Spears)
Matthew Sully, Jr.
John Utt

Five women

Mrs. John Bray

Mrs. William Clark (Clarke)
Mrs. J. W. Green
Mrs. Alexander Placide
Mrs. John Utt

Four boys

Master Green
Master Henry Placide
Master Sully
Master M. Sully

Four girls

Miss Caroline Placide
Miss Jane Placide
Miss Sully
Miss S. Sully

TWENTY-SEVENTH SEASON
Placide and Green Company
August–October 1810

This was the same company, with a few changes. No visiting stars
appeared this season. One local amateur performed.

Fifteen men

Austin
Barton
Thomas Caulfield

Six women

Mrs. William Clark (Clarke)
Mrs. J. W. Green
Mrs. Alexander Placide

William Clark (Clarke)   Mrs. David Poe
Collins   Mrs. John Utt
Foster   Mrs. Charles Young
J. W. Green
J. (?) Jones
M'Donald   *One boy*
Alexander Placide
Hopkins Robertson   Master Henry Placide
Rutherford
William Twaits
John Utt   *Two girls*
Charles Young

                                 Miss Eliza Placide
                                 Miss Jane Placide

TWENTY-EIGHTH SEASON
Placide and Green Company
October–November 1810

Although only eight actors are named in the brief advertisements of this season, the company was the same as it had been during the previous season. John Dwyer appeared as visiting star at the end of the season.

Seven men   William Twaits
                                 John Utt
Thomas Caulfield
Collins
Foster   *One woman*
J. W. Green
M'Donald   Mrs. William Clark (Clarke)

TWENTY-NINTH SEASON
Placide and Green Company
August–October 1811

One gentleman amateur played three leading roles.

Seventeen men

William Anderson
Thomas Burke
Alexander Cain
Thomas Caulfield
William Clark (Clarke)
Foster
J. W. Green
Laurent
Alexander Placide
Potter
Hopkins Robertson
James Rose
Smalley
William Twaits
John Utt
Thomas (?) West
Charles Young

Seven women

Mrs. William Clark (Clarke)
Mrs. J. W. Green
Mrs. Alexander Placide
Mrs. David Poe
Miss Thomas
Mrs. John Utt
Mrs. Charles Young

One boy

Master Henry Placide

Two girls

Miss Clark (Clarke)
Miss Placide

THIRTIETH SEASON

Placide and Green Company

October–December 1811

Scenery was painted by Graim and West. The orchestra included: Gallaher, clarinet; Lefolle, violin; Ribes, violin; Taylor, flute. Mrs. Poe died during this season.

Fifteen men

William Anderson
Thomas Burke
Thomas Caulfield
William Clark (Clarke)
Charles Durang
Foster
J. W. Green
Hanner (Hannar)

Six women

Mrs. William Clark (Clarke)
Mrs. J. W. Green
Mrs. Alexander Placide
Miss Thomas
Mrs. John Utt
Mrs. Charles Young

Alexander Placide
Hopkins Robertson
James Rose (Rouse)
William Twaits
John Utt
Thomas (?) West
Charles Young

Two boys

Master Henry Placide
Master Oliver

Three girls

Miss Clark (Clarke)
Miss Eliza Placide
Miss Jane Placide

Notes

Notes

Chapter I, 1784–1789

1. Samuel Mordecai, *Virginia, Especially Richmond, in By-Gone Days* (Richmond, 1860), p. 198.

2. Records of the Common Hall of the City of Richmond, I, 63, Richmond City Hall (hereafter cited as Richmond City Common Hall Records).

3. Ibid., p. 65.

4. Thomas Clark Pollock, *The Philadelphia Theatre in the Eighteenth Century, Together with the Day Book of the Same Period* (Philadelphia, 1933), p. 41.

5. George O. Seilhamer, *History of the American Theatre* (Philadelphia, 1889), II, 106-7.

6. Executive Letter Book, 1783-1786, p. 286, Virginia State Library (hereafter VSL). I am indebted to William M. E. Rachal for directing my attention to this correspondence.

7. VSL. The playbill carries the inscription "This is the earliest known specimen of a Richmond play-bill" and the date *1783*.

8. Mordecai, p. 35; Mary Newton Stanard, *Richmond: Its People and Its Story* (Philadelphia, 1923), p. 55.

9. Seilhamer, II, 90-91.

10. George Clinton Densmore Odell, *Annals of the New York Stage* (New York, 1927-49), I, 226-27.

11. *Virginia Gazette and Independent Chronicle* (Richmond) and *Virginia Gazette, and Weekly Advertiser* (Richmond), Nov. 27, 1784; I quote the latter because it is slightly more detailed.

12. *Va. Gaz. & Wkly. Adv.*, Dec. 11, 1784.

13. Richmond City Common Hall Records, I, 86.

14. Herbert A. Johnson et al., eds., *The Papers of John Marshall*, I (Chapel Hill, N.C., 1974), 305, 306, 316, 319.

15. Unless otherwise specified, dates of performances throughout are from the following: England: Allardyce Nicoll, *A History of Late Eighteenth Century Drama* (Cambridge, Eng., 1927) and *A History of Early Nineteenth Century Drama* (Cambridge, Eng., 1930); other Virginia theatres: Susanne K. Sherman, "Post-Revolutionary Theatre in Virginia," Master's Thesis, William and Mary, 1950; New York: Odell; Philadelphia: before 1800, Pollock, after 1800, Reese D. James, *Old Drury of Philadelphia* (Philadelphia, 1932); Charleston: before 1800, Eola Willis, *The Charleston Stage in the XVIII Century* (Charleston, S.C., 1924), after 1800, W. Stanley Hoole, *The Ante-Bellum Charleston Theatre* (Tuscaloosa, Ala., 1946).

16. Richmond City Common Hall Records, I, 116.

17. Ibid.

18. Odell, I, 226-28.

19. Mordecai, pp. 207-8.

20. *Va. Gaz. & Ind. Chron.*, Sept. 24, 1785. Quesnay is not without fame. His *Mémoire Statuts et Prospectus, Concernant L'Académie des Sciences et Beaux Arts des États-Unis de L'Amérique, Établie a Richemond, Capitale de la Virginie* was published in Paris in 1788. It contains Quesnay's account of his travels and adventures in America, his efforts to establish the academy, of which the cornerstone was laid with considerable ceremony on June 24, 1786, as well as the statutes and regulations of the academy, a prospectus of subscription, and lists of subscribers in both France and America including Lafayette, Jefferson, Tom Paine, Patrick Henry, Governor Edmund Randolph, and Mayor John Harvie.

21. *Va. Gaz. & Ind. Chron.*, Sept. 13, 1786.

22. Pollock, pp. 40-41.

23. Seilhamer, II, 204-5.

24. *Va. Gaz. & Ind. Chron.*, Oct. 28, 1786.

25. Arthur Hornblow, *A History of the Theatre in America from Its Beginnings to the Present Time* (Philadelphia, 1919), I, 169.

26. *Virginia Independent Chronicle* (Richmond), Nov. 22, 1786.

27. Nicoll, *Late Eighteenth Century Drama*, p. 305; Odell, I, 219, 239-40; Pollock, p. 44; Willis, p. 169; Seilhamer, II, 108.

28. Dougald Macmillan and Howard Mumford Jones, *Plays of the Restoration and Eighteenth Century* (New York, 1931), p. 131.

29. Odell, I, 246.

30. Hugh F. Rankin, *The Theatre in Colonial America* (Chapel Hill, N.C., 1960), p. 200.

31. Seilhamer, I, 235 ff., 257 ff.

32. *Va. Gaz. & Wkly. Adv.*, Nov. 8, 1787.

33. *Va. Ind. Chron.*, Nov. 21, 1787.

34. *Va. Gaz. & Wkly. Adv.*, Nov. 29, 1787.

35. Enumeration of plays throughout includes pantomimes and ballets for which titles were given; it does not include dances, recitations, or songs.

36. Nicoll, *Late Eighteenth Century Drama*, p. 311.

37. *Va. Ind. Chron.*, Apr. 2, 1788; *Va. Gaz. & Wkly. Adv.*, Aug. 21, 1788; ibid., Oct. 2, 1788.

Chapter II, 1790-1794

1. Seilhamer, II, 328 ff.

2. Willis, pp. 175-76.

3. Richmond City Common Hall Records, I, 215.

4. *Virginia Gazette, and General Advertiser* (Richmond), Oct. 27, 1790.

5. Ibid., Jan. 5, 1791.

6. Ibid., Jan. 12, 1791.

7. Susanne K. Sherman, "Thomas Wade West, Theatrical Impresario, 1790-99," *William and Mary Quarterly*, 3rd ser. 9 (1952), 10-12.

8. *Virginia Gazette, and Public Advertiser* (Richmond), July 9, 1791.

9. *Va. Gaz. & Gen. Adv.*, Oct. 19, 1791.

10. Ibid., Oct. 26, 1791 (Extraordinary).

11. *Va. Gaz. & Pub. Adv.*, Nov. 12, 1791.

12. *Va. Gaz. & Gen. Adv.*, Nov. 16, 1791.

13. VSL.

14. Odell, I, 401.

15. Ibid., II, 157.

16. Seilhamer, III, 397.

17. *Va. Gaz. & Gen. Adv.*, Aug. 29, 1792.

18. Ibid., Oct. 1, 1792.

19. *Virginia Gazette: and Richmond Daily Advertiser*, Oct. 8, 1792.

20. Ibid., Oct. 9, 1792.

21. Ibid., Oct. 11, 1792.

22. Ibid., Oct. 12, 1792.

23. J. B. Hubbell to Martin Shockley, Jan. 2, 1948.

24. Robert Munford, *The Candidates, or the Humors of a Virginia Election,* a Comedy in Three Acts, edited with an introduction by J. B. Hubbell and Douglas Adair (Williamsburg, 1948); and Courtlandt Canby, ed., Robert Munford's *The Patriots, William and Mary Quarterly*, 3d ser. 6 (1949), 437-503.

25. *Va. Gaz. & Gen. Adv.*, Dec. 12, 1792.

26. Ibid., Dec. 29, 1792.

27. *William and Mary Quarterly*, 3d ser. 6 (1949), 357.

28. *Va. Gaz. & Gen. Adv.*, Sept. 11, 1793.

29. Ibid., Aug. 7, 1793 (Extraordinary).

30. *Virginia Gazette, and Richmond and Manchester Advertiser*, Sept. 19, 1793.

31. Ibid., Oct. 24, 1793.

32. Ibid., Nov. 7, 1793.

33. Ibid., Nov. 28, 1793.

34. *Virginia Gazette & Richmond Chronicle*, Dec. 6, 1793.

35. *Va. Gaz. & Rich. & Man. Adv.*, Dec. 12, 1793.

36. Ibid., Dec. 16, 1793.

37. Ibid., Nov. 25, 1793.

38. *Va. Gaz. & Rich. Chron.*, Dec. 6, 1793.

39. *Va. Gaz. & Rich. & Man. Adv.*, May 22, 1794.

40. *Va. Gaz. & Rich. Chron.*, June 13, 1794.

41. Odell, I, 336.

42. *Va. Gaz. & Rich. & Man. Adv.*, Aug. 28, 1794.

43. Odell, I, 261-62.

44. Roger P. McCutcheon, "The First English Plays in New Orleans," *American Literature*, II (1939), 185.

45. *Va. Gaz. & Rich. & Man. Adv.*, Dec. 15, 1794.

Chapter III, 1795–1799

1. *Richmond and Manchester Advertiser*, Oct. 15, 1795.
2. Willis, p. 264.
3. *Richmond Chronicle*, Oct. 24, 1795.
4. *Rich. & Man. Adv.*, Oct. 29, 1795.
5. *Rich. Chron.*, Nov. 7, 1795.
6. Ibid., Nov. 17, 1795.
7. Ibid., Nov. 21, 1795.
8. Ibid., Dec. 5, 1795.
9. *Rich. & Man. Adv.*, Dec. 23, 1795.
10. Odell, I, 405.
11. Arthur Hobson Quinn, *A History of the American Drama* (New York, 1943), p. 72.
12. Odell, I, 376.
13. Ibid., p. 371.
14. Ibid., p. 373.
15. Ibid., p. 448.
16. *Va. Gaz. & Gen. Adv.*, Nov. 23, 1796.
17. Ibid., Nov. 30, 1796.
18. Willis, p. 202.
19. *Va. Gaz. & Gen. Adv.*, Dec. 14, 1796.
20. *Virginia Argus* (Richmond), Dec. 20, 1796.
21. Ibid., Dec. 27, 1796.
22. *Va. Gaz. & Gen. Adv.*, Dec. 28, 1796.
23. *Va. Argus*, Jan. 3, 1797.
24. Ibid., Feb. 17, 1797.
25. Quinn, *History of the American Drama*, pp. 113-14.
26. Pollock, p. 432.
27. Ibid., p. 430.
28. Odell, I, 315.
29. Ibid., p. 448.
30. Pollock, pp. 424, 431.
31. Ibid., pp. 425, 433.
32. Talbot Hamlin, *Benjamin Henry Latrobe* (New York, 1955), p. 86.
33. Ibid., p. 87.
34. Ibid., pp. 87-88.
35. Ibid., p. 88.
36. Ibid.
37. Sherman, "Thomas Wade West," pp. 26-27.

38. Willis, p. 302.

39. Sherman, "Thomas Wade West," p. 27.

40. *Va. Argus*, Dec. 14, 1798.

41. *Examiner* (Richmond), Dec. 24, 1798.

42. Willis, p. 377.

43. Quinn, *History of the American Drama*, p. 126.

44. Ibid., p. 117.

45. *Va. Argus*, Jan. 22, 1799.

46. Ibid., Jan. 29, 1799.

47. Ibid., Feb. 5, 1799.

48. Ibid., Feb. 12, 1799.

49. Ibid., Feb. 22, 1799.

50. Ibid., Mar. 5, 1799.

51. Ibid., Mar. 12, 1799.

52. Ibid., Mar. 15, 1799.

53. Ibid., Mar. 22, 1799.

54. Ibid.

55. Ibid., Apr. 2, 1799.

56. Ibid., Apr. 16, 1799.

57. Ibid., Apr. 19, 1799.

58. Nicoll, *Late Eighteenth Century Drama*, p. 120.

59. *Va. Gaz. & Gen. Adv.*, Apr. 5, 1799.

60. *Va. Argus*, Apr. 16, 1799.

61. Ibid., Oct. 11, 1799.

62. Ibid., Nov. 5, 1799.

63. *Examiner*, Dec. 3, 1799.

64. Sherman, "Thomas Wade West," pp. 27-28.

Chapter IV, 1800-1805

1. Sherman, "Thomas Wade West," p. 28.

2. Quinn, *History of the American Drama*, p. 117.

3. *Examiner*, July 10, 1802.

4. *Va. Gaz. & Gen. Adv.*, Apr. 28, 1802. Of the numerous proliferations of the *Virginia Gazette*, only the Richmond *Virginia Gazette, and General Advertiser* continued beyond 1800. Hereafter in text it is referred to simply as the *Virginia Gazette*, or *Gazette*.

5. Ibid., May 19, 1802.

6. Ibid., May 19, 1801.

7. Arthur Hobson Quinn, *Edgar Allan Poe* (New York, 1941), Chapter 1, "The Heritage"; Appendix, "The Theatrical Career of Edgar Poe's Parents."

8. Sherman, *Post-Revolutionary Theatre*.

9. *Va. Argus*, Oct. 2, 1802.

10. Hoole, p. 8.

11. *Va. Argus*, Oct. 9, 1802.

12. *Petersburg Intelligencer*, Nov. 19, 1802.

13. *Examiner*, Jan. 15, 1803.

14. Quinn, *Poe*, pp. 706-7.

15. *Va. Argus*, Apr. 23, 1803; *Va. Gaz. & Gen. Adv.*, June 22 and July 20, 1803; *Va. Argus*, July 23, 1803.

16. *Va. Gaz. & Gen. Adv.*, July 30, Aug. 24, and Sept. 13, 1803.

17. *Va. Argus*, Oct. 22, 1803.

18. *Va. Gaz. & Gen. Adv.*, Nov. 16, 1803; *Va. Argus*, Nov. 23, 1803; *Va. Gaz. & Gen. Adv.*, Dec. 3, 1803.

19. Quinn, *History of the American Drama*, p. 119.

20. *Va. Gaz. & Gen. Adv.*, Dec. 24, 1803.

21. Ibid., Dec. 31, 1803.

22. Ibid., Jan. 18, 1804.

23. Ibid., Feb. 4, 1804.

24. Ibid., Feb. 8, 1804.

25. Ibid., Feb. 11, 1804.

26. Ibid., Feb. 18, 1804.

27. Ibid., Feb. 25, 1804.

28. Ibid., Feb. 29, 1804.

29. Ibid., Mar. 7, 1804.

30. Ibid., Mar. 10, 1804.

31. Ibid., Mar. 14, 1804.

32. "Letters of William T. Barry," *William and Mary Quarterly*, 1st ser. 13 (1904), 115.

33. *Va. Gaz. & Gen. Adv.*, Mar. 31, 1804.

34. Ibid., Apr. 4, 1804.

35. Ibid., May 2 and 5, 1804.

36. Ibid., May 16, 1804; *Va. Argus*, May 30 and June 13, 1804.

37. *Va. Gaz. & Gen. Adv.*, July 7, 1804.

38. Ibid., July 21, 1804.

39. Ibid., July 25, 1804.

40. Ibid., July 28, 1804.

41. Ibid., Aug. 8, 1804.

42. Ibid., Aug. 18, 1804.

43. Ibid., Aug. 25, 1804.

44. Mordecai, p. 142.

45. *Enquirer* (Richmond), Dec. 25, 1804.

46. Ibid., Dec. 29, 1804.

47. Ibid., Jan. 3, 1805.

48. Ibid., Jan. 18, 1805.

49. Ibid., Feb. 12, 1805.

50. Quinn, *Poe*, pp. 710-11.

Chapter V, 1806–1809

1. *Va. Gaz. & Gen. Adv.*, Jan. 29, 1806.
2. Ibid., Feb. 5, 1806.
3. Ibid., Feb. 8, 1806.
4. Ibid., Feb. 26, 1806.
5. Ibid., Mar. 1, 1806.
6. Ibid., Apr. 30, 1806.
7. Ibid., Aug. 13, 1806.
8. Ibid., July 12 and 30, 1806.
9. Ibid., Aug. 16, 1806.
10. Ibid., Aug. 20, 23, and 26, 1806.
11. Ibid., Aug. 27, 1806.
12. Ibid., Sept. 6, 1806.
13. Ibid., Oct. 8, 1806.
14. Ibid., Dec. 6, 1806.
15. Ibid., Dec. 10, 1806.
16. Ibid., Dec. 24, 1806.
17. Ibid., Dec. 27, 1806.
18. Ibid., Jan. 14, 1807.
19. Ibid., Jan. 21, 1807.
20. Ibid., Feb. 4, 1807.
21. Ibid., Feb. 7, 1807.
22. Odell, II, 181; Quinn, *History of the American Drama*, p. 88.
23. *Va. Argus*, Aug. 10 and Sept. 16, 1807.
24. *Enquirer*, May 17 and 24, 1808.
25. *Va. Argus*, Aug. 9, 12, 23, 26, and 30, 1808; *Enquirer*, Sept. 2, 1808.
26. *Va. Gaz. & Gen. Adv.*, Aug. 12, 1808.
27. *Va. Argus*, Nov. 11 and 15, 1808.
28. Ibid., Dec. 6, 1808; *Enquirer*, Dec. 8 and 10, 1808.
29. *Spirit of 'Seventy-Six* (Richmond), Dec. 27, 1808, and Jan. 17 and 20, 1809; *Enquirer*, Jan. 5, 7, 21, and 31, 1809.
30. *Va. Argus*, Mar. 10, and July 11, 1809; *Enquirer*, July 18, 1809.
31. *Enquirer*, Aug. 25, 1809.

Chapter VI, 1809–1811

1. *Va. Gaz. & Gen. Adv.*, Sept. 1, 1809.
2. Ibid., Sept. 5, 1809.
3. Ibid., Sept. 15, 1809.
4. Ibid., Sept. 19, 1809.
5. Ibid., Sept. 29, 1809.
6. Ibid., Oct. 3, 1809.
7. Odell, II, 315.

8. Ibid., I, 301.

9. Hoole, p. 3.

10. Willis, p. 335.

11. Odell, II, 426.

12. Ibid., p. 391.

13. *Va. Gaz. & Gen. Adv.*, Oct. 20, 1809.

14. Ibid., Nov. 7, 1809.

15. Ibid., Nov. 17, 1809.

16. Ibid., Dec. 1, 1809.

17. *Va. Argus* (Extra), Dec. 5, 1809.

18. *Va. Gaz. & Gen. Adv.*, Dec. 8 and 12, 1809; *Enquirer*, Dec. 9, 1809.

19. *Va. Argus*, Dec. 15, 1809.

20. *Va. Gaz. & Gen. Adv.*, Dec. 19, 1809; *Va. Argus*, Dec. 22, 1809; *Enquirer*, Dec. 26, 1809; *Va. Argus*, Dec. 29, 1809.

21. *Enquirer*, Jan. 16, 1810.

22. *Virginia Patriot* (Richmond), Jan. 9 and 11, 1810; *Enquirer*, Jan. 11, 1810; *Va. Argus*, Jan. 12, 1810.

23. Quinn, *History of the American Drama*, p. 272.

24. Ibid., p. 139.

25. Odell, II, 314.

26. *Va. Argus*, Feb. 2, 1810.

27. *Va. Patriot*, May 1 and 4, 1810.

28. Ibid., Aug. 17, 1810.

29. Ibid., Aug. 28, 1810.

30. Ibid., Aug. 31, 1810.

31. Ibid., Sept. 7, 1810.

32. Ibid., Sept. 11, 1810.

33. *Enquirer*, Sept. 18, 1810.

34. *Va. Patriot*, Sept. 18, 1810.

35. Quinn, *Poe*, p. 16.

36. *Enquirer*, Sept. 28 and Oct. 2, 1810.

37. *Va. Patriot*, Oct. 2, 1810.

38. Ibid., Oct. 5, 1810.

39. Ibid., Oct. 9, 1810.

40. Quinn, *History of the American Drama*, p. 155.

41. Odell, II, 237.

42. *Va. Patriot*, Nov. 9, 1810.

43. Ibid., Nov. 13, 1810.

44. Odell, II, 337.

45. *Va. Argus*, Aug. 15, 1811.

46. Ibid., Aug. 19, 1811.

47. *Enquirer*, Aug. 30, 1811; *Va. Argus*, Sept. 2, 1811; *Va. Patriot*, Aug. 30, 1811.

48. *Va. Argus*, Sept. 9, 1811.

49. Ibid., Sept. 12, 1811.

50. Ibid., Sept. 16, 1811.

51. *Va. Patriot*, Sept. 27, 1811.

52. *Enquirer*, Oct. 8, 1811; *Va. Argus*, Oct. 7, 1811; *Va. Patriot*, Oct. 8, 1811.

53. Quinn, *History of the American Drama*, p. 160.

54. Nicoll, *Late Eighteenth Century Drama*, p. 250.

55. *Va. Argus*, Oct. 28, 1811.

56. Ibid., Oct. 31, 1811.

57. Ibid., Nov. 4, 1811.

58. *Va. Patriot*, Nov. 8, 1811.

59. Ibid., Nov. 26, 1811.

60. *Va. Argus*, Nov. 14, 1811; *Va. Patriot*, Nov. 15, 1811.

61. *Va. Patriot*, Nov. 19, 1811.

62. Ibid., Nov. 22, 1811.

63. Ibid., Nov. 26, 1811.

64. Ibid.

65. Ibid., Dec. 3 and 6, 1811; *Enquirer*, Dec. 7, 1811.

66. *Va. Patriot*, Dec. 13 and 17, 1811.

67. Ibid., Dec. 20, 1811.

68. *Enquirer*, Dec. 24, 1811.

69. VSL.

70. *Va. Patriot*, Dec. 27, 1811.

71. Wright, *Modern Language Review*, 14 (1919), 173-82; Nicoll, *Early Eighteenth Century Drama*, p. 113; Willis, p. 206.

72. Odell, II, 192.

Chapter VII, December 26, 1811

1. John P. Little, *History of Richmond* (Richmond, 1933), pp. 120-27; Mordecai, pp. 142-47; Stannard, pp. 104-7.

2. *Enquirer*, Dec. 28, 1811.

3. There were also "Statements" by several prominent citizens who at Ritchie's request recounted their personal experiences of the holocaust, all told with decorum and restraint, mostly repetitious, adding little and correcting nothing. To these may be added the account from Charles Copland's diary. His entry for Dec. 26, 1811, gives further vivid and harrowing details ("Extracts from Diary of Charles Copland," *William and Mary Quarterly*, 1st ser. 14 [1906], 217-30).

4. *Enquirer*, Jan. 4, 1812; *Va. Argus*, Jan. 16, 1812.

5. *Va. Argus*, Jan. 6, 1812.

6. Ibid.; and Jan. 13, 1812.

7. *Enquirer*, Jan. 14, 1812; *Va. Patriot*, Jan. 7, 1812; *Enquirer*, Jan. 9 and 25, 1812.

8. For eulogies, see *Enquirer*, Jan. 2, 4, 25, and 30, 1812; *Va. Argus*,

Jan. 7 and 23, and Feb. 23, 1812.

9. There were also a number of poems inspired by the occasion. The *Enquirer* of January 25, 1812, reprinted from the *Philadelphia Freeman's Journal* an "Ode, occasioned by the late disastrous conflagration of The Theatre at Richmond." It consisted of thirteen stanzas and was signed "Alcondo." The *Virginia Argus* of January 27 published a long "Elegiac Poem" by Thomas E. Birch "dedicated to the Citizens of Richmond." Approximately one hundred lines of heroic couplet signed "S" were published in the *Virginia Patriot* on January 31. A poem of eleven varying stanzas signed "Sedley" appeared in the *Enquirer* on February 1. Among many more, the most interesting is an "Elegiac Ode" by "Porcius" of Washington County, Maryland, which, in some twenty stanzas of fourteen or more lines each, attempts to immortalize in rhyme the names of all who perished in the flames: "Rozier—Lecroix and Nuttall all/Admidst the furious flames they fall" (*Va. Argus*, Mar. 13, 1812). See also *Enquirer*, Feb. 8 and 25, Apr. 3, and Dec. 24, 1812; *Va. Patriot*, Feb. 7, 1812.

10. Hoole, p. 9.

11. *Va. Argus*, Jan. 27, 1812.

12. *Enquirer*, Jan. 16, 1812.

13. Hamlin, p. 28.

14. *Va. Argus*, Jan. 13, 1812.

15. Hamlin, p. 220; *Va. Patriot*, May 7 and 18, 1814.

16. The Rev. George J. Cleaveland to Martin Shockley, Mar. 2, 1973.

17. George D. Fisher, *History of Monumental Church* (Richmond, 1880).

Indexes

Index of Names

Consult Appendix 2 for performers for each season.

Index of Titles